Evolution of Human Behavior

Agustín Fuentes
University of Notre Dame

New York   Oxford
OXFORD UNIVERSITY PRESS
2009

Oxford University Press, Inc., publishes works that further
Oxford University's objective of excellence
in research, scholarship, and education.

Oxford   New York
Auckland   Cape Town   Dar es Salaam   Hong Kong   Karachi
Kuala Lumpur   Madrid   Melbourne   Mexico City   Nairobi
New Delhi   Shanghai   Taipei   Toronto

With offices in
Argentina   Austria   Brazil   Chile   Czech Republic   France   Greece
Guatemala   Hungary   Italy   Japan   Poland   Portugal   Singapore
South Korea   Switzerland   Thailand   Turkey   Ukraine   Vietnam

Library of Congress Cataloging-in-Publication Data
Fuentes, Agustin.
Evolution of human behavior / Agustin Fuentes.
p. cm.
Includes bibliographical references and index.
ISBN 978-0-19-533358-9 (paper/main)
ISBN 978-0-19-533359-6 (hardback)
1. Behavior evolution—Textbooks.
2. Human behavior—Textbooks.   I. Title.
BF698.95.F84 2009
304.5—dc22
2008019392

Printing number: 9 8 7 6 5 4 3 2 1

Printed in the United States of America
on acid-free paper

Evolution of Human Behavior

Contents

PREFACE   xi

1 The Relevance of Understanding Human Behavioral Evolution   3

Theories and Hypotheses about Behavioral Evolution: Why
Are They Relevant?   5

Evolution Is Frequently Misunderstood   5

We Need to Understand Who We Are   6

Practical Issues such as Medicine and Public Health Can
Benefit from an Understanding of Behavioral Evolution   7

Misunderstanding Human Behavioral Evolution Can Result in
Potentially Dangerous Ideas   8

A Simple Example of Behavioral Evolution   11

Mutation   13

Gene Flow   13

Genetic Drift   14

Selection   14

Development   14

Why Give This Example?   14

**2 Why We Behave Like Humans: Historical Perspectives
and Basal Assumptions**   16

Charles Darwin and the *Descent of Man*   17

Alfred Russel Wallace and the Evolution of the Mind   19

Between Darwin and Sociobiology   21

Spencer, Baldwin, and Morgan: Biology, Psychology, and the
Behavioral Evolution of the Human Mind   21

The Modern Synthesis   24

Washburns' New Physical Anthropology, and the Emergence
of an Evolutionary Anthropology of Behavior   26

Tinbergen's Four Questions and Their Impact on the
Understanding of Behavior 28

The Revolution of Sociobiology, Kin Selection, and Selfish Genes:
The New Synthesis 29

Hamilton and Kin Selection 30

Robert Trivers and Reciprocal Altruism 31

E.O. Wilson, Evolutionary Sociobiology and the
Autocatalysis Model 32

Dawkins and the Selfish Gene 34

Suggested Readings 36

**3 Modern Perspectives for Understanding Human Behavioral
Evolution: A Review of Basic Assumptions, Structures,
and Practice** 37

Human Behavioral Ecology 38

Basic Overview of HBE 39

Evolutionary Psychology 44

The Adapted Mind 45

Goals and Methods 47

Contrast with SSSM Specific Approach 48

Gene–Culture Coevolution (or Dual Inheritance Theory) 52

Memetics 57

Summing Up 59

Suggested Readings 63

**4 Basic Bones and Stones: What Do We Know About
the Record of Human Evolution (as of 2008)?** 64

Comparative Primatology Establishes a Baseline
for Human Behavior 64

Very Brief Summary of Human Fossil Record (~5 mya → Present) 68

The Early Australopithecines 71

The Pleistocene Hominins 76

The Genus *Homo* 79

Very Brief Summary of the Cultural Record and Behavioral
Inferences (~2.6 mya → Present) 86

Late Pliocene/Early Pleistocene Forms 86

Pleistocene Hominins—Early 88

Pleistocene Hominins—Late 91

Suggested Readings 94

**5 A Survey of Hypotheses and Proposals of Why We
Behave Like Humans** 95

Why Select These Proposals? 95

Summaries of Specific Hypotheses/Proposals 97

Suggested Readings 126

6 Discussing the Proposals 127

The Comparison Tables 129

A Brief Discussion on Shared Components and
Differences in the Six Basic Categories 129

Cooperation 129

Conflict 149

Food 151

Environmental and Ecological Pressures 152

Sex and Reproduction 154

Specific Behavioral Factors 155

Of Trends and Patterns 157

Suggested Readings 160

**7 Twenty-First Century Evolutionary Theory/Biology and
Thinking about the Evolution of Human Behavior** 160

Adding to Our Toolkit—Using Four Dimensions of Evolution 160

Revisiting Tinbergen's Ontogenetic "Why" 163

Four Other Approaches in Evolutionary Biology/Theory 165

Phenotypic Plasticity and Ecological Impact/Context: Moving
Beyond Norms of Reaction 165

Developmental Systems Theory 169

Niche Construction 172

Biocultural Approaches to Studying Modern Humans 177

Can Adding These Perspectives to Existing Practice
(as Outlined in Chapters 2 and 3) Impact the Way We Formulate
and Test Hypotheses/Conceptualizations of Human
Behavioral Evolution? 180

What Practices and Perspectives Should Be Removed or
De-emphasized? 180

What Practices and/or Perspectives Cross All of
These Categories? 182

What Perspectives Should Be Expanded? 184

Suggested Readings 186

8 A Synthesis and Prospectus for Examining Human Behavioral Evolution   187

A Set of Modest Proposals Emerging from Chapters 1 to 7: Seeking the Broad and the Minute Foci   188

Looking at the Areas of Overlap and Interest from Chapter 6   191

Cooperation Commonalities   192

Cooperation Factors that Deserve Further Examination   201

Conflict Commonalities   203

Conflict Factors that Deserve Further Examination   208

Diet/Food Commonalities   211

Diet/Food Factors that Deserve Further Examination   213

Ecology/Environment Commonalities   213

Ecology/Environment Factors that Deserve Further Examination   216

Sex/Reproduction Commonalities   219

Sex/Reproduction Factors that Deserve Further Examination   224

Specific Behavior Commonalities   225

Specific Behavior Factors that Deserve Further Examination   231

A Modest Proposal for a General Framework of Our Evolutionary History   232

Between Approximately 2 Million Years and 500,000 Years Ago   233

500,000–45,000 Years Ago (Give or Take 10,000 Years)   234

45,000 Years Ago Through Today   235

9 Problem of Being a Modern Human and Looking at Our Evolution   238

Benefits and Flaws in This Prospectus   238

Merging Approaches and Perspectives   238

How Do We Test This and Why Are Testable Hypotheses Important?   240

The Difficulties We Encounter When Reconstructing Our Evolutionary Path and Its Underlying Causes/Patterns   242

Basic Educational and Paradigmatic Biases and the Problems These Bring   242

Human Niche Construction Matters   244

Everyday Life, Gender, and Cultural Anthropology Matter   246

Epilogue: Anthropology, Science, and People   249

Some Notes on the Value of Integrative Anthropological
Approaches   249

Getting Past Conflicts between Researchers Studying
Human Behavioral Evolution   251

The Importance of Understanding the Relationships
between Religion, Science, Politics, and Explanations
for the Evolution of Humanity   252

APPENDIX: RELATED TITLES FOR FURTHER REFERENCE   254

GLOSSARY   258

BIBLIOGRAPHY   262

INDEX   277

Preface

We live in a time when pundits argue that natural disasters, such as hurricane Katrina, and such realities as the frequency of warfare and sexual abuse strip away the veneer of civilization and reveal our inner animal, the beast at the heart of humanity. Popular authors present naïve proposals for the biological basis of human behavior at the same time that nearly one half of U.S. citizens do not believe that humans have evolved over time. Most people think that the term "survival of the fittest" means "bigger is better" and that the toughest, meanest fighters win the biological struggle for life. Clearly, a large part of the general public has a poor understanding of human evolution, and even in broader academic circles that understanding is not always much better. This is in part because public and academic discussions frequently employ a simplified view of evolutionary processes ignoring substantial social complexity and focusing on relatively uncomplicated, often biologically deterministic, explanations. At the same time, there are also scholars who do not see why *any* investigation into biocultural trends and patterns of evolutionary change is important to human society today. This book hopes to demonstrate that both of these perspectives are incorrect; evolution matters but it is complex.

Despite the popular misunderstandings and limitations in some academic circles, there remains a great diversity of perspectives at play in the quest for insight into the evolution of human behavior. Within the social and behavioral sciences, recent innovations in evolutionary theory combined with an expansion in genetic methodologies, fossil finds, and ethnographic studies have produced a variety of hypotheses and models for understanding the emergence of humanity. The holistic approach of evolutionary anthropology is particularly well suited to act as a stimulus for a synthesis of these varying perspectives.

In this book, I present a synthesis of the structural similarities and differences across published hypotheses/proposals for the evolution of human behavior. My goal is to elucidate common themes and patterns and move forward toward a more integrated perspective(s) on human behavioral evolution. I contend that these identifiable commonalities, projected through an anthropological lens, can also add to our understanding of the complex relationships between our evolutionary past and modern human behavior to help us tackle the widespread ignorance and confusion surrounding the topic.

Even without an extensive synthesis of hypotheses, there already exists a commonly held view among science-based academics regarding the evolution of our species: that the genus *Homo* (humans) is approximately 2 million years old and that manipulation of our environment is a core facet in human evolution; that culture (however defined) has been and remains integral to human evolutionary success and that both cooperation and competition significantly influenced patterns in human evolution. Control of groups and individuals through social and linguistic means is a major component of human evolution and language, and a system of complex communication has facilitated hyper-rapid change and adaptation in a manner not available to other organisms. Cooperation and competition between the sexes play an important role in shaping human evolutionary history and patterns. Conflict negotiation and peaceful interactions are also probably important in human evolution, and while warfare is significant in human history, it might be a more recent development associated with agriculture and sedentism.

While an overwhelming majority of researchers agree that human evolution involves a biocultural system, there remains contention over how one models and envisions the integration and interactions of biology, culture, and behavior, and what relevance this might have to living humans. The conflux of researchers and perspectives regarding human behavioral evolution results in some agreements and many disagreements but few integrated proposals incorporating or acknowledging various perspectives and viable suggestions for testable elements.

Because science moves forward by innovation and enhancement of existing perspectives, we have to constantly be evaluating, and possibly incorporating, emerging perspectives that modify, challenge, or simply expand current views and theory. This suggests that as we obtain new finds in the fossil record, achieve greater physiological and genomic understandings about the connections between behavior, biology, and experience, learn more about human behavioral and cultural diversity, and produce new or innovative insights into evolutionary and ecological theory, we must update notions about evolutionary patterns and histories. Today, in the first decade of the twenty-first century, the pace of increases in knowledge in these areas is quickening, and our theory and proposals for human behavioral evolution must keep pace. The process of scholarly discovery cannot be static, even when dominant paradigms hold sway for multiple decades. Pushing the edges of current beliefs is one of the core values in scholarship and one of its most important contributions to humanity.

This book focuses on examining human behavioral evolution in a comparative and theoretical perspective. Rather than present a dogmatic assertion that there is one way to understand how human behavior evolved, I present an overview of ideas, paradigmatic approaches, and major hypotheses and proposals. In the opening chapter, I lay the case for why it is important to investigate and conceptualize the evolution of human behavior. Chapters 2 and 3 provide the historical and theoretical background and context for the investigation into the evolution of human behavior. Chapter 4 is a brief overview of the human fossil record. In Chapters 5 and 6, I review and discuss the major hypotheses for human behavior and in Chapter 7, I present current innovations in evolutionary theory. In the final chapters, Chapters 8 and 9, I present a synthesis, discuss my own views, and conclude with how I think we can best achieve an integration of perspectives for understanding and investigating human behavioral evolution.

In this book we address the following questions:

- Why do we ask questions about the evolution of human behavior?

- What are the major ways in which such questions have been asked over the last few centuries?

- What are the main perspectives current researchers use to ask such questions?

- What do we know about the human morphological evolutionary record and what does it tell us about human behavioral evolution?

- How does what we know about humans as primates influence our understanding of human behavioral evolution?

- What are the major proposals and hypotheses, regarding both specific behaviors and general patterns, for the evolution of human behavior?

- What commonalities/main points emerge from comparing these proposals/hypotheses and what can these tell us about human behavioral evolution?

- What additions to our theoretical toolkit enhance our ability to conduct inquiries into human behavioral evolution at the start of the twenty-first century?

- What do I, as author of this book, propose as an overview for human behavioral evolution?

ACKNOWLEDGMENTS

I would like to extend my thanks to my colleagues, Thad Bartlett, Carola Borries, Greg Downey, Hope Hollocher, Lee Gettler, Andreas Koenig, Kelly Lane, Daniel Lende, James Loudon, Nick Malone, Katherine C. MacKinnon, Thom McDade, Jim McKenna, Rahul Oka, Catherine Panter-Brick, Michael Park, Elsworth Ray, Emily Schultz, Karen Strier, Carel van Schaik, Bob Sussman, Richard Wrangham, Matthew A. Wyczalkowski, and many others for conversations that helped me think through these ideas. I also want to thank the Department of Anthropology at the University of Notre Dame and Mark Roche, the former Dean of the College of Arts and Letters, for support, encouragement, and time to write. I am especially indebted to Phyllis Dolhinow and David Wake for starting me really thinking about evolutionary theory.

Extra special thanks go to Janet Beatty of OUP for years of encouragement and support and for both understanding why anthropology is so important and why writing about it has to be engaging. This book would not have been completed without the excellent assistance of Cory Schneider, Assistant Editor, and Mary Araneo, Managing Production Editor, at OUP, and the team at Newgen Imaging Systems (P) Ltd. Thanks also for the excellent and thorough critiques of various drafts by the reviewers: Robin Bernstein, The George Washington University; John Kingston, Emory University; James J. McKenna, University of Notre Dame; Michael Alan Park, Central Connecticut State University; Karen L. Schmidt, University of Pittsburgh; Roger Sullivan, California State University, Sacramento; and, Andrea Wiley, Indiana University.

I thank my father, Victor Fuentes, for guiding me along the path of scholarship and intellectual development and my mother, Elizabeth Fuentes, for showing me the responsibility and impact of being a teacher. Finally, I thank Devi Snively for listening to my musings and helping me think about the relevance of evolution and human behavior for the last 15 years.

Evolution of Human Behavior

CHAPTER 1

The Relevance of Understanding Human Behavioral Evolution

> It was thus a prevailing, if not universal, belief of early writers on evolution, and one that crept well into the twentieth century, that not only did behavior evolve, but it also functioned as a principal instrument of species modification. (Robert Richards 1987, p. 70)

Behavior matters. It is what humans do. We have a self-awareness, a cognitive complexity, and an ability to reflect on ourselves, which is not available to other animals. Our behavior affects not just ourselves, but the entire globe in a dramatic fashion. To understand our behavior, we must examine not only the current behavior we exhibit, but also why we do so and how patterns of behavior have arisen over the course of our evolutionary history. Understanding the evolution of human behavior is important both in an academic context and in a practical one.

We know a great deal about the evolution of the human body over the last ~7–9 million years since our lineage diverged from the lineage leading to chimpanzees. We know that we are part of a specific lineage (subfamily Homininae) and part of the larger group of primates we call apes (superfamily Hominoidea) (Figure 1.1).

We have a good idea about the timing of major morphological changes such as the emergence of bipedal anatomy (4–6 million years ago), increases in body size (~2 million years ago), increases in brain size and complexity (2–0.3 million years ago), and the emergence of human bodies that exhibit a fully modern form (~200,000 years ago). We know that the earliest human forms originated on the African continent and that over the last ~2 million years our ancestors and we have been moving around that continent and out across all of the others. We know these details about the evolution of humans because of the fossil and archeological records and the ability to reconstruct

4

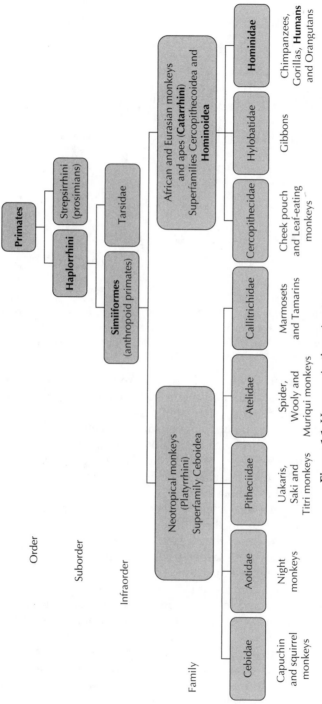

Figure 1.1 Humans in the primate taxonomy.

geographical and phylogenetic histories via DNA sequence changes and patterns. However, the focus of this book, the evolution of human behavior, leaves a much more opaque trail. To reconstruct this trail, we have to speculate and hypothesize about patterns in the past. Few facts are available for scientific analyses and testing; so we are left to construct models and propose scenarios that both explain the outcomes we can measure, usually via modern human behavior, and provide some connection to the processes of evolutionary change as we understand them.

THEORIES AND HYPOTHESES ABOUT BEHAVIORAL EVOLUTION: WHY ARE THEY RELEVANT?

How we propose and assess ideas about human behavioral evolution matter. They impact what people see as natural for humans, where we think we are headed as a species, what kind of behavior we expect from our fellow citizens, and the expectations of our own behavior toward them.

Evolution Is Frequently Misunderstood

In the biological context, "evolution" refers to changes across generations in biological characteristics. These changes may lead to more complexity, or to less. Neither does evolution produce a better set of organisms in any aesthetic sense, nor does it produce a product that is intrinsically better than earlier forms. It simply reflects the pattern of organic change over time in response to processes that alter biological facets of organisms such that in a given environment or set of environments those organisms with particular traits leave more offspring, on average, than do others with different sets of traits.

But loosely used, "evolution" frequently implies that change is purposeful, leading toward something better, and that it is progressive. It is especially dangerous from a political point of view when "change" and "better" are used to describe the role of evolution in contemporary settings as it leads to the ultimate idea that superior humans can or should be the outcome of our evolution. Unfortunately, our society tends to prioritize biological explanations as more "core" than cultural explanations. We see biology as "fact" based and culture as "fuzzier." It is almost impossible to even agree on a definition or measure of culture, while at the same time we have many specific quantifiable definitions and assessments of our biology.

In this book, we will be especially interested in those behavioral patterns that have central relationships to the evolution of our lineage (the genus *Homo*) and our species (*Homo sapiens*). But is behavior a biological trait? Can evolution act on behavior in the same way that it acts on the shape of your foot? Yes and no. This is the area in which even the best researchers begin to encounter problems with mixing the strict and the loose use of the term "evolution." It has long been accepted that if behavior has some form of genetic or biologically heritable component it can be acted on by evolutionary processes in the same way as any part of our body. If behavior impacts the rate or pattern of reproduction (sending copies of one's genetic material into the next generation) it can affect evolutionary change.[1]

But is all behavior influenced by evolution? Does not behavior get progressively more complex and "better" over time? Can we not train ourselves to perform "better" in most behavioral tasks? Do human societies get more complex over time? One can easily see how behavior in a biological evolutionary sense and behavior in a colloquial "evolutionary" sense can become confused with one another. This is a dangerous problem that is tied to our misunderstanding of the terms "nature" and "nurture."

Many people still believe that biology tells us what is "natural" (from nature, all that is not human altered) and cultural patterns tells us what is "nurtural" (emerges from the actions of humankind). So if behavior evolves in the biological sense then the biological facets of that behavior are the most important (or natural). Unfortunately, this is an incorrect assumption. Humans are biocultural beings with such a tight interweaving of our biological and cultural selves that disarticulation of purely biological facets of behavior from purely cultural facets are nearly impossible, and possibly pointless. We are simultaneously natural and nurtural beings with our role as human individuals tied inextricably to our biological and cultural patterns of development, learning, and behaving. However, we can still try to envision and assess the system and histories under which patterns in human behavior have emerged over our evolutionary past, using tools of both biological and cultural investigation.

We Need to Understand Who We Are

Human beings and the natural world are often seen as antagonists. For example, with the emergence of a broad understanding of global climate change and human exploitation and manipulation of the earth's biotic and abiotic resources, it is difficult not to see humans as a disruption of natural systems. However, there is an important error in this view: humans are a part of nature, not separate from it. Like rats, f lowers, flies, and amoebas, human beings are as natural as anything else on the planet. The major distinction is that we are capable of engineering change and altering landscapes and ecological relationships on a scale that no other organisms can ever match. And we do so with awareness and active intention. There are other ecological engineers on large scales, such as tropical forests and oceanic photosynthetic algae (atmosphere converting/altering), and on small scales, such as beavers creating dams, or earthworms with their patterns of alteration of local soil

---

[1] This theme, inheritance of behavior and behavioral impact on evolution, will be addressed with specific theoretical implications in Chapter 7.

chemistries and physical structure. However, it is our ability to intentionally direct these changes and our ability to decide where, how, and when we enact changes[2] that sets us apart. This capacity of humans to willfully change the world reflects an important part of human behavioral evolution. Seeing our behavioral patterns and their evolutionary histories and trajectories as a system, which is part of the earth's biosphere, and sharing similarities and differences with other such systems allow us to discard the erroneous notion of humans as being somehow outside of nature and the natural world and of our actions being opposed to some idealized "natural order." The opposite of natural is not "man-made."

I have argued elsewhere (Fuentes 2006) that

> We are animals, specifically mammals. We can feel like an ape because we are apes.... However, we are not chimpanzee apes.... Rather, we are human apes, a particular kind of ape that manipulates ecosystems across this planet and is capable of intense cruelty and amazing compassion via symbol, language, niche construction, and interaction with other animals and ourselves.

Being a particular kind of ape, one with immense capabilities to alter global and local ecologies for ourselves and other organisms, gives us a starting point for understating our behavioral histories and capabilities; we are primates. Being primates, we also know that our base adaptation is social (Sussman and Chapman 2004, Silk 2007). Being apes, our social adaptation involves slightly more neuro-cognitive complexity than in most other primates, meaning we are able to do a bit more with our social minds (Dunbar and Shutlz 2007). This expansion of the *social mind* into a particular *cultural mind* might be the most significant shift between our lineage and the other apes (Herrmann et al. 2007). Since most of what we do is behavior (as with all species), and our behavior is rooted in a primate context, modified and filtered through millions of years of evolutionary change relative to other primates, a focus on hypotheses and proposals as to how those changes occurred might provide us insight into what we do and why we do it. For this reason alone, it matters very much what people propose as explanations for human behavioral evolution.

Practical Issues such as Medicine and Public Health Can Benefit from an Understanding of Behavioral Evolution

The recent and growing interest in evolutionary medicine and biocultural approaches to medicine and public health are directly tied to an understanding of our evolutionary histories. Research into a wide array of health issues

---

[2] This is not to say that we are always aware of our changes or their impacts. Many ecological impacts go unnoticed or are unintentional by-products of our actions. My point here is that we are in greater control and have greater capabilities to engineer the ecosystem than do other organisms on this planet.

from sleeping behavior and stress to adult onset diabetes, to human–monkey pathogen exchange—all connect in important ways with facets of our behavioral evolutionary history.

For example, anthropologist James McKenna's research into the importance of the behavior of parents co-sleeping with their infants illustrates the role of broad behavioral patterns in primate and human evolution and what emerges when such patterns come into conflict and disjuncture with some modern cultural interpretations of what is "normal" for parents and offspring (McKenna and Gettler 2007). McKenna began with comparative studies of nonhuman primates, assessing the spatial and physical interactions between mothers, other caretakers, and infants. Moving to humans, he focused on the patterns of sleep and spatial and physical interactions through the course of nighttime activity in modern humans and the evidence for such patterns throughout our evolutionary history. Over 20 years of comparative and laboratory research strongly supports the conclusions that co-sleeping has a very long history in primates and humans and that there are substantial health and behavioral benefits for adults and offspring derived from sleeping in close physical and social contact. However, he also realized the changing contexts of modern cultural behavior such as drug and alcohol abuse, obesity, and other health issues that can alter and influence the contexts and facets of co-sleeping. This ongoing research appeared in a variety of scholarly academic publications and was translated for a broader audience and disseminated in an accessible book format, and through television and other media avenues for public consumption (McKenna 2007). This type of application of research into the evolution of human behavior has a direct and important impact on elements of human health such as sudden infant death syndrome, parental–offspring emotional bonding, childhood social and biological development, and parental stress reduction and health.

By no means will all of the ways in which we construct questions and explanations about human behavioral evolution always have some direct implication for human health or well-being. But, it is likely that the way we envision our investigations and present our outcomes has the potential to impact its applicability and usability by a broad set of applied scientists and the public at large. However, this also brings with it some specific dangers relative to public presentation of human evolutionary research.

Misunderstanding Human Behavioral Evolution Can Result in Potentially Dangerous Ideas

Creationist and essentialist perspectives are major constraints on our abilities to think critically about human behavior (Scott 2005).[3] Creationism,

[3] See The National Center for Science Education web site for a more in-depth discussion of this topic: http://www.natcenscied.org/

and the related perspectives of extreme essentialism[4] and complete social constructivism,[5] are challenges and obstacles to thinking in an integrative fashion about human behavioral evolution. These perspectives rely on the concept that we have no need to seek answers about modern behavior in any aspects of the past and biological processes and that all is explained by a particular sociocultural belief, a pattern of political/economic/experiential factors, or a single human, biological, nature. I lump creationism and essentialism together because they occur in the religious and the secular alike. Their underlying theme, namely that our past, or our present, is more or less set and can be fully known, is dangerous because it inhibits inquiry. Believing we already know all the answers to why we do what we do as humans is dangerous; it constrains our ability for introspection and information sharing, the two core facets of humanity.

Just as dangerous as the creationist and essentialist perspectives, and possibly harder to detect, are the misrepresentations of processes and patterns in human evolution. The acceptance of slavery for centuries, the genocide of native peoples across the Americas, the racist eugenics movements, and the wave of anti-immigrant legislation in the United States during the early part of the twentieth century all had a strong foothold in misunderstandings and misrepresentations of human evolution and biology. We now know these views and practices are wrong as biological, social, moral, and political propositions. Knowledge of the human genome disproves the presence of more than one biological race in modern humans and extensive analyses show that there are no innate intelligence differences between social groups. Biological and ethnographic datasets show that humans vary substantially in many ways, but we are all *H. sapiens* and no living group of humans has an evolutionary (i.e., genetic) advantage over any other. There is no concrete evidence for any truly unique biological characteristic that distinguishes one human social/cultural group from all others despite *centuries* of trying to find such differences. However, this does not always stop researchers from proposing faulty "evolutionary" scenarios for human differences.

On October 17, 2006, the BBC web site posted a story about a work by Oliver Curry, a postgraduate researcher in the Darwin@LSE group of the London School of Economics. The story, entitled "human species may split

[4] From Platonic Idealism, essentialism is basically, in its extreme form, the notion that there is an inherent set of fixed defining characteristics for a category, in this case a known, fixed human nature; a static, single way of being human. By creationism and essentialism I am referring to extreme deterministic views, not to any given religion or religious belief in general. In fact, I believe that dialogue across theological, philosophical, and evolutionary perspectives is extremely important in understanding and investigating human behavior (see Epilogue).

[5] Complete social constructivism is the view that the individual and sociocultural–political contexts are the only agents that have any real bearing on understanding human behavior. This extreme view is not really that actively utilized by researchers interested in human behavior, and its more moderate forms are actually very beneficial to the social sciences, especially when combined with evolutionary perspectives into a form of constructivist evolutionary approaches.

in two" was a review of Curry's hypothesis that socioeconomic, mating, behavioral, and technological trajectories will result in two distinct species of humans by the year 3000. Sexual selection and behavioral shifts would result in one "upper class" species of coffee colored, 6½-foot-tall humans in which males have large penises and females have pert breasts. The other species would be short, stocky, and dim-witted "lower class." He compares the outcome to the two races of humanity portrayed by H.G. Wells, the eloi and morlocks, in his fantasy novel *The Time Machine*. Is this all human evolution has in store for us? Apparently not:

> Dr Curry warns, in 10,000 years time, humans may have paid a genetic price for relying on technology. Spoiled by gadgets designed to meet their every need, they could come to resemble domesticated animals. Social skills, such as communicating and interacting with others, could be lost, along with emotions such as love, sympathy, trust and respect. People would become less able to care for others, or perform in teams. (http://news.bbc.co.uk/go/pr/fr/-/2/hi/uk_news/6057734.stm)

The ability to employ critical thinking skills is essential when respected mainstream news media report these kinds of pseudoscientific "research" results. A basic grasp of human evolutionary history in regard to social behavior, mating patterns, distribution of body size and shape, the appearance of modern socioeconomic hierarchies, and rates of morphological change in humans and our recent ancestors demonstrate this "research" result to be as fantastical as H.G. Wells' novel (but not nearly as innovative).[6] Understanding the structure and components of human behavioral patterns and their potential evolutionary pathways facilitates tackling the mystery of our past and its relationship to the present and future with the appropriate toolkit. Using what we know about the evolution of behavior makes a contribution to deciphering why we do what we do and can have broad social implications. It can also allow us to understand why such pronouncements as those by Dr. Curry are not an accurate reflection of critical and analytical evolutionary scientific inquiry.

Beyond this basic critique of pop science and on to the level of future projection, it is relevant as to what kinds of questions we ask and how we formulate our answers about human behavioral evolution. The global increasing densities, escalating violence and conflict, and growing economic disparities across human populations are serious behavioral issues that we must analyze and, hopefully, develop policies to address. Those policies could be influenced by understandings of human potential, human histories, and human behavioral trajectories. Thus, the critical toolkit we bring to bear on such endeavors, both asking and answering questions about human behavioral evolution, and assessing the pronouncements of others, may

---

[6] In fact, Dr. Curry's pronouncements are strikingly similar to the ideas about the future of human evolution put forward shortly after Darwin published the *Origin of Species* and to those promulgated by eugenicists throughout the twentieth century.

have implications on aspects of popular opinion and even governance. I am not making the argument that one should base social policy on results from investigations into human behavioral evolution, rather that such results should be available as information sources for our academies and populace such that we have a more robust toolkit with which to assess the proposals and decisions made by those in power regarding our behavioral potentials and social futures.

A SIMPLE EXAMPLE OF BEHAVIORAL EVOLUTION

So far we have focused on the relevance of the way we think about human evolution, where humans "fit" in nature, and why a critical approach to talking about human behavioral evolution is important. Now let us review a relatively simple example of behavioral evolution to get an idea of the kinds of patterns we can expect in evolutionary scenarios about behavior. This example describes a rapid and human-impacted change in behavioral patterns across generations in two nonhuman social mammals: the silver fox and the domestic dog. The point here is to demonstrate that we do know something about behavioral evolution, and that we can observe it in other organisms and get a hint for the ways in which behavioral systems, not specifically tied to a single genetic sequence or sequences, might be passed across generations (Figure 1.2).

The story of the dog is a story of behavioral evolution. Dogs are highly social mammals that are a part of many human societies. Most hypotheses for the evolution of the domestic dog involve some scenario wherein humans and some ancestral canid are exposed to each other and gradually begin to associate spatially and then socially. The end product is our companion animal and the feral dog that lives in the streets—all of whom share a set of physical and behavioral features that distinguish them sufficiently from other canids to call them a distinct species or, minimally, a subspecies. It is largely the behavioral features, and more recent modifications of form such as breeds, that define the domestic dog. How do we test the hypothesis that dogs evolved behaviorally through association with humans? The archeological record tells us that around 15,000–9000 years ago, canids that look a bit different from wolves or "wild types" appear associated with the remains of human settlements. This tells us the association between humans and ancestral dogs was established by that time; however, it does not tell us about a mechanism for getting from an ancestral canid in association with humans to the modern domestic dog. One way to look for a mechanism, and test this hypothesis, would be to take a wild canid that has not been domesticated and see what happens if you select for particular behavior across many generations. If one can achieve a suite of behaviors like those found in domestic dogs, then the scenario proposed for dog evolution would not be proven per se, but its mechanism would be supported.

In the 1950s, a Soviet scientist, Dimity K. Belyaev began a series of evolutionary experiments that Russian researchers, such as Lyudmila Trut and

Figure 1.2 A: Domestic dogs, showing variation in size, shape, and hair form. Photographs courtesy of Author and Jan Beatty. B: The silver fox is not a dog, but it can be bred to exhibit many dog-like behaviors. Photograph by Monty Sloan, www. wolfphotography.com

her colleagues, continued up to the present. They saw the story of domestication and specifically the domestication of dogs as a likely place to focus study on understanding the patterns of selection at both the phenotypic and genotypic levels.

They noticed that across domesticated animals there were certain behaviors and morphological traits that appeared fairly routinely. If you look at domestic species (such as dogs, sheep, pigs, cats, etc.) you see the behavioral pattern of "tameness" (lack of fear of humans, subordination to human commands/tasks, and actual seeking out of humans for interaction). You also see many physical traits that rarely appear in wild versions of the same animals such as dwarfism, gigantism, piebald coat color, curly hair, curved/rolled tails, shortened tails, floppy ears, and even nonseasonal reproduction.

For over 40 years, the research team conducted experiments on the impact of domestication on silver foxes (*Vulpes vulpes*) (45,000 of them over 35 generations) (Trut 1999). They selected for one behavior: tameness. They only allowed the tamest individuals of every generation to breed (~10–15%

of all animals) such that today they have very tame foxes that whine, cuddle, lick humans' hands, and behave remarkably like domestic dogs. However, along with these behavioral changes, they observed a suite of morphological and physiological ones: more variation in skull shape and size than in wild forms, coat color variation (more than the reddish or grayish morphs in the wild), curled tails, floppy ears, shorter or longer legs, lower levels and peaks of stress hormones, and increased levels of serotonin (a nuerotransmitter that in humans is involved in mood elevation among other things). Trut and colleagues found that many of these changes occurred as favoring "tameness" also favored those pups whose rate of development from pups to adults was variable (most typically slowed down). As developmental patterns became delayed, specific morphological and behavioral trends also emerged. Selection for one suite of behavioral traits resulted in a whole range of physical and behavioral changes that made these foxes, 35 generation later, act and look a lot like domestic dogs. Dogs as we currently know them have only recently undergone the kinds of directed intense breeding that produces the "breeds" we are familiar with. But their "domestication" process emerged from more of a mutual relationship between humans and dogs over the course of the last 15,000 years or so.

Given modern extremes in dog size and behavior one might ask how, evolutionarily, do you get a Great Dane and a Chihuahua from the same ancestral type of animal? First, extensive selection of tameness might have occurred when ancestral dogs hung around human groups, possibly as it led to greater access to food and increased reproductive success. This process, as demonstrated in the fox example, can begin to expose some underlying variation in morphology and behavior—complex developmental linkages and trajectories. But it is also important to note that all of the following processes of evolution play a role.

Mutation

Initially, there needs to be a good deal of variation in the genetic base and this variation must have arisen through mutation. These variants must also in some way be able to affect behavior and developmental patterns.

Gene Flow

Initially, the early domesticated dogs would still be breeding with the wild versions, but over time, as they spent more and more time with humans, they would have less contact and thus less gene flow with wild populations. Restricted gene flow means that other factors, such as selection and drift, can more easily impact the domesticates as their gene pool, and behavioral experiences, become more or less cut off from other populations of the same species in the wild.

Genetic Drift

Once gene flow with wild types is largely cut off the cluster of dogs that spent all their time around humans would only have whatever genetic variation occurs in their population. The gene pool of the domesticates will be more restricted than the wild population. They will also be exposed only to specific behavioral experiences, limited by their group and the humans' actions.

Selection

Over long periods of time we can see those dogs that are tame, associate socially toward the humans, and maybe assist the humans will likely receive more food, shelter, and assistance from the humans than dogs that did not. These dogs are then the individuals who will leave more offspring, and thus their genetic variation, and possibly their behavioral patterns, will become the most represented in the subsequent human-associating (domestic) dog population. It is also possible that humans began to select certain dogs and allowed them to breed while they restricted breeding of the others. If the humans wanted very large dogs, they could select the largest pups and allow only them to breed. Conversely, if the humans want small dogs they can do the same with the small pups, or those with short legs. As in the fox example, humans may also start breeding for behaviors with some heritable component (genetic or epigenetic), such as proclivity either to bark or not bark. In any case, over time, if there is some heritable component to the traits (behaviors and morphology) selected for, dogs produced from such breeding practices will reflect these behaviors or morphology more and more. Of course, there will always be substantial variation in the behavior and morphology of the dogs, as we see even in extreme cases such as Great Danes or Chihuahuas, each of which are the products of centuries of controlled breeding for size.

Development

All of the processes of evolution are tied to the patterns of development and the flexibility that it brings. For example, as with the foxes, when humans select for one specific trait in the dogs, there may be a series of developmental correlates, such as later onset of hormone patterns or decreased levels of hearing response, and so on. These correlates might produce a series of changes not envisioned by the humans, but resulting from the integration of the genetic, developmental, and behavioral systems. Think about the patterns of color, hip structure, temperament, and skull shape in Great Danes and Chihuahuas; all probably carry with them traits that came from the selection for size.

Why Give This Example?

Because, while we do not fully understand all the mechanisms for the connections between behavior and evolution, it is obvious that selection for a given trait, either behavioral or physical, changes many other facets of the organism. Specifically, if the trait being selected is behavioral, there can be a cascade of "side effects" that have substantial behavioral and morphological impacts. This example is "artificial" in the sense that it is human directed and much more intense than could possibly occur in a "wild" population. But it is not truly artificial in that it is an example of selection and can act as a model, albeit speeded up and more focused, of what might occur under free-ranging settings. Traits are interconnected and when one changes, many others may also follow. These changes may be epigenetic (more than just the genes), behavioral, and/or morphological.

A majority of evolutionary scenarios proposed for humanity continue to focus on a few specific traits. It is highly unlikely that human evolution has progressed in such a piecemeal pattern. But maybe, like the foxes, we have systems whose components are changing at different rates. The complex task set out for us in understanding our own behavioral evolution is how to simultaneously use approaches and perspectives that allow for systems and trait analyses to be mutually comprehensible and interactive.

CHAPTER 2

Why We Behave Like Humans

Historical Perspectives and Basal Assumptions

There are very few novel ideas. Most major contributions to scientific (and most analytical and philosophical) endeavors are built on the results of numerous different research strategies and theoretical proposals across long periods of time. Occasionally some individuals are especially good at compiling these disparate threads into coherent systems. Other individuals do on occasion come up with relatively novel ideas or premises that in turn are integrated into ongoing theoretical perspectives or, rarely, radically alter the current paradigm into which they emerge. This chapter is a short primer on the history of the particular ideas that have had the greatest impact in the quest to understand the evolution of human behavior.

In the study of the evolution of human behavior there are many individuals and research programs that have contributed to our modern understandings and methodologies. However, here in the first decade of the twenty-first century we reside amidst one major dominant paradigm that has roots over 100 years old and that has undergone a number of significant changes in the last 40 years. In order to fully understand the primary facets of this paradigm, our modern approaches to assessing and researching the evolution of human behavior, we have to look backwards to the history of ideas and how our current perspectives emerged through time.

While startlingly resilient and widely supported, our dominant paradigm is also malleable and is currently in the process of undergoing some shifting in infrastructure. We will address this shifting in Chapter 7. In this chapter, we will review a few of the prominent people and ideas that had foundational and lasting impacts on how we currently seek to understand the evolution of human behavior. This is by no means a thorough history, rather it is merely meant to be a summary of the main ideas that have had a lasting impact on the infrastructure of our theory and methodologies. The ideas reviewed here are those that have remained most prominent or had major influence on the way in which we structure our thinking about human evolution.

CHARLES DARWIN AND THE *DESCENT OF MAN*

Darwin conceptualized magnitudes of difference between humans ("man" in his terms) and other animals in the arena of the mind. However, these are differences of degree not of kind. Stemming from his focus on natural selection as the process of evolutionary change and the assumption of higher forms being derived from lower types, Darwin saw humans as an expansion on basal traits found in "lower" forms and the higher traits found in the "quadrumana" (apes and monkeys). Human behavior, for Darwin, represents the logical extension of the generalized mammalian and specific primate sociality. However, his bottom line remained that "Man still bears in his bodily frame the indelible stamp of his lowly origin" (p. 913).

In a very real sense, Darwin's view on the evolution of human behavior provides the explicit underpinning for nearly all of the subsequent approaches. He saw sociality and phylogenetic relationships as focal infrastructure for asking question about human behavior. He proposed that natural and sexual selection shaped much of human behavior and even suggested that environmental factors could restrict and/or enhance the appearance of human behavioral complexity. Darwin also believed that the major key to understanding human behavior was the exploration of both the social world of humans and the functioning of the human mind. From even a general reading of the *Descent of Man* one can see that the focal arenas Darwin laid out for the investigation of the evolution of human behavior are almost exactly those areas where the major modern perspectives take their starting points (Sociobiology, Washburnian Biological Anthropology, Human Behavioral Ecology, Evolutionary Psychology, Memetics, and Dual Inheritance Theory—see following sections and Chapter 3). It is almost as if these modern approaches have each selected one or a few of Darwin's focal suggestions as the core focus of their endeavor.

As a major (the major?) proponent of continuity among living forms, Darwin saw a progression from lower animals to humans in the context of the mind (and thus behavior or at least behavioral potential). He also saw all humanity as unified in this potential relative to other life forms. In the *Decent of Man*, Darwin suggests that humans have all the senses of lower animals, all the fundamental intuitions of lower animals, all mental facilities of higher animals, combined with a series of innovations that make the human mind capable of much more than those of other animals. He described these innovations as a stronger ability in imitation, attention, imagination, reasoning, sense of beauty, and language.

Unlike many of his contemporaries, Darwin strongly believed that there were features of the human mind (and thus behavioral potential) shared across the entire species. Darwin noted that the "tastes, dispositions, and habits" within humans were more similar in all aspects of the mind (behavior) than in other types of animals. This held true, according to Darwin, even between the "races" of man, a very unpopular perspective in his day. Which is not to say that Darwin did not see significant differences in behavior and capabilities between human groups, he did, but that these differences were of a smaller order than those between other animals. The differences between human groups he opined were due to environmental and experiential contexts as well as certain biological factors resulting from the action of natural and sexual selection.

For Darwin, the differential expression of human behavioral potential was heavily influenced by ecological, social, and biological factors. For example, Darwin saw social progress as measured by the structural complexity of a population or society as connected to higher functioning of the mind and also linked to higher overall fitness. He went so far as to partially suggest that human groups competing with one another can produce higher levels of cognitive function and thus greater social complexity in the more "fit" group (shades of a multi-level selectionist argument) (see also Wilson and Wilson 2007). Local environments also affected the expression of human behavior. Darwin used the example of (what he considered to be) behaviorally depauperate Eskimos (Esquimaux) to illustrate how harsh environments can stunt the development of complex behavior and social structure. He also suggested that the environment of poverty provided a handicap to those born into it (even those with higher-quality biological bases) due to the associated dearth of material inheritance. In the cognitive context, Darwin used the example of practicing monotheism as a heightened form of cognitive and social functioning that was only facilitated by the most advanced societies.

Differences between the sexes were also a core factor of the evolution and expression of human behavior for Darwin. He believed that sexual selection had a strong hand not only in generating differences between the sexes, in morphology, but also in core aspects of behavior. Women had evolved increased tenderness, less selfishness, better intuition, and more rapid social perception than men. Men were more courageous, pugnacious, and energetic and endowed with more "inventive genius" (p. 867) than women. Darwin saw his "law of battle" at play here. Physical competition between males and nurturing behavior in females were logical extensions of what he had read about social primates and thus he saw them enhanced in the linguistic and super-cognitive humankind. The "battle" that men engaged in made them more acute in understanding the world and achieving positions of eminence through both intellect and physical strength and sheer tenacity. Darwin relied heavily on his cousin Francis Galton's publications (e.g., *Hereditary Genius*) for exemplars of this assertion and concluded that the "average of mental power in man must be above that of woman" (p. 873).

Despite the differences between men and women and between groups of humans Darwin noted than humans share a moral sense at our very core and that this moral sense combined with human intellect made humans dominant above all others. Interestingly, Darwin saw social animals as, at least partially, structurally altruistic "impelled partly by a wish to aid members of their community in a general manner, but more commonly to perform certain definite actions" (p. 913). The human, on the other hand, is "impelled by the same general wish to aid his fellows, but has few or no special instincts" (p. 913). Humans, having intellect, morals, and language did not rely solely on blind instinctive impulses; rather behavior toward others was influenced by experience and reason.

For Charles Darwin human behavioral characteristics are based on mammalian and especially primate social behavioral patterns. During the course of human evolution natural and sexual selection favored increased cognitive capabilities resulting in language, complex social relationships, and moral values. Associated with this is the notion that the power of the human mind exceeds that of any other organism and that change (at least societal change) moves in a progressive sense with the "more fit" groups in humankind moving toward increased moral and social virtue over time. To understand human behavior Darwin saw benefits in studying other mammals, especially primates, in trying to understand the constraints and facilitations inherent in different environments, and in examining the ways in which human groups and sexes vary in identifying how sexual and/or natural selection would have produced such patterns.

ALFRED RUSSEL WALLACE AND THE EVOLUTION OF THE MIND

Like Darwin, Wallace saw human behavior and cognitive capabilities evolving over time under the auspices of natural selection, with the "mind" being the major differentiating factor between humans and other "higher" organisms. To an extent greater than did Darwin, Wallace saw the human mind as fully unique, drawing on basal organization present in "lower" forms in its inception but being unlike any other animal in its current form "placing man apart, as not only the head and culminating point of the grand series of organic nature, but as in some degree a new and distinct order of being." Wallace saw this advancement as resulting in beings who are able to manage and guide nature itself.

The central facets in Wallace's view of the evolution of human behavior overlap extensively with Darwin's. Darwin viewed Wallace's 1864 paper "The origin of human races and the Antiquity of man deduced from the theory of 'natural selection'" as the most eloquent exposition of the development of human behavioral patterns and explicandum for human racial variation (Richards 1987). In this essay, Wallace proposes that the hallmark of the emergence of humanity was the cessation of selection on the body combined with the forceful action of selection on human cognitive abilities. The point in prehistory where this shift in the focus of selection occurs is where he saw humans diverging from the "brute" stock sharing recent common ancestry with the apes.

Once this focus of selection shifted, Wallace proposed that intergroup, or inter "tribe," competition acted to enhance the moral and mental qualities of the more "fit" groups, which over time resulted in the modern human behavioral forms. Those "tribes" or communities, in which individuals are able to construct superior weapons for hunting, have increased types of cooperative endeavors, display heightened social and sympathetic (even altruistic) attitudes toward compatriots, have developed higher mental and moral qualities, and are in turn more "fit." This view highlights both a type of group level competition and a focus on the connection between mental and moral capabilities as the indications of the highest forms produced via evolution by natural selection (both views shared, to an extent, by Darwin).

Wallace saw support for this view in the fact of extreme overlap in post-cranial form between humans and the apes and the subsequent likelihood that the real chasm between humans and apes resulted from selection on the mind and its concomitant impact on the cranium. He also saw support for his position when comparing modern human groups or "races." He used the eurocentric racist views of his day to elaborate on how patterns of selection might act to increase mental and moral powers in some groups and cause the extinction of others. For Wallace the Germanic race and those races of Western Europe are farthest along in the progress of selection toward mental and moral perfection, evidenced by the fact of the "inevitable extinction of all those low and mentally undeveloped populations with which Europeans come in contact" (Wallace 1864). However, Wallace did envision the possibility of enhanced environments resulting in selection on the "lower" races of humans in such a way that they too would improve in the direction of Europeans. In fact, he believed that over time natural selection would result in the enhancement or extinction of all lesser races such that only one human race exhibiting the characteristics of the "noblest of specimens" will remain.

For Alfred Russel Wallace, as with Darwin, the human mind (and thus behavior) evolved under the pressures of natural selection toward a state that emphasizes mental and moral prowess. He saw altruistic and sympathetic behavior toward one's fellow humans as core in this adaptive pattern and competition between human groups ("tribes" or "races") as an essential factor in the evolution of human behavior and cognitive capabilities. To a greater extent than Darwin, Wallace saw a cessation of selection on the human body and human abilities to manipulate and control our environment (and thus selection pressures) as major factors in our evolution. Late in his life, Wallace moved even further along these lines, more or less eschewing the power of selection to affect modern humans and focusing largely on spiritual and metaphysical forces as affecting human development and behavior (Richards 1987).

BETWEEN DARWIN AND SOCIOBIOLOGY

Spencer, Baldwin, and Morgan: Biology, Psychology, and the Behavioral Evolution of the Human Mind

Probably best known, and most maligned, for promulgating a form of social Darwinism, Herbert Spencer contributed more to modern basal perspectives on the evolution of human behavior than many give him credit for. Throughout his life, Spencer espoused a program of "Synthetic Philosophy" regarding humans, a perspective that sought to combine biology, morality, psychology, and sociology in order to most effectively understand human development and behavior. In fact, in the last 40 years of the nineteenth century he authored substantial texts in each of these fields. Thus, in addition to his sociopolitical application of Darwinian perspectives, Spencer also promulgated a multidisciplinary approach to understanding the evolution of human behavior that heavily impacted researchers and philosophers during the latter part of the nineteenth and the first part of the twentieth centuries (Dobzhansky 1972, Richards 1987).

Spencer's quest to understand the evolution of human behavior was goal directed: he sought to explain how natural selection could ultimately produce a moral, utopian society (similar in a sense to both Darwin and Wallace's views, but more explicit in this goal). He worked to construct a set of hypotheses and philosophical propositions that would connect natural selection and this ultimate outcome. Accordingly, he firmly believed that social development in humans is governed by natural laws, and that selection played a substantial role on the formation of societies. He laid out the germination for many of these ideas initially in his book, *Social Statics: Or, the Conditions Essential to Human Happiness Specified, and the First of Them Developed* (1851), prior to Darwin's publication of the theory of Natural Selection. In subsequent years, he began to incorporate facets of Darwin's ideas alongside pseudo-Lamarckian and other evolutionary perspectives into his models for human development and evolution, which he fully laid out in the revised *Social Statics* published in 1892.

At the base of human behavior he saw that humans vary in their behavioral proclivities and moral senses (these senses he divided into selfish instinct and sentiment of sympathy). Underlying this variation he envisioned a pattern of altruistic behavior as core to human success. However, he proposed two ways in which such altruism could arise and become dominant as a human behavioral characteristic. Unlike Darwin and Wallace, Spencer saw the individual expression of altruism as having a selfish motivation. As humans relate to the misery of others (sympathetic response) we act to alleviate others suffering in order to avoid our own (*Principles of Psychology,*

1855 and 1872). Spencer also eventually allowed for a form of altruism that can arise through a series of reciprocally beneficial acts between individuals and then be "selected" for if these exchanges resulted in increased fitness for the participants (*The Principles of Ethics*, 1893). However, Spencer did also agree with both Darwin and Wallace that community or family altruism could arise as behavior within the close group or family and could be widely beneficial. In a sense, Spencer argued that this final type of altruism could arise, much in the way envisioned by Darwin and Wallace, via competition between groups, those having more altruists most likely doing better over all than those with too few altruists. In fact, Spencer went as far as to suggest that the functional adaptation by such groups to social conditions would allow those groups to reduce the impact that challenges of the environment (natural selection) placed on them. This perspective was even cited by the cooperation advocate Petr Kropotkin as evidence in support of his perspectives on the hyper-cooperative adaptation in humans (Richards 1987).

Similar to Darwin and Wallace, Spencer looked to the human mind to localize the unique or most advanced features of humanity. He focused on a human mind that was capable of rapidly adapting to changing and complex social environments. Spencer postulated a "law of intelligence" stating that these complex social environments drove humans toward adaptations of increased intellect and more complex mental states (*Principles of Psychology*). In this pattern Spencer believed that simple or direct selection was insufficient to explain increased intellect and complex mental facilities and that there was also a "formal inheritance of accommodating mechanisms" that arose (in pseudo-Lamarckian fashion) from behavioral adaptation resulting in acquired traits passed across generations (similar to Lloyd Morgan and Baldwin's organic selection below). Herbert Spencer saw the evolution of human behavior as a process that integrated the social and the physical, following both the paradigm of Darwinian selection and the processes of social inheritance of intelligence and adaptive behavior.

During the last decades of the nineteenth and the first of the twentieth centuries, the infusion of Darwin's, Wallace's, and Spencer's ideas into psychology resulted in the first sets of evolutionary psychologists, providing the precursors to many modern perspectives on the evolution of the mind and human behavior. C. Lloyd Morgan and Mark James Baldwin were major figures in this movement. Both men independently came up with a model for human behavioral evolution, currently termed "**the Baldwin effect**," that has a lasting and important impact on modern ideas about how humans develop and evolve behavior.

C. Lloyd Morgan (*Animal Life and Intelligence*, 1891; *Habit and Instinct*, 1896; "Of Modification and Variation," *Science* 4:733–740 (1896)) held that behavior and its associated psychological facilities could be transmitted across generations, that these cognitive facilities could evolve, and that they structured and guided evolution. He proposed that basal behavior in animals (instinct) arose both from the action of natural selection and from the "inheritance of habitual activities intelligently acquired," but denied the continued impact of selection on the minds of modern humans. For Morgan, human minds (brains) were plastic organs capable of rational response and thus not directly (currently) under the pressure of selection. While his broad notion of modification and variation applied to human and nonhuman alike, it has most relevance for the innovation and amplification of human behavior. Morgan's basic argument stated that on facing new challenges those organisms with the most plastic response to exhibiting or learning novel behavior would be naturally preserved relative to those who could not, "learned behavior and acquired modification becomes part of the hereditary legacy." This, along with Baldwin's ideas, constitutes a formal proposal for some (gene)–culture coevolution, in essence what has been termed "organic evolution" or "the Baldwin effect."

Mark James Baldwin could be considered one of the most important contributors to theoretical understanding of the evolution and development of human behavior, and few students in the twenty-first century have ever heard of him. Known almost exclusively for the eponymous "Baldwin effect," Baldwin made major contributions by highlighting the dual and interactive roles of physiology and experience in the development and evolution of behavior. His approach has been termed "evolutionary biopsychology" (Richards 1987) where he sought to integrate physiological, neurological, and psychological factors to develop a theory of "organic selection." For Baldwin all characters were, in part, both congenital and acquired.

Expanding on the perspectives of Herbert Spencer in regards to selection by social environments, Baldwin envisioned a social heredity in addition to physical heredity. For humans these inherited elements included cultural rules, social norms, habits, and so on. Baldwin, in a sense, presents these disparate social elements as competing with one another (preceding the "meme" concept, see Chapter 3) and being reproduced via imitation and application. Once ideas became prominent in a society they constituted a part of the social environment of that society and part of the "selection" pressures on new ideas that emerged. Baldwin saw the social environment as important as the physical in the evolution and development of human behavior (Baldwin 1897).

As with Spencer and Morgan, plasticity of response and inheritance of the subsequent "fit" responses was at the core of Baldwin's ideas. Novel or changing environments (physical and social) resulted in a state wherein "those congenital or phylogenetic variations are kept in existence, which lend themselves to intelligent, imitative, adaptive, and mechanical modification during the lifetime of the creatures which have them" (Baldwin 1896) resulting in a suite of ontogenetically derived characters/behaviors. He also stated that these "ontogenetic adaptations are really new, not preformed; and they are really reproduced in succeeding generations, although not physically inherited" (Baldwin 1896). This is today termed the "Baldwin effect."

Along with the majority of theorists in the late nineteenth century, Baldwin believed that altruism was a core factor in human societies and that its presence was, as promulgated by Darwin, Wallace, and Spencer, due to a form of group selection wherein groups with higher numbers of altruists did better than groups with fewer. Baldwin formalized many of the perspectives of Spencer and others in regard to human behavior with the bottom line being that humans evolved (and are evolving) a capability for wide and ranging plasticity in behavioral responses. However, this plasticity is directed and structured in the context of the social environment in which it occurs and develops.

The Modern Synthesis

The second half of the twentieth century saw the emergence and spread of the "Modern Synthesis" paradigm in evolutionary studies. The discovery of genetic systems and their function, improved the understanding of population level variation, and the innovation/incorporation of mathematical approaches facilitated more in-depth and extensive evolutionary models. This paradigm, combined with dramatic enhancements in fossil human discoveries and the expansion of primatological studies, laid the groundwork for substantial changes in the focus and models for the evolution of human behavior that eventually became formalized in the genic-based sociobiology paradigm of the last quarter of the twentieth century.

The basic tenets of the modern synthesis include a focus on the population (a cluster of individuals of the same species who share a common geographical area and find their mates more often in their own cluster than in others) to study evolutionary change and a focus on the individual as the unit of selection. Evolution is assessed as changes in allele (forms of genes/genetic variants) frequencies over time. Importantly, evolution has neither inherent direction or goal, nor is it necessarily progressive. This is a major distinction, especially in terms of human evolution, from the views held by the major theorists of the nineteenth century. For all of the major proponents of evolution some notion of progressive improvement was at the core of their application of natural selection to human beings (even for Darwin). This improvement more often than not included a progression toward higher morals and ethical conduct and greater degree of "civilization." This perspective is not part of the modern synthesis.

As evolution is seen as allele frequencies changing at the population level over time, the major focus on the new synthesis was the modes of change. Under this rubric, allele frequencies change over time because of mutation, and the evolutionary sorting/mixing processes of gene flow, genetic drift, and natural selection (see Box 2.1 for basic review of genetics). **Mutation** is the only way novel genetic combinations (alleles) are introduced. **Gene flow** is the process by which genetic material and complexes move, or are limited in their movement, through and between populations, largely through migration and nonrandom mating. **Genetic drift** is the process by which random events affect the frequencies of alleles from generation to generation. The new synthesis view of **natural selection** can be seen as the filtering

BOX 2.1
Basic Gene Function

Emerging since the Modern Synthesis we have a very robust understanding of basic genetic processes and a working definition of a gene. We know that DNA and the maternal cellular elements are transmitted across generations. Parents pass on the information for the construction of proteins (as DNA segments) and the regulatory mechanisms in the female gamete (egg) to their offspring. The segments of DNA that contain the "messages" for a given protein are found in the same places in the DNA (and thus on the chromosomes) in all humans. So, at a basic level gene can be defined as a segment of DNA that contains the sequence for a protein. All humans have the same genes, but for most genes there are a number of different nucleotide sequences. Variations in the nucleotide sequences of the same gene are called alleles. These alleles are the basic genetic variation that provide the fuel for evolutionary change.

Although we can say that genes (and their alleles) contain the codes for proteins, the relationship between genes and traits is extremely complex. There is a multitude of complex chemical interactions within the cell, within the nucleus, between cells, and throughout organisms that make most one-gene to one-trait analogies pretty unrealistic. For example, your hands are composed of numerous substances coded for in your DNA. However, your hands themselves are not the direct product of a "hand gene." Rather, they are the product of a complex developmental program in which DNA plays an important, but not exclusive, role.

We can envision "genes" as having four different general types of causal relationships with traits. First, a gene may simply contain the code for one protein (or one set of related proteins if there is more than one allele). This is a simple "one gene–one protein" model. Second, a group of genes may work together to produce one effect, be it a complex protein or even a specific trait composed of multiple proteins. This is a polygenic effect, and it is a common way for genes to work. Third, one gene may have many effects on a number of different traits and/or systems. This effect is called pleiotropic, and it is also quite widespread. Finally, it is quite common for a given gene to have both polygenic and pleiotropic effects within an organism. However, there is another level of complexity, remember that each gene can have more than one allele, so in all of the above cases the same gene can be producing slightly different proteins in different individuals.

Many factors influence the development of an organism, including chemical and physical patterns, internal and external environmental influences, and physical constraints on shape and size, in addition to the instructions for proteins laid out in the genes and the regulatory processes carried out by DNA. From the time of conception (the successful joining of two gametes) epigenetic (outside of the DNA) developmental processes are occurring. Slight changes in temperature, fluctuating chemical environments, and the misreading of chemical cues in addition to variation in the patterns of transcription and translation produce slightly differing outcomes for each individual organism. However, even with all of these variables, the general patterns of development are remarkably consistent time after time. This is due to the pressures of natural selection. Developmental systems that produced widely varying results each time would not do very well when the environments were relatively stable (from generation to generation) or if the variable results produced organisms that could not walk, eat, or reproduce. Understanding both genetics and evolutionary processes combined with the realization that each individual organism develops from the union of a pair of gametes allows us to understand how we can have so much variation (needed as fuel for evolutionary change) and yet great stability (results of adaptations) at the same time. The variation is in the details and the stability on the general form and function.

No two individuals are identical. Even when the exact same segments of DNA are involved (such as in clones or identical twins), there are still many complexities in the ways that genes are expressed. Genes may have multiple types of effects; developmental patterns and changing or shifting environments can alter the outcomes of organismal growth, and mutation can occur. The sheer number of variables that go into the expression of genes and the development of organisms ensures that no two individuals, even genetic copies, will have the exact same phenotype.

of phenotypes (and their genotypes) by factors in the environment, resulting in an overrepresentation of better fit phenotypes (and their associated genotypes) within a population in a given environment over time. The better fit phenotypic variants are considered to be best adapted to the specific environment. The traits they carry that help them do well in the environment are called **adaptations**. In the new synthesis, there is an understanding that the **genotype** (genetic matter) does not generally interact directly with the environment, rather that the **phenotype** (morphology and behavior) interacts with the environment, and the genotype is affected by the phenotype's success in a given environment. Success, or "fitness," is measured as total successful reproductive output of the individual, and thus the copies of her/his genetic material that pass across generations.

Washburns' New Physical Anthropology, and the Emergence of an Evolutionary Anthropology of Behavior

After the Study of Fossils and living animals, when theories have taken definite form, then experiments should be planned. Particularly the importance of adaptive complexes and the precise nature of adaptation can be advanced far beyond the level of individual opinion.–(Sherwood Washburn 1951)

We are primates, products of the evolutionary process, and the promise of primatology is a better understanding of the peculiar creature we call man. (Sherwood Washburn 1973)

Starting in the early 1950s the anthropologist, Sherwood Washburn, inspired by a myriad of field experiences, laboratory research, and the emergence of the Modern Synthesis proposed a "New Physical Anthropology" (Washburn 1951). This prospectus argued for Physical Anthropologists to move away from a focus on classification and **typological approaches** to a discipline that incorporated evolutionary theory, the emerging field of genetics, and the use of primate models to understand both human morphological evolution and the evolution of human behavior. Throughout the 1950s, 1960s, and 1970s, Washburn and many of his students approached the evolution of human behavior through the dual lens of primatological and morphological studies. A main facet of this approach was the notion that the social and the biological are intertwined and that evolutionary theory and genetic studies can provide the context for the datasets from behavioral (anthropological and primatological) and morphological (paleontological/anatomical) investigations into humanity.

His new physical anthropology (or "biological anthropology") paradigm produced a majority of the prominent field primatologists of the 1960s, 1970s, and 1980s, the majority of whom looked to the nonhuman primates as models to understand facets of human behavior and evolution (Kelley and Sussman 2007). They sought out primate patterns and universals, behavioral particulars in certain primates, and the possibilities for human behavioral novelty (Washburn and Jay 1968, Washburn and Dolhinow 1972).

For example, themes such as aggression and social dominance were seen as representing a continuum across the primates with human behavior having roots in the nonhuman primate repertoire. In this paradigm the evolution of human behavior is in large part studied by examining the patterns and adaptation of the living primates.

This approach also influenced the tenor and trajectory of molecular and morphological studies looking into the evolution of human behavior. Evolutionary models from primatological and genetic datasets could be applied to modeling human evolution using the fossil record and modern human behavior. For example, a prominent focus on the selective impact of savannah life on early humans came in part from Washburn's proposal of savannah baboons as human models. Throughout the middle of the twentieth century, associations between behavior and morphological and genetic complexes became increasingly evident and anthropologists of the Washburn School began to focus in on their application to the understanding of human behavior.

These anthropological research trajectories of the 1960s and 1970s produced an evolutionary approach in anthropological studies of human behavior. However, this evolutionary anthropology incorporated, to an extent, ecological and ethnographic traditions in anthropology in addition to the burgeoning studies in primatology and molecular anthropology to result in a focus on human variation (plasticity) in behavior as a hallmark of the species. The famed biologist Theodosius Dobzhansky epitomized this emergent pattern in the quote:

> As theoretical possibilities, one can envisage that man might be genetically determined as aggressive or submissive, warlike or peaceful, territorial or wanderer, selfish or generous, mean or good. Are any of these possibilities likely to be realized? Would the fixation of any of these dispositions, so that they become uncontrollable urges or drives, increase the adaptiveness of a species which relies on culture for its survival? I believe that the answers to these questions are in the negative. (Dobzhansky 1972)

The evolutionary anthropology perspective mixed the common themes of plasticity in behavioral response and the importance of social structure from the approaches of the late nineteenth and early twentieth centuries with the novel information from primatological and molecular studies and evolutionary theory (including population genetics) arising from the Modern Synthesis.

Tinbergen's Four Questions and Their Impact on the Understanding of Behavior

At the same time that the focus on morphology and behavior was emerging in evolutionary anthropology, a separate group of practitioners was also presenting a set of methodologies and hypotheses about behavior; **ethology**. This group was the ethologists, characterized by the work of such luminaries as Konrad Lorenz and Niko Tinbergen. The ethologists were focused on the expression and development of animal behavior as measured though observation. While their focus extended to humans (the work of Eibl-Eibelsfeldt, for example) their methods and general perspectives were rooted in the observational study of the behavior of vertebrate animals (fish, birds, and mammals primarily).

Relevant to our history here, Niko Tinbergen published an influential paper in 1963 entitled "On aims and methods of ethology." In this paper Tinbergen lays out the core point that when asking a "why" question about any given behavior (such as "why does the man duck when he hears a loud noise") there are actually four distinct (but interconnected) versions of the "why." The first is the immediate motivation "why." This is called the *proximate* explanation. What stimulus/context/occurrence was it that elicited the behavior? The answer to this "why" question involves the actual action of the mechanism of response. In the case of a man ducking, the proximate answer is that the noise stimulated his ears that sent a message to the brain initiating a behavior.

The second "why" is concerned with the development of the behavior. What experiences, social and physical, across an individual's life span contributed to the exhibition of a particular behavior? This is called the *onto-genetic* explanation. In the case of the ducking man, this could be that he has heard sounds like this in the past and associates them with flying objects or attempts to injure him, so he responds via experience by ducking. It could also be that there is a set of physiological factors that have developed over the course of his life that have been trained to respond to loud noise by rapidly altering the profile of the body.

The third "why" deals with the evolutionary history of the organism. This is the *phylogenetic* explanation and is concerned with the evolutionary history of the individual the species, the genus, and so on. This question seeks an answer in the patterns and changes over the course of evolutionary time in the lineage leading to the individual in question. In the ducking man's case, the evolution of auditory sensory systems and the limbic system in mammals combined with the evolution of predation avoidance strategies in primates and early humans results in his ducking at the stimulus of a loud noise.

Finally, the last "why" deals with function. How does the behavior impact the individual's ability to survive and reproduce? How does it impact the individuals Darwinian "fitness"? This explanation is termed the ultimate answer and is considered to be the question most directly aligned with the action of natural selection. In the case of the ducking man, the ducking serves to decrease his chance of injury and thus preserving his energy and ability to contribute to the gene pool of the subsequent generation.

In the purest form, the goal is to be able to examine all "why" facets of a behavior and not confuse them. This way, if the answers are relatively consistent we can generate a very robust explanation of the development, context, function, and evolution of a behavior. However, in the study of humans it can become very difficult to keep the explanations separate. Our cognitive abilities provide a sense of intentionality that can confound proximate and ultimate explanations. Although all four questions are intended to be equal in explanatory power and relevance, in modern perspectives there is frequently a bias toward the value of the ultimate, or functional, answer (Stamps 2003), which is seen as the most important "level" of analysis in terms of evolutionary understanding (the quest to find human adaptations) (Barrett et al. 2002). The primacy of interest in Tinbergen's ultimate question combined with a series of mathematical models and perspectives on the role of kin and altruism that arose in the 1960s and 1970s laid the foundation for the most pervasive and influential contribution to the study of the evolution of human behavior since the early 1900s: Wilsonian Sociobiology.

THE REVOLUTION OF SOCIOBIOLOGY, KIN SELECTION, AND SELFISH GENES: THE NEW SYNTHESIS

Among the most significant events in the behavioral and biological sciences of the late twentieth century was the publication of E.O. Wilson's text

Sociobiology[1] (1975). This book along with the perspectives contributed by William Hamilton and Robert Trivers used, expanded, altered, and redefined many of the ideas and models proposed for understanding human behavioral evolution from Darwin through Washburn and the ethologists. Ubiquitous in this "new synthesis" perspective was the primacy of ultimate explanations, a reliance on relatively linear mathematical models to model natural selection of behavior, and reduced concern with the physiological and genetic details of the mechanisms for behavioral adaptations.

Hamilton and Kin Selection

One of the most important assumptions in the sociobiological approach is **kin selection**, the behavioral favoring of your close genetic relatives (Hamilton 1964). While Darwin, Wallace, and Spencer all described a scenario similar to kin selection, modern kin selection hypotheses needed the genetic perspective of the Modern Synthesis to come to fruition. Kin selection was a hypothesis formally (mathematically) proposed by William Hamilton to explain the dilemma posed by altruism. **Altruism,** or acts that have a net loss of fitness to the actor but a net gain in fitness to the receiver, does not make sense if organisms benefit by maximizing their own fitness. Darwin, Wallace, Spencer, and others frequently invoked a form of **group selection,** natural selection acting at the level of intergroup competition, to explain why altruism occurs. Emerging from the Modern Synthesis and continued theoretical work in genetics throughout the middle of the twentieth century was an increasingly negative view of group selection (Williams 1966). The focus of selection became solely fixed on the individual. However, the idea of kin selection offers a simple equation that predicts when an individual organism might behave in a manner that looks altruistic. This equation is $r \times b > c$, with r = genetic relatedness between the actor and receiver of the behavior, b = the fitness benefit to the receiver, and c = the fitness cost to the actor. If the individual who receives the benefit from a behavior that costs fitness to the actor is a relative, then a certain percentage of the actors genotype (depending on the degree of relatedness) also benefits form the action. Relatedness is then calculated as a simple percentage of relationship given a sexual reproducing system. As we are diploid (offspring inherit half of their genome from each parent) each offspring is assumed to share 50% of the unique genetic component of each parent while an uncle or aunt is then related at 25% to an actor. In this model, the relatedness (shared unique genetic component) decreases as "relatives" become more genetically distant from the individual. Because close relatives (parents, offspring, siblings)

---

[1] It is important to point out that the term "sociobiology" had been in use since the 1940s to describe approaches toward understanding social behavior through biological mechanisms. Wilson co-opted the term and it is now almost exclusively used to refer to his specific paradigm rather than the more general use.

share much of their genotype, we would expect behaviors among them to be seemingly altruistic, as they frequently appear. As individuals are more distantly related, we would expect to see less and less seemingly altruistic behavior among them. This simple equation and its associated assumptions about genetic systems form an integral core of the sociobiological approach to understanding the evolution of human behavior.

Robert Trivers and Reciprocal Altruism

While kin selection offers an explanation for why apparently altruistic acts occur between related individuals, we are still left with the substantial problem that in humans and other animals unrelated individuals act in what appear to be altruistic manners. In 1971 Robert Trivers published a paper entitled "the evolution of reciprocal altruism" in which he updated ideas that had been around since Darwin's time, specifically Spencer's notions of altruism arising from mutually reciprocated acts. Trivers, as did Hamilton, formalized these ideas as mathematical models and then derived a series of predictive assumptions arising from the model.

The basis of the **reciprocal altruism model** is that unrelated organisms can enter into relationships that can be characterized as fitness value exchanges. Using a simple Mendelian genetic system as a basis, Trivers presents a mathematical equation that outlines the relationship variables between an actor and a recipient in a series of reciprocal exchanges; he used a **prisoner's dilemma** style "payoff matrix." In a prisoner's dilemma, two players are given the options to cooperate or compete with each choice's payoffs depending on the choice of the other player.

While the core of the hypothesis revolves around the frequency and symmetry of potentially altruistic situations, there are actually three main conditions that are relevant in the potential selection for reciprocal altruism: that there be many opportunities for altruistic action during the lifetime of the actors, that a given actor repeatedly interacts with the same small set of individuals, and that pairs of altruists are exposed "symmetrically" to altruistic opportunities such that over time two such actors are able to render roughly equivalent benefits to each other while incurring roughly compatible costs. It is these three conditions in the context of various biological parameters that can set the stage for the selection (evolution) of a reciprocal altruistic system. Some of the biological parameters include length of lifetime (chances of reciprocal altruism rise with longevity), dispersal pattern (low dispersal rate also favors reciprocal altruism), and degree of mutual independence (group living animals are more reliant on one another more frequently than solitary ones). Other important biological factors include presence and type of parental care, dominance hierarchy structure, and aid in combat. If the three primary conditions are met and the biological parameters set favorable conditions, Trivers predicted that reciprocal altruism will evolve as an adaptation in that population.

This set of ideas is especially important as it had substantial influence on theoreticians since the 1970s and forms one of the main bases for models of animal and human behavior in many hypotheses. Trivers himself proposed that a major human adaptive psychological system evolved out of the need to manage the complex temporal and social facets of reciprocal altruism and that behavior and emotions such as friendship, moralistic aggression, gratitude, sympathy, guilt, rules for exchange, and cheating emerged from this (see Chapter 5). Like Darwin and Spencer, Trivers makes a strong case that human emotions are the result of an adaptive psychological complex; however, unlike Darwin and Spencer, he invokes a genetic calculus and creates a mathematical model tied to the process of reciprocal altruism to serve as the assessment of function and a predictor of the target of selection.

E.O. Wilson, Evolutionary Sociobiology and the Autocatalysis Model

The publication of the book *Sociobiology* created a firestorm in the quest for understanding the evolution of human behavior. While its general content reflected a compendium of current theory and hypotheses in evolutionary biology and animal behavior, the last chapter dealt specifically with humans ("man" in Wilson's words). Proponents and detractors, to this day, wrangle over the details, impact, intent, and content of that last chapter of the text entitled "Man: From Sociobiology to Sociology." Wilson starts the chapter inviting the reader to see humans from the perspective of a Martian zoologist coming to earth. He attempts to provide what he considers a nonbiased external view, a natural history of the mammal *Homo sapiens*, with the intent of assessing our biogram, our sociobiology. Whether or not one considers his attempt a success, the contents of the chapter lay the modern foundation for the majority of investigators researching the evolution of human behavior today. While much of what Wilson proposes had already been stated, in various forms, from the late 1800s through the early 1970s, his major contribution was to compile them all and present a relatively unified prospectus for "man's" behavioral evolution.

At the root of Wilson's proposal are a set of basal assumptions. The main assumptions include the concept that behavior can be modeled using the analogy of Mendelian genetic systems, that natural selection is the architect of functional behavior (behavior that can potentially impact fitness), and that "genes" (or some genetic units) promoting a variety of social behaviors have been selected over time in humans. To support these assumptions, Wilson relies heavily on analogy to social insects (where he is a world renowned expert), comparison with nonhuman primate studies, and a few anthropological ethnographic accounts (an area where he is not an expert). Wilson also assumes that humans, in their modern state (the last ~10,000 years or so), have undergone a form of ecological release thus allowing for the observed huge variation in social structure across the planet.

Wilson identifies what he considers to be a set of unique characteristics in humans, such as enormous social plasticity, true language, continuous sexual activity/receptivity by females across the menstrual cycle, a universality of marriage and incest avoidance, a core role for reciprocal altruism and barter systems, and a cooperative sexual division of labor. Associated factors include the primacy of the nuclear family as the basal social unit, male dominance, a disassociation of sexual behavior and fertilization, and a possible genetic predisposition in individuals to different societal roles. Social elements such as religious beliefs, magic, and totemism are presented as arising from processes of group selection in response to environmental pressures. Territoriality, xenophobia, aggression, bravery, and success in warfare for males are also traits that have been favored by both individual and group selection. Finally, the human penchant for conformity and indoctrinability are also proposed to have arisen from both group and individual level selection (see also Wilson and Wilson 2007).

The specific model that Wilson puts forward to explain his theses is the **autocatalysis model** of human evolution (see also Chapter 5). This model represents a compilation of the main hypotheses of human evolution and the fossil datasets available by the early 1970s. The model states:

> when the earliest homnids[2] became bipedal as part of their terrestrial adaptation, their hands were freed, the manufacture and handling of artifacts was made easier, and intelligence grew as part of the improvement of the tool-using habit. With mental capacity and the tendency to use artifacts increasing through mutual reinforcement, the entire materials-based culture expanded. Cooperation during hunting was perfected, providing a new impetus for the evolution of intelligence, which in turn permitted still more sophistication in tool using, and so on through cycles of causation. At some point, probably during the late *Australopithecus* period or the transition from *Australopithecus* to *Homo*, this autocatalysis carried the evolving populations to a certain threshold of competence, at which the hominids were able to exploit the antelopes, elephants, and other large herbivorous mammals teeming around them on the African plains. Quite possibly the process began when the hominids learned to drive big cats, hyenas, and other carnivores from their kills. In time they became the primary hunters themselves and were forced to protect their prey from other predators and scavengers. (Wilson 1975, pp. 567–568)

The model goes on to state the premises that the shift to big game hunting accelerated the process of mental evolution and that the sexual division of labor forms the baseline for modern humanity. That is, males and females form special bonds (eventually being formalized as marriage) and males become specialized in hunting with females staying at home bases or households to care for children and forage for vegetable foods.

---

[2] Wilson uses the term "Hominids" to describe all members of the lineage that diverged from the African apes and from which humans arose. Many modern researchers use the term "Hominin" for this group reflecting the change in taxonomy initiated by genetic and morphological analyses. See Chapter 4.

Following the initial iterative processes of the autocatalysis model resulting in cognitively modern humans, Wilson suggests that sexual selection and multiplier effects of cultural innovation and network expansion facilitated the evolution of a variety of modern behavioral patterns. He also points to changes in population densities, the ubiquitousness of warfare, and multifactorial economic systems as drivers in social evolution in modern humans. Finally, he envisions that "mankind" will eventually reach an ecological steady state (by the end of the twenty-first century) and the internalization of social evolution will be nearly complete. At this point he suggests that the social sciences and humanities will by necessity become branches of biology and that the true understanding of what it means to be human, and how we came to be, will be made evident through the mature study of evolutionary sociobiology.

Wilson's model and assumptions have been incorporated wholly or via piecemeal in various forms and expanded on over the last 30 years by researchers in the biological and social sciences, and even by some philosophers. Today all of the four major approaches to the study of human behavioral evolution explicitly tie their origin to Wilson's prospectus and use, at least in past, most of the basal assumptions inherent in his model with changes/modifications as datasets increase and theoretical perspectives alter (see Chapter 3).

Dawkins and the Selfish Gene

At approximately the same time that E.O. Wilson was presenting the premise of his *Sociobiology*, the British biologist Richard Dawkins published a small book that has since been frequently partnered with many of the lasting premises of sociobiology. This book was a manifesto of genic selection entitled *The Selfish Gene*. Building on the work of Williams (1966) Dawkin's core premise is that the primary unit for understanding natural selection is the "gene," the replicating sequences of heritable information that reside in the DNA.

Dawkins proposes that evolutionary change is best envisioned as competition for reproduction (relative representation across generations) among discrete "genes." Rather than seeing the whole organism or the group as units where selection acts, Dakwins envisions genic level selection. Here a gene's products (structural, regulatory, catalytic, or behavioral) compete with other similar genes and do so with differential success in different environments; thus changes in gene frequencies across time (evolution) occurs due to competition between genes not organisms or groups. However, this is not to say that individuals or groups do not compete, rather that the ultimate explanation for their competition is best sought at the level of the gene. Individuals are envisioned as "survival machines" for their genes and carry the composite of these genes' products. Environments act on this composite and thus the different genes' contributions. In this way, differential survival

Spencer	Darwin....Wallace	Wallace	Darwin	Spencer
Social Statics 1st Ed	Natural Selection	Origin of human n races	Descent of Man	Social Statics Revised
1851	1859	1864	1871	1892

Lloyd-Morgan.....Baldwin		Washburn		Tinbergen
Organic Evolution "Baldwin effect"	Modern Synthesis	New Physical Anthropology	Ethology	4 Questions for Behavior
1896	1930–1950s	1951, 1973	1940–60s	1963

Hamilton	Williams	Trivers	E.O. Wilson	Dawkins
Kin Selection	no group selection	Reciprocal altruism	Sociobiology	Selfish gene
1964	1966	1971	1975	1976

Figure 2.1 Darwin–Dawkins Timeline.

(reproduction) by organisms is actually differential success by various gene products and therefore those genes themselves are what is passed with greater or lesser frequency into subsequent generations.

Along with this genic level perspective, Dawkins also proposed an explanation for human cultural innovation and change: the existence of "memes," self-contained replicating units of cultural information. He sees these memes as operating similar to genes and using human minds as vehicles for their propagation. In this context, common and prominent cultural patterns are seen as successful "memeplexes" or composites of memes, just as physical or behavioral adaptations can be seen as resulting from geneplexes or sets of successful genes (see Chapter 5). While this extreme reductionist focus on genic (and memic) selection does not agree with the use of group level selection arguments for human behavioral traits in "sociobiology," it does fit well with many of the basal assumptions and ties directly to the Hamilton and Trivers mathematical systems for kin selection and reciprocal altruism.

All four of these perspectives, kin selection, reciprocal altruism, sociobiology, and the selfish gene, intertwine to produce a shared basis, a set of common understandings about evolutionary systems, that underpin the four major approaches to examining behavioral evolution[3] (see Figure 2.1 for overview). In the following chapter we review each of these approaches and provide examples of how they go about examining the evolution of human behavior.

SUGGESTED READINGS

Baldwin, James, M. (1896) A new factor in evolution. *American Naturalist* 30:441–451.

Darwin, Charles (1871) *The Descent of Man and Selection in Relation to Sex*. London: John Murray.

Dawkins, Richard (1976) *The Selfish Gene*. Oxford: Oxford University Press.

Richards, Robert (1987) *Darwin and the Emergence of Evolutionary Theories of Mind and Behavior*. Chicago, IL: University of Chicago Press.

Trivers, Robert (1971) The evolution of reciprocal altruism. *Quarterly Review of Biology* 46(10):35–57.

Wallace, AR. (1864) The origin of human races and the antiquity of man deduced from the theory of "natural selection." *Journal of the Anthropological Society of London* 2:clviii–clxxxvii (access at: www.wku.edu/smithch/wallace/S093.htm)

Washburn, Sherwood (1951) The new physical anthropology. *Transactions of the New York Academy of Science* 13 (2d ser.):298–304.

Washburn, Sherwood (1973) The promise of primatology. *American Journal of Physical Anthropology* 38:177–182.

Wilson, EO. (1975) *Sociobiology: The New Synthesis*. Harvard: Belknap Press.

---

[3] However, see Wilson and Wilson (2007) for a recent acceptance and inclusion of multilevel selection in sociobiology.

CHAPTER 3

Modern Perspectives for Understanding Human Behavioral Evolution

A Review of Basic Assumptions, Structures, and Practice

Today the dominant approaches to asking questions about the evolution of human behavior take the perspectives and hypotheses of Wilson's sociobiology, Hamilton and Trivers' kin selection and reciprocal altruism, and the Dawkinsian genic selfishness as baseline assumptions. They tend to incorporate Darwinian ideas as modified by the Modern Synthesis and interpreted through the eyes of these theoreticians, resulting in a basal perspective of Neo-Darwinian (ND) Sociobiology [called Human Sociobiology by some (Laland and Brown 2002)]. In addition to this basal ND-Sociobiology, the four other main approaches are Human Behavioral Ecology (HBE), Evolutionary Psychology (EP), Gene–Culture Coevolution/Dual Inheritance Theory (DIT), and Memetics.

Each approach is rooted in a Neo-Darwinian history but their interpretations of what this means vary from approach to approach. All focus on natural selection as the architect of behavior and tend to de-emphasize other processes of evolution arising from the Modern Synthesis (such as gene flow and genetic drift) or more recent contributions to evolutionary theory (such as developmental and epigenetic processes, see Chapter 7) as having significant agency in causing behavior (in an evolutionary sense). At least two of them, HBE and EP, rely heavily on Tinbergen's four questions in framing their hypotheses, especially the distinction between ultimate and proximate levels of explanation. In this chapter, we will review the basic premises and predictions inherent in each of the four approaches and then compare them alongside ND-Sociobiology.

HUMAN BEHAVIORAL ECOLOGY

HBE, sometimes known as Darwinian anthropology, derives from an integration of the field of behavioral ecology, facets of ecological anthropology, the main theses of sociobiology, and practices in human ethology. Directly borrowing from general behavioral ecology and with a focus on behavioral strategies, there remains an emphasis on optimality models in the creation of hypotheses and on the search for Evolutionary Stable Strategies (ESS) as examples of adaptive patterns.

Behavioral ecology is the study of behavior from ecological and evolutionary perspectives with the goal of linking ecological factors and adaptive behavior (Krebs and Davies 1997). By obtaining a general understanding of how aspects of ecology challenge organisms, one can model ways in which organisms might deal with these pressures through behavior as well as morphology. In other words, the behavioral ecological approach seeks to understand the selective pressures on organisms and hypothesize about how the behaviors and behavioral patterns they exhibit today have arisen in response to current and past ecological pressures.

General socioecological pressures on organisms can be divided into five main arenas, such as nutrition, locomotion, predation, intraspecific competition, and interspecific competition. Nutritional ecology refers to the pressures that organisms face in obtaining sufficient food and water. The challenges of locomotion involve how an animal moves about.

Predation is considered an important selective force. If an organism is eaten, its reproductive success is drastically diminished, to say the least. The pressure of predation is thought to be so important in the evolution of behavior that it is often proposed as one of the reasons that many animals live in groups. This idea is referred to as the selfish herd concept. If an individual is in a group, the odds of its being eaten are lessened by the number of other individuals in the group. In addition, with more eyes and ears, predator detection increases. On the other hand, the larger the group, the easier it is for predators to detect it. However, in humans, few researchers invoke predation as a major component in selection pressures (but see Hart and Sussman 2005). Intraspecific competition refers to contests among members of the same species or even the same group. Interspecific competition refers to contests between different species for the same resources (e.g., competition between monkeys and birds over the same fruit source). A distinction is also made between what is called contest competition and scramble competition. Contest competition occurs when the resource being fought over can be monopolized by one or more individuals. For example, if there is a relatively small, prized fruit tree, one or a few individual monkeys can potentially dominate in controlling access to it and keep others away. The contest is then between individuals or groups to see who can hold on to the tree and defend it from others. Scramble competition occurs when a resource is not effectively defendable by one or a few individuals (e.g., a whole orchard of fruiting trees), and thus all individuals are really racing against time to see how much fruit they can gather before it is all gone. Each of these types of competition exerts slightly different pressures on organisms. Consequently, we would expect that behavioral adaptations to these pressures would also vary.

Basic Overview of HBE

At its core, HBE is based on determining how ecological and social factors affect behavioral variability within and between populations through the study of function. This is an integration of biological and ecological approaches that is seen as an addition to, or expansion on, investigations of causation, development, and historical constraints already existent in the social sciences. HBE utilizes a form of "**ecological selectionist logic**" deriving from Neo-Darwinian (sociobiological) understanding of selection combined with a focus on specific types of ecological pressures that affect energetic expenditure/gain (as per the five main ecological pressures) as it relates to potential fitness of individuals. HBE poses the question "what ecological forces select for, or favor, a specific behavior or set of behavioral patterns in question?" Here, the focus is often on **strategies** of behavior; patterns of behavioral response that emerge via selection and result in fitness benefits in a given ecological context. To answer this question, HBE focuses on individual's energy return rate (net ratio of energy in/out), mating success, social status, health, and survivorship as proxies for direct fitness measures, and/ or the direct impact on an individual's fitness as the prime assessment tool (Smith 2000, Laland and Brown 2002, Barret et al. 2002). In examining the patterns and outcomes of human action, HBE frequently approaches the analysis of behavior in a piecemeal manner. Each behavior or behavior pattern (hunting, food sharing, alloparenting) is seen as a unit with its concomitant costs and benefits in regard to individual fitness. Piece by piece analyses of behavioral factors provide a context for the creation of straight forward analytical models to generate testable hypotheses about selective pressures and the efficacy of behavioral responses. These models include a focus on "decision rules" or conditional strategies that are exhibited dependent on ecological and social conditions.

A basal assumption of optimality-striving underlies these models. **Optimality theory** dictates that in a given system with multiple variants, selection will push the system toward optimal solutions (patterns of behavior that maximize fitness). Those variants with lower success (as measured by direct or indirect fitness values) will eventually disappear from the system, leaving only the more successful variants. Over time, these become the most common in the population, leaving a majority of the individuals in that population optimally (or near optimally) suited for the local challenges. Optimality models are created for specific situations, data are collected on real populations, and then those data are compared to the outcomes predicted by the model. The results (goodness of fit) can then be used to examine the contexts, costs, and benefits to various behaviors and strategies available to humans. This practice results in a focus on covariation of behavior and socioecological environment and a focus on behavioral variation as *adaptive* responses to ecological challenges.

However, HBE practitioners recognize that most systems do not operate at optimality and thus optimality models are used as yardsticks to identify other constraints in the system that might be maintaining/causing suboptimal responses. A good example of this is the recent work by Sear and Mace (2008) who compared 45 studies to examine the effects of kin (in addition to the mother) on child survival. They found that in most cases strict (optimal) models of kin selection (see Chapter 2) were only moderately supported. Their assessment showed that although "help from kin may be a universal feature of human child rearing, who helps is dependent on ecological conditions" (Sear and Mace 2008). They show that kin interactions are not always beneficial to children and that variation in strategies of kin support is an important area for future research.

Given that behavior is seen as a suite of adaptive responses (or at least potentially fitness-costly behavior) HBE sees flexibility in individual behavior as an outcome of individuals striving to optimize lifetime reproductive success (fitness maximizing) in a diverse array of ecological contexts. This stems from the basal premise that humans display broad "**adaptability**" (the degree to which a species can survive and reproduce in a wide variety of environments). HBE practitioners assume that humans have a strong "evolved" ability to weigh (selective) costs and benefits and respond accordingly. Therefore, real-world living involves a series of adaptive trade-offs and HBE is interested in how these trade-offs are operationalized in humans, especially how they result in variable and flexible behavioral strategies across human groups and ecologies. However, this does not necessitate conscious decision making in the sense of actual fitness accounting systems. Rather, it assumes the selection for generalized mechanisms in the human brain that enable humans to make decisions tied to fitness and selection contexts when faced with behavioral choices stemming from ecological challenges (domain-general modules rather than domain-specific ones, see the section on Evolutionary Psychology).

Given this orientation, HBE practitioners tend to see much of human "culture" as emerging, at least in part, from a fitness maximization program. Collections of behavioral patterns and practices (cultures) develop because humans are flexible opportunists under a wide array of ecological selection pressures. Such models are justified because humans are likely to be approaching optimality maximizing strategies (though not necessarily 100% successfully because of ecological and other constraints); therefore, game theory models and approaches can help in investigating and describing the decision-making processes that result in human behaviors. When considering human behavior and cultural variation, HBE practitioners focus on the measurable and observable behavioral outcomes rather than beliefs, values, and emotions. While these psychological/psychosocial factors are accepted as important to the individuals being observed, it is the quantifiable measures of behavior (actions, not beliefs or sentiments) that HBE considers most useful in measuring lifetime reproductive success, or some proxy thereof, in relation to ecological variables.

Traditionally, HBE approaches involved the study of human populations thought to have been under relatively similar ecological pressures for long periods of time or at least minimally impacted by industrial and postindustrial economic/technological developments or urban culture. This practice was based on the assumption that these populations are more representative of a "generalized" human state before the recent radical changes brought about by the industrial revolution and technological mechanization. Because of this, it is assumed that these populations will most closely reflect adaptive responses to specific local ecological challenges, and thus be most amenable to the type of modeling used in HBE. Whereas urban dwellers in a developed nation are relatively divorced from generalized linear selection pressures such as foraging and related ecological challenges (or at least the modeling of such pressures in modern developed contexts is substantially more complex), ecological intermediaries such as complex cash economies, high-quality invasive health care, and structural insulation from climate pressures create obstacles to the basic modeling approaches in HBE. However, some recent research in HBE focuses on more transitional sedentary agricultural, pastoralist, and general rural populations, thus expanding the comparative dataset used in assessing behavioral strategies and their ecological contexts (see, e.g., Gibson and Mace 2005, Leonetti et al. 2005, and review in Sear and Mace 2008).

HBE has a suite of inherent and explicit assumptions that frame its inquiries and methodologies. Many of these are shared with other approaches and most stem directly from traditional ND Sociobiological approaches. These include the following assumptions:

- Humans are under pressures from natural selection currently, and behavioral patterns exhibited today may reflect adaptations to current, or recent, pressures.
- Complex socioecological (behavioral) phenomena in humans can be effectively studied via a reductionist approach (examining behavior or behavioral strategies piecemeal).
- The behavioral diversity evident across human populations is largely the result of diversity in contemporary socioecological environments.
- Adaptive relationships between behavior and environment may arise from many different mechanisms.
- As humans are capable of rapid shifts in phenotype (via behavior), they are likely to be well adapted to most features of contemporary

environments and to exhibit relatively little **adaptive lag** ("left-over" adaptations to prior environments that may be maladaptive in the present context).

• If adaptive modules do occur in the brain/mind, they are domain-general for broad problem solving rather than domain-specific to certain behavioral patterns and ecological challenges.

In practice, HBE follows a few specific patterns that differ from some of the other approaches to the understanding/assessment of the evolution of human behavior. As already noted, HBE's primary tool is a focus on measuring the differences in reproductive success (or some fitness proxy) between individuals relative to the behavioral strategies they follow. This involves substantial use of mathematical modeling to generate testable predictions/hypotheses to assess the outcomes of said strategies relative to optimality model predictions and to help explain why such behavior might not reach optimal levels but still be highly beneficial (sometimes referred to as **satisficing**). HBE also exploits what has been termed "the phenotypic gambit," a black-box approach to the actual mechanisms of evolution of behavioral responses. That is, HBE is not necessarily concerned with the specific physiological or psychological mechanisms involved in that pattern's adaptation or inheritance. This approach takes a calculated "risk to ignore the generally unknown details of inheritance, cognitive mechanisms, and phylogenetic history that may pertain to a given decision rule and behavioral domain in the hopes that it does not matter to the end result" (Smith 2000). HBE considers this a justified approach as the end product (fitness) is the prime relevant factor and as long as the predictive models work with relatively high success, the actual mechanisms are irrelevant to the overall evolutionary model. For example, we do not need to understand how a given behavior is generated physiologically and employed psychologically as long as we can observe and measure its exhibition and impact on fitness. If it increases fitness we assume it will spread in the populations and if it does, the model is supported regardless of our understanding of the developmental and ontogenetic mechanisms underlying the behavior.

Example

Hawkes, Kristen and Bliege Bird, Rebecca. (2002) Showing off, handicap signaling, and the evolution of men's work. *Evolutionary Anthropology* 11: 58–67.

Hawkes and Bliege Bird tackle a complex question in the evolution of human behavior from the HBE perspective incorporating concepts from animal behavior and evolutionary theory with ethnographic datasets and basic models of energetic input/output. While this is an overview study, they highlight all of the major factors in HBE in making their case and demonstrate its application.

The problem they set out to assess is the role of risky big-game hunting by human males. In many societies, human males provide a substantial percentage of the nutritional requirements through animal protein acquired during hunting of large animals. However, hunting large animals can be a costly exercise in terms of energy and safety; therefore, the hunters incur fitness costs. The conundrum is then, "why do males hunt large game"? At first glance, one might assume that there is an easy explanation: males incur high risks hunting big game because they (and their mates and offspring) receive very high caloric (energy) returns from successful hunts. This was an accepted explanation for much of the twentieth century. However, Hawkes and Bliege Bird review ethnographic data sets from South America, Africa, and Asia that demonstrate that males (and their mates and offspring) regularly share hunted meat with their group and do not necessarily (or even frequently) achieve relatively larger caloric payoffs than other group members. This creates an evolutionary problem: if the costs of big-game hunting (risks/energy) outweigh the benefit (caloric return) due to food sharing, why does this behavior occur with high frequencies in many forager groups across different environments and ecologies?

Hawkes and Bliege Bird briefly note that two previous hypotheses have been put forward explain this problem (reciprocal altruism and tolerated theft) and then go on to propose their own: costly signaling/show-off hypothesis. Reciprocal altruism (see Chapter 2) suggests that the hunter may not get an immediate payoff for sharing meat but at a future time will achieve some "in-kind" payment either in the form of meat or assistance that will balance out his initial investment (fitness loss) by providing a fitness benefit. However, ethnographic overviews show that "quantitative records of meat distributions over time often find claimants continuing to get shares whether or not they ever supply them, and hunters continuing to supply more meat even when others are deeply in their debt" (Hawkes and Bliege Bird 2002). This suggests that it is not at all clear that this behavior is a case of reciprocity, although there might be multiple "currencies" at play. Tolerated theft, proposed by Blurton-Jones (1984) notes that "sharing could result if resources came in large but divisible lumps, but not to everyone at once, and if consumers were prepared to press claims for a share according to the nutritional value of the resource to them" (Hawkes and Bliege Bird 2002). However, it is not clear that this pattern of distribution is supported by the majority of ethnographic examples. Hawkes and Bliege Bird, while acknowledging the potential explanatory power of the two preceding hypotheses, put forward their explanation as the best fit.

In short, this hypothesis proposes that "men establish and maintain their relative social standing by showing off their hunting prowess." Men hunt primarily to acquire prestige that in turn translated to aspects of fitness enhancement. Hawkes and Bliege Bird base this proposal on Zahavi's handicap principle (Zahavi 1975) and the costly signaling hypothesis. These hypotheses argue that very costly signals could be selected for if they impart a set of information from the producer of the signals to the audience that in turn benefits the fitness of the producer. A classic example would be that of the peacock tail; the male has a tail that causes him clear costs in terms of energetic investment and antipredator abilities. However, the fitness payoff to offset the costs comes through the "display" of his vigor to peahens who then select him over less impressively displaying males for mating. Thus, reproductive benefits potentially outweigh the energetic and predation costs of the large flashy tail.

Hawkes and Bliege Bird argue that "more than its value as a source of nutrition, meat is a medium of communication through which the hunter transmits information to potential mates, allies, and competitors" regarding his prowess and abilities (2002). They review studies of forager peoples around the world to show support for this pattern, especially demonstrating from two forager groups (the Meriam Islanders and the Hadza) that greater meat distribution or hunting prowess is not correlated with caloric return. They then go on to review studies of chimpanzee hunting to demonstrate that males use hunting to compete for status, laying a hominoid (apes and humans) ancestral potential for humans to expand on. Through the acquisition of weaponry, complex tool technologies, and language, large-game hunting became available to humans (not to other apes) as did a means for the propagation of prestige (language and material display). This then enabled show-off behavior to appear as a behavioral strategy in humans and over time led to its selection due to the benefits conferred on males who practiced it. They also provide explicit and optimal reason for why meat makes a good signal in such a system. Their basic conclusion is that showing off has been selected "as a strategy to compete effectively for social advantage in a world where honesty is at a premium and political alliances substitute for body size and canine weaponry in gaining the advantages of status" (2002). With social advantage being collected in fitness benefits either in the form of mating access, social alliances, child-rearing assistance, or related social factors.

EVOLUTIONARY PSYCHOLOGY

The basic goal of EP is understanding the evolution of psychological mechanisms resulting in human behavior. Arising both from psychology and aspects of evolutionary theory, EP can trace its roots to Darwin's focus on emotions and behavior, to Spencer and his ideas about patterns in evolution, and especially to Baldwin and Morgan's (see Chapter 2) ideas about organic evolution and the role of psychological adaptations in human behavioral evolution.

Throughout the twentieth century, cognitive and experimental psychology underwent a variety of incarnations ultimately diverging into different schools more or less aligned with/interested in evolutionary biology and anthropology. During the 1970s, a hybrid form of psychological and evolutionary anthropological approaches emerged following the trajectory of Wilson's Sociobiology and, to an extent, the underlying premises of Chomsky's concept of a universal grammar (Barkow et al. 1992). EP seeks to meld together the focus on natural selection and adaptation in sociobiology with the concepts of universal cognitive/psychological modules as human adaptive characters to present scenarios for the psychological mechanisms involved in the expression and evolution of human behavior.

Like HBE, there are practitioners from various disciplines; however, in the case of EP, the prominent allied participants are from anthropology and psychology as opposed to anthropology and biology (as in HBE). There are also a number of slightly divergent views on what EP is and how it is situated and practiced. Since its inception, proponents of EP have contrasted it to the **Standard Social Science Model** (SSSM) (see later section) as a positivist integration of the biological and social sciences rather than as a deconstructive "humans as blank slates" model. This contrast, combined with a focus on the **Environment of Evolutionary Adaptiveness** (EEA; see later section), lead many followers of the EP perspective to claim their perspective as the logical outcome of Wilson's sociobiological paradigm and call for the folding of the social sciences and humanities into adaptationist biological perspectives.

The Adapted Mind

In the seminal volume of EP, *The Adapted Mind*, the main thesis of EP is laid out: culture is generated by information processing mechanisms situated in human minds. These mechanisms are the "elaborately sculpted product of the evolutionary process." In essence, to understand the relationship between biology and culture, we must understand the architecture of the human evolved psychology (Barkow et al. 1992). The *mind* (information processing description of the brain) is characterized by a set of *design features* (modules) that have been constructed to resolve *adaptive problems* through the process of *natural selection* resulting in *functionally organized* minds (modern human minds) (Barkow et al. 1992). Accordingly, "Evolution by natural selection provides a coherent and unified explanation of human social evolution and adaptation" (Barrett et al. 2002).

Under this rubric, EP is the "study of the evolved information processing mechanisms that allow humans to absorb, generate, modify and transmit culture—the psychological mechanism that take cultural information as input and generate behavior as output" (Barkow et al. 1992). In short, EP is "the adaptationist program applied to the study of the human mind/brain" (Symons 1992).

The Adapted Mind lays out a set of central premises for the EP perspective:

• That there is a universal human nature that exists primarily at the level of evolved psychological mechanisms, not necessarily expressed cultural behavior.

- That these evolved psychological mechanisms are adaptations constructed by natural selection over evolutionary time.
- That the evolved structure of the human mind is adapted to the lifeways of Pleistocene hunter-gatherers, not necessarily to modern circumstances (as we spent 99% of our evolutionary history as Pleistocene foragers and less than 1% in modern contexts).

Because of the third point above, practitioners of EP are very concerned with modeling the EEA. Originally proposed by Bowlby (1969), this concept refers to the period of time in which humans underwent the majority of their adaptation. Organisms have a functional organization produced via the action of selection over time, their set of adaptations (this organization) are designed to exploit the enduring or most challenging properties of the environment in which they evolved. As the genus *Homo* spent the majority of its evolutionary trajectory in the Pleistocene (1.8 million years ago until ~10,000 years ago) existing in forager groups with limited technology (relative to modern day), this is then the EEA for humans. Our adaptations should reflect the pressures of the generalized Pleistocene forager lifeways (see Chapter 4), which are not necessarily the same as in modern industrial/agricultural environments. These adaptations in the mind would then be apparent across the species (human universals) and be geared toward solving problems faced during the Pleistocene by small bands of foragers/hunter-gatherers. This leads to the possibility that these adaptations are "out of step" with modern selective pressures due to the rapidity of radical changes in technologies, residence, and subsistence patterns over the past 10–20,000 years. This produces a type of "adaptive lag" where human cognitive adaptation may be nonadaptive or even maladaptive in modern contexts.

Barrett et al. (2002) provide an updated version of the EEA relative to the initial proposals in Barkow et al. (1992). They state that the EEA can be best seen as a "statistical composite of the adaptation-relevant properties of the ancestral environments encountered by members of ancestral populations" (Barrett et al. 2002). In this sense, the EEA is still the sum of selection pressures that have operated on humans during the Pleistocene. EP practitioners, in general, are aware of problems with a monolithic EEA concept: that evolution is a mosaic process and that humans create their environment to a certain extent. Recently, some researchers argue for shifting the focus from the EEA and acknowledge that some modern human behavior can be adaptive or reflect adaptation to modern contexts and use the concept of the **"adaptively relevant environment"** (ARE) (Irons 1998). In this case, the ARE is considered to be just those features of an environment that an organism must interact with to achieve reproductive success. Thus, only a few key features need be present, not whole environments, and therefore some environmental pressures can continue through from the Pleistocene to modern times in various forms. Alternatively, certain pressures may remain, but their proximate triggers have altered over time. For example, male risky behavior in hunting may not be displayed in modern contexts but male risky behavior in acts of bravado or show-off displayed in these modern contexts may reflect similar selection pressures.

Goals and Methods

The main methodological point of EP is that natural selection cannot select for behavior per se but for the mechanism(s) that produce behavior. Thus, the goal of EP is to identify the selection pressures that have shaped the human psyche over evolutionary time and to test whether human psychological mechanisms actually show features that one would expect if they were designed to solve these particular adaptive problems. This approach assumes that the human psyche is composed of a set of adapted "domain-specific modules" or "mental algorithms" rather than a set of generalized mechanisms (such as in HBE) that can cope with a whole range of adaptive problems. The brain/mind is seen as a wholly functional tool in its evolution, with the caveat that some behavior can be nonfunctional as a by-product of the lack of fit between functional modules and current environments. In this context, the EP approach does not look necessarily for reproductive benefits (fitness measurements) but rather indications of "good design" pointing to the operation of selection in the past and then to identify the specific design features (psychological mechanisms) of human psychological adaptations.

The basic assumptions of EP then include a concept of cognitive modularity, a primary role for historicity (the EEA) and adaptive specificity in response to particular selection pressures, and a role for environmental novelty in explaining the potential "poor-fit" of some human behavior in the modern context. Owing to these elements, measuring fitness based on current behavioral outcomes can be misleading as the behaviors in question may result from modular adaptation to EEA type conditions, not modern ones.

At its core, the basic approach of EP asks three questions:

1. What selection pressures are most relevant to understanding the adaptive problems under consideration?
2. What psychological mechanism has evolved to solve that adaptive problem?
3. What is the relationship between the structure of these psychological mechanisms and human culture?

Associated with and underlying these questions are the assumptions that learning is a Darwinian process, that human behavior and psychology are the products of evolution, and that clarity about the Tinbergian level of explanation (see Chapter 2) is a must when investigating human behavior. Ultimate and proximate explanations must be kept distinct and understood in different terms. In this context, it is evident that EP investigates the design and architecture of cognitive mechanisms and their relationships (fit) to modeled selection pressures as opposed to HBE, which investigates the manner in which human phenotypic expression influences reproductive outcomes.

In their review of the structure and intent of EP, Laland and Brown (2002) identify major methodological goals based on the premise that evolved, domain-specific, psychological mechanisms are adaptations that underlie human behavior, and the EEA model is used to identify selection scenarios (adaptive problems) for the evolution of the said mechanisms. These methods are

1. The use of evolutionary theory to develop models of adaptive problems that the human psyche had to solve.
2. The attempt to determine how these adaptive problems manifested themselves in Pleistocene conditions (EEA) and try to model the specific selection pressures (ARE).
3. To identify/catalogue the specific information processing problems that must be solved if the adaptive problem is to be overcome, and develop a computational theory—a very specific, empirically testable hypothesis(ses) about the structure of the information processing mechanisms.
4. To use the computational theory to determine the design features necessary for solving the adaptive problems and then develop model(s) of the structure of such cognitive programs(s).
5. To eliminate alternative models with experiments and field observation.
6. To compare model against patterns of behavior exhibited in modern conditions.

In the more recent overviews of EP, some practitioners make an explicit linkage to the methods and outcomes of HBE as potentially being complementary to EP (Barrett et al. 2002). These views are more likely to highlight phenotypic plasticity as core human adaptation than are other more conservative EP approaches. In fact, Barrett et al. (2002) go as far as to argue that EP can best be envisioned as a broad theoretical umbrella that can include HBE and Dual Inheritance Theory (DIT, see later section) in the quest to understand human behavior from an adaptationist perspective (a primacy of natural selection as architect of function).

Contrast with SSSM Specific Approach

Since its inception, practitioners of EP have positioned EP as a counterbalance to something they refer to as the SSSM (Barkow et al. 1992, Gaulin and McBurney 2004). Followers of the EP perspective see the SSSM as the antithesis of their endeavor: they describe it as one that is practiced by cultural anthropologists, "humanist" biologists, and other social constructivists who believe that mental organization of the adult is absent in the infant and must be acquired from their social world and that biological construction goes on in the womb, but it is complete except for growth at birth with social forces being the main agents responsible for the remaining construction of the individual (Barkow et al. 2002). This is a polemic view and not vociferously espoused by all EP practitioners, but often referred to nonetheless.[1]

The argument against the SSSM is as follows:

1. The SSSM argues for blank slate, the irrelevance of biology, and the existence of general purpose learning mechanisms.

2. The SSSM misunderstands the nature of development drawing false dichotomy between nature and nurture, which always work together.

3. The SSSM drives a wedge between the social and natural sciences (by disregarding the possibility of biological adaptation as playing a major role in the development and display of behavior).

4. The SSSM lacks overarching theory of design (EP has it and explains why people respond to their environments in the ways that they do).

There is also the contention that the SSSM misconstrues or ignores Tinbergen's levels of analysis in approaches to understanding behavior. In an extreme case, in their textbook of EP, Gaulin and McBurney (2004) use the "fallacy of Margaret Mead and Infinite malleability" to drive home this point. This is (in their view) the assumption that humans have a very generalized "nature" and that cultural variations and social development are the main factors in explaining why humans do what they do. Their point is that "human nature" is not infinitely variable and much of the cultural variation can be explained in terms of facultative responses to local conditions. They state that genetically based traits are often highly responsive to local condition and much of the human behavior is facultative but emerging from adapted modules/complexes in the human brain/mind. EP then positions itself as the alternative, science-based, logical methodology to understand the origin and meaning of human behavior relative to the SSSM.

Example

Schmitt, David P. (2005) Sociosexuality from Argentina to Zimbabwe: A 48-nation study of sex, culture, and strategies of human mating. *Behavioral and Brain Sciences* 28:247–311.

---

[1] I personally find this characterization of the SSSM a "straw-man" concept espoused by "classic" EP practitioners such as Barkow, Cosmides, and Tooby, and in textbooks such as the one by Gaulin and McBurney. The SSSM as they propose is an overly simplistic assertion regarding the state of nonadaptationist perspectives in the social sciences of the first decade of the twenty-first century. In general, one can see this as a response to the polemics of these discourses during the 1980s. While there are few practitioners of the SSSM as characterized by these authors today, the use of the SSSM as a combative counter-structure for the purpose of comparison remains common in many EP arguments.

In this study, Schmitt expands on previous work by evolutionary psychologists examining sexuality. Here, sexuality is defined generally as the number of partner preference and mating style preference and expressed as a continuum from extreme monogamy (one exclusive sexual partner) to extreme polygamy (many partners). To assess this, Schmitt and his team employ the Sociosexual Strategies Index (SOI), which is a self-reported measure used to examine differences in human mating strategies. High SOI scores indicate tending toward polygamy/promiscuity and low SOI scores show a tendency toward monogamy. The SOI was implemented as part of the International Sexuality Description Project (ISDP) and was translated into 25 languages and administered to 14,059 individuals in 48 countries to create the main dataset for this study. The evolutionary problem tackled the following questions: do human mating strategies appear as universal across cultures?, are intersexual differences universal?, and can variation in mating strategies be explained by extant theories of parental investment (including theories of sexual strategies and strategic pluralism) or the constructivist/biosocial "social structures" theory?

The goals of the project were to assess the cross-cultural validity of the SOI, to examine the distribution of sociosexuality (mating strategies) cross-culturally including universal patterns, and to assess explanatory theories/hypotheses regarding the degree of differentiation in sociosexuality.

The methods included distributing the SOI to participants who were largely college students in their respective countries, including some non-student community members in a small subset of the countries surveyed. Participants received either course-credit or a small payment for participation. Student return rate was ~95% and community return rate was ~50%. The SOI consists of seven questions that result in a mosaic representation of sociosexuality that can be individually assessed and/or reported as a composite score. In addition to the SOI data, marriage, sexuality, and demographic information were also collected from archival materials. Additional self-reported measures of sexual behavior and "mate poaching" likelihood were also collected.

The basic results were reported in descriptive and tabular form with substantial statistical analyses to clarify trends and patterns and to guide interpretation. From these results, Schmitt states that the SOI seems to be a reliable measure of within-culture variation in self-reported sociosexuality (cumulative SOI score accounting for ~39–45% of all variation in responses). Schmitt also makes the case from the data that the SOI works adequately well across cultures as mean national scores are validated and thus their comparison across cultures provides a good comparative tool. Specific findings include the following:

• Cultures with more women have higher male promiscuity and thus higher sociosexuality rates (SOI scores).

• Cultures with more men have lower sociosexuality rates and tend toward monogamy.

- Cultures in which early reproduction is common have decreased socio-sexuality rates.
- Cultures with higher fertility also have decreased sociosexuality rates.
- Cultures in environments that create infant-rearing stress have decreased sociosexuality rates.

Schmitt also finds that across cultures, males tend to have higher sociosexuality rates than females, reflecting an evolutionary history of sex differences (interestingly, Latvia, Slovakia, and Switzerland do not exhibit this trend). Schmitt suggests that these sex-difference results in the ISDP are the "largest and culturally most robust ever documented in the domain of sex and mating," leading to the statement that men possess "psychological design features that reliably lead to higher levels of sociosexuality" (supporting sexual strategies theory). However, he also notes that the results of the ISDP suggest that cultural variants do impact intersexual differences especially in the context that cultures with increased gender equality have raised female sociosexuality rates and less difference between males and females in their SOI scores. However, he cautions that these score are not likely to become equal regardless of gender equality.

Given these results, Schmitt finds that the study strongly supports sexual strategies theory and strategic pluralism theory, and that even the social structure theory can impact sociosexuality to an extent. Conclusions that emerge from the study are that the "patterning of sociosexuality across nations suggests that human mating systems as a whole are adaptively responsive to at least two aspects of the local ecology." In cultural contexts with male-biased sex ratios, there is an adaptive shift toward monogamy ("perhaps in response to the sexually selective desires of women"). In contexts of a female-biased sex ratio, promiscuity is more common ("in response to the sexually selective desires of men") (support for sexual strategies theory). Schmitt also concludes that mating systems appear to adaptively respond to specific ecological stress (support for strategic pluralism theory). In high-stress local environments, the mating system shifts toward monogamy as an adaptation whereas in low-stress environments the system "tends to shift toward unrestricted sociosexuality—at least those aspects of sociosexuality linked to adult forms of sexual promiscuity." Although adaptive shifts in sociosexuality occur across mating systems as a whole, the evolved mating desires of men and women within those systems are not necessarily identical. The universal sex differences presented in the study (according to Schmitt) suggest "that men and women possess psychological design features that cause at least moderately sized sex differences in sociosexuality to reliably emerge across all ecological contexts (at least those tested in the ISDP)." He does, however, note that the degree of sexual differentiation can depend on a number of sociocultural/sociopolitical factors (some support for social structure theory).

It is important to point out that Schmitt is aware of the limitations of this type of study. He explicitly notes the inherent limitations of self-reported data, of a sample that is primarily composed of college students, and that all the data come from nation state populations (assumedly living in "developed" contexts) as opposed to data from forager or tribal/horticultural populations.

GENE–CULTURE COEVOLUTION (OR DUAL INHERITANCE THEORY)

As a direct descendant of Spencer's "formal inheritance of accommodating mechanisms" and Lloyd Morgan and Baldwin's organic evolution/Baldwin effect (see Chapter 2), gene–culture coevolution or DIT holds the basal perspectives that culture is evolutionarily important, that culture evolves in a Darwinian fashion, and that understanding gene–culture coevolution is the key to understanding human behavior. The main thesis and methods rely on the premise that "evolution provides the ultimate explanation for why organisms are the way they are," that simple mathematical models are "a form of meditation on nature without peer" (Richerson and Boyd 2005), and that culture and genes provide "separate but linked systems of inheritance, variation and fitness effects" (Smith 2000). Proponents see DIT as a solution to the quandary of modeling, in an evolutionary sense, human plasticity in behavioral response and the overriding role of cultural patterns in everyday human life. DIT offers a hybrid approach utilizing methods of analysis from biological evolution to examine biosocial patterns in humans. Because of the reliance on a particulate view of cultural behavior and its focus on mental/cognitive facets of human behavior, the DIT perspective has been referred to by some non-DIT practitioners as "a cross between memetics and evolutionary psychology, with a little mathematical rigor" (Laland and Brown 2002).

The modern development of DIT has been primarily through the work of Robert Boyd and Peter Richerson, with core contributions by Wilson and Lumsden (1981), Cavalli-Sforza and Feldman (1973), and others. This perspective seeks to meld cultural behavior with sociobiological functionalist perspectives in order to understand the multiple contexts of inheritance and selection of behavior in humans. Boyd and Richerson (2005) outline five primary components that form the infrastructure of the DIT perspective. These are the following:

- Culture is information that people acquire from others by teaching, imitation, and other forms of social learning.
- Culture change should be modeled as a Darwinian evolutionary process.
- Culture is part of human biology.
- Culture makes human evolution very different from the evolution of other organisms.
- Genes and culture coevolve.

Boyd and Richerson provide a basal definition of culture utilized in DIT models that enables them to see culture as a set of information in a way similar to seeing the genetic code as a set of information. In this definition, culture is described as "information capable of affecting individual's behavior that they acquire from other members of their species by teaching, imitation, and other forms of social transmission." In this perspective, culture is an evolving pool of ideas, beliefs, values, and knowledge that is learned and transmitted between individuals, similar to the gene pool concept in population genetics. The core notion with this culture definition/gene pool metaphor is that the interactions and interconnections between culture variants and genetic variants consist of a bidirectional interface that shapes the evolution of human behavior. **Cultural "units"** are then modeled as discrete packages or as particles (called "culturgens" by Lumsden and Wilson 1981, and "culture variants" for Boyd and Richerson). These units can be beliefs, behaviors, or other cultural elements and are seen as acting roughly analogous to genes and alleles (variant forms of genes) in the context of population genetics and their relationship to evolutionary patterns. That is, the analogy is to the process of natural selection resulting in varying frequencies of genetic variants (genes/alleles) across generational time.

DIT holds that it is specifically culture itself, and the capacity for culture, that separates humans from other animals and that this difference results in a novel synthesis of selection at biological and cultural levels. In short, DIT assumes that "cultural evolution is fundamentally Darwinian in its basic structure" (Richerson and Boyd 2005). Natural selection, as an evolutionary process, is seen as driving culture change across generations. For example, DIT proponents argue that humans seek prestige and that its acquisition reflects a form of cultural fitness just as reproductive success or net energy accumulation results in biological fitness in natural selection models. Thus, cultural variants that augment prestige will be "selected for" and achieve substantial representation in subsequent cultural generations relative to variants that do not facilitate increased prestige. In this scenario, cultural variant units (similar in many ways to Dawkinsian memes, see below) compete with one another, much as genes/alleles do in a selfish gene selection scenario (Dawkins 1976, see Chapter 2). Here, genetic units and culture units are seen as analogous targets of selection and thus competition between such units (in either biological or cultural realms) results in differential representation of better "fit" variants in subsequent generations. Boyd and Richerson make a point to suggest that genes and culture are **"obligate mutualists"** and that modeling their coevolution is necessary in order to best envision the evolution of human behavior.

For this perspective of selection of cultural units to work a number of assumptions must be met. The core assumption being that culture is a nongenetic system of inheritance of learned/transmitted social information (which DIT proponents define it as). The spread and inheritance of cultural information (in the form of culture variants, or units of culture) can then be affected by multiple forces including natural selection, individual decision making, and transmitter influence or prominence. Both cultural and biological influences affect the transmission of cultural variants. However, Darwinian evolution (natural selection) is the dominant pattern of shaping variation in cultural information. **Codetermination** (or dual inheritance and interaction of biological and cultural units) thus arises from the mutual engagement of biological and cultural factors: human behavior is jointly shaped by genetic, cultural, and environmental influences simultaneously.

This main premise assumes that the process of natural selection as proposed by Darwin and Wallace and as modified through the Modern Synthesis and the various enhancements of the latter half of the twentieth century is the best model for viewing cultural change. According to the DIT perspective culture exhibits the requirements for natural selection to occur. There is variation in cultural units/behaviors. These units/behaviors are heritable through a number of pathways. Different cultural variants do more or less well in given cultural and environmental contexts resulting in differential success, thus mimicking fitness effects of genes and phenotypes. Thus, because of the analogous nature of culture and genetic systems, cultural change can be analyzed using Neo-Darwinian methods.

Structurally, DIT relies on vigorous use of mathematical models to describe and predict patterns and changes in culture variants brought about via natural and cultural selection. These models assume that there is a form of cultural inheritance. In this inheritance pattern, genes and environment account for some variation in cultural units but social transmission is the primary avenue for cultural variation. The infectious, information-based transmission pattern of cultural variants allows for rapid change that can potentially affect selection pressures on genes as well as culture. Given this pattern, there are two types of selection: cultural selection and natural selection. Cultural selection is the process by which culture variants increase or decrease in frequency dependant on rates and patterns of adoption by individuals, giving different culture variants relative fitness value. Natural selection (biological selection) can change cultural variant frequencies through differential survival of individuals expressing different cultural variants. In cultural selection, various types of bias exist and impact the relative success of cultural variants. These biases in transmission include experiential biases, the social context in which the individual finds her-/himself, the genetic predisposition/situation of the individual exhibiting the variant, and so on. All of these biases can be seen as environmental influences that can impact the resultant frequencies of cultural variants.

However, it is important to note that high cultural fitness need not correspond with high fitness values for natural selection. The widespread use of contraception in developed nations is a good example of a cultural variant at odds with biological fitness. As cultural inheritance can differ from genetic inheritance in modes of transmission (lateral as well as cross-generational) its evolutionary dynamics may also differ from those of genes (conferring cultural success rather than biological success). This means that cultural evolution can result not only in biologically adaptive behavior but also in biologically nonadaptive behavior. Even maladaptive behavior is possible, given modern societal complexities (much as with the adaptive lag seen in EP and Baldwin's organic evolution). Also, like EP, DIT assumes that cultural evolution is integrated in and constrained by evolved psychological propensities.

Example

Soltis, J., Boyd, R., and Richerson, P.J. (1995) Can group functional behavior evolve via cultural group selection? An empirical test. *Current Anthropology* 36:473–494.

In this example, the authors tackle the vexing problem of humans seeming to exhibit group-level behaviors that benefit the group but not necessarily individuals. This appears to be related to the fact that humans display much greater levels of intragroup (beyond kin-biased) cooperation than do other animals. Both of these patterns are contrary to the basal expectations of Neo-Darwinian selection theory. The authors, taking a DIT perspective, pose the question: Can group functional behaviors (those that benefit the group) evolve by cultural group selection? They use ethnographic datasets, a mathematical model and cultural selection theory in deriving their answer, which is "yes" (with a caveat, see below).

Soltis et al. argue that cultural group selection is analogous to genetic group selection (as envisioned by both Darwin and E.O. Wilson) but acts on cultural rather than genetic differences between groups. In this case, competing cultural variants will bestow varying levels of fitness (group proliferation and/or maintenance versus group extinction) relative to their level of utilization by different groups. The authors argue that cultural variation is more prone to group selection than genetic variation and that this leads to humans exhibiting cooperation at a much higher level than other animals.

To test their assertions, they derive a model for cultural group selection and then use ethnographic data from the island of New Guinea (including Papua, the Indonesian half of the island) to test the predictions of the model. They chose this area because it offers "high-quality ethnographic descriptions of peoples that had not been pacified by a colonial administration." Their model has three prerequisites for cultural group selection to act:

- There must be observable cultural differences between groups.
- These differences must have an effect on group persistence or proliferation (group "fitness").
- These differences must be heritable (transmitted across time and generations).

In addition to these basal requirements, groups should most likely be small and migration between them limited. Or, if the groups are larger, some form of biased cultural transmission must maintain differences between the groups. The example of a biased transmission they provide is that of food taboos and their associated beliefs regarding purity and ethnic markers that act to keep group members and cultural variants from excessive admixture.

In testing the model, Soltis et al. define a group as a "territorial population that can conduct warfare as a unit." They then propose three questions for the empirical tests:

- Do groups suffer disruption and dispersal at a rate high enough to account for the evolution of any important attributes of human societies?
- Are new groups formed mainly by fission in groups that avoid extinction?
- Are there transmissible cultural differences among groups that affect their growth and survival, and do these differences persist long enough for group selection to operate?

They use five cultural regions and over 100 groups in their assessments. They examined rates of group extinction, looking at the number of extinctions in each area, the number of years over which the extinction took place, and the number of groups among which extinctions took place. Extinction was defined as when all members of a group had been killed or assimilated into another group. They also looked at the rates and patterns of new group formation due to fissioning of extant groups. Finally they examined cultural variation in detail in three cultural units made up of multiple groups (The Mountain Ok, the Faiwolmin, and the Tor).

The results provide initial support for their model of group cultural selection. Soltis et al. found that group disruption and dispersal are common, with extinction rates ranging from 2% to 31% (median ~10%) for the five culture areas. New groups did form usually from the fissioning of existing groups. There was cultural variation amongst local groups in the areas; however, the connection between this variation, its longevity, and its relationship to differential extinction or proliferation of groups was not clear. Using a modified formula from population genetics with the data from their overview, Soltis et al. calculate predicted rates of cultural change that could result from cultural group selection. From this equation they derive a minimum of 500 years and a mean time of 1000 years for the replacement of one cultural variant with a more favorable one due to cultural group selection (based on variation in extinction rates). Because of the rapidity of much cultural change and given this time period (20–40 generations), Soltis et al. suggest that many of the cultural variants that show up as different between groups are not the result of cultural group selection. However, the results also suggest that "group selection, perhaps in concert with other processes, is a plausible mechanism for the evolution of widespread attributes of human societies over the long run." So, while cultural group selection may not explain much rapid cultural change or many of the small differences between related cultures, it may have played a substantial role over the evolution of humans in select-ing and refining some of the more common behavioral variants (large-scale cooperative patterns, for example) ubiquitous in human groups.

MEMETICS

Richard Dawkins (1976) posited "memes" as cultural replicators, and pre-sented them as existing in a parallel, cultural, system roughly analogous to his view of selfish genes. Shortening the Greek *Mimeme* (imitation) to "meme" (because he wanted a term that sounded like "gene") he defined **memes** as "tunes, ideas, catch-phrases, clothes fashions, ways of making pots or of building arches" (Dawkins 1976). Susan Blackmore (2003) echos this position stating the

> every story you have ever heard, and every song you know, is a meme. The fact that you drive on the left (or perhaps the right), that you drink lager, think sun-dried tomatoes are passé, and wear jeans and a T-shirt to work are memes. The style of your house and your bicycle, the design of the roads in your city and the colour of the buses—all these are memes.

Memes, then are cultural units/ideas, and are seen as analogous to viral elements infecting human minds and "trying" (as in selfish genes) to repli-cate as much as possible. Proponents of Memetics argue that because memes have variation, are inherited/transmitted/acquired and produce differen-tial fitness (either for themselves and/or their hosts), they are best exam-ined/modeled using Neo-Darwinian natural selection. They have longevity, fecundity, and a degree of copying fidelity just like Dawkinsian "genes" and thus the "selfish meme" system runs in a similar, and parallel, fashion to the selfish gene system.

While memes are similar to the concept of cultural variants in gene–cul-ture coevolution/DIT (see earlier text) they are distinct in that they are seen as having a "life cycle" more akin to viruses. DIT culture variants are more analogous to genetic segments that code for structural elements (genes), whereas memes are generally modeled more along the lines of viruses whose goal is purely reproduction of themselves. They are aggressively compet-ing with other memes to utilize the human mind as a vehicle for replica-tion. An extreme example that is commonly used is that scholars are just a library's way of making more libraries (assuming "library" can be seen as a meme). Memes are also seen as occurring in structurally different forms. There can be "copy the product" via imitation memes and "copy the instruc-tions" memes, which involve more than just imitation. These different types of memes result in different types of inheritance/transmission patterns.

While memes are "selfish" replicators, they can have beneficial effects for their human hosts. Innovative cultural ideas, such as tool use and agri-cultural practices are seen as clusters of memes that have positive fitness values for their hosts. These clusters of memes are called "**memeplexes**" and can be best described as cultural trends, patterns and beliefs. However, just as with individual memes, most memeplexes do not necessarily provide fitness benefits to their hosts. Memeticists often use the example of organized religion as a powerful selfish memeplex. According to memeticists, inherent in religious belief are a series of structures that help replicate the memeplex, discourage rejection of the memeplex, and encourage disdain or xenophobia regarding other similar memeplexes (other religions in this case).

Dennet (1991) argues that cultural evolution/complexity is due to memes and occurs via natural selection with better "fit" memes/memeplexes (more efficient replicators) becoming overrepresented over time in human cultures. He sees humans as a "particular sort of ape infested with memes," suggesting that the evolution of human behavior is best understood by examining the memic selection involved. Blackmore (1999) sees memes as drivers for much of human cognitive evolution. She proposes that the expansion in the human neocortex is a result of feedback from memic evolution and competition. Memes facilitated the selection for an expanded cognitive function (and thus morphological change) in the brain. With regard to human self-awareness, Blackmore (2003) states that

> The illusion that we are a conscious self having a stream of experiences is constructed when memes compete for replication by human hosts. Some memes survive by being promoted as personal beliefs, desires, opinions and possessions, leading to the formation of a memeplex (or selfplex).

Blackmore also suggests meme–gene coevolution (as in DIT above), where memes and genes affect one another's fitness.

With regard to the evolution of human behavior, memeticists propose that understanding cultural phenomena (behavior) can be best accomplished by viewing the problem from the perspective of the "meme" (as with Dawkinsian selfish gene perspective). Cultural traits (memeplexes) evolve both as a result of their utility to individual humans (increasing fitness to humans using them, thus selecting for continued use) and also because they facilitate their own propagation (memeplexes that create high fitness for themselves but not necessarily for the humans using them). Owing to meme–gene coevolution, certain memeplexes may have substantial impact on human morphology and behavior over the course of human evolution. The methodology of Memetics consists primarily of developing explanatory models for the evolution of these memeplexes. To date, there remains little formal hypothesis testing in Memetics.

Example

Blackmore, Susan. (2003) The evolution of meme machines. In Meneghetti, A. et al., Eds. *Ontopsychology and Memetics*. Rome, Psicologica Editrice, pp. 233–240.

Susan Blackmore presents a memetic solution to the problem posed by large human brains. Why did one lineage of hominins undergo such an expansion in the neocortex relative to other similar lineages? The brain is expensive to construct and maintain, therefore has a high cost. We assume that cost is outweighed by the benefit of cognitive function, but how did the cognitive power of the mind arise during human evolution?

According to Blackmore, the perfection of true imitation by early hominins on our lineage was the major turning point in the evolution of cognitive function. Other related forms could practice certain types of imitation, but not to the extent of our ancestors. Once true imitation was a part of the toolkit our ancestors were able to acquire and transmit useful skills, such as hunting, preparing food, and making/controlling fire.

> As these early memes spread, it became increasingly important to be able to acquire them. So people who were better at imitation thrived, and the genes that gave them that ability, and the bigger brains it required, spread in the gene pool.

She goes on to propose that as individuals became better and better at imitation, there was enhanced selection for increases in brain size and neurological complexity/cognitive power as a result of feedback system between the imitation and its enhancement of individual fitness. Once high-quality imitation is ubiquitous in this population of hominins, competition amongst memes becomes heightened and expanded. So alongside of the human fitness enhancing memes, we also begin to see a variety of other selfish memes such as personal adornment and proto-religious behavior that might be energetically costly but not fitness beneficial for the early humans.

Under this scenario, the early humans who were the better imitators (better cognitive abilities) had the best chances of survival due to correct acquisition of beneficial memes (but also in the processes acquire and propagate the purely selfish memes). These "better imitators" are also the preferred mates because of their edge in overall survival. Blackmore concludes

> This means that sexual selection, guided by memes, could have played a role in creating our big brains. By choosing the best imitator for a mate, women help propagate the genes needed to copy religious rituals, colourful clothes, singing, dancing or painting, depending on the direction memetic evolution has taken. By this process, the legacy of past memetic evolution becomes embedded in the structures of our brains and we become musical, artistic and religious creatures. Our big brains are selective imitation devices built by and for the memes, as much as for the genes.

SUMMING UP

Table 3.1 provides a comparative overview of the five prominent approaches to examining the evolution of human behavior. ND-Sociobiology forms the

TABLE 3.1

Overview of the Dominant Approaches to the Evolution of Human Behavior

	ND-Sociobiology	HBE	EP	DIT	Memetics
Focus of selection	Gene/individual/group	Individual/behavior	Individual/behavior/psychological mechanism	Individual/group/gene/culture variant	Meme/gene
Measure of natural selection	Reproductive success or proxy measure of fitness	Reproductive success or proxy measure of fitness (energetic balance)	Potential/predicted impact on reproductive success/fitness	Potential/predicted impact on genetic and cultural fitness	Potential impact on genic and memic fitness
Method for asking questions	Genic functionalism-construct genic level fitness enhancing/optimality models, test data against them	Test data against optimality models, ecological expectations/prediction models from behavioral ecology	Construct selection scenarios and describe predicted fitness increasing strategies, test with datasets	Construct mathematical and conceptual models and simulations, sometimes test with datasets	Construct selection scenarios, controlled thought experiments
Main underlying causes for evolution of human behavior	Genetic evolution produces both human general behavioral capacities and specific behavior patterns/strategies	Behavior and behavioral strategies arise from adaptation to ecological and other selective pressures	Psychological mechanisms (and thus behavior) arose/arise though adaptation to pressures of the Environment of Evolutionary Adpativeness (Pleistocene) and Adaptively Relevant Environments	Gene-culture coevolution results in patterns of complex, symbolic and linguistic human behavior	Selfish meme replication and meme-gene coevolution result in most human behavior

(continued)

Basic premise	Humans are very complex and highly social animals whose behavior is best analyzed via Neo-Darwinian approaches	Humans, while highly adaptable, can be modeled using same premises as other animals, socioecological contexts drive most selection pressures	Human universals and human behavioral strategies are reflections of adapted modules (psychological mechanisms) in the mind	Humans are under genic and group selection for physical and cultural traits; culture and genetics coevolve via natural selection	Memes/memeplexes are primarily responsible for human behavioral variation and culture
Datasets	Ethnographic datasets, observations, comparisons with other animals especially primates, fossil record	Behavior observations, physiological and ecological measurements, ethnographic datasets	Questionnaires, surveys, interviews, demographic and behavioral datasets, public records	Ethnographic datasets, Outcomes of mathematical models	Popular ethnography, survey and interviews, general cultural information

Note: All perspectives have natural selection as their primary evolutionary force.

main outline from which the others draw much of their framework. However, each has its own distinctions separating it from ND-Sociobiology. The common thread is the almost complete reliance on Natural Selection as the main architect of function at both biological and cultural levels. The focus of all five is on a functionalist approach emphasizing those current behaviors that are expected to arise/have arisen via the action of selection (which could also be maladaptive as a result of adaptive lag, gene–culture coevolution, or memeic selection). Other processes of evolutionary change and the possible role of nonfunctional or nongenetic, or nonmemetic developmental processes in the generation and modification of human behavior (see Chapter 7) are generally downplayed or not addressed in hypotheses developed by these perspectives. That is, in each perspective, behavior is seen primarily as an adaptation resulting from the actions of natural selection, a focus on Tinbergen's functional or ultimate causation questions. The main differences in the approaches come in the focal target of selection (gene vs. individual vs. group, and genic only vs. gene–culture coevolution). While all do have genic selection as their theoretical underpinning, in practice, all five use behavior and/or behavioral strategies as a proxy measure for genic expression such that their actual tests rely on the assessment of behavior with an assumption that the bases of the behavior are at some level tied to selection for some genic elements (actual genes, adaptive psychological mechanisms, specific physiological traits, etc.). DIT and Memetics also explicitly argue that selection acting on cultural elements (culture units or memes) can also affect genic patterns.

Other differences between the perspectives are found in the relative degree of adaptive lag, with EP proposing that most human adaptations are to a broadly conceived EEA such that many of them may not be the best fit with current selection pressures (thus the "adaptive" lag) (Laland and Brown 2006). While all the perspectives acknowledge the role of cultural complexity, DIT and Memetics prioritize the actions of natural selection on culture variants (or memes) as core factors relative to the other perspectives. Measures of natural selection vary with ND-Sociobiology and HBE relying more on field-based quantitative outcomes relative to the other three. However, even ND-Sociobiology and HBE rely more on proxy measures of fitness than actual measures of reproductive success. The other three focus more on qualitative and theoretical outcomes based either on mathematical models (DIT), interviews, laboratory studies, and thought experiments or other heuristic reasoning models. In part, this lack of direct measures of selection is due mainly to human longevity and the difficulties in conducting long-term studies or matching behavioral data to accurate paternity and demographic records in most populations.

Missing from HBE, EP, DIT, and Memetics is much of the evolutionary anthropological approach pioneered by Sherwood Washburn. In the over 50 years since Washburn proposed his "New Physical Anthropology," there has been an explosion in the paleoanthropological data base, resulting in a series of important changes and enhancements of the scenarios for human physical (and social) evolution. Unfortunately, ND-Sociobiology is the only one of these perspectives to regularly exploit both the fossil and archeological records and primate studies as comparative tools. Of the other four, HBE does occasionally incorporate fossil/archeological/primatological datasets (Hawkes et al. 2003) and EP uses assumed Pleistocene selection pressures as its baseline, but neither EP, DIT, or Memetics regularly use fossil or cross-species comparisons in their construction of scenarios and hypotheses for the evolution of human behavior. In the next chapter we will review the current state of knowledge regarding the pattern and major elements in human evolution.

SUGGESTED READINGS

Barkow, Jerome H., Cosmides, Leda, and Tooby, John. Eds. (1992) *The Adapted Mind: Evolutionary Psychology and the Generation of Culture.* New York: Oxford University Press.

Dennett, D. (1995) *Darwin's Dangerous Idea.* New York: Simon and Schuster.

Hawkes, Kristin and Paine, Richard R. (Eds.) (2006) *The Evolution of Human Life History.* Santa Fe, NM: School of American Research Press.

Richerson, Peter J. and Boyd, Robert. (2005) *Not by Genes Alone: How Culture Transformed Human Evolution.* Chicago, IL: University of Chicago Press.

CHAPTER 4

Basic Bones and Stones

What Do We Know About the Record of Human
Evolution (as of 2008)?

In this chapter, we briefly review three main bases for assessing the evolution of human behavior: primate-wide trends, an overview of the human and human ancestor fossil record, and a general review of what indications exist for human material culture from the archeological record.

COMPARATIVE PRIMATOLOGY ESTABLISHES A BASELINE FOR HUMAN BEHAVIOR

In using comparative primatology to facilitate exploration of the evolution of human behavior, we are looking for three types of patterns: primate-wide trends, hominoid-wide trends, and unique hominin or human characteristics. **Primate-wide trends** are those behaviors or behavior patterns that occur in all, or most, primates. We assume that their universal presence in members of the order primates indicates that they are primitive traits that have maintained themselves in all cases due to their selective benefits. **Hominoid-wide trends** are those behavior patterns that we see in all, or most, hominoids (apes) but not in other primates. We assume that these behavior patterns arose since the evolutionary split between the hominoids and other primate lineages in the earliest Miocene, about 22 million years ago (mya). These behaviors are those that distinguish the apes and humans from other primates. Finally, looking at our primate relatives and ourselves, we will find that many behaviors occur only in humans, not in other primates. These behaviors are unique to humans and thus have arisen since our split with the apes in the terminal Miocene, about 6 mya. Looking at these trends allows us to establish a baseline in reconstructing the evolution of our behavior. Most of these basal behavior patterns stem from living in groups and negotiating the social relationships that group living creates.

In all primates, and in many mammals, the behavioral interactions between a mother and her infant establish the parameters for the offspring's later social relationships. Compared to other mammals, primates have a very long infant dependency period, the period during which the infant is wholly reliant on others for nutrition, movement, thermoregulation, and protection. In primates, due to the long dependency period, there is a particularly strong mother–infant bond. This bond is characterized by very close spatial association (for years in human, ape, and some monkey societies), frequent physical and vocal contact, and the exposure of the infant to the mother's behavior and association patterns. The infant not only gains nutrition and protection from the mother but also acquires information about other group members, foods, ranging patterns, and behavior habits. All female primates (and males in many species) have the behavioral capability to exhibit a set of caretaking behaviors. What type of behavior an individual exhibits depends on her or his previous life experience (ontogeny). Infants act as a strong stimulus and always seem to generate much interest from members of a group; however, if a female has not had previous experience observing her mother or other group members handle infants, or if she herself has never interacted with young individuals, she may feel the stimulus but not be able to exhibit behavior that results in successful infant caretaking. We can also expect that in many species the selection pressures for successful caretaking potential would be stronger on females than on males due to the fact that females give birth and must lactate and provide food if the offspring is to survive.

Most primates live year-round in relatively cohesive groups, typically consisting of more than two adults and related offspring. Frequently, there are multiple adult females and males, although sometimes there is only one male and multiple females. In a few species there are groups with one adult female and multiple adult males. In about 3–5% of primate species, groups typically consist of one female, one male, and their offspring (Fuentes 1999, 2002). Some primates, primarily prosimians and a few anthropoids, are also found in what is referred to as a dispersed social group. In this pattern, individuals rarely gather in the same place at the same time, but their individual home ranges, the areas they use regularly, overlap substantially. These individuals know each other and frequently interact via scent marking or vocalizations but rarely engage in face-to-face behavioral interactions (Nekaris and Bearder 2007).

Because primates live in groups and interact with one another frequently, social tolerance is extremely important. One important way in which individuals establish relationships with one another is through the use of space and a type of contact behavior called grooming. Space use is an important indicator of the type of relationship between individuals. If individuals are frequently in close spatial association, we can say they have a tolerant and probably affiliative ("friendly") relationship. If two individuals avoid one another or engage in conflict over the use of the same area, we can say that they are less tolerant of one another and have an agonistic ("unfriendly") relationship. An important way in which primates establish and cement affiliatative relationships is through mutual grooming. Obviously, this behavior has a hygienic function, but primates groom far more frequently than would be required for simple hygiene (McKenna 1978). The physical contact involved in grooming appears to have a beneficial effect on both the groomer and the groomee. Especially in times of tension or strife, grooming can reduce stress and cement relationships. Individuals may spend more time grooming those with whom they want to associate, or they may refuse to groom those with whom they have agonistic relationships. The directionality of grooming can also be important. All primates groom—it is a primate-wide behavior pattern—but they vary in the extent of social grooming (Sussman and Garber 2007).

Most primate species exhibit a pattern of differential access to resources within the social group. The set of relationships that results in different relative abilities to acquire desired goods/resources is called **dominance**. If an individual is dominant or has a high rank, he or she can gain a favored resource more easily than an individual who is less dominant or lower ranking. The measure of access to desired resources by different individuals relative to one another is called a dominance hierarchy and can take a variety of forms. Some species have relatively linear hierarchies, wherein one or a few individuals have priority access over most or all of the other members of the group. However, in most primate societies, dominance relations are contingent on coalitions and alliances between group members. Even in relatively linear systems, high-ranking individuals usually have one or more allies in the group with whom they interact frequently and who provide social support in contests for resources or even in direct physical fighting (Bernstein 2007).

In many primate species, adult males and adult females have separate dominance hierarchies. Frequently, in one-on-one contests for resources, males are dominant over females, especially if the males are larger (sexually dimorphic). However, environmental and social selective pressures do result in systems in which females are dominant and in which males and females are codominant (Gould and Sauther 2007). Dominance is not a trait inherent in an individual; it is a social role that he or she occupies for a time. Primates move through different dominance ranks and roles throughout their lives, and each primate species has a slightly different pattern by which individuals attain dominance or interact with one another in the competition for resources. Because dominance hierarchies are found primarily in adult primates, the system is one that young individuals have to learn to negotiate ontogenetically.

Dispersal patterns are extremely important to these aspects of group living and dominance systems. In most primate species, members of one sex disperse, and members of the other sex are **philopatric** (stay in the natal group). Members of the philopatric sex then have genetic relatives who live in the same group and theoretically have an investment in their survival (according to the kin selection hypothesis). Members of the dispersing sex have to enter a group in which they have no relatives and thus must forge relationships with non-kin. In some primate species, both sexes leave their natal groups, resulting in few kin bonds except those between mothers and offspring. Dispersal also has another cost: time spent alone, outside of a group. It is highly likely that dispersal can be very costly in an evolutionary sense, because the individual does not get the benefits of living in a group and may be more susceptible to predation and less able to compete for access to food. In some primate species, individuals of one or both sexes move among multiple groups during their lifetime, making and breaking alliances and relationships across groups and time. In some species, different types of groups exist within the same population.

Both cooperation and conflict play major roles in the lives of primates. Alliances and coalitions are core in social groups, and primates use social negotiation to establish, reinforce, and disrupt these relationships. Because dominance relationships are pervasive in primate societies, serious fighting for resources usually does not occur. There are fights, but the overall time and energy spent engaging in serious aggression, for most species, tend to be quite low (Sussman and Garber 2007). This is not to imply that conflict is not important. It has been argued that social relationships between individuals are so important that the potential damage caused by conflict is serious and must be repaired. Many primate species display some from of reconciliatory behavior wherein they repair damage to relationships caused by conflict (Aureli and de Waal 2000, Arnold and Aureli 2007).

Comparative primatology then shows that humans are derived from a general primate base that includes high sociality and group living, with long periods of infant dependency. It is also complex dominance relationships, reliance on grooming or some form of social interaction to negotiate relationships, and forming alliances and coalitions within the group that are common patterns across most primates. Learning of social behavior is an important component of individuals' ontogeny and genetic relationships and intersexual relationships vary between individuals in a group depending on group type, dispersal patterns, and social and demographic history of the group. Also, while aggression takes place, mutual tolerance and/or social negotiation are common within group patterns. These are all the basal patterns for primates; thus we can assume that human behavioral patterns are derived from these initial contexts. Therefore, our hypotheses for the evolution of human behavior start with these patterns and do not need to explain their origin as that origin is deeper in primate history than the time of appearance of humans.

In addition to primate-wide trends, there are also some more specific hominoid-(ape) wide trends that are salient in our assessment of human behavioral evolution as they provide a baseline for the taxonomic subgroup within the primates to which humans (and our ancestors) belong. All three of the African hominoids (gorillas and both species of chimpanzee) occur primarily in some variant of multimale/multifemale group that exhibits variable cohesion and group/subgroup size along a continuum. This variation is likely related to resource distribution, population density, and intraindividual sociality. The African hominoids exhibit a degree of arboreality, but also rely heavily on terrestrial locomotion and interaction patterns (Robbins 2007, Stumpf 2007). The Asian great ape, the orangutan, while generally occurring in small groups or as individuals, currently does not frequently occur in multimale/multifemale groups. However, orangutans do form large groups in captivity, at provisioned sites, and at particularly resource-rich sites (although there is usually only one adult male present at a time) (Knott and Kahlenberg 2007). Given the overall similarities of the large-bodied hominoids in response to resource distribution, it is possible that all current grouping patterns are derived from a more gregarious multiadult group composition in the past (Fuentes 2000). Chimpanzees and orangutans use simple wood, bone, and unmodified stone tools for foraging in a variety of manners and it is very likely that tool use, in a more complex manner than with other primates, is an ancestral pattern for all hominoids (Panger 2007).

Despite these hominoid-wide commonalities, there is also an important behavioral distinction between humans and other hominoids that is of particular relevance to the investigation of human behavioral evolution: the ability to use symbolic/linguistic communication. Apes trained in human sign language show little or no evidence for semantic or syntactic structure with combination of signs and most "signing" interactions involve only acquisitive motivation (Rivas 2005; however, see Savage-Rumbaugh and Lewin 1994). Tetsuro Matsuzawa and colleagues (2006) summarize the cognitive development of chimpanzees and demonstrate that chimpanzees are extremely adept at memorizing images and learning image sequences (such as number sequences) with an almost photographic memory recall. When challenged with visual sequence recognition tasks, chimpanzees outperform (in speed of completion and ability to memorize long sequences) humans significantly. Matsuzawa and colleagues suggest that this results from a trade-off involved with the acquisition of symbolic communication and language. In this proposed trade-off, humans lose the hominoid ability for immediate visual memory recall and gain the ability to convey much larger and more complex types/sets of information.

VERY BRIEF SUMMARY OF HUMAN FOSSIL RECORD (~5 MYA → PRESENT)

In this chapter, I refer to humans and all their ancestors and relatives *after* the split with any other ape lineage as the "**hominins**." The humans' closest African ape cousins (the gorilla and chimpanzees, the other members of the subfamily *Homininae*) are referred to as *hominines* and the orangutans as *ponginines* (members of the subfamily Ponginae). This is not the most widely used naming system—at least not yet. Some researchers continue to call all humans and human ancestors after the split with the African apes "hominids." I will not use that system here because the current genetic, molecular, and fossil data do not support it (Begun 1999, Fuentes 2006).

All the hominins share a number of unique physical traits (see Table 4.1). These include modifications in the pelvic girdle and lower limbs that make them capable of effective bipedal locomotion. Changes in the upper arm and vertebral column indicate that weight is borne by the legs. Hominins also have smaller canine teeth than do other members of the family Hominidae (great Apes), a forward-placed **foramen magnum** (the hole where the spinal column enters the skull) and no (or a dramatically reduced) **shearing complex** (a characteristic ape condition in which the lower first premolar is somewhat sharpened or flattened from rubbing against the upper canine as the mouth closes). While many of these traits were developed in hominins by 4 mya, the large brain that characterizes modern hominins (humans), does not appear in the fossil record until the last 1.5 million years.

There are a number of early fossils that are potential hominins and are found in rocks dating to between 6 and 4 mya (Table 4.2). *Orrorin tugenensis* consists of fossils of postcranial bones unearthed in Kenya and dated to approximately 6 mya (Senut et al. 2001). However, it remains unclear whether this find is a hominin. There are some teeth, a jaw fragment, a partial humerus, a **phalange** (finger bone), and three partial femurs. The scientists who found the fossils point to the thick molar enamel on the *Orrorin*

TABLE 4.1

Characteristics of the Hominins (Modified from Fuentes 2006)

Cranial Characteristics	Postcranial Characteristics
• Canine teeth relatively small and incisiform [relative to other members of the family Hominidae and subfamily Homininae (chimpanzees and gorillas)] • A forward-placed foramen magnum • No, or a dramatically reduced, shearing complex between the lower premolar and the upper canine. • Premolar 3 (mandible) double rooted (bicuspid) • Molars with thick enamel • Mastoid process present • Temporal origins forward on cranium • Parabolic dental arcade	• Modifications to the pelvic girdle and lower limbs making them capable of effective bipedal locomotion, changes in the upper arm and vertebral column indicating that weight is borne by the legs — angled femur, center of gravity medial and forward, distal end indicates "knee locking" — foot (pes) double arched; big toe (hallux) relatively nonabductable — phalanges of pedal digits 2–5 shorter — wide flaring iliac blade, os coxae broad and short

TABLE 4.2

Early Hominine and Hominin Fossils (Modified from Fuentes 2006)

Species	Location	Date (mya)	Main characteristic
Possible early Hominins			
Orrorin tugenensis	E. Africa	~6	Thick molar enamel, possible hominin
Sahelanthropus tchadensis	N. Central Africa	~7–6	Relatively small canines with no shearing complex, and thick molar enamel, possible hominin
Ardipithecus ramidus	E. Africa	5.8–4.4	Thin molar enamel, relatively large canines, forward-placed foramen magnum
Early Hominins			
Australopithecus anamensis	E. Africa	4.2–3.9	Large molars with thick enamel, relatively large canines and sectorial premolar, most likely biped, long arms
Australopithecus afarensis	E. Africa	3.9–3.0	Large molars with thick enamel, relatively large canines and semisectorial premolar, bipedal anatomy, long arms
Australopithecus bahrelghazali	N. Central Africa	3.3	Mandible fragment only
Kenyanthropus platyops	E. Africa	3.5	Single cranium, relatively small teeth, thick molar enamel

teeth. Most hominins have thick enamel on the molars, but chimpanzees and gorillas do not. However, the one canine fossil of *Orrorin* appears to be relatively large and ape-like. The team that found *Orrorin* also suggest that the characteristics of the fossil femurs indicate that *Orrorin* was minimally frequently bipedal (Galick et al., 2004). They also note that elements of its bipedal anatomy are similar to those found in modern humans but somewhat different from those found in some later hominins, suggesting that *Orrorin* might be a direct ancestor of humans.

Sahelanthropus tchadensis is represented by a fossil cranium found in Central African nation of Chad and dated to between 6 and 7 mya (Brunet et al. 2002). The fossil displays a mix of hominine-like and potentially hominin-like features. The canines are relatively small and the enamel on the molars relatively thick. The cranium has prominent brow ridges, a feature associated with later hominins, yet a small brain case. The researchers who discovered the fossil propose that the neck muscles' assumed attachment to the occipital bone (the back of the skull) and other basal cranial areas suggest that this organism moved bipedally. Because of the limited sample size (the cranium published in 2002 and a partial mandible and some teeth found in 2004) and the time it probably lived (6–7 mya), this fossil is hard to place relative to the later hominins. It could be a hominine whose descendants are either African apes or hominins, or it could be the remnant of an extinct lineage. However, the lack of a shearing complex weakens the potential for *Sahelanthropus* to be ancestral to the gorilla or chimpanzee lineages (Brunet et al. 2005).

The Aramis site in northern Ethiopia has produced many fossils, representing multiple individuals, dated to approximately 4.4 mya (White et al. 1994). These fossils include many dental fragments, upper limb bones, some cranial remains, and a partial skeleton. The Aramis fossils are classified as *Ardipithecus ramidus* (literally, "ground ape at the root"). They may represent a species near the base of the hominin divergence from the other African hominine lineages (chimpanzees and gorillas). Assessing fossil pollens and other fossil remains associated with these finds, researchers concluded that Aramis was a woodland, or forested, environment 4.4 mya, suggesting that *Ardipithecus* was a forest dweller. The *Ardipithecus* fossils display a number of late Miocene ape-like traits, such as a flat cranial base, thin molar enamel, large canine teeth, and substantial facial prognathism (forward-jutting face). However, the foramen magnum is much farther forward under the skull than one would expect in a quadruped, and the humerus does not demonstrate the specific structures associated with weight bearing that are common to quadrupedal hominoids. Therefore, researchers concluded that *Ardipithecus* used a form of bipedal locomotion (White et al. 1994). In 2001, more fossils from this species were discovered (Haile-Selassie 2001) but were older and possibly a distinct subspecies of *A. ramidus* (named *A. ramidus kadabba*). This find consisted of fossils from at least five different individuals dating to between 5.8 and 5.2 mya. *A. ramidus kadabba* had anatomical structures that suggest bipedality and that it lived (as did its later relative, now called *A. ramidus ramidus*) in a forested environment (Haile-Selassie 2001). These three genera and species (*Orrorin*, *Sahelanthropus*, and *Ardipithecus*) are the earliest possible hominins that we have fossil evidence for, and aside from possibly having bipedality and being forest dwelling, they tell us little about our behavioral evolution.

The Early Australopithecines

Fossils assigned to the genus *Australopithecus* are undisputably considered to be those of hominins. Seventy-eight fossils from two sites near Lake Turkana in Kenya are classified as *Australopithecus anamensis*. These fossils, 4.2–3.9 million years old, represent the earliest species in the genus *Australopithecus*. The *A. anamensis* fossils are primarily dental fragments and some cranial and postcranial remains. The lower limbs suggest that this species was bipedal (Leakey et al. 1995, 1998; Ward et al., 2001). The molars are large and have thick enamel. However, *A. anamensis* displays large canine teeth, a slight canine/premolar shearing complex, and a sectorial premolar (a lower premolar that exhibits side-to-side compression due to its role as a shearing surface for the upper canine tooth). The fossils also suggest a large range in body size in this species; there may have been sexual dimorphism, with males being larger than females, and canine dimorphism. This dimorphism suggests possible behavioral differences between sexes. (Table 4.3.)

By far the best-known early hominin is *Australopithecus afarensis*. Represented by fossils making up over 70 individuals from multiple sites in East Africa, this species is found from ~3.9 to 3 mya. *A. afarensis* shares a number of primitive traits with *Ardipithecus* and *A. anamensis*. The canines are fairly large compared to those of later hominins; the lower first premolar is semisectorial (partially compressed side to side); and the tooth rows are parallel (as in *A. ramidus* and *A. anamensis* but unlike those of modern humans). However, the canines of *A. afarensis* are smaller than those of earlier hominins, as is the canine/premolar shearing complex. The large size and thick enamel of the molars are characteristics that reflect similarities to earlier forms, such as *A. anamensis* and *O. tugenensis*, as well as to later hominins. The size of the cranium in this species is fairly small, with a brain about 420 cc in volume. This is only slightly larger than one would expect for a generalized hominoid (ape) with the body size of *A. afarensis* (Figure 4.1).

A reconstruction of the bones in the lower body of *A. afarensis* indicate frequent, if not obligate, bipedal locomotion. However, the arm bones are longer than in later hominins, and some researchers suggest that the phalanges (finger and toe bones) are relatively curved (Stearn 2000), as in the earlier hominins (such as *Ardipithecus* and *A. anamensis*). Long arms and curved phalanges are associated with arboreal movement in hominoids. There is also a set of fossil footprints from Laetoli in Tanzania that date to 3.6 mya. Most researchers have attributed these footprints to *A. afarensis*. Analyses of the footprints in a 23-m-long stretch suggest that two (and maybe a third) individuals strolled, bipedally, across this open area with short, slow strides. It is also evident that the two individuals differed in height and body size, and are frequently reconstructed as a male and a female. While *A. afarensis* was bipedal, we do not know how much time it spent exclusively on the ground. It lived in a savanna and woodland environment, and it is very possible that this species utilized both terrestrial and arboreal environments, walking bipedally on the ground and moving with all four limbs through the trees (although the lack of an opposable big toe could limit the type of arboreality exhibited) (Conroy 1997, Stern 2000 Simpson 2002).

Most (but not all) researchers believe that this species exhibited extreme sexual dimorphism. Females were about 110 cm (3.6 feet) and males nearly 150 cm (4.9 feet) tall. Males may have weighed twice as much as females. If these estimates are correct, *A. afarensis* ranks among the most sexually dimorphic of all primates (about equal to the gorilla in this respect). However,

TABLE 4.3

Plio-Pleistocene Hominin Fossils (Modified from Fuentes 2006)

Species	Location	Date (mya)	Main Characteristic
Paranthropus aethiopicus	E. Africa	2.6	Hyper-robust, few fossil fragments
Paranthropus boisei	E. Africa	2.2–1.3	Robust, MQ of 2.7, canines that appear like incisors (incisiform)
Paranthropus robustus	S. Africa	2–1.3	Robust, MQ 2.2, brain >500 cc (30.5 cubic inches)
Australopithecus africanus	S. Africa	3–2.4	Gracile, MQ 2.0, slightly prognathic face
Australopithecus garhi	E. Africa	2.5	Large incisors, long femur, possible tool association
Homo habilis	E. and S. Africa	2.4–1.6	Large incisors, MQ 1.9, ~600 cc (36.6 cubic inches) brain, Olduwan tools
Homo rudolfensis	E. Africa	2.4–1.6	Large body size, MQ 1.5, ~700 cc (42.7 cubic inches) brain, Olduwan tools
Homo erectus	Africa, Eurasia	1.8–~.25	Brain 727–1251 cc (883 cc—54 cubic inches avg.) increasingly complex tools (Acheulean) Moved out of Africa. Robust compared to modern humans
Other possible forms			
Homo ergaster	Africa	1.8–2.6	Same as *Homo erectus*
Homo antecessor	Europe (Spain)	~.8	Same as *Homo erectus*
"Archaic" human forms			
"*Homo heidelbergensis*"	Africa, Europe, Asia?	600,000–200,000	Robust, thick cranial walls, separated supraorbital tori Brains >1000 cc (>61 cubic inches)
"*Homo neanderthalensis*"	Europe, Middle East	300,000–27,000	Brains avg 1400 cc (85.4 cubic inches) midface prognathism retromolar gap very large incisors
Modern human form			
Homo sapiens	Global	~160,000–present	Brain avg 1350 cc (82.4 cubic inches); canine fossa, MQ 0.9; high, rounded cranium; chin, no retromolar gap

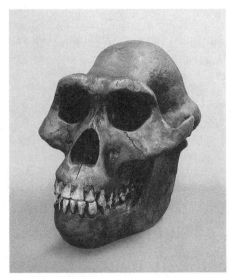

Figure 4.1 This skull is a representation of the early hominin *Australopithecus afarensis.* (Sculpted reconstruction courtesy of BoneClones™, www.boneclones.com.)

some paleoanthropologists and anatomists suggest that analyses of *A. afarensis* have exaggerated its sexual dimorphism. At least one comprehensive overview of the *A. afarensis* materials suggests a degree of dimorphism just slightly greater than that found in modern humans and chimpanzees (see Simpson 2002).

There are two other hominins found during the same time period as *A. afarensis.* There is one hominin fossil (a mandible) from the site of Koro Toro in the country of Chad in north central Africa, usually placed in a separate species named *Australopithecus bahrelghazali,* but there is too little information available to make an accurate assignment to a particular species. A series of fossil remains west of Lake Turkana, Kenya (a near-complete cranium, a maxilla, and some teeth) dating to approximately 3.5 mya were named *Kenyanthropus platyops* (Leakey et al. 2001). These finds suggest that there were at least two or three, if not more, types of hominins living in Africa between 3 and 4 mya (Leakey et al. 2001). This early hominin could also have made the fossil footprints at Laetoli.

There remains debate over the specific relationships among early hominin taxa and several different possible phylogenies are proposed. The relationships between *O. tugenensis, S. tchadensis,* and both *Ardipithecus* subspecies, on the one hand, and later hominins, on the other, remain unclear. Although the available data support the notion that *A. anamensis* is ancestral to *A. afarensis,* this is not definitive. The bottom line is that we do not know how many early species existed or how the early species are related to later ones. However, most researchers do posit *A. afarensis* as ancestral to later forms (including the lineage of humans). Even if not directly on our lineage there is a high likelihood that it shares a very recent common ancestor and thus basal patterns of behavior with the earliest members of the human lineage. What do we know about those patterns of behavior?

A. *afarensis* fossils are found in areas that were primarily mixed savanna and woodland environments during the periods of 4–3 mya. These hominins shared their habitat with a range of herbivorous bovids, a number of medium-sized and smaller mammals (pigs and rabbits, for example), and several carnivores (primarily big cats and hyenids). These environments were rich in grasses, shrubs, root and tuber plants, and fruiting and nonfruiting trees. Temperatures varied across the year but were never as cool as those of the temperate world today.

Microscopic analyses of the fossil A. *afarensis* molars reveal a combination of tiny pits, striations, and smooth areas that reflects a diet composed of fruits, leaves, nuts or grains, and a variety of tubers and roots. The thick enamel on the molars and the relatively large size of the incisors also support these general dietary assumptions. It is probable that A. *afarensis* also took advantage of the animal foodstuffs available in its environment, including insects, birds eggs, small mammals, and reptiles. There were probably some opportunities to scavenge the remains of carnivore kills as well. It remains unclear whether animal matter made up a very large portion of the diet of these early hominins.

There is no direct evidence that A. *afarensis* modified stone, bone, or wood to use as tools, but there is strong comparative evidence for at least some tool use. All the living apes except the gibbons use modified objects in foraging. Given that all hominids use tools of some sort, it is very likely that tool use is a primitive characteristic that was shared by the common ancestor of modern hominids that was an ancestor of A. *afarensis* as well. A. *afarensis* may have used sticks and grasses to forage for insects and may have used stones to crack nuts, but these assertions are speculative.

There is debate about the grouping patterns and social behavior of A. *afarensis*. Although the males are thought to have been much larger than the females, the canine teeth of both sexes are similar in size, a combination (sexual size dimorphism and canine monomorphism) that is rare in living primates. Generally, highly sexually dimorphic primates are found in grouping patterns in which either one adult male lives with many adult females and offspring or many adult males and females and young live in the same group. The latter type of group is the most common in primates today. Similar-sized canines are most often found in modern primates that live in small groups (usually averaging one male and one female plus young), but they occasionally show up in multiadult groups as well. One of the few fossil indicators of social behavior we have is the A. *afarensis* site of AL-333 at Hadar, which appears to consist of up to 13 individuals (including 4 infants) at a single locale and deposited in a single event. This provides tentative support for a multiadult grouping pattern in this species and thus as a baseline for subsequent species (including humans).

We know that many kinds of behavior are found among all primates, and we can assume that many of these patterns characterized *A. afarensis*. They probably moved as a group, ranging over large areas of their environment. Most likely, they engaged in mutual grooming and a good deal of socializing that may or may not have involved various kinds of gestural and vocal communication. Given that predators were quite common, it is likely that some form of antipredator strategy was practiced. The strategy may have been to run away, or it may have involved individual or group defense. Given their body size and lack of physical weaponry, avoiding predation was probably an important element (selective factor) in the life of *A. afarensis* (Hart and Sussman 2005).

The Pleistocene Hominins

During the Pleistocene (~2 mya until ~10,000 years ago) there are at least three genera of fossil hominins. The genus *Paranthropus* is currently grouped into three species dating to between 2.7 and about 1 mya. *Paranthropus* fossils display **megadontia**, meaning that they have larger postcanine teeth (molars and premolars) than would be expected for the size of their bodies. These forms also have adaptations consisting of massive chewing structures. The two other genera during this time period include the genus, *Homo* (humans) and the last few species of the genus *Australopithecus*. By the middle Pleistocene (~1 mya) all members of *Paranthropus* and *Australopithecus* had gone extinct and *Homo* began to spread across the planet. Because *Paranthropus* and *Homo* were coexistent and potentially shared similar environments and ecologies for over 1 million years, their differences and similarities may be important in understanding the evolution of human behavior (Figure 4.2).

Dating to about 2.7–2.3 mya, the earliest fossil representative of *Paranthropus* (*P. aethiopicus*) is a cranium that shows a number of derived characteristics relative to earlier hominins (such as *A. afarensis*) (Walker et al. 1986). It has a broad, "dish-shaped" face, almost no forehead, widely flared zygomatic arches (the "cheekbones"), a pronounced sagittal crest, extreme facial prognathism, and very large molar teeth. The single complete cranium of *P. aethiopicus* has a braincase of approximately 410 cc (25 cubic inches), no larger than those of earlier hominins.

One of the best studied hominin fossil species is now known as *Paranthropus boisei*. This species is known from multiple fossils, all from East Africa, dating from just over 2–1.3 mya. Most of these fossil finds are of cranial and dental remains with a few postcranial bones associated with the species. *P. boisei* appears to have been somewhat sexually dimorphic, with males weighing about 49 kg and standing nearly 137 cm tall and females weighing about 34 kg and 124 cm tall (McHenry and Coffing 2000). The dimorphism in this species seems less dramatic than in earlier hominin forms.

P. boisei displays many of the same chewing adaptations as *P. aethiopicus*. Using the measure of **megadontia quotient (MQ)** (a measure of premolar/

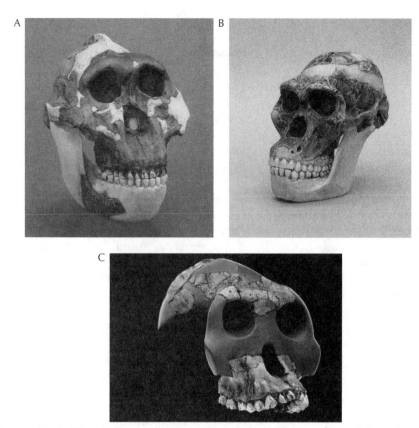

Figure 4.2 A: The skull shows the massive chewing adaptations of *Paranthropus boisei* (sculpted reconstruction courtesy of BoneClones™, www.boneclones.com). B: The skull shows a young *Australopithecus africanus* (sculpted reconstruction courtesy of BoneClones™, www.boneclones.com). C: The only existing cranial fossil of *Australopithecus garhi* [© 1999 David L. Brill (Original housed in National Museum of Ethiopia, Addis Ababa)].

molar tooth area relative to body size) suggests that *P. boisei* had the largest teeth relative to body size of any hominin. Their MQ is 2.7, indicating that their postcanine teeth are more than two and a half times larger than we would expect for their size (modern humans have an MQ of about 0.9) (McHenry and Coffing 2000). High MQ is thought to represent adaptations for massive chewing strength/force. Estimates place the brain size of *P. boisei* between 410 and 530 cc, giving them an **encephalization quotient** (brain to body size ratio for mammals) of about 2.7 (slightly higher than earlier hominins and higher than most primates). Unlike earlier hominins, *P. boisei* (and *Paranthropus robustus*, see below) had very small incisors and canines. These are characteristic of later hominins and members of the genus *Homo*. In addition, unlike earlier forms, *P. boisei* had a relatively parabolic tooth row, with the tooth rows diverging slightly at the back of the mouth. This characteristic is also shared with humans and not with earlier hominins.

The final *Paranthropine, P. robustus*, is found in South Africa dating to between 2.3 and 1.3 mya and is well known from fossils representing more than 100 individuals. *P. robustus* females were approximately 110 cm tall and weighed about 32 kg. Males were about 132 cm tall and weighed approximately 40 kg (McHenry and Coffing 2000). Sexual dimorphism in this species was very similar to that in *P. boisei* and in later hominins. Members of this species share many cranial features with *P. boisei*; however, the *P. robustus* braincase appears to have been slightly larger than that of *P. boisei* (about 530 cc), and the resulting EQ is also higher (3.0). *P. robustus'* MQ of 2.2 is slightly smaller than that of *P. boisei* (McHenry and Coffing 2000). The arms of *P. robustus* were longer than the legs, but the feet and hands displayed remarkable similarities to those of later hominins (humans). Because *P. robustus* and *P. boisei* are found in areas and times where we also find stone tools, and because their hands are similar to that of modern humans, these hominins may have been tool users, possibly tool makers.

The tenure of the last member of the genus *Australopithecus* found in South Africa, *Australopithecus africanus*, remains contentious. There is little dispute that they existed between 3 and 2.4 mya, but some researchers have proposed dates as old as 3.5 mya for some of the fossils attributed to the species.

The species is known from fossils representing more than 50 individuals from South Africa. *A. africanus* exhibited sexual dimorphism similar to that in the genus *Paranthropus*. Females stood approximately 115 cm tall and weighed about 29 kg, and males reached 138 cm in height and weighed about 41 kg. Cranial capacity ranged from low 400s to low 500s cc, with a mean of about 454 cc. *A. africanus* had an EQ of about 2.7, making them comparable to *P. boisei*.

Their incisors are small, as are the canines, and the premolar and molar teeth are substantially smaller than those of *Paranthropus*, giving *A. africanus* an MQ of 2.0 (McHenry and Coffing 2000). The arms of this species are longer than the legs, as in other early hominins, and the big toe is slightly divergent and mobile (less so than in apes, but similar). These characteristics suggest that *A. africanus* may still have moved around in trees.

In 1999, a group of scientists reported the discovery of a new species of *Australopithecus* in the Bouri geological formation of Ethiopia (Asfaw et al. 1999). They called this find *Australopithecus garhi*. Dating to 2.5 mya, the fossils consist of at least a few individuals and include cranial and dental fragments. Upper and lower limb bone fossils were also found in the same general area and dated to approximately the same time.

Numerous characteristics of this species set it apart from other previous fossil hominins. *A. garhi* has extremely large premolars and molars; in fact, they are at the upper end in size even relative to *Paranthropus*. However, because the incisors are also very large, the relative size of the postcanine teeth is smaller than in *Paranthropus*. Despite the large molar teeth, *A. garhi* does not share most facial features shared by members of the genus *Paranthropus* associated with massive chewing apparatus. Instead, *A. garhi* shares a set of primitive traits in the face and palate with *A. afarensis*, but it is distinguished from that species by its different dentition (Asfaw et al. 1999). If the limb bones found in rocks of the same age at nearby sites are correctly associated with this species, then *A. garhi* displayed a longer femur relative to the humerus than earlier hominins (a characteristic of humans), but an upper-arm to lower-arm ratio very similar to that of *A. afarensis*. Although represented by only a few fossils, this australopithecine appears to exhibit a constellation of traits not seen in any other hominin although some researchers are inclined to lump them with *Paranthropus* (Skinner and Wood 2006).

In addition to the surprising morphology of *A. garhi*, this fossil hominin is found in relative association with evidence of tool use and meat eating. Researchers found several fossils of mammalian bone with cut marks clearly made by stone tools in rocks of roughly the same age and nearby the *A. garhi* finds (de Heinzelin et al. 1999). Unfortunately, the stone tools that made the cut marks on the bones were not found at the site. About 100 km (62 miles) to the north, at the Gona site, researchers have found simple stone tools dated to 2.6 mya. Pointing out that natural outcrops of raw materials for stone making appear to be limited, researchers suggest that the users of the stone tools may have transported them over large distances rather than discarding them at the site (de Heinzelin et al. 1999). Regardless, if the cut marks on the bones are the work of the only hominin known from that site (*A. garhi*), it would be the earliest example of cultural processing of animal food in the fossil record.

The Genus *Homo*

Hominins with relatively large brains, differently shaped faces, and slightly smaller teeth show up in the fossil record starting around 2.4 mya, and stone tools appear alongside them. There remains significant debate over whether these fossils should be assigned to the genus *Homo* or the genus *Australopithecus* and how many species are actually present (Wood and Collard 1999). The earliest potential fossils of the genus *Homo* are often classified as two separate species, *Homo habilis* and *Homo rudolfensis*. Both display a mix of primitive and derived characteristics, but each one does so differently.

The majority of early *Homo* fossils are placed in the species *H. habilis*. These date from a little more than 2 mya to approximately 1.6 mya and are found in both East and South Africa. The fossils include both cranial and postcranial material, including elements of both the upper and lower limbs. Similar or slightly smaller than *Paranthropus*, *H. habilis* females stood nearly 100 cm tall and weighed about 32 kg. Males were about 131 cm in height and weighed about 37 kg. The few cranial fossils have a relatively prognathic face, no sagittal ridge, large incisors, and smaller postcanine teeth

(MQ = 1.9) (Conroy 1997, McHenry and Coffing 2000). The fingers appear slightly curved and strongly built. Some suggest that the arms of *H. habilis* are relatively primitive (showing similarities to those of *A. afarensis* and *A. garhi*), but other researchers argue that there is too little fossil information to support such an assessment (Asfaw et al. 1999). The pelvic girdle and legs of *H. habilis* display bipedal adaptations similar to those seen in *Paranthropus*. However, the one fossil foot associated with this species is a mix of primitive and derived traits and appears to retain some potential climbing adaptations (Wood and Collard 1999).

Six cranial remains attributed to *H. habilis* provide estimates of brain size, which range from 503 to 661 cc with a mean of 601 cc (McHenry and Coffing 2000). *H. habilis* therefore has both a relatively and an absolutely larger brain than the *Paranthropus* species. Evidence from endocasts (fossil impressions of the shape of the brain) suggests that a certain part of the human brain associated with speech in modern humans, called Broca's area, may be present in *H. habilis*.

In addition to the fossils attributed to *H. habilis* found in East Africa, there is another set of fossils possibly belonging to a larger hominin dating to between 2.4 and 1.7 mya. At first, these fossils were associated with *H. habilis*, with the notion that the species might be highly variable or extremely sexually dimorphic. However, currently some researchers place them in their own species, *H. rudolfensis* (Wood 1992). The majority of *H. rudolfensis* material comes from a dozen or so fossils, with very little postcranial material. Researchers still debate whether the postcranial material that does exist belongs to this species or to *Paranthropus* (Wood and Collard 1999, McHenry and Coffing 2000). If this is a true species, then its members are much larger than members of *H. habilis*, and present a very different picture of an early member of the genus *Homo*.

H. rudolfensis females may have been as tall as 150 cm (nearly 5 feet) and weighed as much as 51 kg, making them larger than any previous hominins and putting them well within the size range of modern humans. Males were probably taller [160 cm (5.3 feet)] and heavier (up to 60 kg). The one relatively complete cranial fossil associated with this species suggests a brain size of 736 cc, by far the largest for any hominin living before 1.8 mya. The face is broad and flat, there is no distinct brow ridge, and there is a sagittal ridge. The postcanine teeth exhibit megadontia and are absolutely larger than those of *H. habilis*, but because of the larger body size of *H. rudolfensis*, the premolars and molars are relatively smaller (MQ = 1.5) (McHenry and Coffing 2000) (Figure 4.3).

Between 1.8 and .04 mya, the fossil record for the genus *Homo* began to diversify and became increasingly complex. Beginning approximately 1.8 mya, the fossil record shows growing "humanness" in our ancestors, as they move into new geographical regions, change in shape, and demonstrate a wider and richer array of material culture. There is currently substantial debate over the classification of the fossils of the genus *Homo* dating to between about 1.8 and 0.04 mya. All scientists agree that these fossils come from members of the genus *Homo*, but they disagree on how many species are represented and how they are related to modern humans. There are three main perspectives in this debate. These are that all members of the genus *Homo* occurring between roughly 1.8 and 0.3 mya are one species (*Homo erectus*) that transitions into *Homo sapiens*. This species originated in Africa at the end of the Pliocene and dispersed throughout Africa, Eurasia, and Eastern Asia. In this model, some gene flow occurred in *H. erectus* populations as they moved around the Old World, and all of these populations are generally ancestral to modern humans. The second perspective is that the genus *Homo* included at least three or more species between 1.8 mya and modern times, and there were repeated movements out of Africa. In this model, only one lineage (or species) gives rise to modern humans, but there is contention as to which species that is and what the timing of the speciation events were. The perspective holds that all fossils of the genus *Homo* from about 1.8 mya through the present day are members of the same species, *H. sapiens*. Here the assumption is that as a species *H. sapiens* has been quite variable over time and that we (*H. sapiens sapiens*) are its current representatives.

In general, all of the *Homo* fossils dating from between about 1.8 and about .3 mya are differentiated from the late australopithecines, *Paranthropus* and the earlier forms of *Homo* by larger brains, larger bodies, less sexual dimorphism, and in size, shorter arms relative to the legs, longer legs relative to the body, reduced absolute and relative postcanine tooth size, and a diversification in the material record. There are also differentiations (on a smaller but still discernable scale) between some of the fossils that exist after 0.3 mya and up until 15–27,000 years ago (see below). However, the vast

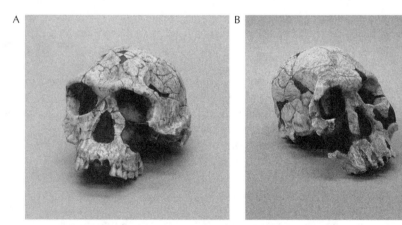

Figure 4.3 A: The skull shown is most often classified as *Homo habilis* (sculpted reconstruction courtesy of BoneClones™, www.boneclones.com). B: The skull is the main representative of the species *Homo rudolfensis* (sculpted reconstruction courtesy of BoneClones™, www.boneclones.com).

majority of fossils from 200,000 years ago through the present are considered to be members of the species *H. sapiens*.

The *Homo* fossils between 1.8 and 0.3 (generally assigned to *H. erectus* and possibly 1–2 other species) exhibit some general patterns. Females weighed, on average, about 51 kg and stood about 160 cm (5.3 feet) tall; males weighed about 66 kg and stood about 180 cm (5.9 feet) tall. Measurements of 26 fossil crania from Africa and East Asia indicate that *H. erectus* had an average cranial capacity of about 883 cc, with a range of 727 to 1251 cc (Conroy 1997). Their postcranial anatomy was similar to modern humans in many respects, although with higher bone density and greater overall skeletal robusticity. There are only a few fossils of hand bones, but those that are available do not show strong curvature of the phalanges. The shape of the cranium is long and low, with projection of the frontal bone, called a brow ridge, or supraorbital torus. Some of the fossils have a sagittal keel, a raised area where the parietals meet mid-cranium, and most have a pronounced ridge at the rearmost point on the occipital bone. The mandibles are robust compared to those of modern humans, and there is no protruding chin.

There remains some contention as to which hominins moved out of Africa, when they did so, and why. In one scenario, early members of the genus *Homo* (*H. habilis* or *H. rudolfensis*) expanded throughout, and out of, Africa approximately 2 mya, taking stone tool technology with them. Over time, populations moved around Eurasia and Africa, gradually evolving into the morphologies we associate with *H. erectus* and then into early *H. sapiens* (moving through the possible species *Homo antecessor* and *Homo heidelbergensis* according to some researchers). In versions of this scenario, the East Asian branch of *H. erectus* became relatively isolated and did not contribute significantly to the more modern forms. In these versions, the African ancestral from is termed *H. ergaster* (rather than *H. erectus*) and subsequently gives rise to *H. antecessor* and *H. heidelbergensis* in western Eurasia. This scenario has modern *H. sapiens* evolved from African populations about 200,000 years ago.

In a second scenario, the species that expanded throughout and out of Africa about 1.8 mya was *H. sapiens*, giving our species a very ancient origin in Africa. In this case, all the fossils found in Africa, Asia, and Eurasia dating to 1.8 mya or more recently belong to a single species, *H. sapiens*.

Which of these scenarios is correct? We have a diverse set of fossils in the genus Homo from ~2 million years, exhibiting numerous similarities and differences. Some argue that the morphological differences are not great enough to justify placing the fossils in different species, and others argue that these differences, in combination with the disparate locations of the finds, are sufficient to warrant species-level distinctions. Which scenarios one ascribes to depends on how you classify species in the fossil record and how you envision the evolution of many populations over large geographical distances. What is certain is that by approximately 1.8 mya hominins had expanded from East and South Africa into new areas of Africa and Eurasia. As members of the genus *Homo* were doing this, their brains were getting a bit larger, their postcanine teeth a bit smaller, and their use and manipulation of material objects was increasing.

The fossils of the genus *Homo* found in Africa and Eurasia dating from about 500,000 to 100,000 years ago exhibit morphological changes from the characteristic patterns of *H. erectus* [mostly due to thinner cranial bones and slightly larger cranial capacities (brains sizes)]. Depending on the dates, their locations, and certain morphological characteristics, some of these fossils are called either archaic *H. sapiens*, *H. heidelbergensis*, or *Homo neanderthalensis*. It is potentially difficult to pinpoint an exact dividing line between "anatomically modern" humans and these archaic humans. However, there are specific and marked changes in the cranium that do arise relatively quickly in the fossil record and that serve to distinguish "moderns" from "archaics."

Some "archaic" humans appear to have coexisted side by side with modern humans until fairly recently. Neanderthal fossils are found in areas of Europe and the middle east dating to as recent at 24,000 years ago, and recently a suite of incompletely fossilized remains of possible archaic humans were found on the Indonesia Island of Flores dating to as little as 12,000 years ago. The Flores finds were that of very short statured individuals (~1 m in height) with extremely small brains (approximately 380 cc). Some researchers argue that these are microcephalic and/or diseased pygmy modern humans whereas others point to their overlap with many *H. erectus/ ergaster*-like characteristics and the commonality of Island dwarfism in other mammals to suggest that they are a new species of Hominin (*Homo floresiensis*) that also coexisted until recently with modern humans. If these archaic forms are indeed separate species (and not merely variants or subspecies of *H. sapiens*) then apparently multiple species of humans did coexist until more recently than previously believed (Brown et al. 2004, Falk et al. 2005, Skinner and Wood 2006).

Anatomically modern human (*H. sapiens sapiens*) fossils are first found ~150–200,000 years ago in Africa. We have a high, rounded cranium, with the widest point on the sides above the midpoint of the skull. The cranium has an almost vertical frontal bone (forehead) and a highly flexed cranial base and a face that is pulled in under the cranium, nearly flush with the frontal bone. Overall, modern humans tend to be less robust than the archaic forms. Modern human's mean cranial capacity is about 1400 cc but ranges from 1000 to 2000 cc. This range of normal function is equal to the entire cranial capacity of *H. erectus*! This suggest that there has also been some sort of physio-neurological change such that pure brain size has less of an impact on function once above a basal size (probably about 1000 cc).

Modern human's teeth are the smallest of any of the hominins relative to body size, with a MQ of only about 0.9, and we have a distinct canine fossa (the indentation in the maxilla where the root of the canine tooth causes

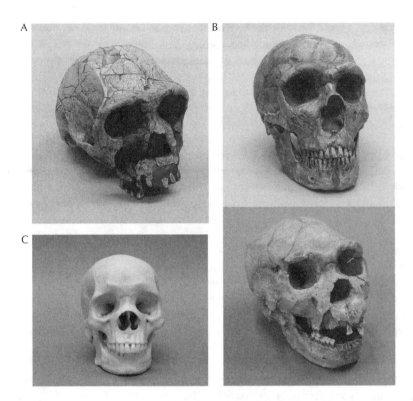

Figure 4.4 A: The skull shows a classic reconstruction of *Homo erectus* (sculpted reconstruction courtesy of BoneClones™, www.boneclones.com). B: The skull typifies many of the characteristics of Archaic *Homo sapiens* (sculpted reconstruction courtesy of BoneClones™, www.boneclones.com (both photos)). C: Modern *Homo sapiens* have a high forehead and rounded cranium, distinct from earlier forms (sculpted reconstruction courtesy of BoneClones™, www.boneclones.com).

a bulge). Unlike the late archaics or Neanderthals, anatomically modern humans have no retromolar gap (a space on the mandible behind the third molar). Finally, we have a chin. The bony protrusion where the two halves of the mandible join results from the collision between the changing shape of the cranium and face and the pressures and physical forces exerted by the chewing muscles (Figure 4.4).

Skinner and Wood (2006) note that the current life history patterns of humans (very long infancy and juvenile dependency, long adult life, and its associated morphological correlates) is significantly different from that of our closest relative, the African apes. They reviewed the hominin fossil record utilizing the species and genera reviewed here to examine whether or not modern life history-associated variables (body size, brain mass, dental formation and eruption) emerged as a package or separate events. Their findings

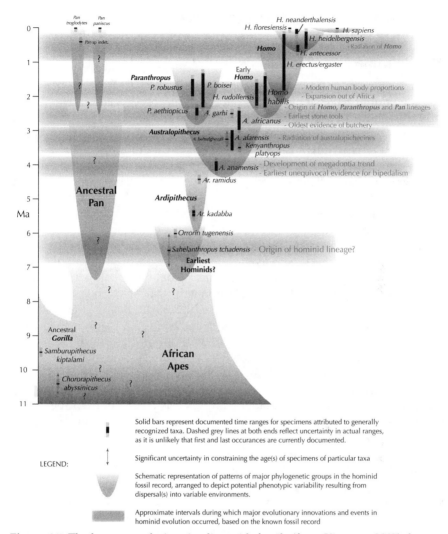

Figure 4.5 The human evolution timeline with fossils (from Kingston 2007) demonstrates the distribution of fossils over time and place.

suggest that each of these life history-related variables is not present in any hominins prior to early *Homo*; however, the timing and sequence of their appearance varies across the humans fossil record, and appear full blown only in modern humans (although some archaic *Homo* forms come close). Although this is a morphological measure of development and thus life history patterns, it has implications especially in regards to hypotheses for the evolution of human behavior tied to developmental life stages and the processes and encumbrances of human growth and development (Hawkes and Paine 2006) (Figure 4.5).

VERY BRIEF SUMMARY OF THE CULTURAL RECORD AND BEHAVIORAL INFERENCES (~2.6 MYA → PRESENT)

Late Pliocene/Early Pleistocene Forms

Given the general morphology associated with *H. habilis*, we may surmise that they might have slept in trees and possibly foraged and moved about arboreally, but it is more likely that terrestrial bipedality was the primary mode of locomotion. If *H. rudolfensis* is a valid taxon, it is unlikely they used the arboreal environment as much as *H. habilis* due to the structures of the lower limbs potentially associated with this taxa. The limb morphology of *Paranthropus* also indicates a reliance on primarily terrestrial locomotion and exploitation. However, there is no reason that all these hominins could not have also exploited arboreal foodstuffs and possible other aspects of the arboreal environment (as even modern humans do in many locales).

In modern humans, the brain requires approximately 20% of the entire energy intake of the body, and as the body gets larger, the amount of energy required to run the brain increases. It appears that the absolute and relative size of the brain increased in the early members of the genus *Homo* compared to *Paranthropus* (however, *P. boisei* and *P. robustus* have a slight increase relative to earlier forms). The size increase in the brain (possibly also in body size for *H. rudolfensis*) would have come with an increase in the metabolic cost. The cost appears to rise dramatically in later members of the genus *Homo* (see below), but it may have its beginnings in early *Homo*. If this is the case, then we would expect to see the diets of these early members of the genus *Homo* improving in quality and increasing in calorie content. The fastest way to implement such changes is to increase the amount of animal protein or high calorie/carbohydrate plant materials in the diet.

There is ample evidence that many types of large carnivores lived in East and South Africa, and late Pliocene/Early Pleistocene fossil sites have revealed the stone tool processed remains of small bovids and other animals in association with the types of tools we think early *Homo* made. At these sites, animal bones (primarily limb bones) have indications that meat was cut off them, as well as bones that have been crushed and had their marrow extracted. Increasing the amount of meat and marrow in the diet could have helped solve the problem posed by larger brains and bodies. However, there is little evidence that early *Homo* or *Paranthropus* hunted prey or even consumed large amounts of meat. It is more likely that they scavenged from predator kills or chance encounters with dead animals. A larger portion of caloric intake was probably made up of high-quality vegetable sources of proteins and carbohydrates, such as underground storage organs (roots and tubers) and nuts and other fatty fruits. It remains unclear exactly how these early members of the genus *Homo* foraged, but it is likely that they revisited food-rich sites, engaged in some small scale hunting and scavenging, and used tools to enhance their ability to process animal and plant foods.

On the basis of comparisons with all the living apes, it is assumed that simple tool use is common to all the hominins. However, we do not see any evidence that organisms actually modified stone to change its structure and function until approximately 2.5 mya. Modified stones, referred to as Olduwan types, have been found at numerous sites in East and South Africa. In the **Olduwan tool industry**, very simple modifications were made to certain types of rocks to produce sharp flakes and edged choppers. There is no evidence that any organism other than hominins has ever independently produced such tools.

The earliest stone tools were unearthed near a site where we find *A. garhi*, at about 2.5 mya and later tools are found at sites associated with either *H. habilis*, *H. rudolfensis*, *P. boisei*, or *P. robustus*. However, we have not actually found an Olduwan tool in a fossil hand, but we do find more early *Homo* in close association with Olduwan tools than *Paranthropus*. Given their larger brain size, many researchers assume that early members of the genus *Homo* made Olduwan tools. However, there is no evidence to counter the hypothesis that *Paranthropus* and possibly *A. garhi* also made Olduwan tools. *Paranthropus* and *Homo* were more or less sympatric with one another, appear to have similar dietary patterns, locomotary patterns, and hand morphologies, and therefore may have shared elements of material culture or at least copied or stolen from one another.

Making and using such tools could have enhanced hominins' ability to acquire and process foods and otherwise modify their surroundings. These dietary and environmental improvements, in turn, may have facilitated the ongoing changes that led to the later forms of *Homo*. If this ability to make and use tools to modify their environment and meet its challenges was successful, then it is in the latest Pliocene (likely with members of the genus *Homo*) that we see the advent of biocultural evolution, the interaction of somatic and extrasomatic material elements to meet selective challenges.

H. habilis and *H. rudolfensis* would have lived in social groups, as did the other hominins. However, as their brains grew in size over time and their ability to use and modify more and more objects in their environment increased, it is likely that the level and quality of their social interactions and communicative abilities became more complex. Making stone tools, searching for and gathering the raw material for those tools, hunting or scavenging for meat, and extracting and processing nutrient-rich plant foods are more effectively conducted in social groups. In addition, coordinating these types of activities across time and among a number of individuals requires a fairly advanced communication system (most likely more complex that that of modern chimpanzees). It is also possible that the threat of predation was a pressure driving grouping, social and communicative behavior (Hart and Sussman 2005).

From 2.4 until ~1.3 mya, the distribution of early *Homo* fossil finds in Africa is similar to that of *Paranthropus*. In fact, many sites that have yielded *Paranthropus* fossils also turn up fossils attributed to *H. habilis* or *H. rudolfensis*. These sites occur in a variety of habitats, including lakesides, savannas, woodlands, and semiforested areas. The fossil record indicates that the genus *Homo* went on to expand around and out of Africa and the genus *Paranthropus* went extinct. Any relationship between the success of the genus *Homo* and the extinction of the genus *Paranthropus* would obviously involve multiple factors. However, until recently the most often used explanation for the *Homo* and *Paranthropus* relationship (success versus extinction) is Robinson's dietary hypothesis: that members of the *Homo* were generalist foragers (eurytopic) and the members of the genus *Paranthropus* were specialist foragers (stenotopic) and thus ecological pressures of changing environments favored *Homo* (Wood and Strait 2004, Ungar et al. 2006).

Dental and related fossil analyses indicate that *Paranthropus* was not particularly **stenotopic** (a dietary specialist) and that *Homo* not more **eurytopic** (dietary generalist) than *Paranthropus* (Wood and Strait 2004). Wood and Strait (2004) demonstrate that the Robinson's dietary hypothesis is not supported across a majority of morphological and ecological variables—both genera appear relatively eurytopic. If this is the case, then dietary strategies and flexibility in foraging behavior may not fully account for the differential survivorship between the two genera.

Pleistocene Hominins—Early

It is during the earliest Pliocene that members of the genus *Homo* expand around and out of Africa, and by 1.3 mya or so are the only hominin genus left standing. About 1.6–1.4 mya, a new type of stone tool technology appears in the fossil record, first in East Africa and then throughout the rest of Africa, in western and central Eurasia, and in at least one location in East Asia. These **Acheulian tools** were more complex and diverse than earlier forms and were added gradually to the toolkits of *Homo*. An important characteristic of the Acheulian toolkit is bifacial flaking, a process that produced strong, sharp edges with better control in the making than Olduwan tools. The Acheulian tools were made in a variety of forms and sizes and included bifaces, flakes, and sometimes choppers similar to those of the earlier Olduwan tradition. Surface wear analyses indicate that the Acheulian tools were used to process plant materials, meat and skins/hides and possibly to modify wood and bone (Figure 4.6).

Acheulian tools do not show up at all fossil *Homo* sites. It may be that the members of the genus *Homo* who moved out of Africa and into Eurasia some 1.8 mya did so prior to the invention of Acheulian tools and the subsequent innovations in tool types did not reach many Far Eastern populations. Alternatively, it may be that *H. erectus* populations in East and Southeast Asia relied heavily on high-quality vegetable/wood matter (like bamboo) for tools, which would leave little or nothing in the fossil record. It is highly likely that all Pleistocene *Homo* populations used biodegradable material such as wood, bamboo, and probably bone to make tools, but since there is so little evidence in the fossil record, we do not know what these tools were or how they were used.

Figure 4.6 A: Olduwan stone tools are the first types of modified stones found (from Kristie Cannon-Bonventre/Anthro-Photo). B: Acheulian stone tools are more complex and harder to make than Olduwan tools (from Tim Laman/Anthro-Photo).

Another biocultural innovation associated with Pleistocene *Homo* is the controlled use of fire. There is evidence of the use of fire from sites around Eurasia dating to 0.5–0.3 mya. There is also some controversial evidence of fire use from before 1 mya in East Africa and about 1 mya in South Africa. It is possible that *Homo* began to use fire before 0.5 mya, but we currently do not have firm factual support for this conjecture. Evidence for controlled use of fire appears regularly in the archeological record by about 0.5–0.3 mya, so we can hypothesize that in at least some locations, *Homo* were using fire earlier than that.

There is no direct evidence of the construction of shelters prior to about 0.3 mya or so. However, given the widespread distribution of Pleistocene *Homo*, the environmental obstacles they had to face, and their other material innovations, it is not unreasonable to imagine that they may have built temporary shelters in times of cold or wet weather. Over-water travel is also thought to be relatively recent; however, the dates for the tools and fossil remains found on the Indonesian island of Flores suggest otherwise. Even at the lowest sea levels between islands in Southeast Asia, at 0.9–0.8 mya *H. erectus* would have had to cross at least 19 km of water to get to the island from its nearest neighboring land mass (Arribas and Palmqvist 1999). This is also the island where the recent *H. floresiensis* is found (see above).

Models of the changes in metabolic rates between early *Homo* and *H. erectus* show that because of increases in body size, especially in females,

H. erectus would have had much higher energetic, or caloric, requirements—perhaps as much as 35% higher—than earlier hominins (Aiello and Wells 2002). Larger body size conferred advantages for Pleistocene *Homo* (increased niche exploitation possibly increased the effectiveness of prey collection and predation avoidance, allowed individuals to carry greater loads, and resulted in more effective thermoregulation and water utilization). However, the size increase has costs, namely, the higher energy requirements to "run" the larger body. Pleistocene *Homo* had to consume more calories than earlier hominins. In addition to larger body sizes there is also evidence that extended infant dependency and loss of infants' abilities to grasp carriers resulted in increased infant carrying costs (increasing the cost of locomotion by as much as 16%) (Wall-Scheffler et al. 2007). The increase in brain size from the early Pleistocene forms until reaching modern size at ~300,000 years ago also would have required a ratcheting up of caloric quality and intake.

The increase in energy requirements suggests that a change in dietary patterns accompanied (or arose just prior to) the appearance of *H. erectus/ ergaster*. Aiello and Wells (2002) hypothesize that this dietary change took the form of greater reliance on animal protein and other high-energy food resources (see also O'Connell et al. 2002). A morphological correlate of the predicted change in dietary patterns is that estimated gut sizes are smaller in *H. erectus* than in earlier hominins (as is the case in modern humans). Because digestion and gut tissue are relatively expensive in terms of energy expenditure, there may have been an evolutionary trade-off between gut size and brain size in *H. erectus*. As brain size increased, gut size decreased, partially offsetting the higher calorie requirements of the brain (Aiello and Wells 2002). But having a smaller gut, in addition to having smaller teeth and jaws, makes it more difficult to process low-quality, easily available foods (namely, plants), giving added impetus to the shift toward high return food (such as meat eating) and/or to increased pressure to develop novel and more effective processes tools/behaviors. The fossil record does provide evidence of an increasing utilization of tools for food processing and eventually evidence of hunting and/or highly effective scavenging activities.

If *H. erectus* was shifting to a greater reliance on hunting and on gathering high-quality plant material, then the pressures for cooperative social living would have been even greater than they were for earlier hominins. As caloric requirements go up, the costs of reproduction, especially lactation, also increase. Lactation may have been as much as 45% more costly (energetically) in *H. erectus* than in earlier hominins (Aiello and Key in Aiello and Wells 2002). The appearance of aged individuals in some early and mid- Pleistocene sites also suggest that cooperative assistance to the elderly may have been present in even relatively early Pleistocene *Homo*. There is no direct evidence for the size of *Homo* social groups, but on the basis of comparisons with modern foragers they are assumed to be relatively small and mobile.

Early and mid-Pleistocene *Homo* were armed with a material culture that allowed them to exploit a wide array of food sources and to modify stones, wood, and other items. They had relatively large brains and large bodies. They moved over great geographical distances and ventured into new lands, habitats, and climates. We do not know if they spoke to one another, but must have had some form of complex communications system (at least relative to other hominoids and hominins).

Pleistocene Hominins—Late

Some information on *Homo* material culture and behavior comes from the time between 500,000 and 200,000 years ago from a few finds in Africa, Europe, and east Asia. However, much more material information comes from Neanderthal and other archaic *Homo* sites from between 300,000 and about 20,000 years ago.

Acheulian and other more basic tool kits remained in use up to relatively recent times, but between 400,000 and 200,000 years ago, some archaic populations displayed new and more complex tool-making abilities. By 400,000 years ago, archaic humans were using wood spears and hunting large game in an organized fashion at a site in present-day Germany (Dennell 1997). Other wood spears may have been used in eastern Africa at an even earlier date. Archaic humans may also have organized group hunts and ran large game animals over cliffs at Atapuerca, Spain. *Homo* were using and controlling fire, if not producing it themselves by this time period and there is evidence from sites in Eurasia and East Africa, that shelters of wood and possibly hide were built.

Starting in Africa and spreading to parts of Eurasia by 200,000 years ago, is a new tool-making technique called the **Levallois technique**, providing higher quality end products that can be refined for a wide variety of uses. In many of the later archaic or Neanderthal sites, we see a further refinement of stone tool making called the Mousterian industry. There are at least 60 known types of Mousterian tools. This increase in the type of tools and in their size range meant that tools could be used for a broader array of activities, opening up new opportunities.

Throughout the Pleistocene, there is evidence of continued use of animal matter in the diet, along with a broadening of the types of foods eaten and the methods used to acquire them. Although it is assumed that some early/mid-Pleistocene *Homo* were capable of large game hunting (maybe *H. antecessor*, Arsuaga et al. 1997), later Pleistocene *Homo* were doing so regularly by 400,000 years ago, as shown by spears and other tools associated with assemblages of bones from deer, bison, elephants, and other large mammals. Having more tools allowed archaic humans to apply them to more uses, such as enhanced scraping, piercing, puncturing, and gauging. Tool kits from different sites and geographic locations are different, even when the same general techniques were used, suggesting regional cultural variation, partly as a function of the types of materials available.

In late-Pleistocene *Homo*, there is evidence for cooperative hunting and complex tool production, which require coordination and communication, but there are no clear signs of how they thought or if they used spoken language to communicate. There is evidence that they may have provided assistance for injured or aged individuals, that they buried some of their dead, and that they may have had some items of personal or group adornment. The high number of healed injuries and the appearance of relatively aged individuals in the fossil record (especially for Neanderthal sites) has been interpreted as suggesting the presence of care for the aged and infirm. However, there are only a few aged individuals in the fossil record and the fact that we also see healed injuries in nonhuman primate species that have no communal care may contradict this view. In Europe and the circum Mediterranean region more than 35 burial sites associated with archaic *Homo* have been discovered. In those, material and skeletal evidence suggests that Neanderthals excavated an area and placed the body of a deceased individual in a hole, sometimes in specific positions, and sometimes containing material items such as tools and flowers. Some of the mid- and late-Pleistocene fossils, in Africa and across Eurasia, show evidence of defleshing, especially from the skull, after death. Although initial interpretations usually focused on cannibalism, it is also possible that other forms of postmortem practices were at play (Walker 2001).

Although fossils that we call anatomically modern humans are found ~150,000 to 200,000 years ago, the material culture that we associate with the advent of modern humanity does not become common in the archeological record until approximately 60,000 to 40,000 years ago. Regardless of why these changes occurred, by the end of the Pleistocene we begin to see a new level of complexity in tools, in hunting and foraging behavior, and in symbolic and individual expression. It is also only with extremely recent *H. sapiens sapiens* that we see the social complexity and environmental modification on a massive scale that characterizes humanity today.

Between approximately 50,000 and 17,000 years ago, the tool kits become more complex and incorporated items that substantially enhanced the physical capabilities of humans. The advent of blade tools and microflakes substantially increased the capabilities of stone tools including increased technical ability to modify nonstone items. Tools could now be efficiently hafted to wood or bone handles. Wood, ivory, and bone was carved to produce very small tools, such as fishhooks and needles. Blade tool kits varied from location to location, and not all modern human groups used them. Some retained older stone tool kits, and some used other, nonstone materials as their main tools. The *atlatl*, or spear thrower, and the barbed harpoons are examples of the types of innovative tools from this time period. Both of these items expanded the power of humans to exploit their own morphology and the surrounding environment in ways that no other animal on the planet can. By at least 22,000 years ago we have evidence from gravesites in Eurasia of sewn clothing and shoes. These new tool kits did not appear de novo. The Mousterian industry included some crude blades and a wide variety of smaller tools that were effective for working wood and bone. The blade tool industry of the Upper Paleolithic emerged from the Mousterian industry of the Middle Paleolithic, which in turn emerged from the Acheulian and even Olduwan industries of the Lower Paleolithic. The Upper Paleolithic industries were extensions and elaborations of prior patterns, not novel creations.

The advent of new tool technologies and the movement of humans into new environments opened up a variety of possibilities for the expansion of dietary patterns. Fine points and small tools enhanced the collection of fish and other marine and terrestrial small, hard-to-capture organisms. At coastal sites across all continents, there was intense exploitation of marine organisms, especially fish and shellfish, and occasionally marine mammals as well. The wider range of tools combined with continuous use of fire also allowed for substantial food processing. Macro- and microprocessing combined with cooking food reduces the stress on the jaw and teeth and also ameliorated many plant chemical defenses. Strength-enhancing tools such as the atlatl and the bow and arrow allowed for hunting from a distance, reducing the danger to individual humans and at the same time increasing the effectiveness of hunting and the overall return on each hunt.

By at least 50,000 years ago in Africa and Australia, fossil sites are increasingly associated with items of nonfunctional symbolism, or art. By 20,000 years ago, art and symbolism are ubiquitous in human fossil sites. This early modern human "art" ranges from etchings on cave walls and marks on the handles of tools to elaborate cave paintings and complex carved figurines. Images include both abstract forms and clear and accurate representations of animals and humans. There are even hybrid figures with mixed human and animal features. Sometimes single colors are used and at other times multiple pigments are exploited (Figure 4.7).

It is widely assumed that these images had cultural meaning to peoples who made them. How and why humans developed the ability to create pigments and to then apply them to surfaces in complex and aesthetically

Figure 4.7 Early human art, such as these cave paintings, indicates an explosion in symbolic representation.

imaginative ways remains a difficult question. These patterns may be the material mark of the emergence of belief systems and cultural attempts to understand the world and the place of human beings in it. The symbols may have been related to beliefs about hunting or foraging, about the changes in the seasons, or about events that had occurred in the past. Because of the variations in theme, in materials used, and in location, there are probably multiple explanations for the creation and use of art and symbol across both space and time. It is hard to image how such symbols could exist without some means of complex communication. Although it is highly likely that archaic humans and even older members of the genus *Homo* used some form of fairly complex communication, no concrete evidence supports such assertions. However, the symbolic expression associated with modern humans is generally seen as being associated with linguistic properties.

Many of the human remains dating to 40,000 years ago or less are in the form of burials. Modern humans buried their dead in a variety of patterns and with varying kinds and quantities of grave goods. In addition to burials, many modern human groups practiced some form of postmortem modification. These practices ranged from dismemberment to defleshing to placement of the body in specific positions. Some of the defleshing and anatomical modification patterns may reflect nutritional cannibalism, but most modifications were probably ritualistic.

The material record indicates that before approximately 20,000 years ago humans did not live in very large groups, nor were they consistently sedentary. However, between 20,000 and 10,000 years ago, those patterns changed, and by 5000 years ago, large population centers had emerged, along with the beginning of the political, economic, and social structures we have today. The emergence of agriculture, socioeconomic class distinctions, and clear and materially demarcated gender distinctions are all aspects of our most recent past (Adovasio et al., 2007).

SUGGESTED READINGS

Adovasio, J.M., Olga, S., and Jake, P. (2007) *The Invisible Sex: Uncovering the True Roles of Women in Prehistory*. New York: Smithsonian Books.

Campbell, C.J., Fuentes, A., MacKinnon, K.C., Panger, M., & Bearder, S.K., Eds. (2007) *Primates in Perspective*. New York: Oxford University Press.

Ciochon, Russel, L. and Fleagle, John, G., Eds. (2006) The Human Evolutions Source Book (2nd edition). In *Advances in Human Evolution Series*. Upper Saddle River, NJ: Pearson Prentice Hall.

Conroy, G.C. (2004) *Reconstructing Human Origins: A Modern Synthesis* (2nd edition). New York: Norton.

Kingston, J.D. (2007) Shifting adaptive landscapes: Progress and challenges in reconstructing early hominid environments. *Yearbook of Physical Anthropology* 50:20–58.

CHAPTER 5

A Survey of Hypotheses and Proposals of Why We Behave Like Humans

This chapter summarizes a set of proposals that have been put forward to explain all or some aspects of human behavioral evolution. The 38 proposals presented here emerge from the perspectives reviewed in Chapter 3 [Human Behavioral Ecology (HBE), Evolutionary Psychology (EP), Dual Inheritance Theory (DIT), and Memetics], from general ND-Sociobiology, from evolutionary anthropology, and from affiliated disciplines such as anthropology, biology, and psychology. I start the summaries with the proposals of Darwin and E.O. Wilson as they are highly influential and form a basis for the derivation of much current thinking about human behavioral evolution. This is not a fully comprehensive list of all the proposals for aspects of human behavioral evolution, but it is very representative of the major views and discussions in the field.

WHY SELECT THESE PROPOSALS?

In conducting this overview, I focus on proposals that evoke a grand narrative of human behavioral evolution *or* focus on evolutionary mechanisms and/or scenarios for *specific* patterns of human behavior. The 38 I chose can mostly be more accurately considered proposals than strict hypotheses,[1] although some are formulated as specifically testable hypotheses. The reason I use the term "hypothesis" is because each of these are treated by their authors, and others, as a starting point and/or basal explanation for

---

[1] In this case a strict definition of a hypothesis would be an explanatory statement that is structured so that it is possible to clearly and quantifiably test its outcome resulting in replicable refutation or support of the assertions.

the evolution of human behavior, either a specific trait/pattern or human tendencies in general. Each of the 38 proposals has been used to develop further predictions and assertions about behavior and adaptive (or maladaptive) strategies in humans. These proposals are their proponents' ideas about how human behavior (or aspects of it) came to be; therefore they are hypotheses in the loosest sense, but not always in the scientific sense (in that not all come with testable predictions).

In selecting which proposals about human evolution to include, I developed a set of justifications for inclusion and a methodology of comparison. The proposals must originate from researchers who publish their findings in scholarly and peer-reviewed journals and have worked in a field that has a general stake in investigating human behavioral evolution (traditionally anthropology, biology, psychology, and occasionally, sociology and philosophy). In the case of proposals for specific patterns, such as grandmothering or embodied capital, I looked to well-known (often cited) articles primarily (but not exclusively) originating from practitioners of the dominant paradigms reviewed in Chapter 3. For the broader, less trait-specific proposals, I looked to published narratives that have influenced the way researchers think about asking questions regarding human behavioral evolution (e.g., the Environment of Evolutionary Adaptiveness or the Human Behavioral Phenome scenarios). Selected works had to have been cited by other researchers as sources of information about human behavioral evolution (with exceptions for articles published in 2006 or 2007) and they had to be published in either peer-reviewed journals or as books from reputable (generally academic) presses.

Once selected, the content of each proposal was assessed based on its first published appearance, or most well-known appearance, (main citation) and additional published elements that augmented or clarified specific aspects of it. I summarized the main gist and the main points relative to human behavioral evolution, and extracted the main structural elements according to a classification system involving six main categories based on basic assumptions in behavioral ecology and evolutionary anthropology (cooperation, conflict, dietary practice/food, ecological/environmental pressures, sex and reproduction, other specific behavior patterns) and 81 components within those six categories (drawn from the contents of the proposals themselves). Chapter 6 provides the details on this comparative overview, while this chapter provides the summary of each without comparative commentary.

I want to repeat that I am not suggesting that this chapter provides a complete overview of all the rational proposals for the evolution of human behavior. I am sure that I have inadvertently left out some relevant proposals, included some that others might argue do not qualify. However, I have made a concerted and largely successful effort to capture and present a realistic and accurate overview of the main perspectives and proposals circulating amongst researchers interested in this area. Hopefully, the structure of this book will enable future readers to add additional proposals/hypotheses to the list and assess them along these lines for themselves. It is also my intention that readers interested in pursuing this further will use this chapter as a jumping-off point to follow up with these proposals/hypotheses, go to the original literature and read for themselves to capture all of the detail and facets that these short summaries, by definition, will miss. Each hypothesis is summarized in ~200–400 words in the following manner: title, main citation(s), general summary, main points, and additional relevant citations (if any).

SUMMARIES OF SPECIFIC HYPOTHESES/PROPOSALS

Name: Darwin's views on the evolution of human behavior: Mental Powers, Intellectual and Moral Affinities, and The Races of Man (Chapters III, IV, V, and VII in *The Descent of Man*)

Main Citation(s):
Charles Darwin (1871) *The Descent of Man and Selection in Relation to Sex.* London: John Murray.

Summary: There is a trajectory in the evolution of humanity from a state of brute savagery to higher civilization. Modern human groups represent various levels of this progressive scale. The basic senses, emotions, and social behavior found in animals, especially the social (anthropoid) primates, forms the ancestral baseline for human development. Selective pressures throughout the course of the evolution of humans since their derivation from ancestral ape-like stock (and continuing today) have favored a mental prowess that has resulted in the ability for language and related complex cognitive powers. Emerging from these cognitive powers is a moral sense and system of values that acts to distinguish humans from all other animals. In fact, it is this moral sense that in its highest form leads to the adoption and practice of the "golden rule" (do unto others as you would have them do unto you), which acts as the primary principle of human morality and in turn leads to a sincere regard for the welfare and happiness of other humans (and even other animals). Within modern human societies, the descendants of those with greater intelligence/capabilities/virtue will become a majority via selection as will groups of humans (populations/cultures) whose collective attributes confer such selective advantages. The differences between such groups (between "racial groups" in Darwin's terminology) have arisen primarily via isolation, adaptation to local environments, and sexual selection.

Main Points: Human behavioral characteristics are based in mammalian and especially primate prosocial behavioral patterns. However, during the course of human evolution, selection favored increased cognitive capabilities resulting in language, complex social relationships, and moral values. Associated with this pattern is the capacity for altruism, intragroup cooperation, intergroup conflict, group extinction due to natural selection, altruistic punishment, and a progressive sense of humankind moving toward increased moral and social virtue.

Name: Sociobiology

Main Citation(s):

Edward O. Wilson (1975) *Sociobiology: the New Synthesis*. Harvard: Belknap press (Chapter 27: Man: from sociobiology to sociology).

Summary: The basal assumptions are that early humans lived in small territorial groups with male dominance and possibly matrilineal kinship; hunting was important but it is not clear which individuals did the majority of hunting early on. Wilson proposes the *autocatalysis model* to explain the evolution of humanity. This model involves

1.   A strong baseline of behavioral flexibility in anthropoid primates.
2.   Evolution of bipedality resulting in freeing of the hands, which led to increased material manipulation and a stimulation of intelligence and cognitive abilities.
3.   Continued increases in material culture and complexity (possibly including hunting), which resulted in increased levels of cooperation (intragroup) and thus social complexity.
4.   Continued interaction and enhancement of material culture and intelligence combined with increasing division of labor between the sexes.
5.   The above points resulted in the multiplier effects of cultural evolution/complexity combined with strong sexual selection on males and females and a strong role for intergroup aggression and warfare to produce the patterns we see in modern humanity.

Main Points: Stemming from the predictions of sociobiology and the autocatalysis model, humans display

1.   Plasticity of social organization, more so than any other organism, that is best explained by prevalence of genes/genetic systems promoting plasticity.
2.   Systems of barter and reciprocity: a true reciprocal economy.
3.   Bonding, sex, and the division of labor: the nuclear family is the building block for humans societies, the loss of overt signals of female cycling estrus and continual receptivity characterize sexual interactions, and kinship is complex.
4.   Multiple social roles, with possible genetic dispositions in different people to fill the roles.
5.   Pervasive language and symbol use.

6. Ritual and religion, and culture as a hierarchical system of environmental tracking devices including selection/competition between cultural variants (see Memes hypothesis).

7. Ethics and morality reflecting an innate moral pluralism.

8. A state wherein most human groups are territorial and xenophobic.

Name: Man the hunter

Main Citation(s):
Sherwood L. Washburn and C.S. Lancaster (1968) The evolution of hunting. In Richard B. Lee and Irven DeVore, Eds. *Man the Hunter*. Chicago, IL: Aldine Publishing Company, pp. 293–303.

Summary: Human hunting, done by males, is "based on a division of labor and is a social and technical adaptation quite different from that of other mammals." "It is a way of life, and the success of this adaptation (in its total social, technical, and psychological dimensions) has dominated the course of human evolution for hundreds of thousands of years. In a very real sense our intellect, interests, emotions, and basic social life—all are evolutionary products of the success of the hunting adaptation." (p. 293)

Main Points: A set way of life that involves division of labor between male and female (male hunts), sharing according to custom, specific (hunting) cooperation among males, planning, knowledge of many species and large areas, technical skill. Additional points include females as main caretakers of young, males as providers of meat and sharing with females who gather vegetable matter, male enjoyment of hunting and killing (innate aggression), the evolution of handedness (skill specialization and brain lateralization), and language being a part of this package as well. These points imply intrasexual and interage group sharing and cooperation, general intragroup cooperation and sharing, innate male "killer instinct" ("man is naturally aggressive and he naturally enjoys the destruction of other creatures" p. 299), one male and one female plus offspring as basal unit of human family and associated incest taboo, exogamy, possible female infanticide, and loss of estrus, and possible/limited intergroup cooperation.

Other Citations:
Richard B. Lee and Irven DeVore, Eds. (1968) *Man the Hunter*. Chicago, IL: Aldine Publishing Company.

Name: Meat eating/Humans the hunters

Main Citation(s):
Craig B. Stanford and Henry T. Bunn (2001) *Meat-Eating and Human Evolution*. Oxford: Oxford University Press.

Summary: The acquisition and consumption of meat is a core factor in the evolution of humanity. Meat was acquired by early humans through both hunting and pirating ("power scavenging") and the meat was shared amongst group members. Increased meat consumption in the genus *Homo* is associated with larger, more energy demanding brains, stone tools (which were probably used to butcher carcasses), and increasing social and techno-logical complexity.

Main Points: Meat acquisition was a major causal factor in the successful trajectory of the genus *Homo*. The increase in use of meat resulted in increased defense of resources (central location territoriality), stone tool use, and development (related to meat acquisition, and processing). Other correlates (from Foley, see the reference listed in 'Other Citations') include physiological adaptations for "feast" or "famine" (thrifty genotype), high rates of intragroup sharing, high rates of intergroup conflict (territoriality and hostility), male cooperation/bonding, "risk prone" behavior in males (show off/handicap—related to hunting, possible group protection/intergroup aggression, and sexual selection), flexibility in foraging behavior and increased intragroup information transfer.

Other Citations:
Robert Foley (2001) The evolutionary consequences of increased carnivory in hominids. In Craig B. Stanford and Henry T. Bunn, Eds. *Meat-Eating and Human Evolution*. Oxford: Oxford University Press, pp. 305–331.

Katherine Milton (1999) A hypothesis to explain the role of meat-eating in human evolution. *Evolutionary Anthropology* 8(1):11–21.

Name: Cooking, tubers, and male guarding

Main Citation(s):
Richard W. Wrangham, James Holland Jones, Greg Laden, David Pilbeam, and Nancy Lou Conklin-Brittain (1999) The raw and the stolen: cooking and the ecology of human origins. *Current Anthropology* 40(5):567–594.

Summary: The use of fire for cooking appears early in the history of the genus *Homo* [~1.9 million years ago(mya)]. Associated with cooking is a focus on foods that have a high return when cooked (such as underground storage organs and other plant foods, as well as meat). As cooking requires a delay in the consumption of food, accumulations of food were valuable and subject to theft. This set up a producer–scrounger dynamic. Males, because of their body size, could steal (scrounge) from females as a foraging strategy; in response, females evolved a counterstrategy of bonding/partnering with males who could act as effective protectors. Resulting from this scenario is a suite of physical and behavioral characteristics associated with pair bonds, strong sexual selection/competition, and increased efficiency of resource exploitation.

Main Points: Cooking appears early in human evolution (~1.9 mya with *Homo erectus/ergaster* in Africa). Central place foraging along with delayed consumption (storage/accumulation) of high return plant foods created a set of "dietary packages" (p. 568) amenable to both theft and sharing (see Winterhalder 1996, below, for broader treatment of scrounging and sharing).

Theft and sharing occurred, with males (being larger and aggressive) acting as main thieves and females controlling the processing of food. Females chose to form bonds with males capable of protecting their food investments (and offspring) resulting in pair bonds and the antecedent to the nuclear family. Increased access to nutrition allowed for rapid body and brain growth in size along with a variety of anatomical and behavioral characteristics that appear over a short period of time (100,000–1,000,000 years). Associated characteristics include extended or continuous female receptivity (or at least attractivity), sexual division of labor, food sharing (intragroup and/or intra-kin and intersex), reduced same-sex alliances, increased heterosexual alliances, sexual coercion of females by males, innate male aggression and intrasexual competition, and females as the primary "cooks" (food processors) in human evolution since *H. erectus*.

Other Citations:

T. Hatley and J. Kappelman (1980) Bears, pigs, and Plio-Pleistocene hominids: a case for the exploitation of below ground food resources. *Human Ecology* 8:371–387.

B. Winterhalder (1996) Social foraging and the behavioral ecology of intragroup resource transfer. *Evolutionary Anthropology* 5(2):46–57.

Name: Demonic males/infanticide/body guard

Main Citation(s):

Richard W. Wrangham and Dale Peterson (1996) *Demonic Males: Apes and the Origins of Human Violence*. New York: Houghton Mifflin Company.

Summary: Male hominoids (specifically the great apes and humans) utilize specific patterns of aggressive behavior to increase their potential fitness. Males form cooperative bonds with related males to defend territory (resources) and females. This territorial defense involves monitoring of neighboring groups, occasionally resulting in intergroup aggression and potentially lethal conflict/confrontations. In intragroup interactions, males may use the threat of aggression to control/coerce females in sexual relationships. Males also may engage in infanticidal attacks both intra- and intergroup as a sexual strategy and as resource defense. While these behaviors may not necessarily be fully expressed given cultural and other proximate variables in humans, men maintain an evolutionary heritage including potentially lethal aggressive tendencies developed from these broader hominoid-evolved strategies. Females are expected to have developed counterstrategies to these patterns of male behavior.

Main Points: Males are inherently aggressive due to an evolutionary history of aggressive behaviors resulting in higher fitness values. Males within a group have a high degree of relatedness (are kin), engage in intragroup same-sex cooperation, intersexual aggression/coercion, and may practice infanticide. Conflict between different groups of males (intergroup) may be extremely violent and potentially lethal. Males will patrol/monitor group range boundaries to minimize losing conflicts and maximize winning conflicts (imbalance of power). Females develop counterstrategies to cope with male aggression, such as hidden cycling and mating with multiple males (paternity confusion) and pair-bonding with single males (bodyguard formation).

Other Citations:

Martin Daly and Margo Wilson (1988) *Homicide*. New York: Aldine de Gruyter.

Sarah L. Mesnick (1997) Sexual alliances: evidence and evolutionary implications. In P.A. Gowaty, Ed. *Feminism and Evolutionary Biology: Boundaries, Intersections, and Frontiers*. New York: Chapman and Hall, pp. 207–260.

Carel P. van Schiak and Charles H. Janson (2000) *Infanticide by Males and Its Implications*. Cambridge: Cambridge University Press.

Richard W. Wrangham (1999) Evolution of coalitionary killing. *Yearbook of Physical Anthropology* 42:1–30.

Robert Ardey (1966). *The Territorial Imperative*. New York: Atheneum.

Name: Cruelty as adaptive

Main Citation(s):

Victor Nell (2006) Cruelty's rewards: the gratifications of perpetrators and spectators. *Behavioral and Brain Sciences* 29:211–257.

Summary: The expression of cruelty, especially in males, is a human adaptation. Deep prehuman and then protohuman evolutionary history is permeated with the development of a predatory adaptation. With the appearance of hunting in Pliocene hominins there is an "emotional loading" of cruelty in forager society resulting in "powerful emotions—high arousal and strong affect—evoked by the pain-blood death complex" (p. 211). True cruelty emerges about 1.5 mya as a hominin "behavioral repertoire that promoted fitness through the maintenance of personal and social power" (p. 211). The practice of cruelty results in fitness benefits in solving problems of survival and reproduction in forager, pastoral, and urban societies. Modern and historical cultural elaborations of cruelty in war, sacrificial rites, and as entertainment illustrate the crosscultural stability of the uses of cruelty for punishment, amusement, and social control. The modern human enjoyment of cruelty is a culturally elaborated manifestation of the predatory adaptation.

Main Points: Cruelty is a behavioral by-product of an evolutionary history of predation and is driven by reinforcers that derive from adaptations to efficient hunting/aggression. Males are the primary actors in cruelty although females may also exhibit it. Cruelty requires the intention (cognitive ability) to inflict pain and is associated with complex cognitive functions and (minimally) protolanguage. Cruelty is exclusively a hominin behavior, and appears as a specific adaptation with *H. erectus* (~1.5 mya). Controlled use of cruelty and aggression (intra- and intergroup) results in the accumulation of power.

Other Citations:
Richard W. Wrangham and Dale Peterson (1996) *Demonic Males: Apes and the Origins of Human Violence.* New York: Houghton Mifflin Company.

Name: Tribal social instincts

Main Citation(s):
Peter J. Richerson and Robert Boyd (2005) *Not by Genes Alone: How Culture Transformed Human Evolution.* Chicago, IL: The University of Chicago Press.

Summary: Climate fluctuations and related varying selective regimes, hominin technological advances, increased ability to imitate, and cultural transmission led to increasing social complexity in the genus *Homo* throughout the Pleistocene. With the advent of anatomically modern humans, we see full gene–culture coevolution [encompassing five elements: (1) Culture is information that people acquire from others by teaching, imitation, and other forms of social learning; (2) culture change can be modeled as a Darwinian evolutionary process; (3) culture is part of human biology; (4) culture makes human evolution very different from the evolution of other organisms; and (5) genes and culture coevolve, Boyd and Richerson 2005, pp. 3–4]. By 100,000 years ago, gene–culture coevolutionary pressures between culturally variable groups gave rise to a predominance of "cooperative, socially marked groups" (p. 214) where symbolic markers involved language, dress, ritual practice, and so on. Humans thus developed a set of "uniquely human social instincts" (p. 235) stemming from the expectation of living in symbolically marked groups (or tribes). These groups can be larger than small foraging groups as symbolic ties can conglomerate various groups over larger areas of space. This "tribal" psychology includes behavior such as intragroup cooperation (including intra-larger symbolic metagroup), strong kin selection and altruism between members of same symbolically marked group, individuals striving for both status and group norms, shame and guilt along with moralistic punishment for not following group norms, and conflict between symbolically marked groups (and metagroups).

Main Points: A conflux of climactic, cognitive, and biological variables resulted in the appearance of complex human ultrasociality and subsequent gene–culture coevolution. Humans developed a set of tribal social instincts resulting in groups and metagroups unified through the common use of symbol and ritual markers and shared histories. These instincts result in intragroup cooperation and intergroup conflict resulting in group selection, intensive use of symbols for identification with and against groups, intra-symbolic-group altruism, intra- and intergroup competition for status, and moralistic punishment of nonconformists.

Other Citations:
Robert Boyd and Peter J. Richerson (2005) *The Origin and Evolution of Cultures.*
New York: Oxford University Press.

Name: Ratcheting effect and culture

Main Citation(s):
Michael Tomasello (1999) The human adaptation for culture. *Annual Review of Anthropology* 28:509–529.

Summary:

> Human cultures are historical products built up over many generations...the most distinctive characteristic of human cultural evolution as a process is the way that modifications to an artifact or a social practice made by one individual or group of individuals often spread within the group, and then stay in place until some future individual or individuals make further modifications and these then stay in place until still further modifications are made. (p. 512)

Tomasello refers to this process of pooled knowledge and subsequent multiple modifications as a "ratchet effect." Individual and group innovations throughout the evolution of the genus *Homo* are replicated and performed more or less faithfully by other members of the group until a novel modification emerges to "ratchet" (improve upon) or otherwise alter their efficiency and function. Substantial ratcheting potential occurs during childhood imitative learning and is uniquely human due to our complex social cognition, which emerged at some point between 2 and 0.3 mya. This results in a system wherein "human beings not only pooled their cognitive resources contemporaneously, they also built on one another's cognitive inventions over time" (p. 526).

Main Points: The genus *Homo* evolved specific cognitive abilities involving imitation, learning, and sharing that facilitated the pooling and augmenting of cultural (cognitive, material and historical) resources. Associated with this ability are intragroup cooperation, cooperation across age–sex classes, potential intergroup cooperation, a core role for language and complex semantic exchange, extensive caretaking of young with the potential for multiple caretakers or interactants with young.

Other Citations:
E. Herrmann, J. Call, M.V. Hernandez-Lloreda, B. Hare, and M. Tomasello (2007) Humans have evolved specialized skills of social cognition: the cultural intelligence hypothesis. *Science* 317:1360–1366.

Name: Human behavioral phenome

Main Citation(s):
Paul Erlich and Marcus Feldman (2003) Genes and cultures: what creates our behavioral phenome? *Current Anthropology* 44(1):87–107.

Summary: "Over the last 40,000 years or so, the scale of cultural evolution has produced a volume of information that dwarfs what is encoded in our genes" (p. 94). This species-wide cultural complex (information) and its resultant modification of global and local ecologies results in a system wherein the majority of influence shaping the modern human behavioral phenome (what we "do") comes from environmental influences (with "environment" meaning all environments encountered by human beings from the womb to death). Human evolution has created a physiology capable of extensive cognitive and social complexity and thus the majority of influences shaping human behavior come from the exposures and responses throughout the lifetime of the individual rather than any specific biological adaptations for particular behaviors.

Main Points: The small number of actual genes (<30,000) in the human system suggests that nongenetic cultural factors predominate in the causal underpinning of most human behavior for at least the last 40 kya (kya—thousand years ago) and possibly longer. All behavior is the result of biological and environmental factors, but with humans, cultural contexts and their environmental correlates are the primary interactants with individuals and groups in the creation of human behavior. Associated with this pattern are extensive flexibility and plasticity in behavior, cooperation and information sharing intra- and intergroup, aggression/conflict intra- and intergroup, kin selection, empathic altruism, and no single way to most effectively be human.

Other Citations:
Paul Erlich (1999) *Human Natures: Genes, Cultures and the Human Prospect.* Washington, DC: Island Press.

Name: Memes

Main Citation(s):
S.J. Blackmore (1999) *The Meme Machine.* Oxford: Oxford University Press.

R. Dawkins (1976) *The Selfish Gene.* Oxford: Oxford University Press.

D. Dennett (1995) *Darwin's Dangerous Idea.* New York: Simon and Schuster.

Summary: Human cultures are constructed of memes, which according to the *Oxford English Dictionary* are defined as "An element of a culture that may be considered to be passed on by nongenetic means, esp. imitation." Memes are ideas, concepts, and patterns of behavior that can occur either individually or in clusters (called memeplexes). Memes, like genes, are subject to natural selection such that at any given time the memes, memeplexes, and memetic variants are undergoing competition and certain memes/memeplexes (or variants thereof) increase in prevalence due to their "selective" advantage over others in a given cultural environment. It is therefore argued that ideas/practices/patterns that are ubiquitous in human cultures can be best seen (and modeled) as highly successful memeplexes (or "adaptations" in Darwinian terms). Modern human culture(s) (the total sum of all extant memes) arose from earlier, less complex meme clusters in our ancestors. With the increasing complexity of information transfer and the use of symbol and language throughout the evolution of the genus *Homo*, meme diversity increased and culture complexified. However, memes and genes need not display concordant fitness values in the populations in which they co-occur as memes replicate extra-somatically unlike genetic material.

Main Points: Memes, or units of human cultural behavior, undergo a process of natural selection in cultural environments. Information transfer, social complexity, and the reliance on extra-somatic means of environmental manipulation are core aspects allowing the propagation of memes and memeplexes. Thus, as the genus *Homo* evolved more complex cognitive, symbolic, and material patterns memes became more numerous. Behaviors common across human populations such as cooperation, xenophobia, religious beliefs, social roles, morality, ethics, and civil responsibilities, can be seen as particularly successful memeplexes. Such behaviors/patterns are reproduced extensively because they either facilitate biological fitness, or they consist of specific cultural fitness enhancing mechanisms, or have "viral-like" properties that foster selfish replication of themselves within human cultures in the absence of biological benefits for humans.

Other Citations:

http://www.susanblackmore.co.uk/memetics/index.htm

http://www.jom-emit.org/

Name: Culture/bursts of innovation

Main Citation(s):

Ian Tattersal (1998) *Becoming Human: Evolution and Human Uniqueness.* New York: Oxford University Press.

Summary: The appearance of a unique modern human cognition was a recent, and abrupt, event. This event occurred soon after the appearance of modern *Homo sapiens* in the fossil record (~120–200 kya or so) and the acquisition of this unique cognition results in an emergent quality that endows humans with the ability to make more rapid and complex extra-somatic responses to a myriad of challenges as compared to other primates or our recent ancestors. This modern human cognition is *in addition* to the already complex cognition evolved by ancestral members of the genus *Homo* (prior to modern forms), but it is a novel state not simply resulting from fine-tuning of previous patterns. It is derived from underlying primate and hominin physiological patterns but expanded and augmented in a way that had not been present in previous forms. The climax of this emergent quality is the plasticity and flexibility in human individual and social response.

Main Points: Environments of the Pliocene and Pleistocene did not shape modern human behavior; rather, the novel cognitive abilities that emerge abruptly, as an exaptation, from hominin physiology with modern humans outstrip previous behavioral abilities in members of the genus *Homo*.

The scope and contents of modern human symbolic, linguistic, and behavioral repertoires result in complex individual and group plasticity in response to environmental and social challenges.

Other Citations:
Ian Tattersal (2004) Emergent behaviors and human sociality. In R.W. Sussman and A.R. Chapman, Eds. *The Origins and Nature of Sociality.* New York: Aldine de Gruyter, pp. 237–248.

Name: Sociality and variability selection

Main Citation(s):
Richard Potts (2004) Sociality and the concept of culture in human origins. In Robert W. Sussman and Audrey R. Chapman, Eds. *The Origins and Nature of Sociality.* New York: Aldine de Gruyter, pp. 249–269.

Summary: Substantial environmental fluctuations throughout the Pleistocene provide the critical context in which humans evolved. Humans display startling flexibility and versatility in behavior. The context in which the genus *Homo* evolved effectively "decoupled the human organism from any single ancestral environment" (p. 260). This resulted in a suite of characteristics in humans, such as increases in brain size, increased complexity in material culture, and intensification of social interactions. Increases in symbolic activity and the appearance of language create a feedback system that results in the enhancement of material and social cultural patterns. Emerging from this feedback are human cultural patterns including economic pair-bond systems (marriage), trade and exchange networks, and increasingly complex bonds of social reciprocity. All of which create the context in which modern cultural institutions can emerge. In sum, "the origin of cultural capacities distinctive to living humans embellished the chances of adapting to environmental instability" (p. 263).

Main Points: Variable environments during the evolution of the genus *Homo* resulted in selection favoring behaviorally flexible adaptive patterns. This flexibility combined with the feedback systems enabled by symbolic cognitive processes and language resulted in the emergence of the myriad of complex sociocultural patterns we see in humans today. Associated factors include intra- and intergroup cooperation, intrasexual and across age group cooperation, a core role for information transfer, and the use and sharing of complex symbol and coding systems.

Other Citations:
Kathleen R. Gibson (2005) Epigenesis, brain plasticity, and behavioral versatility: alternatives to standard evolutionary psychology models. In S. McKinnon and S. Silverman, Eds. *Complexities: Beyond Nature and Nurture.* Chicago, IL: University of Chicago Press, pp. 23–42.

Richard Potts (1998) Environmental hypotheses of hominin evolution. *Yearbook of Physical Anthropology* 41:93–136.

Richard Potts (1999) Variability selection in hominid evolution. *Evolutionary Anthropology* 7(3):81–96.

Name: Primate plasticity
Main Citation(s):
Adrienne L. Zihlman and Debra R. Bolter (2004) Mammalian and primate roots of human sociality. In Robert W. Sussman and Audrey R. Chapman, Eds. *The Origins and Nature of Sociality.* New York: Aldine de Gruyter, pp. 23–52.

Summary: Nonhuman primates display a high degree of variability and plasticity of response in their social behavior relative to other mammals. Anthropoid nonhuman primates (monkeys and apes) display individual behavioral variability to a greater extent than other organisms. As humans are anthropoid primates, their evolutionary history begins within a baseline of pronounced social complexity and behavioral plasticity. The development of an extended childhood and extensive cooperation at the community level along with an elaborate information transfer system facilitates the emergence of human complexity from primate-wide antecedents. Modern human social complexity and behavioral diversity then emerge through selection for increased and enhanced behavioral complexity and variability.

Main Points: Primates are highly variable in their social behaviors and therefore humans are as well. Modern human social complexity and society emerged though a series of selective events favoring an expansion and enhancement of primate variability and social behavioral complexity. Associated patterns include individual behavioral plasticity, group-level behavioral plasticity, broadscale potential for complex cooperation between individuals and within communities, communal social care of slowly developing young, cooperation across age/sex groups, and the assumption of selection pressures to enhance such patterns in human evolution.

Other Citations:
Agustin Fuentes (2007) Social organization: social systems and the complexities in understanding the evolution of primate behavior. In C. Campbell, A. Fuentes, K. MacKinnon, M. Panger, and S. Bearder, Eds. *Primates in Perspective.* Oxford University Press, pp. 609–621.

Agustin Fuentes (2004) It's not all sex and violence: integrated anthropology and the role of cooperation and social complexity in human evolution. *American Anthropologist* 106(4):710–718.

Richard Potts (2004) Sociality and the concept of culture in human origins. In Robert W. Sussman and Audrey R. Chapman, Eds. *The Origins and Nature of Sociality.* New York: Aldine de Gruyter, pp. 249–269.

J.B. Silk (2007) Social component of fitness in primate groups. *Science* 317:1347–1351.

Edward O. Wilson (1975) *Sociobiology: The New Synthesis.* Harvard: Belknap Press.

Name: Epigenetic cognitive plasticity

Main Citation(s):

Kathleen R. Gibson (2005) Epigenesis, brain plasticity, and behavioral versatility: alternatives to standard evolutionary psychology models. In S. McKinnon and S. Silverman, Eds. *Complexities: Beyond Nature and Nurture.* Chicago, IL: University of Chicago Press, pp. 23–42.

Summary: "Creativity, versatility and advanced learning capacities are primary hallmarks of the human mind" (p. 23). This pattern of human flexibility and adaptability reflects "the neural plasticity and epigenetic processes that shape the maturing brain" (p. 38) of modern humans. This also endows humans with the ability to create mental constructions that allows humans to combine and recombine experiences, previous actions and concepts to create novel concepts and actions in response to novel problems. Humans are able to do this in ways that no other organism can. Given the exploitation of diverse and variable habitats/ecologies by the genus *Homo* over hundreds of millennia, the epigenetic and plastic nature of human cognitive processes can be seen as an adaptive response.

Main Points: "The human brain is an epigenetic and functionally plastic organ" (p. 38) that has emerged over evolutionary time from already socially complex primate ancestral states through the pressures of variable environments and ecologies. Human mental construction features plastic and creative processes that give rise to the multitude of human social behavior and societies today. Associated factors include a core role for complex information transfer in human evolution, exposure to multiple complex environments throughout the evolution of the genus *Homo*, a lack of specialized "modules" in the brain, and a core role for epigenetic development and neural plasticity in fostering the creation and use of mental constructions.

Other Citations:

Richard Potts (2004) Sociality and the concept of culture in human origins. In Robert W. Sussman and Audrey R. Chapman, Eds. *The Origins and Nature of Sociality.* New York: Aldine de Gruyter, pp. 249–269.

Name: Reciprocal altruism

Main Citation(s):

Robert Trivers (1971) The evolution of reciprocal altruism. *Quarterly Review of Biology* 46(10):35–57.

Summary: Humans display a wide range of seemingly altruistic behavior. These actions are most likely forms of reciprocal altruism. Reciprocal altruism involves a system wherein one actor assists a recipient in return for the present or future assistance of the recipient. In an evolutionary sense, this implies giving up ~X fitness value and receiving ~X fitness value in return. Humans appear to be particularly altruistic; therefore strong evolutionary pressure favoring reciprocal altruism must have played major roles in the evolution of the genus *Homo*. This importance of altruistic acts in the human system may have established a "selection pressure for psychological and cognitive powers which partly contributed to the large increase in hominid brain size during the Pleistocene" (p. 54). In humans, altruistic systems are highly susceptible to cheating; therefore a complex psychological system that regulates reciprocal altruism has evolved. This psychology is seen in elements such as friendships and emotional bonds, moralistic aggression, gratitude and sympathy, guilt, dishonesty, hypocrisy, complex learning from others, and other mechanisms for subtle cheating and the detection of such cheaters. This psychology is described by Richard Alexander (below) as the underpinning of human morality (moral systems are systems of indirect reciprocity) that acts to unite groups via internal moral cohesion and specifically excluding and directing this cohesion against other such groups.

Main Points: Humans are practitioners of substantial reciprocal altruism. In the evolution of the genus *Homo*, strong pressures favored the emergence of a complex psychology to contextualize and make use of reciprocal altruistic patterns. This psychology explains much of modern human behavior and society. Associated factors include: selfish cheating orientation when possible, cooperation with both kin and non-kin, the use of moralistic aggression as punishment, developmental plasticity of those traits regulating altruistic and cheating behavior, intersexual cooperation and conflicts, and cooperation and conflict across age/sex classes.

Other Citations:
Richard D. Alexander (1987) *The Biology of Moral Systems*. New York: Aldine de Gruyter.

Name: Altruistic punishment

Main Citation(s):
Ernst Fehr and Simon Gachter (2002) Altruistic punishment in humans. *Nature* 415:137–140.

Summary: Human cooperation cannot be fully explained by reliance on kin selection, selfish signaling theory, or reciprocal altruism. However, if altruistic punishment (defined as individuals punishing others at potential fitness cost to themselves with no specific individual gain) is common in a population there can be a flourishing of cooperation in that human society. Negative emotions toward defectors (those who "free ride" on cooperation of others) are the proximate mechanisms that elicit the altruistic punishment behavior. The evolution of substantial cooperation in modern human societies can be largely explained by focusing on the structure and causal factors underlying altruistic punishment.

Main Points: Humans cooperate at high levels and the maintenance of this cooperation cannot be fully explained by kin selection, signaling, or reciprocal altruism theories. Altruistic punishment, stimulated by negative emotions toward cheaters in a cooperative system, maintains cooperation in human populations. Associated factors are a predominance of cooperation in human groups, including amongst large groups of non-kin, maintained by aggressive punishment of non-cooperators and the potential presence of nonselfish behavior associated with both cooperation and altruistic punishment.

Other Citations:
Karl Sigmund, Christoph Hauert, and Martin A. Nowak (2001) Reward and punishment. *Proceedings of the National Academy of Sciences USA* 98:10757–10761.

Name: Tit-for-tat cooperation

Main Citation(s):
Robert Axlerod and William D. Hamilton (1981) The evolution of cooperation. *Science* 211:1390–1396.

Summary: Cooperation between unrelated individuals is difficult to explain in an evolutionary perspective. However, using a prisoner's dilemma game scenario one can demonstrate that cooperation based on reciprocity can develop within populations and become an evolutionarily stable strategy. In the prisoner's dilemma, players can cooperate or defect (with variable costs or payoffs depending on the opponent's choice of play). Reciprocity develops when organisms adopt a tit-for-tat strategy where the probability of play (cooperate or defect) in any given encounter is based on the history of interactions between interactants. This strategy mandates that an organism will copy the last "play" (defection or cooperation) by his opponent in their previous meeting. Thus, if the opponent cooperated previously, the player cooperates, and vice versa. If practiced in an iterated prisoner's dilemma scenario, the tit-for-tat strategy has higher payoffs than any other and thus is the favored strategy for any individual, upholding a "selfish gene" perspective even with high rates on cooperation between non-kin. This pattern of reciprocal cooperation based on tit-for-tat strategy can help us understand much about organisms' (including humans') behavior including territoriality, mating and disease.

Main Points: Tit-for-tat strategies practiced in an iterated prisoner's dilemma scenario demonstrate that cooperation can evolve even in a population of selfish organisms. Cooperation between non-kin need not be explained by group-level selection or any other means aside from an emphasis on individual (selfish) advantage. This perspective along with Robert Trivers' reciprocal altruism and more complex agent- based modeling approaches in Axelrod (1997) can potentially explain the high rates of cooperation and conflict in human organisms.

Other Citations:
Robert Axlerod (1984) *The Evolution of Cooperation*. New York: Basic Books.

Robert Axelrod (1997) *The Complexity of Cooperation: Agent Based Models of Competition and Collaboration*. Princeton: Princeton University Press.

Robert Trivers (1971) The evolution of reciprocal altruism. *Quarterly Review of Biology* 46(10):35–57.

Name: Conflict negotiation

Main Citation(s):

Frans B.M. de Waal (2000) Primates—a natural heritage of conflict resolution. *Science* 289:586–590.

Jessica C. Flack, Michelle Girvan, Frans B.M. de Waal, and David C. Krakauer (2006) Policing stabilizes construction of social niches in primates. *Nature* 439:426–429.

Summary: "When survival depends on mutual assistance, the expression of aggression is constrained by the need to maintain beneficial relationships. Moreover, evolution has produced ways of countering its disruptive consequences" (p. 586). Nonhuman primates engage in reconciliation behavior after conflict to repair the damage to valued social relationships. Because humans are also primates, we can say that "Without denying the human heritage of aggression and violence...research demonstrates an equally old heritage of countermeasures that protect cooperative arrangements against the undermining effects of competition" (p. 590). Throughout the course of human evolution as social complexity increases so does the pattern of conflict negotiation. Humans have evolved complex behavioral sets to ameliorate or repair the damage caused by interindividual aggressive conflict. Among these sets are both behaviors for reconciliation that act to repair damage caused by conflict and those for "policing tendencies" that act to control conflicts and influence the structure of social networks.

Main Points: Conflict negation and reconciliation is an important component of human evolution and modern human behavior. Humans have evolved a psychology that deals with inherent and ubiquitous interindividual aggression via the development of a set of behavioral patterns and strategies. Humans cooperate extensively to negotiate conflicts and repair/ameliorate the potential damage to social relationships caused by aggression between individuals. In primate societies (especially humans) some individuals may take on "policing" roles that act to stabilize and maintain social structures. Associated factors include a prevalence of both intragroup conflict and cooperation and cooperation between same and differing age and sex groups.

Other Citations:

F. Aureli and Frans B.M. de Waal (2000) *Natural Conflict Resolution.* Berkeley: University of California Press.

Frans B.M. de Waal, (1996) *Good Natured.* Cambridge, MA: Harvard University Press.

Name: Cooperation—a general pattern

Main Citation(s):

Agustin Fuentes (2004) It's not all sex and violence: integrated anthropology and the role of cooperation and social complexity in human evolution. *American Anthropologist* 106(4):710–718.

Bruce M. Knauft (1991) Violence and sociality in human evolution. *Current Anthropology* 32(4):391–428.

John. M. Watanabe and Barbara B. Smuts (2004) Cooperation, commitment, and communication in the evolution of human sociality. In Robert W. Sussman and Audrey R. Chapman, Eds. *The Origins and Nature of Sociality.* New York: Aldine de Gruyter, pp. 288–312.

Summary: Human cooperation represents an intensified and complexified form of nonhuman primate cooperation. Modern human sociality and society intrinsically represents a progressive intensification of social cooperation. The evolution of the genus *Homo* is characterized by increasingly complex social and cooperative engagements facilitated by malleable individual behavior strategies and multilevel selection in the context of complex cognitive, symbolic, and linguistic behavioral interchanges. Complex cooperation within and potentially between groups is a major adaptation of humankind.

Main Points: Cooperation has a prominent role in the evolution of modern humans. Complex information sharing, social interactions, and mutual reliance on multiple individuals foster a niche wherein cooperation amongst individuals can provide evolutionary benefits. Associated factors emerging form this proposal include intra- and intergroup cooperation, an important role for multilevel selection, symbolic culture, language, and information sharing, and that peaceful interactions are common amongst human groups.

Other Citations:

Bruce M. Knauft (1994) Culture and cooperation in human evolution. In Leslie E. Sponsel and Thomas Gregor, Eds. *The Anthropology of Peace and Nonviolence*, pp. 37–67. Boulder, CO: Lynne Riener.

Eliott Sober and David S. Wilson (1998) *Do Unto Others: The Evolution and Psychology of Unselfish Behavior.* Cambridge, MA: Harvard University Press.

Name: Cooperative Breeding model

Main Citation(s):

Sarah B. Hrdy (2005) Evolutionary context of human development: the cooperative breeding model. In C.S. Carter, L. Ahnert, K.E. grossmann, S.B. Hrdy, M.E. Lamb, S.W. Porges, and N. Sachser, Eds. *Attachment and Bonding: A New Synthesis.* Cambridge, MA: The MIT Press, pp. 9–32.

Summary: Allomaternal assistance formed a main aspect of human adaptive response in the Pleistocene evolution of the genus *Homo*. Biological and classificatory kinship systems and reciprocal trade networks/sharing between and within groups enabled a broad set of caretakers and learning experiences for developing offspring. This helped offset potentially high infant mortality and depends on complex cognitively active engagement between infants and caretakers.

Main Points: Cooperative breeding represents a core factor in human social evolution. Appearing during the evolution of the genus *Homo* (expanding on ape-like mothering systems), this system includes multiple caretakers for young (intragroup), high intragroup cooperation, potential for some inter-group cooperation, cooperation across age/sex classes, some form of language, and/or complex information transfer between young and caretakers and amongst members of humans groups.

Other Citations:
Sarah B. Hrdy (1999) *Mother Nature: A History of Mothers, Infants and Natural Selection*. New York: Pantheon.

Name: Multilevel selection
Main Citation(s):
David S. Wilson and Eliott Sober (1994) Reintroducing group selection to the human behavioral sciences. *Behavioral and Brain Sciences* 17(4):585–608.

Summary: "Humans can facultatively span the full range from self-interested individuals to 'organs' of group-level 'organisms'" (p. 585). Human behavior not only results from the balance between levels of selection (genic, individual, group) but it can also alter their relationship "through the construction of social structures that have the effect of reducing fitness differences within groups, concentrating natural selection (and functional organization) at the group level" (p. 585). Complex social structures and the cognitive abilities in humans result in shared knowledge and group/community level cohesion and behavior such that group selection can be important even among large groups of unrelated individuals.

Main Points: Social complexity, extensive interactions within and between groups of humans produces a context wherein multilevel selection results in widespread cooperative patterns in humanity. Associated factors include cooperation intra- and potentially intergroup within populations and substantial complexity of social structures, communication systems, and information sharing.

Other Citations:
Eliott Sober and David S. Wilson (1998) *Do Unto Others: The Evolution and Psychology of Unselfish Behavior*. Cambridge, MA: Harvard University Press.

Wilson, D.S. and Wilson, E.O. (2007) Rethinking the theoretical foundation of sociobiology. *The Quarterly review of Biology* 82(4):327–348.

Name: Inherent morality
Main Citation(s):
Marc Hauser (2006) *Moral Minds: How Nature Designed Our Universal Sense of Right and Wrong*. New York: Harper Collin Publishers.

Summary: Despite substantial variation in modern human social norms, there is an underlying similarity via a common biological infrastructure that allows for the development of complex human beliefs and morality in all human groups. Humans posses an inherent "grammar" (biological template) for morality, much as we possess an inherent grammar for language (ala Chomsky). This potential for a system of morality is pluralistic in that there are many specific moral systems across human cultures, and our inherent grammar simply ensures that all humans have the toolkit to acquire and use the moral system that they are enculturated in. This inherent morality is based on the simple recognition and action systems of social vertebrates, the more complex social contexts, cooperation, and conflict negotiation of primates, but it is most complex and diverse in humans. This suggests that in the course of human evolution various selection pressures expanded the context and capabilities of the "moral grammar." In Hauser's perspective, the universal moral grammar emerges in a fashion similar to language and the immune system: underlying physiological/neurological infrastructure is enabled and shaped by lifetime experience producing a phenotype (behavior) that is culturally/experientially contingent.

Main Points: Humans are endowed with "a moral instinct, a faculty of the human mind that unconsciously guides our judgments concerning right and wrong, establishing a range of learnable moral systems, each with a shared set of unique signatures" (p. 423). This moral instinct is based on our vertebrate, mammalian, and primate phylogenic history and specifically expanded in our hominin evolutionary trajectory. This implies that human groups are capable of a wide array of extensive social cooperation (morals, ethics, actions) based on a universal biological infrastructure (broadscale intragroup cooperation and information transfer) and that aspects of human evolution differentiated the potential extent of such infrastructure relative to other primates and related forms.

Other Citations:
John Rawls (1971) *A Theory of Justice*. Cambridge, MA: Harvard University Press.

Name: Morality and cognition
Main Citation(s):
Ursula Goodenough and Terrence W. Deacon (2003) From biology to consciousness to morality. *Zygon* 38(4):801–819.

Summary: All social animals have prosocial orientations that enable cooperative interactions; however, human cognitive capabilities allow them to exceed all other organisms in the extent of cooperation and social complexity in that they have morality. During the evolution of the hominins, particularly the genus *Homo* "culture has masked the need for certain genetically encoded (phylotypic) primate mental pathways and these have degraded," resulting in a neurological system where "The freed-up brain space has been reconfigured, again genetically, to generate minds adept at learning symbolic language and hence acquiring cultural information" (p. 811). Once this occurred, humans achieve a unique sense of self-awareness that results in moral experience. Four primary virtues compose the bulk of this moral experience: humaneness/compassion, fair mindedness, care, and reverence. Morality is an emergent property associated with primate-wide prosociality, particular patterns in human evolution, and the resultant cognitive infrastructure.

Main Points: Human morality emerges from generalized primate prosocial complexity transfigured and engaged by human capacities for symbolic language, culture and religion. In the course of human evolution, basic cognitive capabilities expanded, facilitating the acquisition of the moral experience and thus shaping modern human behavior. Associated factors include an extensive potential for cooperation of all types, a primary role for language and complex information transfer, an emphasis on reciprocal altruism and altruistic punishment, the creation of communities based on moral codes, and the concomitant widespread sharing of information and material based on moral codes and structures.

Other Citations:
Terrence W. Deacon (1997) *The Symbolic Species: The Co-Evolution of Language and the Brain.* New York: W.W. Norton.

Name: Affect hunger

Main Citation(s):
Walter Goldschmidt (2006) *The Bridge to Humanity: How Affect Hunger Trumps the Selfish Gene.* New York: Oxford University Press.

Summary: "Affect hunger is the urge to get expressions of affection from others" (p. 47) and its physiological infrastructure and resultant behavior lies at the core of humanity. It is an expansion and enhancement of the biosocial mother–infant/caretaker–infant bond in primates such that such relationships are sought and reciprocated with multiple sources throughout the life of the individual. The affect hunger in humans combines with human cognitive capabilities (language, symbol, culture) to facilitate the emergence of human communities and societies over the course of the evolution of the genus *Homo*. Diverging from individualistic/selfish-gene-based strategies, the human adaptive zone has become one that emphasizes flexibility of behavior, communal interactions, and cooperation, and the cooption of the physiology of attachment into a broader series of biocultural patterns of connection and interactions between people. The primary human adaptation then is the integration of attachment physiology with cognitive and social complexity in the context of an organism that uses extra-somatic means of manipulation for engaging environmental pressures. The result is a species (*H. sapiens*) that has the capacity to extensively manipulate the material world and "to see, to understand, and to share our understandings" with other humans (p. 149).

Main Points: Basal attachment physiology and behavioral flexibility in primates is enhanced and expanded in the human lineage. This attachment hunger combined with increased cognitive complexity (language, symbol, culture) facilitates extensive collaboration between individuals and a series of relationships not seen in other organisms. This pattern, beginning early in human evolution, has enabled humans to adapt to diverse environments and tackle a myriad of novel social and ecological challenges. Associated factors include extensive cooperation intra- and potentially intergroup, cooperation within and between age/sex classes, sharing of information and goods between individuals, substantial behavioral flexibility, and primary roles for language and symbol in establishing and reinforcing the biocultural relationships between humans.

Name: Niche construction

Main Citation(s):
F.J. Odling-Smee, K.N. Laland, and M.W. Feldman (2003) *Niche Construction: The Neglected Process in Evolution*. Monographs in Population Biology 37. Princeton: Princeton University Press.

Summary: Niche construction refers to the ability of organisms to functionally modify the relationships with their environments such that the pattern and context of selection pressures are altered. This is a dynamic process resulting in ecosystem engineering, organisms modifying not only their environments but also other organisms' environments, and the creation of ecological inheritance such that adaptation relies both on natural selection and niche construction. In other words, as organisms evolve they "drag part of their own environments along with them, thereby transforming their own adaptive landscapes" (p. 367). In humans "ontogenetic processes, culture and counteractive niche construction in general have consistently damped out a population's need for a genetic response to changes in a population's environment" (p. 367). Thus, over the course of the evolution of the genus *Homo*, populations initially responded to selection pressures with niche construction and subsequently via cultural tradition and social complexity. Because human cultural and biological selves are integrated, humans interact with selection pressures via a phenogenotype, wherein physiological and cultural factors are not necessarily separable from one another. With the emergence of increasingly complex cognitive, social, symbolic, and linguistic patterns and their associated "ratchet" effects (see Ratcheting culture hypothesis), humans have increased the intensity and significance of niche construction on their own evolution (and thus behavior).

Main Points: The human phenogenotype is a biocultural entity with complex, shared cognitive information and inherited resources. As the role of niche construction increases in impact and significance for human evolution, patterns of social behavior such as cooperation, social complexity, and conflict can be explained in terms separate from basal assumptions about kin selection, reciprocal altruism, and selfish-genic behavior. Associated factors include cooperation and conflict stemming from inherited environments and mutualisms rather than just genic selection, sharing of information and materials as important in human evolution, and substantial cross age/sex group transmission of information (mostly intragroup).

Name: Environment of Evolutionary Adaptation (EEA)—the adapted mind

Main Citation(s):

Jerome H. Barkow, Leda Cosmides, and John Tooby, Eds. (1992) *The Adapted Mind: Evolutionary Psychology and the Generation of Culture.* New York: Oxford University Press.

Summary: There is a universal human nature seen at the level of evolved psychological mechanisms (frequently represented using a metaphor of domain-specific "modules" in the brain). These evolved psychological mechanisms (modules) are adaptations arising largely from selection pressures associated with the environments and life ways of Pleistocene hunter-gatherers (the EEA) and not necessarily reflective of modern environments. However, by adapting various domain-specific modules to combat specific classes of problems, the resultant overall pattern is a high degree of adaptive flexibility in human response to environmental pressures. These adaptations arose throughout the evolution of the genus *Homo*, but specifically later *H. erectus* and *H. sapiens* and make up the underpinning of much modern behavior. These general EEA conditions included living in small foraging groups (or bands) united by kinship ties. Strong biological kinship ties reduced chances of intragroup lethal conflict and enhanced kin reciprocity within groups and between neighboring groups who exchanged members. Cooperative reciprocal relationships could occur between neighboring groups sharing local areas and uniting against other such clusters. Human cultural behavior and cultural variation today is seen, in part, as the EEA psychological adaptations being expressed in novel modern environments radically altered from our Pleistocene past.

Main Points: Humans evolved psychological mechanisms as adaptation in response to selection pressures from a Pleistocene hunter-gatherer lifestyle. These adaptations form a universal human nature underlying what we see expressed as modern human behavior. However, this human nature is a set of psychological mechanisms adapted to Pleistocene environments and therefore may display variable fit with modern contexts. Major factors include: strong kinship-based cooperation and strong reciprocal altruism between cooperators who are not biological kin. Amongst unrelated/non-cooperator groups one can expect high levels of xenophobia and aggression. Aggression, lethal violence, sexual patterns, and many other evolutionarily important behaviors are mediated both by kinship ties and by mismatches between Pleistocene and modern environmental pressures.

Other Citations:

John Bowlby (1969) *Attachment.* New York: Basic Books.

Donald Symons (1979) *The Evolution of Human Sexuality.* New York: Oxford University Press.

Name: Egalitarianism/hunting

Main Citation(s):

Christopher Boehm (1999) *Hierarchy in the Forest: The Evolution of Egalitarian Behavior*. Cambridge, MA: Harvard University Press.

Christopher Boehm (2004) Large game hunting and the evolution of human sociality. In Robert W. Sussman and Audrey R. Chapman, Eds. *The Origins and Nature of Sociality*. New York: Aldine de Gruyter, pp. 270–287.

Summary: The acquisition of animal meat and fat is important in the evolution of human sociality and cooperation. Humans have an innate propensity for fatty foods and therefore the acquisition of meat in large packages became a focal target during the course of the evolution of the genus *Homo*. However, there is a large variance associated with the acquisition of large game (or large meat sources) and therefore humans have developed important variance reduction strategies (sharing) over time. These cooperative sharing behaviors are derived from morally based cultural rules reinforced through social control, giving rise to relatively egalitarian groups and moralistically mediated conflict management. Neither kin selection nor reciprocal altruism effectively explain these behavior patterns, rather between-group selection for intragroup group cooperation appears to offer support for these patterns.

Main Points: Human hunting/gathering of large meat sources has created a set of selection pressures favoring intragroup cooperation and sharing. This arises not from kin selection or reciprocal altruism, rather it is a product of intergroup competition and selection for effectively cooperative and egalitarian groups. Associated with this scenario is intragroup cooperation and sharing, intergroup competition, political egalitarianism, familial pair-bonding, and moralistic social-sanctioning as conflict management.

Name: Grandmothering

Main Citation(s):

Kristin Hawkes, James F. O'Connell, Nicholas G. Blurton-Jones, Helen Alvarez, and E. L. Charnov (1998) Grandmothering, menopause, and the evolution of human life histories. *Proceedings of the National Academic Science USA* 95:1336–1339.

Summary: Beginning potentially as early as *H. erectus* and certainly by the last 50 kya, human females have developed a slower senescence and a cessation of reproductive cycling midway though life. This allows for older females to assist their female offspring in the raising and provisioning of their children. As there is a sexual division of labor and females primarily focus on gathering high return vegetable items (such as underground storage organs) and human infants have a long dependency period, this assistance is primarily in the form of food sharing and caretaking behaviors.

Main Points: Human females have evolved a cessation of reproductive cycling (menopause) and long postmenopausal lives, allowing them to assist their kin in raising offspring. This assistance takes the form of substantial food sharing [especially of high-quality plant foods (plant underground storage organs, USOs)] between female relatives (and potential intragroup sharing in general) and cooperative caretaking of highly dependant offspring. Associated factors include sexual division of labor, important dietary role of USOs, cooperative caretaking amongst female kin, food sharing amongst female kin and potentially intragroup sharing.

Other Citations:
Kristin Hawkes, James F. O'Connell, Nicholas G. Blurton-Jones (2003) Human life histories: primate trade-offs, grandmothering socioecology, and the fossil record. In Peter M. Kappeler and Michael E. Pereira, Eds. *Primate Life Histories and Socioecology*. Chicago, IL: The University of Chicago Press, pp. 204–227.

Name: Embodied capital/hunting

Main Citation(s):
Hilard Kaplan, Jane Lancaster, and Arthur Robson (2003) Embodied capital and the evolutionary economics of the human life span. In James R. Carey and Shripad Tuljapurkar, Eds. *Life Span: Evolutionary, Ecological, and Demographic Perspectives*, Supplement to *Population and Development Review*, 29. New York: Population Council.

Summary: "Embodied capital theory... combines the basic structure of life-history theory as developed in biology with the formal analytical approach developed in the analysis of capital in economics" (p. 152). In a physical sense embodied capital is bone, tissue and organs, and so on and in a functional sense it is speed, strength, skill, and so on. Human behavior (and adaptations) can then be seen as emerging from "a trade-off between investments in one's own embodied capital and reproduction, and the quantity–quality trade-off becomes a trade-off between the embodied capital of offspring and their number" (p. 156). The human digestive system is adapted for meat and low-fiber plant tissues. During the course of the evolution of the genus *Homo*, there is a shift toward increased meat in the diet (hunting). Given an embodied capital perspective, the following trends emerged: The skill and long learning process involved in hunting combined with complex food sharing and a sexual division of labor resulted in a large percentage of nutrition being generated by male investment (hunting), and combined with the complex nature of human childcare (long growth and dependency periods) resulted in enhancing the sexual division of labor (female's focus on less dangerous efforts and greater childcare). There is systematic variation in response to environmental variation by human bodies and behavior such that as environments change, the distribution and "spending" of capital also alters.

Main Points: Human adaptations and behavior can be seen as a trade-off between investment in one's own embodied capital and the embodied capital of offspring. In humans, the focus on meat consumption, hunting and long childhood dependency results in substantial sexual division of labor, intragroup food sharing, male–female cooperation, and a human ability to adaptively respond in behavior and physiology to variable environmental conditions.

Name: Male showing off

Main Citation(s):

Kristen Hawkes and Rebecca Bliege Bird (2002) Showing off, handicap signaling, and the evolution of men's work. *Evolutionary Anthropology* 11:58–67.

Summary: Humans are unique among primates in that males may contribute a substantial portion of the food consumed by the group. Most meat is accumulated via hunting and most hunting is performed by males. However, in many cases the meat from hunts is distributed amongst group members, and the hunter's own kin do not necessarily gain a higher percentage than do other members of the group. It is possible that the prowess (high-risk behavior, significant meat capture and distribution) displayed by successful male hunters acts as a signal of the male's social and physical quality by which other group members (allies and competitors) and potential mates (group females) can assess him.

> More than its value as a source of nutrition, meat is a medium of communication through which the hunter transmits information to potential mates, allies, and competitors. If men hunt to display their relative quality, then the benefits they earn for that effort come not from exchanges of meat for other goods and services, but from the different ways that others treat them in light of the quality they reveal. Others use the information of hunting reputations to their own advantage in the numerous decisions of social life. (p. 61)

Hunting and other high-risk behavior may serve a function of a signal "showing off" the human male's abilities as a member of the group. This pattern arose during the evolution of the genus *Homo* and solidified with the large-game hunting of more recent forms of *H. sapiens*.

Main Points: Human male "show-off" high-risk behavior may have evolved as hunting large animals became a focus of competitive display during the evolution of the genus *Homo*. Males can signal their social and physical value to other group members via engaging in high-risk behavior that has potential benefits for the group (such as hunting and subsequent meat sharing). Associated factors include sexual division of labor, male participation in high-risk behavior, food sharing and intragroup cooperation, conflict/competition between males via show-off behavior, and conflict/competition between females over high-value males.

Other Citations:

K. Hawkes (1991) Showing off: tests of an hypothesis about men's foraging goals. *Ethology Sociobiology* 12:29–54.

A. Zahavi (1977) The cost of honesty (further remarks on the handicap principle). *Journal of Theoretical Biology* 67:603–605.

Name: Nomadic forager model

Main Citation(s):
Douglas Fry (2006) *The Human Potential for Peace.* New York: Oxford University Press.

Summary: Basic tit-for-tat reciprocity, kin selection, and basal aggression models for human behavior are not supported by extant forager populations. Because the majority of our evolution occurred as humans lived a foraging lifestyle, generalized social patterns associated with ethnographic studies on nomadic foragers are robust indicators of basic social patterns in humans. Small local groups mixing and interacting within a larger population united by symbolic and linguistic commonalities, a strong emphasis on sharing and cooperating, individual autonomy, egalitarian social structure, sexual division of labor (with males doing most hunting), social punishment and social conflict negotiation, devaluation of physical aggression, and loose territoriality are all factors that have emerged over the course of the evolution of the genus *Homo*, specifically *H. sapiens*. A dominant basal pattern is that humans have evolved a "tremendous potential for getting along and dealing with conflict without violence" (p. 241) and that this pattern underlies much of the range of modern human behavior.

Main Points: Specific adaptations for negotiating social complexity and the challenges of a forager lifestyle have resulted in humans exhibiting high levels of intra- and intergroup cooperation, sharing, and a social complexity that favors interindividual social negotiation over aggression. While aggressive conflict and lethal aggression do occur between individuals and on occasion between groups, the more recent pattern of lethal conflict between populations is not rooted in our evolutionary patterns (but is facilitated by our cooperative abilities).

Name: Mother–infant baby talk

Main Citation(s):
Dean Falk (2004) Prelinguistic evolution in early hominins: Whence motherese? *Behavioral and Brain Sciences* 27:491–541.

Summary: Motherese, the gestural/vocal exchanges between mothers and infants in humans has a central role in the evolution of language. Arising during the evolution of the hominins, specifically leading up to the genus *Homo*, motherese forms the basis of protolanguage.

> The central thesis regarding motherese is that bipedal mothers had to put their babies down next to them periodically in order to go about their business, and that prosodic vocalizations would have replaced cradling arms as a means for keeping the little ones content. (p. 503)

In this scenario, mothers foraged relatively alone and/or with a small number of other individuals (much as with chimpanzees today). The type of foraging required females to set infants down as the infants could not cling by themselves. To keep the infants quiet (predation pressure) and to maintain the bond between mother and infant, females use vocal and gestural interactions that form the basis of protolanguage in subsequent hominin species and eventually language in humans.

Main Points: Motherese is the basis for the evolution of protolanguage and language in hominins and humans; therefore the mother–infant bond and the emergence of motherese is at the root of human social complexity facilitated through linguistic means. Associated factors in this scenario are that mothers are the main caretakers, that there is a sexual division of foraging, that females park infants, that there is little or no cooperative care during foraging, and that females foraged in small groups or independently.

Name: Man the hunted

Main Citation(s):

Donna L. Hart and Robert W. Sussman (2005) *Man the Hunted: Primates, Predators, and Human Evolution.* New York: Basic Books/Westview Press.

Summary: During the evolution of the hominins and the lineage of the genus *Homo*, predation was a major selection pressure. This predation pressure is a significant component of the ecological and psychological environments in which humans evolved. The threat of predation is related to human sociality (living in relatively large social groups with flexibility in social structure), increased cognition/information sharing (shared knowledge as defense against predation), possible group defense, or the potential for cooperation to avoid predation (use of sentinels, careful selection of sleeping sites, coordinated defense). This perspective assumes that meat capture via hunting was not a predominant factor in hominin behavioral evolution until later *Homo* forms and that aggressive or violent behavior was not necessarily fitness enhancing for humans and our ancestors.

Main Points: Hominins faced substantial predation pressures and these selective forces helped shape the behavior of the genus *Homo*. Associated factors include living in large socially flexible groups, substantial information sharing, cooperation intragroup and intersex, strong selection for interindividual affiliation, and no selection for aggression or aggressive behavior arising from hunting.

Other Citations:

Robert W. Sussman and Paul A. Garber (2004) Rethinking sociality: cooperation and aggression among primates. In R.W. Sussman and A.R. Chapman, Eds. *The Origins and Nature of Sociality*, New York: Aldine de Gruyter, pp. 161–190.

Name: Bonding pair/human bonding

Main Citation(s):

Cort A. Pederson (2004) Biological aspects of social bonding and the roots of human violence. *Annals of New York Academic Science* 1036: 106–127.

Warren B. Miller and Joseph Lee Rodgers (2001) *The Ontogeny of Human Bonding Systems: Evolutionary Origins, Neural Bases, and Psychological Mechanisms.* Boston, MA: Kluwer Academic Publishers.

Summary: Humans form a wide variety of strong social bonds, beyond the mother–infant bond, as adults. Many mammalian species, including humans, have a specific set of underlying neurological and physiological correlates associated with bonding. Pair-bonding and bonding with unrelated conspecifics has been favored in humans as an important factor in potentially mutual fitness enhancement. During the evolution of the genus *Homo* the underlying physiological factors are united with human cognitive complexity to facilitate the appearance of a wide variety of bioculturally based emotional bonds with unrelated individuals including mates. This bonding allows for complex sensations of group unity and cooperation. Dysfunction occurring during the development of the individual can result in malformation, erratic formation, and exhibition of this underlying bonding pattern.

Main Points: Humans bond with related and unrelated individuals in a complex biocultural manner that integrates underlying physiologies with human cognitive abilities to create types and patterns of interindividual bonding to an extent not seen in other organisms. This physio-emotive bonding has allowed humans to have extremely complex group structure and cooperation; but it also facilitates aberrant and violent behavior when developmental patterns are disrupted.

Other Citations:

C.A. Pederson Ahnert, L., Anzenberger, G., Belsky, J., Draper, P., Fleming, A.S., Grossmann, K., Sachser, N., Sommer, S., Tietze, D.P., and Young, L.J (2003) Group report: beyond infant attachment: the origins of bonding later in life. In C.S. Carter, L. Ahnert, K.E. Grossmann, S.B. Hrdy, M.E. Lamb, S.W. Porges, and N. Sachser, Eds. *Attachment and Bonding: A New Synthesis* Cambridge, MA: The MIT Press, pp. 385–428.

Name: Male provisioning/monogamy

Main Citation(s):

Owen Lovejoy (1981) The origin of man. *Science* 211:341–350.

Owen Lovejoy (1993) Modeling human origins: are we sexy because we're smart or smart because we're sexy? In Tab Rasmussen, Ed. *The Origin and Evolution of Humans and Humanness.* Boston, MA: Jones and Bartlett Publishers, pp. 1–28.

Summary: As the hominins diverged from the broader ape lineage, the average interbirth interval increased due to conspecific competition for maximum behavioral plasticity (long learning periods). This led to restricted mating pairs and males who provided more quality food items (high fat and/or protein content) in addition to other male reproductive investment being favored by selection. Such males were most successful if bipedal and paired with females who had a concealed ovulation and demonstrable fat stores (visible as body form). Active choice by both sexes led to a reduction of intragroup male–male aggression, and an increase in monogamous mating and heterosexual pair-bonding that led to overall higher-group cohesion. This pattern set the stage for the evolution of the genus *Homo* who capitalized and expanded on these patterns.

Main Points: Male–female pair-bonding underlies human social structure. As male–female pair-bonding evolved in hominins (and specifically the human lineage) the pattern resulted in efficient bipedality and hunting/ high energy food collection by males, male provisioning and a sexual division of labor, increased infant-dependency and thus long learning and behavior plasticity, concealed ovulation, and strong intragroup cooperative patterns in groups made up of multiple nuclear (one male-one female-offspring) units.

Name: Sham menstruation/symbol

Main Citation(s):
Camilla Power and Leslie Aiello (1997) Female proto-symbolic strategies. In Lori D. Hagar, Ed. *Women in Human Evolution*. London: Routledge, pp. 153–171.

Summary: Increased brain size (encephalization) in the genus *Homo* placed considerable reproductive stress on females. Humans evolved concealed ovulation, ovulatory synchrony, and accentuated menstruation as a fertility indicator to raise levels of male reproductive investment. Females then began using coalitionary behavior involving cosmetic/symbolic manipulation of menstruation (sham menstruation) and artificial synchrony to enhance and control their physiological signals, which in turn creates a preadaptation for ritual. Greater use of symbolism, including taboos regarding menstruation, male hunting and sexual activity, and others related to a sexual division of labor cascaded into broader symbol use and modern human complexity of symbolic behavior.

Main Points: Human symbolic behavior and reliance on cooperative use and manipulation of symbols/concepts emerges from female coalitionary manipulation of menstruation signals to enhance male investment in their offspring. Associated factors include female cooperation, sexual division of labor, concealed ovulation, and the use of symbol to manipulate physiological signals.

Name: The mating mind

Main Citation(s):
Geoffrey Miller (2006) *The Mating Mind: How Sexual Choice Shaped the Evolution of Human Nature*. London: Doubleday.

Summary: The human mind (and thus much of human behavior) evolved "not just as survival machines, but as courtship machines." Sexual selection (via a costly signaling mechanism) played a major role, in addition to natural selection, acting on variation in hominin intelligence and neurological structure resulting in selection for behavioral flexibility, and increased social intelligence (creativity) via increased brain size and complexity. The human mind (as reflected in creativity, language, tool use and so on) is seen as a set of fitness indicators reflecting "good genes" or a "healthy brain" indicating high benefits despite the physiological costs of large brains. Selection is primarily by females for males, but because of the enormous amount of shared genetic material between the sexes, the benefits and genetic/physiology of large brains are shared by both sexes. Many complex human social/behavioral capabilities arise from the challenges of courtship (sexual selection) imposed by female choice on males, including the evolution of fairness and morality.

Main Points: Sexual selection is a major driving force in human behavioral evolution, with polygyny as ancestral human mating pattern and serial monogamy emerging. Other factors include; mating strategies between males and females, human mate choice focused on the mind (behavior) as quality indicator, cooperation and conflict between the sexes, increasing behavioral variation/complexity over time, concealed ovulation, female–female cooperation,and male–female pair-bonds.

SUGGESTED READINGS

Each of the publications cited for the proposals/hypotheses.

CHAPTER 6

Discussing the Proposals

When the 38 proposals from Chapter 5 are compared with one another a set of commonalities and differences emerge that might help us better approach the examination of human behavioral evolution. The similarities across these proposals might give us some insight into where theoreticians agree and thus where we might find robust assertions and assumptions about human behavioral evolutionary trends. These can act as a base for future investigation.

We have to be careful when assessing the differences between these proposals as they can arise from the different foci the proposals seek to explain, from differences in viewpoints/perspectives of the originators of the proposals, and from different interpretations of human evolutionary datasets. Therefore, some of these differences are not directly comparable. However, in some of these differences we might find important elements that enable us to highlight ways to integrate the proposals for understanding human behavioral evolution. In Chapter 8 I will try to synthesize the information emerging from this comparison (Chapters 5 and 6) with the information reviewed in Chapters 2–4 and the perspectives in Chapter 7 to propose just such a model for looking at human behavioral evolution.

The proposals reviewed in the previous chapter arise from the various perspectives outlined in earlier chapters and all share a common generalized Darwinian evolutionary underpinning, although the individual originators of the proposals have a diverse array of interpretations of exactly how evolutionary patterns and processes occur and are modeled (see Chapters 3 and 4 for those comparisons). The majority of these authors do rely on a broadly shared sequence of hominin evolution in regards to social behavior. This basic pattern is succinctly illustrated by John Cartwright

(2000; Figure 6.9) in his text *Evolution and Human Behavior*, and can be summarized as follows:

Ancestral hominins lived in one-male groups with multiple females, which characterized male dominance, in open or mixed grassland/woodland environments with resources that varied seasonally. Group size began to increase as cooperative hunting and food sharing began to emerge; this led to male kin coalitions and multimale/multifemale groups. Increased nutritive intake facilitates increased brain size. Increasing brain size co-occurs with increasing group size and its cognitive requirements. This also leads to increasing need for information processing abilities as home range sizes increase and seasonality and environmental variation increase concomitantly. This favors further behavioral flexibility and increased success at hunting and enhanced protein/caloric intake in general. This also favors increased longevity and group size, which in turn allows for increased reciprocity (reciprocal altruism) and kin selection. Increased encephalization leads to more dependent, slowly maturing infants, raising costs of reproduction for females and further leading to an increase in paternal care (possibly involving male provisioning). All this leads to stronger male–female bonds, concealed ovulation, and other forms of cooperation and conflict between the sexes.

It is obvious that many of the proposals in Chapter 5 agree with much in this summary but challenge certain aspects of it. Others discard this approach and propose very different patterns. However, the basic assumptions about increasing group size, increased encephalization, increased behavioral complexity, increased cooperation, an increase in nutritional requirements, and conflict and negotiation between the sexes are common to nearly all proposals for human behavioral evolution. These are potentially supported by elements in the fossil record, but only a few of the many assumptions about behavior are well supported. Support comes from the fossil and archeological record for increased encephalization and behavioral complexity, growing group size, and increased nutritive requirements (see Chapter 4). The assumptions in Cartwright's scenario that do not have support or have equivocal support from the fossil record and comparative primatology include uni-male grouping as ancestral, male dominance as central, relative importance of hunting early in human evolution, types of intragroup relationships, male–female relationships, and whether or not reproductive cycling is truly "concealed" in human females (see Chapter 4).

All scenarios and proposals for human behavioral evolution should have some connectivity to the actual fossil evidence and their underlying paradigmatic assumptions should be clear. What I intend to do in this chapter is to examine the similarities and differences in the 38 proposals from Chapter 5 in order to extract a framework of patterns that will enable comparison to the fossil and archeological records, different paradigmatic viewpoints/models, and a broader synthesis of approaches (in Chapter 8). Cartwright (2000) suggests that "there is room for both approaches" (referring to his Evolutionary Anthropology, a melding of Sociobiology and HBE, and Evolutionary Psychology) in the quest to understand human behavioral evolution. I agree and would add that there is room for more than just those two approaches if we intend to propose truly viable scenarios and models for human behavioral evolution. Let us see what emerges from the comparison of the proposals from Chapter 5.

THE COMPARISON TABLES

The hypotheses are compared across six general categories of core factors having between 10 and 18 components per category (81 in total) (Tables 6.1–6.6). A mark in the grid denotes which components of which categories are core or main explanatory factors for each hypothesis/proposal. The components reflect basic concepts common to the main paradigmatic approaches (Chapters 2–4) and elements that appear in the hypotheses. I only marked a component as salient to the proposal if it was explicitly stated or overtly implied in the description of the proposal in the main or the additional sources (citations). The categories are:

1. Type of cooperation
2. Type of conflict
3. Ecological/Environmental pressures
4. Sex and reproduction
5. Dietary practice/food
6. Specific behavior patterns.

One could argue that there are more categories that could be assessed; however, food, sex, the environment, behavior, and cooperation/conflict are the prime drivers in ecological and behavioral analyses of organisms across the animal and plant kingdoms and therefore provide a sufficient basis for comparisons. Further specificity in categories would reduce the potential to compare across so many diverse proposals.

A BRIEF DISCUSSION ON SHARED COMPONENTS AND DIFFERENCES IN THE SIX BASIC CATEGORIES

Cooperation

Nearly all of the 38 see some form of cooperation as central to human behavioral evolution. Intragroup cooperation occurs as a main factor in nearly 100% of the scenarios proposed. There is little to no debate that within group cooperation has been an important component in human evolution; this illustrates and reinforces a distinction between human and other primates/social mammals in the kind and intensity of intragroup cooperation enabled by our cognitive capabilities. Not all of these proposals link cooperation within

TABLE 6.1

Cooperation Patterns

	CP Contingent	CP General	CP Between Kin	CP Non-Kin	CP Same Sex	CP Different Sex	CP Across Age Groups	CP Intragroup	CP Intergroup	CP Hunting	CP Food Sharing	CP Punishment	CP Child Rearing
Darwin	x							x				x	
Wilson			x			x		x	x	?	x		
Cooperation-general		x						x	x		x		
Man the hunter					x	x	x	x	?	x	x		
Meat eating					x male			x		x	x		
Cooking/mate guarding			x			x		x			x		
Demonic males			x		x	x							
Cruelty										?		?	
Tribal social instincts			x		x	x		x				x	
Ratcheting language						x	x	x	?				x
Human behavioral phenomenon		x	x			x		x	x				
Meme								x					
Bursts of innovation								x					
Variability selection	x				x	x	x	x	x		x		

Primate plasticity	x			x	x	?			x
Epigenetic cognitive plasticity				x	x				x
Reciprocal altruism	x	x	x	x	x		x	x	
Altruistic punishment	x	x	x	x	x		x	x	
Tit for tat	x	x	x	x					
Conflict negotiation		x	x	x	x				
Cooperative breeding			x female	x	x	?		x	x
Cooperation/Multilevel selection				x	x	?			
Inherent morality				x	x	x			
Morality/cognition			x	x	x	x		x	
Affect hunger		x	x	x	x	?	x	x	?
Niche construction		x	x	x	x	?	x		
EEA-adapted mind	x	x		x	x	?			
Egalitarianism/hunting		x		x	x		x	x	
Grandmothering		x	x	x	x		x		x
Embodied capital/hunting				x	x		x	x	
Male show off				x	x		x		x

(continued)

TABLE 6.1
Continued

cooperation patterns (handwritten)

	CP Contingent	CP General	CP Between Kin	CP Non-Kin	CP Same Sex	CP Different Sex	CP Across Age Groups	CP Intragroup	CP Intergroup	CP Hunting	CP Food Sharing	CP Punishment	CP Child Rearing
Nomadic forager								x	x		x		
Mother–infant babyspeak							x						
Man the hunted						x		x			x		
Bonding pair				x		x		x					
Sham menstruation					x	x							
Male provisioning/ monogamy				x		x		x			x		
The mating mind			x		x								x

TABLE 6.2
Conflict (CF) Patterns

	CF Intragroup	CF Intergroup	CF Same Sex	CF Different Sex	CF Across Age Groups	CF for Resources	CF for Mates	CF Interspecific Hominin	CF Interspecific Mammal	CF in Cultural Variables/Units
Darwin		x				x	x			
Wilson		x				x	x			
Cooperation-general										
Man the hunter		x				x				
Meat eating		x				x				
Cooking/mate guarding			x	x		x	x			
Demonic males		x	x	x		x	x			
Cruelty	x	x	x							x
Tribal social instincts		x								x
Ratcheting language										
Human behavioral phenomenon	x	x								
Meme										x
Bursts of innovation										
Variability selection						x				

(continued)

TABLE 6.2
Continued

	CF Intragroup	CF Intergroup	CF Same Sex	CF Different Sex	CF Across Age Groups	CF for Resources	CF for Mates	CF Interspecific Hominin	CF Interspecific Mammal	CF in Cultural Variables/Units
Primate plasticity										
Epigenetic cognitive plasticity										
Reciprocal altruism	x	x	x	x	x					
Altruistic punishment	x									
Tit for tat	x	x	x	x	x					
Conflict negotiation	x		x	x						
Cooperative breeding										
Cooperation/multilevel selection		x								
Inherent morality										
Morality/cognition										
Affect hunger										

Niche construction

EEA-adapted mind

Egalitarianism/ hunting

Grandmothering

Embodied capital/ hunting

Male show off

Nomadic forager

Mother–infant babyspeak

Man the hunted

Bonding pair

Sham menstruation

Male provisioning/ monogamy

The mating mind

TABLE 6.3

Environment/Ecological Patterns

	Specific Environment	Variable Environments	Food Stress	Predation	Competition with Other Human Groups	Competition with Other Hominins	Competition with Other Mammals	Disease	Nutritional Stress—Brain	Nutritional Stress—Body Size	Human–Environment Mutual Mutability
Darwin					x						
Wilson					x						
Cooperation-general		x									
Man the hunter			x		x						
Meat eating			x		x		x		x	x	
Cooking/mate guarding	x		x						x	x	
Demonic males				x	x						
Cruelty											
Tribal social instincts		x			x						
Ratcheting language		x									
Human behavioral phenomenon		x									x
Meme	x										
Bursts of innovation		x									
Variability selection		x									x

Primate plasticity				
Epigenetic cognitive plasticity	x	x		x
Reciprocal altruism	x			
Altruistic punishment				
Tit for tat			x	
Conflict negotiation		x		
Cooperative breeding			x	
Cooperation/multilevel selection			x	
Inherent morality				
Morality/cognition				
Affect hunger		x		x
Niche construction		x		x
EEA-adapted mind	x		x	
Egalitarianism/hunting	x	x	x	x
Grandmothering		x		

(continued)

TABLE 6.3
Continued

	Specific Environment	Variable Environments	Food Stress	Predation	Competition with Other Human Groups	Competition with Other Hominins	Competition with Other Mammals	Disease	Nutritional Stress—Brain	Nutritional Stress—Body Size	Human—Environment Mutability
Embodied capital/hunting		x	x						x	x	
Male show off			x								
Nomadic forager	x										
Mother–infant babyspeak											
Man the hunted				x							
Bonding pair											
Sham menstruation			x			x			x	x	
Male provisioning/monogamy										x	
The mating mind									x		

TABLE 6.4
Food/Diet Patterns

	Meat	Male Provisioning Main Source	Female Provisioning Main Source	Underground Storage Organs (USOs)	Cooking	Food Theft	Food Sharing: Kin	Food Sharing: Non-kin	Food Sharing: Intragroup	Food sharing: Intergroup	Hunting	Gathering	Mixed Collection
Darwin													
Wilson		x											
Cooperation-general	x								x				
Man the hunter	x								x		x	x	
Meat eating	x								x		x		
Cooking/mate guarding			x	x	x	x	x		x			x	
Demonic males													
Cruelty													
Tribal social instincts													
Ratcheting language													
Human behavioral phenomenon													
Meme													
Bursts of innovation													
Variability selection									x				x
Primate plasticity													
Epigenetic cognitive plasticity													
Reciprocal altruism													
Altruistic punishment													
Tit for tat													

(continued)

TABLE 6.4
Continued

	Meat	Male Provisioning Main Source	Female Provisioning Main Source	Underground Storage Organs (USOs)	Cooking	Food Theft	Food Sharing: Kin	Food Sharing: Non-Kin	Food Sharing: Intragroup	Food sharing: Intergroup	Hunting	Gathering	Mixed Collection
Conflict negotiation													
Cooperative breeding													
Cooperation/multilevel selection													
Inherent morality													
Morality/cognition													
Affect hunger									x				
Niche construction													
EEA-adapted mind	x												
Egalitarianism/hunting	x							x	x		x		
Grandmothering			x	x			x		x			x	
Embodied capital/hunting	x	x							x		x		
Male show off	x	x									x		
Nomadic forager								x	x		x	x	
Mother–infant babyspeak												x	
Man the hunted									x				
Bonding pair											x		
Sham menstruation													
Male provisioning/monogamy	x	x					x						
The mating mind													

a group to successful competition with other groups, although a focus on intergroup conflict and intragroup cooperation is a common assumption (see Conflict below).

Approximately 20% of the proposals explicitly rely on intragroup cooperation between kin in their scenarios, whereas nearly as many (~17%) see cooperation between non-kin as core. Nearly a third (~30%) propose same-sex cooperation as central to their predictions. In each of these cases, the perspectives on altruism, kin selection, and reciprocal altruism are important. Nearly 30% of the proposals see cooperation across age groups as important. This again is a rare pattern across mammals (although somewhat more common in highly social mammals) and highlights the possibility that immature humans have substantial social and ecological agency, perhaps more than in other organisms (even chimpanzees). This is an element to keep in mind as immatures are usually ignored in the construction of evolutionary scenarios except for the noting of the costs of raising them. If immature hominins were contributing significantly to cooperative interactions (foraging, child rearing, defense/vigilance) they too could be a force in human adaptability and success. Because humans cooperate in such extensive manners, any hypotheses or attempt to explain human behavioral evolution requires that such high levels of cooperation be explained.

Interestingly, about 50% of the proposals see male–female cooperation as central to human behavioral evolution. This makes a good deal of sense, as successful modern humans rely heavily on such cooperative systems. However, popular discussions about human behavioral evolution, and even some traditional ones, focus largely on competition or the "battle between the sexes" as central to their explanations of behavioral patterns. In a large part this may be due to the physiological differences between the sexes, and to the importance of sex differences in many nonhuman animals. However, while there may be evolutionary strategy differences between males and females in general, in humans it might be the remarkable ability for collaboration between the sexes that facilitates our ability to do so well relative to other organisms. This is especially significant when one considers the very dependent human infants and the costs of infant rearing in humans relative to other mammals and even other primates. Many of the proposals reviewed here suggest that both same-sex and heterosexual cooperation played a significant role in creating human behavioral patterns.

Interestingly, most of the hypotheses did not see cooperative hunting as core to their scenarios (about 10%). This is likely due to debates about the timing of hunting in human evolution and its relative nutritional impact on hominins (see Chapter 4). There is little debate that large-scale hunting is important in recent human evolution, but it is not clear what the time depth of this is and how much cooperation between hunters drove other evolutionary patterns or was the by-product of other adaptive strategies and behavior. It is worth noting, however, that there is a small cluster of hypotheses that specifically focus on hunting as a prime variable in human evolution and

TABLE 6.5

Sex/Reproductive Patterns

	Monogamy	Polygyny	Polyandry	Polygynandry	Mother as Caretaker	Multiple Caretakers	Kin Caretakers	Non-kin Caretakers
Darwin								
Wilson	x							
Cooperation-general						x		
Man the hunter								
Meat eating								
Cooking/Mate guarding	x							
Demonic males	x			x	x			
Cruelty								
Tribal social instincts								
Ratcheting language						x		
Human behavioral phenomenon						x		
Meme								
Bursts of innovation								
Variability selection								
Primate plasticity						?		
Epigenetic cognitive plasticity						x		
Reciprocal altruism								
Altruistic punishment								
Tit for tat								
Conflict negotiation								
Cooperative breeding						x		
Cooperation/ Multilevel selection								
Inherent morality								
Morality/cogntion								
Affect hunger						x		
Niche construction								

Female Caretakers	Female and Male Caretakers	Infanticide	Sexual Selection	Concealed Ovulation	Continuous Female Receptivity	Continuous Female Advertisement	Nuclear Family	Male Advertisement
			x					
			x	x	x	x	x	
x		x of females	x	x			x	x
			x					
x		x	x	x				
x		x	x	x	x	x	x	
							x	

(*continued*)

TABLE 6.5

Continued

	Monogamy	Polygyny	Polyandry	Polygynandry	Mother as Caretaker	Multiple Caretakers	Kin Caretakers	Non-kin Caretakers
EEA-adapted mind								
Egalitarianism/ hunting	x							
Grandmothering						x female	x female	
Embodied capital/ hunting								
Male show off								
Nomadic forager								
Mother–infant babyspeak					x			
Man the hunted						?		
Bonding pair	x							
Sham menstruation								
Male provisioning/ monogamy	x							
The mating mind				x	x	x		

that doing so has a tradition that extends back to the earliest models for human evolution.

Cooperative food sharing appears as an important factor in a third of the proposals. This is expected, given what we know about the importance of food sharing in modern humans and the archeological evidence of such sharing. However, not many of the proposals go into any depth about what this implies in the sense of niche construction (see Chapter 7) and or nutritional access relative to age and sex. Also, the actual behaviors involved in food sharing are not usually discussed. For example, whether such sharing was widespread and social or whether it was more competitively based. Was it similar to social canids (wolves, for example) and many apes where female–infant sharing is common and among adults sharing occurs mainly only between main social partners, or was it more broadly distributed across members of a group? Was it something that appeared to be sharing but really emerged from scramble or contest competition (Chapter 3), was it tolerated theft, or was it really egalitarian sharing? Depending on how food was shared and who shared what, hominins might reflect a radical departure

Female Caretakers	Female and Male Caretakers	Infanticide	Sexual Selection	Concealed Ovulation	Continuous Female Receptivity	Continuous Female Advertisement	Nuclear Family	Male Advertisement
				x	x	x		
							x	
x								
x								
x			x					x
x								
							x	
				x		x		
x				x	x	x	x	
	x		x	x	x			x

from what we see in other organisms. This also can tell us a good deal about how humans deal with the diverse sets of ecological/nutritional/physical challenges posed by their foraging environments.

Some of the proposals (~13%) see cooperative punishment as important in our evolution. This is not too prevalent, but it is worthy of notice as the ideas around cooperative punishment can be central to thinking about the mechanisms of altruistic behavior, reciprocal altruism, and kin selection. Also, cooperative punishment combined with complex information exchange and the potential for linguistic manipulation might be quite important when thinking about mechanisms for some facets of human social organization.

Cooperative child rearing, noted in approximately 17% of the proposals, is not mentioned much at all. In sex and reproduction (below), multiple caretakers are noted as a core component in nearly a quarter of the proposals. However, the majority of the proposals do not link cooperative child rearing and multiple caretakers as a form of cooperation. That is, the multiple caretakers are seen largely as same-sex cooperation (female–female) or in a few cases as heterosexual cooperation. The possibility of older immatures and

TABLE 6.6

Specific Behavior Patterns

	Symbol	Language	Male Dominance	Sexual Division of Labor	Social Pair Bond: Heterosexual	Social Pair Bond: General	Male Cruelty and Punishment	Male Bodyguard
Darwin	x	x						
Wilson	x	x	x	x	x			
Cooperation-general	x	x						
Man the hunter			x	x	x			
Meat eating				x				
Cooking/mate guarding			x	x	x			x
Demonic males			x	x	x		x	x
Cruelty		x	x				x	
Tribal social instincts	x	x			x			
Ratcheting language	x	x						
Human behavioral phenomenon	x	x						
Meme	x	x						
Bursts of innovation	x	x						
Variability selection	x	x			x	x		
Primate plasticity	x	x			x	x		
Epigenetic cognitive plasticity	x	x						
Reciprocal altruism		x			x	x		
Altruistic punishment								
Tit for tat								
Conflict negotiation								
Cooperative breeding		x						
Cooperation/ multilevel selection	x	x						
Inherent morality	x	x						
Morality/ cognition	x	x						

Memes	Humans as Predator	Humans as Prey	Male Provisioning	Female Provisioning	Tool Use	Status Acquisition	Ethnocentric Xenophobia	Flexible Behavior	Fixed Behavior
					x		x		
					x		x	x	
	x		x		x				x male hunting
	x		x		x				
				x	x				
	x						x		x male aggr
	x				x	x			x male aggr
?					x	x	x	x	
					x			x	
?								x	
x						x		x	
					x			x	
					x			x	
					x			x	
								x	
									x patterned reciprocity
									x moral grammer
									x moral codes

(continued)

TABLE 6.6

Continued

	Symbol	Language	Male Dominance	Sexual Division of Labor	Social Pair Bond: Heterosexual	Social Pair Bond: General	Male Cruelty and Punishment	Male Bodyguard
Affect hunger	x	x			x	x		
Niche construction	x	x						
EEA-adapted mind	x	x		x				
Egalitarianism/ hunting				x	x			
Grandmothering				x				
Embodied capital/ hunting				x	x			
Male show off	x			x	x			
Nomadic forager				x				
Mother–infant babyspeak		x		x				
Man the hunted	x	x						
Bonding pair		x			x	x		
Sham menstruation	x	x		x				
Male provisioning/ monogamy				x	x			?
The mating mind		x			x			x

juveniles also participating in child care (could fall under cooperation across age groups above) also seems worthy of consideration as it occurs frequently in modern human societies and again would act to draw some distinctions between human evolutionary patterns and those of other animals in the area of care for immatures. This would also establish the need for a greater investigation into the distribution of costs and benefits of child rearing in addition to casting a broader net regarding the types of behavioral strategies available to our ancestors. One might also wonder why there is not more theoretical focus placed on this subject/possibility?

Finally, the role that intergroup cooperation plays in human behavioral evolution has largely been ignored. The general assumption (a popular assumption at least, and one common to basic ND-Sociobiological approaches) is that the likelihood of intergroup cooperation is low and/or unlikely. Depending on how one interprets the proposals reviewed here, intergroup cooperation shows up in between 9% and 30% of them. Even E.O. Wilson in his formulation of human sociobiology leaves open the possibility

Memes	Humans as Predator	Humans as Prey	Male Provisioning	Female Provisioning	Tool Use	Status Acquisition	Ethnocentric Xenophobia	Flexible Behavior	Fixed Behavior
					x			x	
					x			x	
								x adaptive flex	x evold modules
	x		x						
				x					
	x		x						
	x		x						
			x	x					
		x						x	
	x		x		x			x	x monogamy
					x	x		x	

for intergroup alliances. The fossil evidence for intergroup cooperation is equivocal and the dominance of competition models (especially competition for limited resources) in evolutionary thinking (see Chapters 2 and 3) seems to make this an unlikely possibility. However, that it does emerge in some of the proposals, that cooperation seems to be such a major element in human evolution, and that we do not really know the relationships (genetic or otherwise) between groups of hominins sharing local and regional areas suggests that this theme probably deserves more careful examination/consideration, especially at the level of local and regional communities.

Conflict

The overall occurrence of intragroup conflict as a major factor in hypotheses (~15%) is not very strong, but with such a strong focus on intragroup cooperation, this is not surprising. As such, I think the proposals suggest not that there are no high rates of conflict within groups, but rather that these conflicts are, on average, low intensity and/or of low/negligible fitness costs. The majority of the proposals reviewed either ignore conflicts between group members or assume that if they occur the conflicts are of minimal fitness impact. When intragroup conflict does emerge, it is in the hypotheses that are framed in the context of intragroup competition such as reciprocal altruism, altruistic punishment, tit-for-tat strategies, and the like. Again, this seems to be differences in paradigmatic perspectives with differential weight placed on intragroup conflicts as having selective or fitness-based impacts.

Given the low frequency of focus on intragroup conflict, it is not surprising that same-sex, heterosexual (both ~18%), and across age group (~8%) conflicts are all relatively rare as core elements in the proposals. But this seems quite understandable in the context of the overwhelming domination of intragroup cooperation as the meta-theme in hypotheses about the evolution of human behavior. Competition between the sexes emerges in a more nuanced form in sex and reproduction (below) rather than at the general level of intragroup competition.

Interestingly, despite its overwhelming appearance in popular reports and its role as a main assumption in many discussion of human "nature," intergroup conflict appears as a core element in only approximately 27% of these hypotheses. Again, this number may be lower than expected, in part due to the fact that although some hypotheses focus exclusively on group competition, many others might assume that it is inherent and thus not explicitly or implicitly acknowledge it. This is likely to be the case as both Darwin and E.O. Wilson, whose ideas form the backbone for most proposals of human behavioral evolution, explicitly saw intergroup competition as a major factor driving human behavioral evolution. However, it does remain interesting that such conflict is not a necessary assumption or requisite for approximately 2/3 of the proposals reviewed here.

One might ask why intergroup conflict is such a prominent and popular aspect of ideas about human evolution and behavior? It might be related to the relatively significant role that Darwin's and E.O. Wilson's specific ideas about human behavioral evolution have on public opinion. We can also look to the very prominent contributions to popular and academic culture and philosophy by Hobbes, Malthus, and Adam Smith. Their prominent conceptualizations of limited good and the inherent conflict that it entails is a particular motif that is pervasive in our society. Interestingly, this is an area of information where fossil and archeological evidence for the majority of hominin evolution is quite equivocal, but where the majority paradigmatic opinion is not. Is it possible that intergroup conflict has not had a core or driving evolutionary impact in human history? It seems to be a prominent part of modern humanity and at least in part associated with recent changes (last 20–10,000 years or so) in subsistence practice, economics and politics. If it has not been a driver in the distant past, could we be moving towards a new phase in human evolution where intergroup competition is a driving factor? We will discuss this topic further in Chapters 8 and 9.

The perception of a more general conflict for resources is as common as is intergroup conflict in the proposals. However, this does not necessarily imply ubiquitous intergroup conflict nor does it describe or infer the kind of conflict (scramble versus contest) in which groups would engage in if they did come into conflict. The conflict for resources also include the possibility of conflict emerging between early humans and other organisms such as large mammals and/or other nonhuman lineage hominin species (such as the coexistence between the genera *Homo* (humans) and *Paranthropus* (see Chapters 4 and 8). One can wonder why reference to such interspecific conflicts seems to be absent from these proposals as the fossil record suggests possible niche overlap not only between hominin species but also between hominins and other primates and possibly other animals as well (see Chapters 4 and 8). It is likely that the competition for resources is such an overarching assumption underlying most evolutionary proposals that a percentage of these hypotheses simply assume that it occurs without needing to recognize it explicitly.

It is important to reiterate that the dominant paradigms of investigation into human behavioral evolution (HBE, EP, and gene–culture coevolution) all follow basic Darwinian and Sociobiological assumptions that intergroup conflict is a driver in social/behavioral evolution. However, E.O. Wilson, in the last chapter of his seminal text, *Sociobiology*, explicitly leaves the door open for intergroup cooperation as a force of evolutionary change as well.

Food

Intragroup food sharing is a dominant factor evident across a third of the hypotheses. As with intragroup cooperation, food sharing in hominin groups seems to be a core aspect that may have facilitated modern human social organization and behavior. In most of these proposals, the sharing focus is not necessarily exclusively between kin; rather, the focus is on intragroup activity in a broader sense. This is not surprising given the extreme commonality of this type of behavior in modern human societies and the proposed benefits that such actions could have had for hominin groups relative to other organisms.

Hunting plays an explicit role in nearly 20% of the proposals, and logically these are primarily hypotheses specifically about hunting or meat provisioning. Meat eating in a more general sense appears in slightly fewer proposals, and contrary to dominant assumptions from the 1960s to 1970s, is not seen as a core facet for most proposals. However, it should be noted that many of the proposals may assume some underlying role for hunting and meat consumption and not explicitly or implicitly include it in the structure of the proposals. Plant underground storage organs are the focus in only two of the hypotheses, but they are gaining increasing attention in paleoanthropological and archeological investigations and models for their potential energetic contribution to hominin diets.

In general, it seems that neither particular food types nor specific foraging strategies play prominent roles in the vast majority of the hypotheses,
but some form of food stress or other resource-limiting factor does appear (at
least as an assumption) in most proposals. Again, this is rooted in behavioral
ecological theory, which assumes competition over resources at some level,
and thus, food acts as a limiting factor for organisms and groups. A good
number of the proposals reviewed here see food stress and food sharing as
potential causal factors or selective elements affecting patterns of human
behavioral evolution. Specific food types, aside from a traditional focus on
meat acquisition and consumption, and foraging strategies by themselves do
not seem as popular as drivers or as central foci for these proposals.

Environmental and Ecological Pressures

Aside from intergroup competition and food stress, which we have mentioned in previous categories, variable environments (appearing in ~29% of
the hypotheses) is the most prominent ecological factor. While Rick Potts
formalizes this in his variability selection hypothesis (1999, 2004, Chapter 5),
the presence of variable environments as important to human behavioral
evolution as a common theme is likely due to the increase in available paleo-
climatic datasets. It is becoming increasingly clear that there were significant
oscillations in the Early-Middle Pleistocene environments and that the geographic spread of the genus *Homo* mandated exposure to a variety of, and
to variable, environments (Kingston 2007). It strikes me as interesting that
while variable environments are in nearly a third of the proposals, explicit
attention to the possibility of mutual mutability between humans and their
environments is not nearly as prominent. This is a theme I will come back
to in Chapter 8.

Unlike prominent hypotheses from the 1960s, few current hypotheses
argue for a specific environment or environments or even a specific set of
environmental characteristics that form a predominantly causal cluster (with
the Environment of Evolutionary Adaptiveness and Male Provisioning/
Monogamy being notable exceptions). Previous assumptions about a clear
transition from forested to savannah habitats with the onset of bipedalism
are not longer supported by the fossil evidence (see Chapter 4); so the association with open environments as providing a structural selective pressure
(tied to the appearance of bipedalism) is no longer in vogue.

As in the food/diet and conflict categories above, food stress (in ~27%
of the hypotheses as an ecological factor) is again reflective of the general
assumption regarding competition and resources. Also, overlapping with
the food/diet section, there is scant mention of specific food types or even
foraging strategies in most of the proposals. Given the potential importance
of variable environments, it is highly likely that hypotheses are going to be
general regarding specific forage targets except when there are direct data
available from analyses of fossil dentition and abrasions/marks on stone tools
and/or animal bones. For example, isotope and striation/damage analyses

on molar teeth are providing evidence for types of diets in hominins as old as approximately 2 million years, and marks on fossil animal bones indicate butchering and processing by hominins (assumedly) well before the appearance of the genus *Homo*. These data are becoming increasingly available (see Chapter 4) but currently, few hypotheses concerned with human behavioral evolution incorporate them.

It is surprising that predation is only noted explicitly by two of the proposals. From a natural history point of view, this is interesting given the body size, locomotary capabilities, and somatic defense capabilities (or lack thereof) in hominins (and even in modern humans) combined with the number, types, and sizes of predators known from the Plio-Pleistocene fauna associated with hominins. These factors suggest that hominins were quite susceptible to predation, and there are mounting data that predators did take hominins (at least in the genera *Australopithecus* and *Paranthropus*) (see Hart and Sussman 2005). However, to counter this and support the absence of predation in many proposals it is also possible that by the time that *Homo erectus/ergaster* was the main (or only) human lineage hominin (1.5 million years ago) predation had ceased to be a major selective factor. However, given the available information on *H. erectus* body size and the carnivore fauna associated with their ranges, this seems less likely than having a more important role for predation in human behavioral evolution. It is also worth noting that predation does appear to play a role for both living large-bodied African apes, the gorilla, and the chimpanzee (Miller and Treves 2007).

Competition with other human groups, which as an environmental factor shows up in just under a third of the hypotheses, is in line with the common assumptions about competition between groups in our species (and our ancestors). Again, however, the actual data are quite limited and this prevalence may reflect societal and paradigmatic assumptions. Comparative data from one of our closest relatives, the common chimpanzee, support the assertion of resource competition between groups but data from the other groups of living large apes (gorillas and the other species of chimpanzee), and from many other primate species, are rather complicated, and thus quite equivocal, in regards to intergroup competition being an ecological factor. Fossil evidence of this type of competition, as we will discuss in Chapter 8, is extremely difficult to come by and therefore there has been a heavy reliance of comparative primatology and general behavioral ecological assumptions in attempts to assess this facet of our evolutionary past.

Possibly, the most glaring absence from all of the ecological proposals is a significant role for disease. Pathogens and disease are not explicitly mentioned by any of the hypotheses and only a few could be read to possibly include these factors as important selective agents (usually measured as good genes or indicators of health in mate choice, for example). A common assumption is that disease as a selective factor was relatively unimportant for much of human evolution because of low population densities. That is, disease impacts may have had pronounced effects at a local level in small populations, but that species-wide or regional impacts were minimal (in an evolutionary sense). Common assumptions hold that the dramatic increases in population sizes and densities of the past 10,000 years are the primary facilitators of important selection roles for pathogens in human evolution. If this is the case, it might be interesting to consider the possibility that pathogens/disease and intergroup completion/conflict (above) are relatively recent (in an evolutionary sense) drivers of human behavioral evolution.

While it is a well-known physiological fact that the human brain (in its current form) is a relatively costly organ, specific roles for energetic/nutritional stressors on the brain, the body, or both appears only in approximately 16–18% of the proposals. This is probably in large partly due to the fact that most hypotheses for human behavioral evolution do not directly incorporate physiological factors into their formulation or their primary selective forces. This illustrates specific disequilibria between hypotheses for morphological and behavioral evolution in humans. However, nearly a fifth of the proposals explicitly give some consideration to how these physiological factors (especially brain growth) might have impacted behavior, particularly in the area of increased/enhanced acquisition of nutritional intake. To be fair, in many of the hypotheses, a general increase in energetic requirements is noted as background but not necessarily incorporated as a specific selective pressure.

Sex and Reproduction

Monogamy as the primary mating pattern appears in approximately 16% percentage of the proposals. Nearly a fifth of the proposals identify the nuclear family as a basal unit in human social organization and there is frequently an assumption of a relatively high level of monogamy in such systems. Specific reference to other mating patterns is very rare in these hypotheses.

A set of behavioral and physiological factors associated with female sexuality and sexual behavior appear in a relatively large number of these proposals. This includes female "continuous receptivity" and sexual advertisement and "concealed" ovulation (where females are able to obfuscate their ovulatory state so as to confuse potential paternity). Recent work challenges both male and female abilities to detect ovulatory state and the fact that there is significant debate on exactly what is meant by "concealed" makes it unclear whether behavioral assessment of ovulatory state is a major factor in human behavioral evolution (as generally stated) (Brewis and Meyer 2005). Given the available data, it is not clear what role ovulatory assessment might play or even whether the conceptualization of a "concealed" ovulation is an accurate representation of humans relative to other primates (Brewis and Meyer 2005). The same can be said for continuous female receptivity and advertisement. These are behavioral states and how one measures and assess them will have substantial impact on their applicability to proposals for human behavioral evolution. The use of female breasts and other body shape cues have been proposed, but there remain a series of problems with such concepts (see Chapter 8).

Interestingly, in the vast majority of vertebrate organisms, males are the sex most likely to perform advertisement behavior or have specific advertisement morphology. This is not reflected in most proposals for the evolution of human behavior. Only one of these hypotheses (the mating mind) specifically proposes male advertisement in the context of sexual selection by females and a few others (male show off and man the hunter, for example) offer male risk-taking behavior and/or hunting as advertisement avenues. Still, this leaves open the possibility that in humans the sexual and mating display patterns may be very different from that of other animals.

Nearly 25% of the proposals have an important role for multiple caretakers for young (implicit in many, but you have to look carefully at assumptions and mechanisms). Some specify sex/age and others do not. In the context of a high focus on intragroup cooperation and food sharing this is not surprising. Females are highlighted as caretakers more often than not. This is interesting as it runs somewhat in conflict with the positioning of the nuclear family as important in the formation of human behavior and social organization.

Sexual selection as specifically formative/influential in the evolution of human behavior is prominent in more than a fifth of the proposals. This is interesting in the light of the commonality of male–female cooperation in the proposals and the slightly lower frequency for male–female conflict. Sexual selection is used to explain many sex differences across mammals in both behavior and morphology. Its impact on humans was held as central by Darwin (who relied on it to explain a large percentage of the "racial" differences he saw in humans) and also by E.O. Wilson. However, many recent theoreticians seem to have lessened its centrality and relegated it to a general underlying assumption.

Given the popularity of infanticide as an evolutionary strategy in the primatological and animal behavior literatures, it remains interesting that it is quite infrequent in the ideas about human evolution. A few of the proposals reviewed here argue for its centrality (Demonic males, for example), but overall it is absent in the majority of hypotheses. The animal behavior and primate literature proponents of infanticide focus on infant killing by males as a reproductive strategy, a perspective that only appears in a few of the proposals here as one possible factor underlying females' drive to form social and sexual (protective) bonds with males.

Specific Behavioral Factors

Symbol and language are given primary driving roles in the evolution of human behavior by over 50% of the hypotheses. A central role for language and symbol in human behavioral evolution is obvious but nonetheless very important as it indicates that at some point there is a substantial difference in both the modality and pattern of evolutionary change in humans relative to other species. The prominence of language and symbol suggests that humans are able to adapt/respond to selective challenges in ways not shared by other organisms (at least not to the extent that humans do it). This is most important in the modeling of behavioral evolution because these modes of response to selective pressures are primarily nonsomatic (or at least not reliant on changes in specific morphological traits) and largely cognitive and thus may not leave easily assessed cues in the fossil record. The role for temporally displaced transfer of information (speaking to one another about past or future actions, for example) in human evolution is not explicitly noted in many of the hypotheses, but one can envision that it was (and is) quite central to human behavior. This level and style of information transfer again creates some problems in drawing analogies between human evolutionary specific pathways/patterns/responses and those of other organisms, at least at the level of group coordination across time and space and in the quality and content of information transfer. While tool use does not factor specifically in most of the hypotheses, the ability to manipulate extra-somatic elements and exploit them in responding to selective pressures underlies many of them.

Few proposals focus on male dominance as a central facet. This seems contrary to popular perceptions of the human past and present. The sexual division of labor, appearing in about 40% of the hypotheses, is a major factor. It is possible that combined with the kinds of cooperation and information exchange in humans, a type of complementary division of labor within groups allows for a more efficient exploitation of the environment and related selective challenges (more on this in Chapter 8). Interestingly, fossil and archeological evidence for the genus *Homo* does not display any obvious sexual divisions of labor until recently in evolutionary time (see Chapter 4). Recent overviews (Adovasio et al. 2007) challenge much in the popular conception of male and female roles in human evolution, and the paucity of positive evidence for early division of labor seems to support this. However, as with intergroup conflict, archeological datasets do support increasing importance of sexual division of labor and distinct (but overlapping) behavioral roles for the sexes as we move closer in time to modern societies.

More than a third of the proposals focus on heterosexual pair bonds as core in human evolution. However, there is not much explicit assessment of the specific behavioral facets of these pair bonds (sexual and social) (See Fuentes 1999, 2002). While pair bonding is frequently associated with monogamous mating, the two are not explicitly tied in many of these proposals and various relationships between mating patterns and bonding patterns are proposed. However, there is a long-held association between heterosexual bonding and the nuclear family. The role of social bonds (both same sex and different sex) emerges as important and may be related to a set of primate-wide trends in social relationships that is expanded and enhanced across human evolution (see Chapter 8).

As in the overview of ecological factors, a much larger percentage of proposals see a role for humans as predators, but only a few see a role for humans as prey in our behavioral evolution. Despite the focus on intergroup competition in a few important hypotheses, specific patterns of xenophobia do not appear to be core for many. It is worth noting that both Darwin and E.O. Wilson did see xenophobia as a core factor in human evolutionary history.

While a few of the proposals focus on specific behavior patterns such as aggression in males, morality in humans, or adapted cognitive modules, a much larger percentage (~40%) focus on flexibility of behavior and behavioral response in and of itself as a significant factor in human behavioral evolution. This is not surprising, given modern human behavioral diversity and plasticity.

OF TRENDS AND PATTERNS

This brief comparison of the proposals results in some of the causal/explanatory components emerging as prominent foci in the proposed patterns of human behavioral evolution. Does this reveal a set of metapatterns and are they the same as those commonly assumed patterns that we reviewed in the prologue to this text?

In the prologue, I laid out a general set of commonly accepted views: that the genus *Homo* (humans) is approximately 2 million years old and that manipulation of our environment is a core facet in human evolution. That culture (however defined—but inclusive of symbol and language) has been and still remains integral to human evolutionary success, and cooperation and competition have both driven and arisen from patterns in human evolution. Control of groups and individuals though social and linguistic means is a major component of human evolution and language and a system of complex communication has allowed for hyper-rapid change and adaptation in a manner not available to other organisms. Cooperation and competition between the sexes also play important roles in shaping human evolutionary history and patterns. Warfare and conflict negotiation are important in human history, but it is fervently debated what the evolutionary role for these elements may be, nor is there any consensus on the role of peace and peaceful interactions in human evolution. While an overwhelming majority of practitioners agree that human evolution involves a biocultural system, there remains contention over how one models and envisions the integration and interactions of biology, culture, and behavior, and what relevance this might have to living humans. At the beginning of this chapter I also summarized a similar, but slightly more detailed, overview put forward by John Cartwright. How did these proposals match those two summaries of the main perspectives in human evolution?

Table 6.7 lists the most prominent commonalities from the proposals. They do support some aspects of the assumptions/agreements in the

TABLE 6.7

The Major Commonalities, in Rank Order of Frequency/Centrality Top to Bottom, Emerging Across the Proposals in Each of the Six Categories

Cooperation	Conflict	Diet/Food	Ecological/ Environmental	Sex/Reproduction	Specific Behavior
Intragroup	Intergroup	Food sharing	Variable environment	Multiple caretakers	Symbol/ language/ tool use
Male–female	Resources	Hunting	Competition with other human groups	Sexual selection	Sexual division of labor
Food sharing	Same/ Different sex		Brain/body energetic costs	Female advertisement/ concealed ovulation/ receptivity	Flexible behavior
Same-sex			Food stress	Nuclear family	Heterosexual pair-bond

TABLE 6.8

A few Factors that Appear in a Few or None of the Hypotheses that May Deserve Further Examination Given the Fossil/Archeological Record and Comparative Primatology

Cooperation	Conflict	Diet/Food	Ecological/ Environmental	Sex/Reproduction	Specific behavior
Intergroup	Intragroup	Plant storage organs	Human- environment mutability	Male advertisement	Pair-bonding in detail (same and different sex)
Across age class	Interhominin		Disease		
	Intermammalian		Predation		

summary above and Cartwright's main points, such as cooperation within groups and competition between groups and the role of symbol and language. Interestingly, when one looks at these patterns in more detail, we see that specific details of cooperation, such as food sharing, division of labor, child care by multiple group members, and pair-bonds might be particularly deserving of further inquiry. The possibility of cooperation between human groups was least addressed and details of potential cooperative behavior across age classes are also ignored for the most part. While flexibility in behavior was a common theme, direct environmental manipulation received less attention than did the stressors of variable environments. And some environmental factors such as predators and disease/pathogens received almost no attention from the hypotheses. Resource stress and competition between human groups received much attention, but competition with other human-like organisms (hominins) and with other mammals did not. The costs of brain and body growth are recognized as possible drivers in behavioral evolution. No specific pattern of mating received more attention than monogamy, but that also received little note. The more important factors seemed to be child rearing, the impact of sexual selection, and patterns of female advertisement and manipulation (the "concealment of ovulation"). Little attention was paid to male advertisement in spite of its commonality as a pattern in the animal world and details of pair bonding are not addressed in great detail (see Table 6.8).

SUGGESTED READINGS

Adovasio, J.M., Soffer, O., and Page, J. (2007) *The Invisible Sex: Uncovering the True Roles of Women in Prehistory.* New York: Smithsonian Books.

Cartwright, J. (2000) *Evolution and Human Behavior: Darwinian Perspectives on Human Nature.* Suffolk, UK: Palmgrave. Chapters 4–11.

CHAPTER 7

Twenty-First Century Evolutionary Theory/ Biology and Thinking about the Evolution of Human Behavior

The Neo-Darwinian Sociobiology perspective and its affiliated approaches of Human Behavioral Ecology (HBE), Evolutionary Psychology (EP), gene–culture coevolution/Dual-Inheritance Theory (DIT), and Memetics, are the primary theoretical tools used to formulate the hypotheses/proposals reviewed/discussed in Chapters 5 and 6. However, these approaches do not reflect the full range of evolutionary perspectives available to theoreticians and practitioners investigating human behavior. To maximize the potential explanatory power and impact of hypotheses and theories exploring the evolution of human behavior, we should include both the current approaches and emerging perspectives in modern evolutionary biology, ecology, and anthropological theory.

ADDING TO OUR TOOLKIT—USING FOUR DIMENSIONS OF EVOLUTION

Jablonka and Lamb (2005) call for a renovation in evolutionary theory at the start of the twenty-first century, a "new" new synthesis in how we model evolution. They argue for recognition of "evolution in four dimensions" rather than a focus on just one. Their main point being that practitioners of traditional Neo-Darwinian approaches, especially sociobiology and its affiliates, focus on one system of inheritance in their models of evolutionary patterns and change: the genetic system of inheritance.[1] Because of this, the majority of hypotheses proposed for scenarios regarding the selection and adaptation of human behavior rely on, or are derived from, perspectives with explanations of ultimate causal factors (Chapter 2—Tinbergen's questions) residing at the genic level, some proxy for genic effect, or an assumption of some "blackbox" linkage to genetics (such as in HBE, Chapter 3). Jablonka and Lamb argue for adding a perspective wherein three other inheritance systems also, potentially, have causal roles in evolutionary change. These other systems are the **epigenetic** (organic systems outside of, or in addition to, the DNA that can affect genetic expression, development, and biological function), behavioral, and symbolic inheritance systems. Epigenetic inheritance is found in all organisms, behavioral inheritance in most, and symbolic inheritance is found only in humans.[2,3] Jablonka and Lamb (2005) state that

- There is more to heredity than genes.
- Some hereditary variations are nonrandom in origin.
- Some acquired information is inherited.
- Evolutionary change can result from instruction as well as selection.

They summarize their position as follows:

> Information is transferred from one generation to the next by many inter-acting inheritance systems. Moreover, contrary to current dogma, the variation on which natural selection acts is not always random in origin or blind to function: new heritable variation can arise in response to the conditions of life. Variation is often *targeted*, in the sense that it preferentially affects functions or activities that can make organisms better adapted to the environment in which they live. Variation is also *constructed*, in the sense that, whatever their origin, which variants are inherited and what final form they assume depend on various "filtering" and "editing" processes that occur before and during transmission. (Jablonka and Lamb 2005, p. 319, italics in original)

In evolutionary history, many new adaptations arise not de novo but rather as by-products of characteristics or components of traits that resulted from selection for very different functions. In many cases, original functions

---

[1] This assertion does not explicitly hold for gene–culture coevolution (DIT) or Memetics as those perspectives focus also on cultural variant/meme inheritance. However, they do use the gene focused natural selection model (Chapter 2) as their process of evolution for both genetic and cultural factors. DIT does go further than Memetics in arguing for different types and levels of information transmission, overlapping with Jablonka and Lamb's perspective (see footnote #2).

[2] Remembering Chapters 3 and 5, one notices significant overlap between Jablonka and Lamb's fourth (or symbolic) inheritance system and the role of cultural/symbolic evolution in the gene–culture coevolution (DIT), especially as proposed by Boyd and Richerson.

[3] Jablonka and Lamb actually make the case that chimpanzees and other apes using sign language are participating in a symbolic system as well. However, the intraspecific transmission of such a system is currently debated.

and structure may or may not be lost. This results in adaptations being mixed structures representing potentially more than one system of inheritance. The three nongenetic systems of inheritance are important in understanding and modeling evolutionary change and patterns of adaptation.

Epigenetic systems are elements that are not directly coded for in genetic sequences or under immediate genetic regulation, but in turn impact gene expression, cellular machinery, tissue interactions, and other chemical and developmental organic processes. Epigenetic effects are involved at both intra- and intercellular levels and range from self-sustaining feedback loop systems with multiple interacting genes and gene products (such as daily and seasonally cyclical/rhythmic changes in physiological state), to the inheritance of specific topological structure within cells, or guided assemble (such as with prion systems like Mad Cow Disease), to chromatin marking and RNA interference (see Jablonka and Lamb 2005 for detailed descriptions of these processes).

All of these types of intra- and intercellular epigenetic inheritance affect the products of genes, the interactions of genes, the structures of cells, and cell–cell interactions, thus potentially impacting behavior and development. They are important ways selection can act without targeting genetic sequences. This challenges the focus on the gene as the sole locus for the generation, storage, and transmission of evolutionarily relevant biological information. As Jablonka and Lamb note "groups are made of individuals, individuals are built of cells, cells contain chromosomes, chromosomes have genes and selection can occur at any of these levels" (2005, p. 342). The higher-level biological structures (epigenetic levels) are integrated elements/systems, more than just the simple sum of genetic products. These structures can pass information across generations and thus are subject to selection.

Behavioral inheritance, according to Jablonka and Lamb, arises from the potential selective advantage of social attention and social learning. Many organisms transmit information via behavior; so the acquisition of behavioral patterns that confer selective benefits can occur through socially learning via observation and the reproduction of behavior. This transmission of information occurs and can be selected without having any linkage to genetic systems that selection can target. Finally, symbolic inheritance comes with language and the ability to engage in information transfer that can be temporally and spatially complex, contain a high density of information, and convey more than material descriptions. This allows for the acquisition and reproduction of a variety of potentially beneficial factors for humans that have no genetic basis or linkage.

Obviously, in the quest to understand the evolution of human behavior, the behavioral and symbolic inheritance systems are of great interest to us. However, the premise that selection can target more than the genetic level, that information transfer occurs at multiple levels, and that instruction (at epigenetic, behavioral, or symbolic levels) can also impact evolutionary change forces a broader heuristic toolkit when constructing hypotheses and building models of human evolutionary patterns. This possibility that "instruction," the passing of nongenetic information or structure across generations, can influence evolutionary patterns as well as selection changes the way we can envision human evolution. Models using this system will by necessity become more complex than the generally linear genetic models of Neo-Darwinian behavioral theory (such as kin selection, for example). However, they may be better attuned to the actual interactions of systems. Specifically in terms of human evolution, this perspective forces a concern with the way in which behavioral and symbolic systems construct and interact with social and ecological niches and how, in turn, these systems interact with epigenetic and genetic systems. Jablonka and Lamb conclude with the following points:

- Heredity is through genes and other transmissible biochemical and behavioral entities.

- Heritable variation—genetic, epigenetic, behavioral, and symbolic—is the consequence both of accidents (random) and of instructive processes during development.

- Selection occurs between entities that develop variant heritable traits that affect reproductive success. Such selection can occur within cells, between cells, between organism, and between groups of organisms.

REVISITING TINBERGEN'S ONTOGENETIC " WHY"

In Chapter 2, we saw that Tinbergen proposed four types of "why" questions that one can use when investigating behavior. With the rise and dominance of ND-Sociobiology, HBE, and EP (see Chapter 3) one of the four "why" questions dropped from many research paradigms and hypotheses; the "ontogeny/development" why (Stamps 2003). This question focuses on factors during the development of the organism that act in a causal/influential manner on a given behavior. In most Neo-Darwinian approaches, this factor is unaddressed in favor of functional (ultimate impact on fitness) or phylogenetic (evolutionarily historical) explanations. In the last decade there has been a resurgence in interest in developmental systems and their relationship to/with behavior. However, few practitioners involved in examining the evolution of human behavior participate in this resurgence or incorporate it into their analyses. It is possible that we are now "poised for a surge in research on topics involving behavior and development" (Stamps 2003), specifically examining whether behavior itself can have substantial impact on development and maintenance of variation in behavioral phenotypes. This renewed interest in the relationship between development and behavior moves the focus off of optimality or single developmental and behavioral trajectories as the ideal targets/products of selection. The concept of selection generally favoring "typical," "normal," or "optimal" phenotypes that are best for all individuals in a population may no longer be a particularly beneficial approach in behaviorally complex organisms (Stamps 2003). Recent work examining behavioral plasticity, niche construction, and developmental systems approaches suggest we should consider research paradigms and approaches that look for "behavioral processes that encourage the development and maintenance of interindividual differences in behavioral, physiological, and morphological traits" (Stamps 2003). Some more recent work in HBE looking at variation in behavioral responses and the possibility that multiple patterns work well within a systems matches well with aspects of this perspective (see Sear and Mace 2008).

Tinbergen's original definition of ontogeny refers to a change in behavior machinery during development of the organism. This definition does not see ontogeny as ceasing at adulthood or development solely as juveniles training for or progressing toward adulthood. Rather, changes in the machinery of behavior can occur across the life span as the individual is constantly developing through different life stages, behavioral contexts, and physiological conditions. The main way in which this approach is envisioned is via the utilization of the **reaction norm** concept as a point of departure. A "reaction norm" is the set of phenotypes (final forms) that can potentially be produced by a single genotype exposed to a variety of different environmental conditions (Schlichting and Pagliucci 1998). Thus, the relationship of phenotypic variation based on environmental pressures can be represented in a relatively simple manner. However, reaction norms are rarely, if ever, as straightforward in genetically similar or even identical individuals living in different environments. Environmental fluctuations, shifting distribution patterns resulting in environmental discordance between generations, specific factors in parental or local group modification of the environment, and other historical and contingent factors can influence the shape and relationships across/between reaction norms. Using the reaction norm distribution/pattern as a "jumping off" point rather than an optimality model with a single or small set of "ideal" outcomes might provide a better toolkit for assessing the potential impact of behavioral factors on evolutionary change. Therefore, dissecting the complexities in the pattern and range of reaction norms might facilitate a greater understanding of the behavioral processes that are "likely to influence the production and maintenance of phenotypic variation within populations" (Stamps 2003).

Humans exhibit a range of behavioral variation broader than that of most other organisms. Most traditional approaches (ND-Sociobiology, for example) favor locating the optimal or ideal behavioral variant and modeling pressures that enable or disrupt movement toward that state. "Optimal" response may not always be possible or even preferable in many contexts. Focusing on the range of behavior exhibited and the development of behavior might offer additional views/perspectives that enhance the traditional approaches. If "extragenetic" behavior processes are common and important contributors to developmental change, then those patterns creating, maintaining, and impacting these behaviors are as important as those genetic factors that influence/affect the phenotype.

In the next section of this chapter we will review four perspectives on behavioral systems and evolution that straddle the boundaries of the traditional Neo-Darwinian approach and fit within the multiple dimension perspective and involve a consideration of developmental contexts and patterns. These approaches are of specific interest to understanding and investigating the evolution of human behavior, especially in regards to patterns of variation and development. They are phenotypic plasticity and its relationship to ecologies, developmental systems theory (DST), niche construction theory, and biocultural approaches in anthropology (see Table 7.1).

FOUR OTHER APPROACHES IN EVOLUTIONARY BIOLOGY/THEORY

Phenotypic Plasticity and Ecological Impact/Context: Moving Beyond Norms of Reaction

Mary Jane West-Eberhard's broad overview (2003) of developmental plasticity and evolution led her to suggest that plasticity is one of the key factors for our understanding of adaptive evolution. She argues, like Jablonka and Lamb (2005) and other prominent evolutionary biologists (Steven Jay Gould and Richard Lewontin, for example), that reducing the processes of development and evolutionary change to genomic levels is not always possible or preferable. Her analyses demonstrate that evolved plasticity in development can allow for the evolution of new or variant, but adaptive, phenotypes without substantial, or even marked, genetic change.

Recent reviews define basic **phenotypic plasticity** as "the production of multiple phenotypes from a single genotype, depending on environmental conditions" (Miner et al. 2005). However, more important than the basic definition is the abundance of evidence that a wide range of organisms express phenotypic plasticity and that this plasticity can be expressed via changes in behavior, physiology, morphology, growth, life history, and demography and can occur in both individual and intergenerational contexts (Pigliucci 2001, Miner et al. 2005). Research into modeling this plasticity, its potential adaptive value and contexts, and its ecological impact all suggest that phenotypic plasticity is a significant factor for many organisms' evolutionary histories and current behavior/morphology.

The focus on plasticity has a long history in behavioral ecology (and is becoming a core factor in modern HBE) where behavioral variation and the ability to alter behavioral patterns in response to ecological pressures is seen as an important factor in adaptability/success. The relative degree of behavioral and developmental plasticity of an organism is often seen as a marker of the organisms' ability to resist rapid environmental changes or its

TABLE 7.1

Summaries of Main Points of the Perspectives Reviewed in this Chapter

	Evolution in Four Dimensions	Phenotypic Plasticity	Developmental Systems Theory	Niche Construction	Biocultural Approaches
Focus of selection	Gene, epigenetic systems, behavioral and symbolic systems	Phenotype and community interactions	Outcome of complex interactions between genic, epigenetic, and behavioral factors	Individual-local ecology interaction (niche)—a focus on Phenogenotypes	Behavior and physiology in interaction
Main underlying causes for evolution of human behavior	Combination of genic, epigenetic, behavioral, and symbolic inheritance systems	High degree of behavioral and developmental plasticity as a marker of humans' ability to face rapid and dynamic environmental challenges	Constant constructing—and being constructed by—demography, social interactions, cultural variations, and manipulation of the environment in intra- and intergroup contexts in addition to the developmental, biological, and ecological factors throughout the course of life history	Tri-inheritance vision model (TIV) wherein human behavior results from information-acquiring processes at three levels: population genetic processes, ontogenetic processes, and cultural processes	Human physiological traits and behavior emerge from interactions within different cultural contexts and patterns in different ecologies
Basic premise	• There is more to heredity than genes • Some hereditary variations are nonrandom in origin	Organisms express phenotypic plasticity that can be expressed via changes in behavior, physiology, morphology,	Evolution is not a matter of organisms or populations being molded by their environments but of organism–environment systems changing over time. This involves joint determination by multiple causes, context sensitivity	• Ecosystem engineering. • Organisms modify their own, and other, organisms' selective environments • Ecological inheritance, including modified selection pressures for subsequent populations	Synthesis and equal valorization of biologically and culturally based assessments of human behavior and health

	• Some acquired information is inherited • Evolutionary change can result from instruction as well as selection	growth, life history, and demography and can occur in both individual and intergenerational contexts	and contingency, extended inheritance, development as construction, distributed control, and evolution as construction	• Is a process, in addition to natural selection, that contributes to changes over time in the dynamic relationship between organisms and environments (niches)	
Forces other than selection at play	Epigenetic, behavioral and symbolic modes of inheritance	Epigenetic plasticity in phenotypic expression and development	Epigenetic and developmental systems, ecological and cultural inheritance	Niche construction interacts with patterns and strength of selection	Behavioral/cultural change and response impacts physiology
Datasets	Genetic, epigenetic, behavioral, and cultural	Genetic, ecological, morphological, physiological, and behavioral	Developmental systems, behavior, physiology	Genetic, behavioral, cultural, ecological	Physiological, behavioral, cultural

potential to successfully invade new areas.[4] Let us briefly review the types of effects that plasticity can have on organism–environment interaction and then localize these patterns in our broader focus on evolutionary patterns (following the review and terminology of Miner et al. 2005).

Many studies have focused on the way in which plasticity alters the relationships between organisms and their environment, both in direct and indirect manners. Direct interactions stimulate plastic responses to both biotic and abiotic pressures. Pressures such as foraging by herbivores inducing changes in plant morphological defenses (increased thorns in Acacia tress in response to increased feeding on them by herbivores, for example), or frog tadpoles responding to predator pressure by modifying foraging activity and by undergoing changes in body form (increased tail length and reduced body size) relative to swimming speed. Abiotic examples include changes in local climate and/or light patterns that result in changes in growth of larvae, feeding structure/patterns, and in other behavioral patterns.

Indirect interactions among multispecies communities can also occur. These happen when interactions between two species spread out into the local ecosystem impacting other organisms. For example, a predator decreasing the density of a prey species can have an effect on a third species that has a relationship with the prey species. Miner et al. (2005) draw from Werner and Peacor (2003) to provide the example of dragonfly and frog larvae and algae. Dragonfly larvae, when present, eat the frog larvae, reducing tadpole density and foraging rates. The fewer tadpole and their reduced foraging rates reduces grazing pressure on the algae, increasing overall algae densities. In this example, plasticity and its impact on interactions can have affects on parameters of competition, **facilitation**[5] (positive interaction between species or potentially between groups within a species) and food webs.

While each of these examples can also be modeled individually in a traditional Neo-Darwinian perspective, the point here is that it may be the plasticity itself, rather than the specific outcomes that are being selected and/or transmitted across generations. That is, the plastic responses may arise from epigenetic or behavioral factors as ontogenetic/developmental responses and not be available to genic level selection in the sense that they may not be passed on, given their tight correlation to specific eliciting environmental

---

[4] In many organisms, this ability is often matched with a generalized and flexible body form or behavioral profile enabling rapid accommodation as well as adaptation. These types of species have also been termed "weed" species for their relative success at colonizing new environments. Interestingly, the two most widespread primate radiations, the human lineage and the papionine/macaque lineage, can both be considered as weed species groups. See also Chapter 8.

[5] Facilitation—positive interaction between species or potentially between groups within a species—also drives evolutionary change. Research from ecology, especially intertidal and plant ecosystems, demonstrates that the interactions between two or more species may alter the selective environments such that each of the groups does better when the other is also sharing the environment (Bruno et al. 2003).

the systems facilitating the plasticity, not the morphological or behavioral responses themselves. Another way in which plasticity can influence evolutionary patterns is as it affects organism's abilities to modify the environment they live in (niche construction, see later). Phenotypic plasticity can result in niche construction (documented in plants, Donohue 2005) and alter or shape patterns within feedback loops such that the organism–environment dynamic is complicated by both the organism's phenotypic plasticity and the mutual interaction and modification between the organism and the environment.

Plasticity need not be always adaptive, nor are the effects of behavioral, morphological, physiological, and life history plasticity necessarily independent. So, within organisms that display many types of plasticity we can see multiple patterns of development for traits that exhibit plasticity, but these may have different impacts ecologically and may be affecting one another (see also niche construction below). This complexity then increases as we consider the consequences of plasticity at whole-community-wide levels. Tying this to the multidimensional approach to evolutionary theory, we can see that plasticity, as noted by West-Eberhard, can act as a major process in organismal and community evolution. While the vast majority of this research is currently conducted on plants and nonhuman animals, we can see that the theoretical implications have salience for ways in which we can model the past and present evolution of human behavior, especially as we look to the fossil record and try to understand how humans ancestors modified and changed their environments and how this feedback changed their bodies/behaviors.

Developmental Systems Theory

DST is proposed as an alternative to what Susan Oyama calls the "developmental dualism" approach (Oyama 2000). The developmental dualism approach is viewing development as having some aspects driven mainly by "internal" causes (genes) and others driven mainly by external causes (environment, or memes/culture variants). Oyama (2000) states that "The developmental systems approach allows us to redraw the overly restrictive boundary around the genes to include other developmentally important influences." The point is not to propose, as in DIT (Chapter 3), two selective systems, one to carry culture and one biology, with the two mirroring one another in their mode of change (selection), coevolving and impacting one another. Rather, DST seeks to trade discrete channels (genes and culture, for example) for interacting systems whose processes give rise to successive generations. DST is an approach that attempts to combine multiple dimensions and interactants utilizing a systems approach to understand development, in the broadest sense, and its evolutionary impact.

Oyama et al. (2001) summarize the main theses of DST in six major points (in italics below). I have added additional explanatory text tying the points directly to our broader consideration of the evolution of human behavior (from Fuentes 2004):

1. *Joint determination by multiple causes: Every trait is produced by the interaction of many developmental resources. The gene/environment dichotomy is only one of the many ways to divide up the interactants in evolutionary processes.* Therefore, explanations assuming the primacy of "genes," their competition for propagation, and their interactions with an environment, while forceful and important avenues for research, are not the only avenues for inquiry into the evolution of human behavior (Dawkins' selfish gene for example, Chapter 2).

2. *Context sensitivity and contingency: The significance of any one cause is contingent on the state of the rest of the system.* Given the complex, bioculturally integrated nature of human lives, the assessment of the evolution of human traits/patterns must take into account various contexts including intra- and intergroup dynamics, multiple patterns of information transmission, and micro- and macromanipulation of the environment and the resulting selection pressures. Single aspects of human behavior or morphology cannot be seen as independent in an evolutionary sense from any others.

3. *Extended inheritance: An organism inherits a wide range of resources that interact to construct that organism's life cycle.* In humans, inherited resources include the memory and experience of group members, the previous manipulation of the area in which the group lives, and the patterns of cultural interaction extant in that population. These extra-somatic factors must be included in the construction of evolutionary hypotheses as they affect, and are affected by gene flow (population/individual movement and mating), genetic drift (chance events altering the composition and behavior of populations), and natural selection.

4. *Development as construction: Neither traits nor representations of traits are transmitted to offspring. Instead, traits are made—reconstructed—in development.* The implication of incorporating this concept in models of human evolution is that human life histories are extended relative to many animals and the symbol-rich social environment in which they exist requires dynamic learning and is primarily socially negotiated (see Chapter 4). Human development is equally affected by somatic and extra-somatic factors interacting with one another during the course of constructing the adult human. The assumption of inheritance of specific, discrete behavioral traits as units that emerge during development is highly questionable. Human development is a biocultural phenomenon (see later sections).

5. *Distributed control: No one type of interactant controls development.* A focus on selection and the basic gene–phenotype–environment relationships while ignoring other dimensions of inheritance (see Jablonka and Lamb, 2005) is unlikely to effectively explain the full range of human evolutionary patterns and processes.

6. *Evolution as construction: Evolution is not a matter of organisms or popula-*
tions being molded by their environments but of organism–environment systems
changing over time. This conceptualization reframes some Neo-Darwinian
perspectives by envisioning human evolutionary patterns as constantly
constructing—and being constructedby—demography, social interactions, cultural variations, complex information transfer, and manipulation of the environment in intra- and intergroup contexts in addition to
the developmental biological and ecological factors throughout the course
of life history.

These six theses make up the core of DST. They reflect a series of con-
tentions that expand on traditional gene-based conceptualizations of development. According to Oyama et al. (2001), genes do not "make" anything
by themselves but are involved in processes requiring many other molecules, contexts and conditions. Additional facets/factors of development are
found at a diverse array of levels from the molecular to the macroecological.
"None is sufficient, and their effects are interdependent. Development never
occurs (and could not occur) in a vacuum" (Oyama 2000). Further, genes
do not "make" organisms or result (generally) in a set of products that create species-specific characters. Rather, "Typical conditions, again at many
scales, contribute to forming these characters, whose uniformity should not
be exaggerated" (Oyama 2000). Genetic, epigenetic, and other interactants
in development can produce or facilitate phenotypic variants, which can be
heritable in a variety of senses (as per Jablonka and Lamb, 2005). DST argues
against the privileging of the DNA or the region within the cell membrane
as the dominant factor(s) in structuring development and stresses the "processes that bring together the prerequisites for successive iterations of a life
cycle." Finally, as with Jablonka and Lamb's prospectus, DST proponents
argue against a reductionist "unit" of evolution (such as that embodied in
the common Neo-Darwinian definition of evolution as a change in allele
frequencies over time). For DST, the "unit" or logical focus for assessing
evolutionary change would be the interactive developmental system: "life
cycles of organisms in their niches." Evolution would then be change in the
constitution and distribution of these interactive developmental systems
(Oyama 2000).

While sounding, initially, quite radical, the DST perspective is reflective
of many current concepts and practices emerging in evolutionary biology
(Stamps 2003, West-Eberhard 2003, Jablonka and Lamb 2005). The "radical"
facet of DST is its strong stance regarding the deprioritizing of the "gene"
and genomic structures (or their "cultural" analogs memes and culture variants, see DIT and Memetics) as the primary or most important factor(s) in
assessing and modeling causal facets and processes of evolutionary change.
This is a direct counter to Dawkinsian and Memetic perspectives (Chapters 2
and 3) and casts a much broader net of actors in evolutionary change than
do traditional Neo-Darwinian perspectives. DST, the four-dimension view,

and phenotypic plasticity approaches do focus more on Tinbergen's "ontogeny" question and on systems of interaction rather than traits. It is precisely these systems of interaction and the concept of mutual organism–environment dynamism that are central to our next perspective, niche construction theory.

Niche Construction

> All living creatures, through their metabolism, their activities, and their choices, partly create and partly destroy their own niches, on scales ranging from the extremely local to the global. (Odling-Smee et al. 2003)

Building on the work of Richard Lewontin (1983), Ernst Mayr (1963), and Conrad Waddington (1959), and even taking from the "extended phenotype" concept of Richard Dawkins (1982), Odling-Smee et al. (2003) formalized and proposed **niche construction** as a significant evolutionary force. Niche construction, the building and destroying of niches by organisms and the mutual dynamic interactions between organisms and environments is a long-accepted occurrence, but only recently has it been proposed as a major force of evolution. Niche construction, according to Odling-Smee et al. (2003) creates feedback within the evolutionary dynamic, where organisms engaged in niche construction significantly modify the selection pressures acting on them, on their descendants, and on unrelated sympatric populations.

Odling-Smee et al. (2003) identify four major consequences and three prime implications of niche construction. Niche construction:

- Impacts/alters energy flows in ecosystems through ecosystem engineering.
- Demonstrates that organisms modify their, and other, organisms' selective environments.
- Creates an ecological inheritance, including modified selection pressures, for subsequent populations.
- Is a process, in addition to natural selection, that contributes to changes over time in the dynamic relationship between organisms and environments (niches).

These consequences of niche construction then have implications. In the context of evolutionary theory, niche construction provides a second role for phenotypes; in the context of ecological theory, the focus on coevolution between organisms and their abiotic/biotic environments promotes closer integration of ecological and evolutionary frameworks (see phenotypic plasticity); and for the study of humans, it provides an important, potentially integrative, framework for connecting evolutionary approaches to the social sciences.

Ecosystem engineering is the simple concept that organisms modify their environments, and simultaneously, the environmental pressures on themselves. "The activities of organisms can result in significant, consistent and directed changes in their local environments" (Olding-Smee et al. 2003). Odling-Smee et al. (2003) provide the example of leaf-cutter ants and their tendency to build giant nests and grow/harvest fungus within them. These nests reach up to 22 cubic meters in size and weigh as much as 44 tons. These nests have dramatic impacts on local ecosystems through soil movement and aeration, and changing local microclimates and nutrient and pH levels in the soils. In this case, the alterations of the niche extend to impact other organisms as well. The local ecosystem can be said to be engineered in part by the ongoing actions of these ants. There are a number of other examples wherein actions by one species alter the flow and movement patterns of energy within ecosystems and even the overall physical structure of said ecosystems.

This ecosystem engineering and other dynamic engagements with the environment can act to alter selection pressures. That is, the niche construction behavior may produce alterations that persist across generations and space such that they, themselves, are a factor creating the pattern and strength of selection pressures. In this way, niche construction is not a maintainer of selection or a subset of ecological variables involved in selection, rather it is a manipulator and constructor of selection pressures: a force of evolution. One classic example provided by Odling-Smee et al. (2003) is that of earthworms (the same example used by Darwin, who spent much of his final years working with these fascinating animals). Through their burrowing activities, earthworms mix organic and inorganic materials in the soils and their castings (excrement) act as major bases/catalysts for microbial activity. Through their behavior, earthworms dramatically alter the structure, chemistry, and ecological profiles of the soils in which they live (a fact known to human gardeners for centuries). Cumulative effects of multiple generations of earthworms engaging in these niche construction activities generate and modify selective pressures not only on themselves but a whole range of sympatric organisms. It is highly likely that many of the interesting earthworm physical adaptations, which seem to lie between those of terrestrial and aquatic organisms are adaptations to the combination of selection and ongoing niche construction in earthworm niches. Ecosystem engineering via niche construction is ongoing and creates, modifies, and structures selection pressures on the niche constructors and sympatric organisms.

The pattern of ecological engineering of earthworms also acts as a stellar example of the third major consequence of niche construction: ecological inheritance. This perspective draws on basic ecological theory, Dawkinsian "extended phenotype" ideas, a mixture of elements from Jablonka and Lamb's epigenetic and behavioral inheritance patterns, and a direct correlation with the DST concept of extended inheritance. In fact, one can even reach back to Baldwin and Lloyd Morgan's organic evolution (Chapter 2) to see progenitors for this outcome of niche construction. Odling-Smee et al. (2003) define this factor as "whatever legacies of modified natural selection pressures are bequeathed by niche-constructing ancestral organisms to their descendants." They envision two distinct, but obviously interactive, inheritance systems wherein a gene pool under pressure from natural selection engages in niche construction activity affecting the local environment. This interactive feedback between the environment and the population results in an ecological inheritance being passed to subsequent generations in the local environment as well as genetic inheritance being passed down across generations (see Odling-Smee et al. 2003, Figure 1.3).

All of the above three consequences—ecosystem engineering, alteration of selection pressures, and ecological inheritance—are relevant to the final consequence: that niche construction results in evolutionary change and is thus a force of evolution. As noted by Lewontin (1983), traditional Neo-Darwinian theory treats adaptations in organisms and the sources of natural selection in the environment as separate spheres, independent of one another. The environment is the problem and the organism presents solutions to that (those) problems. The best solution(s) are then "chosen" and thus are what we call adaptations (Lewontin 1983). However, this traditional view overlooks niche construction, the fact that organisms partially (at least) build and alter their environments. As Odling-Smee et al. (2003) quote from Lewontin (1983) "Organisms do not adapt to their environments; they construct them out of the bits and pieces of the external world." It is clear that during organisms' lives and the challenges they face, they can either change to suit environments or change environments to suit themselves. Integrated, these two elements represent the interactions between niche construction and natural selection (Odling-Smee et al. 2003). There is no "chicken or egg" quandary here. Neither natural selection nor niche construction comes "first;" rather, all organisms, to varying degrees, modify their selective environments and they are able to do so because of the "naturally selected" systems that constitute their beings, and, this relationship is a feedback system as it moves temporally and cross-generationally. This implies a dynamic relationship between organisms and environments that goes beyond the traditional Neo-Darwinian liner perspective of unidirectional (environment→organism) natural selection pressures as mediating/shaping organism–environment interactions.

This perspective has three main implications for evolutionary theory. Feedback must be a component in evolutionary analyses as organisms (phenotypes) and local environments coevolve across time mutually impacting one another and the concomitant selection pressures/parameters. Ecological inheritance forces expansion beyond the genetic mode of inheritance in the construction of evolutionary scenarios and models (as with four dimension, DST, and phenotypic plasticity perspectives). Finally, niche construction allows for acquired characteristics to play a role in the evolutionary process. This view is not new, Lloyd Morgan and Baldwin's organic evolution centered on it. Jablonka and Lamb call it behavioral inheritance, and DST sees it as a component in extended inheritance. Odling-Smee et al.

(2003) see this implication as calling for a focus on learning and behavior in animal niche construction and a possible focus on cultural processes when thinking about human evolution (as with Jablonka and Lamb's behavioral and symbolic inheritance).

Olding-Smee et al. (2003) assert that niche construction can substantially contribute to the social sciences and our study of the evolution of human behavior. They explicitly state that ecological inheritance, especially via material culture, and niche construction in general can occur via cultural means. They state that humans are the "ultimate niche constructors" and that adding niche construction to attempts to understand evolution makes such attempts more complicated (bypassing more simplistic adaptationist accounts), but ultimately this complexity will be more beneficial, and attractive, to researchers looking into human evolution and behavior. Thus, niche construction is of particular relevance to humans as Odling-Smee et al. (2003) see cultural processes as providing a particular vehicle for niche construction; humans are born into a world (local environments) that is largely "constructed" (anthropogenic ecologies) whether they are urban dwellers, hunter/foragers, or nomadic herders. Because of this current state of affairs, they opine that niche construction in general, and ecological inheritance in particular, are likely to have been very important factors in human evolution.

Odling-Smee et al. (2003), building on the work of Laland et al. (2000) and Laland and Brown (2002) propose a model for human genetic and cultural evolution that expands on gene–culture coevolution/DIT models. They propose a **tri-inheritance vision model** (TIV) wherein human behavior results from information-acquiring processes at three levels: population genetic processes, ontogenetic processes, and cultural processes (see Odling-Smee et al. 2003, Figures 6.1c and 6.2). Niche construction in humans emerges from all three of these processes, each of which can impact patterns, contexts, and structure of natural selection. They state

> Much of human niche construction is guided by socially learned knowledge and cultural inheritance, but the transmission of this knowledge is itself dependent on preexisting information acquired through genetic evolution, complex ontogenetic processes, or prior social learning. (Odling-Smee et al. 2003, pp. 260–261)

In all, these processes correspond closely to Jablonka and Lamb's genetic, behavioral, and symbolic inheritance systems. TIV also shares largely with current perspectives in both four-dimensional evolution and phenotypic plasticity wherein selection acts not on specific behavioral traits or strategies but rather on ranges of behavior potential and evolved "aptitudes" that facilitate the acquisition and utilization of behavioral variants (phenotypic plasticity) that are broadly adaptive. Finally, TIV utilizes the concept of culture variants (as in DIT) to model cultural change. Their overall point is that niche construction is particularly salient in humans as culturally based niche construction has the ability to act on selection genetic level, ontogenetic, and cultural levels.[6]

Olding-Smee et al. (2003) do provide some possible avenues for testing the appearance and relevance of niche construction in the human evolutionary record. They demonstrate (through a model) how there are two forms of feedback loop we can expect to see in human evolution from niche construction endeavors. In the first form, niche cultural construction alters the local selection pressures and the population then responds with further (novel) cultural shifts to combat the new pressures. In this case, the pressures are ameliorated with minimal, if any, biological change. The other alternative is when cultural shifts cannot respond fast enough or efficiently enough and genetic/biological change becomes the mode of response. In this case, cultural niche construction may be modifying the patterns of the population's genetic makeup, which in turn may stimulate new pattern of niche construction resulting in continuous mutual feedback. In the more complex version, a third form would focus on ontogenetic processes and react interactively with the first two options. This model suggest that one can look to the human fossil and archeological record and to historical aspects of modern human societies in search of signatures of niche construction.

Among the possible signatures of a niche construction feedback scenario reviewed by Odling-Smee et al. (2003) is the **expensive tissue hypothesis** (Aiello and Wheeler 1995). Hominin guts size decreases as relative brain size increases in the mid-Pleistocene fossil record. Researchers have suggested that cultural practices (hunting, enhanced scavenging) led to an increase in meat consumption, making large guts less necessary (due to the processing and absorption qualities of meat versus plant matter). This shift allows increased energetic investment in brain tissue, which results in large neocortexes that allow subsequent hominins to express even more sophisticated cultural niche construction (such as cooking), resulting in even less demand on extensive gut tissue for absorption of nutrients. Other examples include the well-known case of red blood cell polymorphism and malaria in Mediterranean and West African populations and the appearance of the body louse in human evolution (significant as it lays eggs in human clothing). They also refer to a variant of the tribal-social instincts hypotheses (see Chapter 5) as a possible result of the interaction of human competition, cooperation, group living, and niche construction.

The bottomline contribution proposed by niche construction theory for human evolution is a focus on **phenogenotypes** (the human biocultural

---

[6] Odling-Smee et al. (2003) provide two models that specify (mathematically) their basic premises (Chapter 6 section 6.4; pp. 264–275). Figures 6.4 and 6.5 in Odling-Smee et al. (2003) demonstrate the complexity in outcomes from said models and exemplify how the addition of niche construction element (TIV) to gene–culture coevolution (DIT) models enhances both their potential applicability and the difficulty in applying them with simple datasets.

complex) and multiple processes of adaptation in the context of feedback loops initiated and maintained via niche construction and changing patterns of selection pressures. It is specifically this concept of a biocultural human being that the final emergent perspective has to contribute to this expansion on Neo-Darwinian theory.

Biocultural Approaches to Studying Modern Humans

Emerging as a synthesis of human biology and biological anthropology perspectives, the last two decades have seen an increase in research projects that fall under the generalized heading of "biocultural." The earliest biocultural approaches began with researchers initiating studies of human populations with the assumption that "environment" is more than the external physical conditions surrounding a human population (Dufour 2006), such as Livingstone's (1958) research on malaria and the sickle cell trait in Africa. However, this perspective, of the environment being more than just the physical context, did not become a common component in human biology studies until the last quarter of the twentieth century. Although many anthropologists were looking at human ecology as a complex symbolic and biotic system, much human biology lagged behind in infusing cultural patterns and behavior into their concepts of integrated environments. In general, "biocultural" studies remained heavily focused on the biology of systems but in an attempt correlate the biological variation with variation in the "cultural" environment (Dufour 2006). However, many long-term projects have developed substantial databases of human physiological traits (especially health disorders) correlated with different cultural contexts and patterns.

Anthropology and allied disciplines have demonstrated substantial advances in the understanding of the relationship and interfaces between social structures, cultural behavioral contexts, and human physiology and health. Within this arena of research, there is a focus on comparative approaches to examine health experiences across space and time, ideally linking bioevolutionary approaches and sociocultural fields with medical anthropology in an interstitial position; however, this ideal is seldom fully achieved (Dufour 2006, Panter-Brick and Fuentes, 2008). However, there are several conceptual frameworks in existence that are relevant to the themes of this chapter. In general, those with a focus biased toward the biological see health across populations as shaped by the expression of genetic inheritance and the relative fitness of individuals confronting environmental challenges over evolutionary time (Stinson et al. 2001). For researchers biased toward the social, health experiences are individually and socially constructed often embedded in a hegemonic construction of knowledge (Krieger 2001). The common ground of "biocultural" where both approaches are valorized is advocated by researchers promoting systematic ways of understanding the corelationship of "biology" with "culture", primarily in the evaluation of health disparities within and between populations (Goodman and Leatherman 1998, Hahn 1999, Helman 2001, Kaplan 2004, Dressler 2005, Leatherman 2005, Dufour 2006). This echoes the symbolic dimension of Jablonka and Lamb, the first three premises of DST and the TIV perspective of Odling-Smee et al. (2003). The concept of phenotypic plasticity, and its relation to adaptability, also plays a core role in many of the classic and ongoing studies of human variation in health across and within differing social contexts (Godfrey and Hansen, 2008).

This "biocultural" approach can provide a powerful complement to studies of human behavior, and to our efforts to model the evolution of human behavior. The explicit recognition of mutual engagement between human biology and behavior and a major role of "culture" is central to most of the emerging themes in evolutionary theory as applied to humans; however, the biocultural approach adds a set of methodologies for this integration that is missing from most traditional approaches. It is worth noting that both HBE and gene–culture coevolution/DIT do overlap somewhat, almost by definition, with this biocultural approach. In addition, the focus of niche construction theory on the phenogenotype (and Erlich and Feldman's 2002, "human phenome" see Chapter 5) fits well within the set of assumptions and practices of the biocultural approach. However, while the goal of biocultural studies is to achieve true synthesis and equal valorization of biologically based and culturally based assessment of human behavior and health, they seldom fully achieve that in practice (Panter-Brick and Fuentes, 2008; Dressler, 2008).

A good example of this perspective is the research of Thom McDade in Samoa (McDade 2001, 2002, 2003, 2008). His research examines the relationship between psychosocial stress and the social gradient in health utilizing minimally invasive biomarker methods for physiological assessments in community-based settings. Simultaneously, he highlights the importance of cultural factors in defining social status and its relevance to stress. Taking Selye's (1976) "General Adaptation Syndrome" as a jumping off point, McDade defines "stress" as a process involving interactions between stressors, responses, consequences, and moderators. Stressors are events or situations that disrupt normal functioning and pose "an adaptive challenge to the individual." Responses are the reactions to stressors wherein the individual (and/or his/her physiology) attempts to restore homeostasis, or maintain stability around a new baseline. Responses, while potentially beneficial in the short term, may have deleterious consequences for an individual's health (Sapolsky 2004). Moderators are "the developmental, genetic, or situational factors that contribute to individual differences in the pathways linking stressors, responses, and/or consequences" (McDade, 2008). McDade points out that psychosocial stressors initiate the activation of multiple physiological systems, including neurological and endocrinological pathways, and that it is through these pathways that the stress response and consequences are mediated. Recent reviews demonstrate that stress represents a major means through which our physical and social environments affect human health and behavior.

McDade's research looked at multiple indicators of social status and combined that with physiological measures of stress in Samoan populations. His analyses provide some insight into sources of stress for Samoan adolescent, but his combined observations of youth in Samoa suggested a very complicated set of social dynamics. McDade states

> It was clear that in the context of globalization and local cultural diversification, new markers of social status were beginning to emerge in Samoa, and that tensions and uncertainties associated with reconciling multiple status markers could be an important source of stress. (McDade in press)

He decided to explore the use of models of status inconsistency (the assumption that individuals derive social status from multiple sources) and the possibility that the variation in these factors create social stressors. He examined two distinct social sources, one "traditional" to Samoan society (the presence of a high status "matai" social class in the household) and the other related to globalization/westernization (a more standard economic social status measure), and a set of physiological measures. This approach allowed for dynamic and shifting sets of relationships and local meanings resulting from the integration of cultural elements (the matai system and degree of "western" lifestyle). His results show a significant effect of status incongruity on the physiological measure of stress: adolescents in situations of incongruence had significantly higher indicators of stress than congruent individuals, indicating lower cell-mediated immune function and higher psychosocial stress. However, the simpler summary measure of social status (traditional or western) was not significantly related to the physiological stress level.

McDade states that

> These findings suggest that for the youth of Samoa, discrepancy in two meaningful dimensions of social status—one old (the presence of a matai title in the household) and one relatively new (familiarity with western lifestyles through siblings, friends, travel, and television)—is a significant source of stress. It is worth noting that the direction of incongruity made no difference.

The pattern he reports seems to support that incongruity itself is a source of stress. This is particularly important in the context of assessing human behavior as an integrated system (as in DST) where physiological and social factors are not separate inputs affecting the system but actually entwined dynamic interactors. The products (behavior and physiology) of this interaction are part of an ongoing dynamic interface with broader ecological and cultural contexts as well. Although this is a highly localized and specific example, it has salience in the context of the TIV niche construction model, symbolic and behavioral inheritance systems theory, DIT theory, and, in the historical sense, Baldwin and Morgans' organic evolution.

CAN ADDING THESE PERSPECTIVES TO EXISTING PRACTICE (AS OUTLINED IN CHAPTERS 2 AND 3) IMPACT THE WAY WE FORMULATE AND TEST HYPOTHESES/CONCEPTUALIZATIONS OF HUMAN BEHAVIORAL EVOLUTION?

Yes. Integrating facets of extant theoretical perspectives such as traditional ND-Sociobiology, HBE, EP, DIT, and Memetics with these emerging perspectives can enhance our ability to ask and answer questions about the processes and patterns of human behavioral evolution. However, not all of these perspectives are easily intertwined and in some cases may be relatively contradictory. I suggest that the perspectives covered in this chapter suggest a removal or deemphasis of certain practices, a reinforcement of others, and an expansion of a few specific conceptual tools.

What Practices and Perspectives Should Be Removed or De-emphasized?

In the quest to discover the patterns and processes of human behavioral evolution, in the light of current perspectives on plasticity, development and contingency of systems, the use of optimality models seems to be a relatively weak starting point. Many areas of investigation (including practitioners of HBE and ND-Sociobiology) have already reduced their reliance on optimality modeling as a main tool in the construction of adaptive scenarios, but many behavioral investigations do continue to utilize them. Because of plasticity in behavioral responses, the context sensitivity inherent in development, and the possibilities of multiple successful phenotypes from single genotypes, the notion of optimal patterns becomes a difficult starting point for the development of hypotheses. Multiple inheritance systems and the interdependence of traits further complicate any optimal modeling. This is not to say that optimality models are never of use, rather that the assumption that systems strive toward optimality may be of limited use in trying to model a complex and multimodal system such as the evolution of human behavior.

A focus on the genic level (DNA sequences) as the primary or most important level of selection might misrepresent the patterns of inheritance, development and selection in a behavioral system. Obviously, genic level evolution occurs and is core to the evolution of populations; however, when modeling the evolution of behavioral systems there appears to be a substantial possibility that some evolution occurs without changes to genetic material or without any functional linkage between the changing phenotypes and organisms' genotype. The basal predictions/assumptions of DST and four-dimensional evolution suggest that a focus on selection models privileging the genes will ignore many epigenetic and developmental factors important in behavioral change. Also, biocultural anthropological work demonstrates the complex impact of psychological and social states on physiologies indicating a nonlinear feedback relationship between behavior and physiology. A focus on behavior being rooted in genic selection models may bypass very important causal forces of human biocultural behavior. Shifting cultural contexts and the experientially influenced behavioral responses by humans to them can influence behavioral change across generations without being linked to genic assemblages that favor patterned responses.

The above two suggestions de-emphasize a requisite need for an assumption of "blackbox" linkages between behavioral traits and underlying genetic systems. HBE and ND-Sociobiology approaches to behavioral evolution assume a specific linkage of this manner to enable selection to occur on a given trait. The main Darwinian notion that a trait must have heritable variation to be selected has been, in many cases, converted into the concept that a trait must have some linkage to heritable genetic variation in order for it to be visible to selection. This perspective leads to the assumption of some "blackbox" system linking genes to traits even when the traits themselves are variable and there is no clear evidence of such a linkage. Assuming that there is this direct heritable genetic linkage leads to simplified explanations of behavioral evolution wherein a model of the behavior enhancing reproductive success (thus passing on copies of the genetic sequences underpinning the behavior) is all that is required to explain the ultimate (or bottom line) presence/maintenance of the behavior.

Finally, it is possible that the use of simple proxy measures of fitness, and a reliance on single-trait models, may be misrepresenting behavioral systems. DST, epigenetic systems, and the reality of behavioral plasticity lay out scenarios wherein simple assessment (the use of proxies) of fitness ignores multiple factors in the development and exhibition of behavior that can influence the individual's current and future actions. Because development does not cease at adulthood, and because of the dynamic interplay between the expression of behavior and social context in humans, measuring the potential evolutionary cost of a given behavior, even over some limited portion of the lifetime of the individual, may not reflect the overall impact of the behavior (or behaviors) on the individual's likelihood and capability of passing the behavior across generations. This is not to say that assessing reproductive success is not critical in examining evolutionary patterns, but rather that using such assessments as the only, or necessarily primary, explanatory underpinning of human behavior and behavioral change may be overlooking other factors that contribute to the development and exhibition of the behavior, which also can influence its heritability and patterns of change. The potential impact on reproductive success should not be the only, or necessarily the main, measure of likely maintenance of behavior within a human population. This perspective is not only supported by the views reviewed in this chapter but is also present in EP, Memetics, and DIT, and has its roots in Lloyd Morgan and Baldwin's organic evolution.

What Practices and/or Perspectives Cross
All of These Categories?

Of all the concepts represented in traditional Neo-Darwinian thought and the perspectives reviewed in this chapter, natural selection remains the most prominent and robust. Darwin and Wallace's conceptualization of selection and its subsequent refinements over the last 150 years have stood the test of time and proven to be a core tool in understanding the patterns and processes of behavioral evolution.[7] While there is variation in how central and how dominant a role selection plays in each perspective outlined in this chapter and in Chapters 2 and 3, natural selection plays a prominent role in models and predictions for them all. For ND-Sociobiology, HBE, EP, DIT, and Memetics, natural selection is the only significant force of evolutionary change considered relevant by a vast majority of practitioners. Whereas all would acknowledge other factors influencing genetic and behavioral changes across generations, functional change and ultimate explanations are produced by the action of selection. Gene–culture coevolution and Memetics perspectives emphasize at least an equivalent, or more important, role for selection on behavior (culture units or memes) than on genetic sequences in humans. Sociobiological and Human Behavior Ecological perspectives tend to prioritize the underlying genetic basis for selection, even if it involves a "blackbox" linkage between behavior and genes and the use of proxy measures for genetic fitness. EP focuses on selection as an explanatory tool in modeling the appearance of evolved modules and their associated psychological outcomes, simultaneously incorporating both behavioral and genetic factors without specifically referencing or linking them as units of selection.

In the perspectives from this chapter, Jablonka and Lamb see selection operating at all four dimensions of evolution with differences being in the targets and response patterns of each dimension. However, unlike many of the traditional Neo-Darwinian approaches, they also prioritize structural systems, historical events, and developmental trajectory's roles in shaping and directing the ways in which change can occur and how selection might affect traits. Behavioral plasticity approaches see selection at broader levels than specific traits with the favoring of plastic response systems (such as multiple phenotypes from one genotype). They also see local ecological conditions as a sort of microselection eliciting plastic responses that may or may not have long-term genetic evolutionary impacts on a population. DST acknowledges the importance of selection in shaping systems but raises developmental, historical, and contingent forces to a relatively equal footing in the appearance, expression, and change of traits. This does not devalue

---

[7] Not that natural selection is the only, or necessarily the most potent, force of evolutionary change in behavioral systems, but that its impact has been and continues to be the most prized, measured, and modeled factor in such systems.

the role of selection but adds multiple pathways to the emergence of traits, forcing a more complex approach by adding explanatory (causal) forces to models of evolutionary change (thus selection is not the only "architect" of function). In the niche construction perspective, natural selection shares the main causal (architectural) role in the evolutionary change with niche construction. In this view, niche construction and selection exist in a dynamic nonlinear relationship where both are simultaneously affecting and being affected by one another. Finally, biocultural anthropological approaches are rooted in a natural selection focus most similar to ND-Sociobiology; however, they also see cultural trends and patterns as having immediate and long-term impacts on the expression and development of traits. As with DST and behavioral plasticity approaches, biocultural views endow local ecologies (social and biotic) with a degree of agency in evolutionary change at both behavioral and physiological levels.

Charles Darwin (1871) made a point to highlight the core role for symbolic communication and culture in the lives of humans, as did E.O. Wilson and many evolutionary biologists who have considered human behavioral evolution. Every one of the perspectives reviewed here (including behavioral plasticity as applied to humans) acknowledges human communicative abilities and the use of symbol as a major factor in the evolution and expression of human behavior. However, many of the perspectives vary in their views on the function and current impact of human symbolic communication and culture on behavioral evolution today. Some give it an equivalent (DIT, four-dimensional evolution, niche construction) or even greater (Memetics) role than genetic inheritance systems in modeling human evolution. Others see its causal role in evolutionary change as less than that of genetic systems and see it as emergent from underlying modules (EP) or biological systems (HBE, Sociobiology).

Most of the perspectives reviewed here see the focus on both past and present environments in order to understand the evolution and expression of human behavior as central to understanding human behavioral evolution. EP sees the EEA (past relevant environments during which most human adaptive modules emerged) as the primary locale for understanding evolution, with modern environments more likely to generate maladaptation. HBE sees the present environment as the most important for understanding modern behavior, but like sociobiology, acknowledges that past environments have elicited specific adaptive responses present in modern humans (a phylogenetic effect). DIT views the past as does HBE and ND-Sociobiology, but sees modern cultural contexts as centrally important in shaping human behavioral evolution as well. Memetics sees the modern memic environment as the core factor in behavioral evolution. Evolution in four dimensions and DST see both current and past environments as central without necessarily prioritizing one as more relevant than the other. Niche construction sees a highly dynamic organism–environment system with environments continuously interactive with organisms such that both are constantly changing in response and with one another. This view valorizes past and present equally and gives both primary roles in the explanation of current behavior (as do DST and evolution in four dimensions). Behavioral plasticity approaches look primarily at current environments and their impacts on organisms' phenotypes with (as in nearly all of the perspectives) a strong acknowledgement that past organism–environment interactions have produced adaptive complexes.

Finally, all of the perspectives use some form of "reconstructive scenarios" to propose hypotheses for human behavioral evolution. That is, explanations proposed frequently take the shape of a hypothetical scenario that includes a set of selective factors in an environment (deep past, recent past, or present) that elicited a set of responses, some of which worked well (in an evolutionary sense), and thus were retained in the population (became adaptations). This is a standard format for most of the sciences involved in asking evolutionary questions. However, among the perspectives reviewed here, there are differing emphases on how accurate such scenarios can be, what types of variables can be tested, what qualifies as a test of such hypotheses, and how valuable past scenarios are to understanding modern contexts and behavior. Because of the long life spans in humans and ethical issues surrounding human manipulation, most direct tests (aside from interviews and some observational data collection) are rare in scenarios about modern change/patterns, and testing scenarios about past evolutionary change is limited by the (relative) paucity of human fossils, the availability of archeological information, and our abilities to reconstruct past environments.

What Perspectives Should Be Expanded?

Combining the concepts reviewed in this chapter with the more traditional approaches in Chapters 2 and 3 identifies a number of areas where an expanded focus can better facilitate investigation into the evolution of human behavior. By expanding these foci (below), maintaining emphasis on the perspectives in the previous section and by possibly de-emphasizing certain views (see above), our toolkit for assessing human behavioral evolution will improve.

Many of the current perspectives used in the assessment and analyses of the evolution of human behavior already use multiple loci/levels of selection in their models. DIT, DST, niche construction, and evolution in four dimensions, explicitly acknowledge selection's impact at multiple levels. Other perspectives may include some models that allow for selection beyond the genic level as relevant to human behavioral evolution. However, it is readily apparent from an overview of the human archeological and fossil record that extra-somatic and group and individual behavioral factors constitute a significant portion of our adaptive response potential. Complex cognitive capabilities and language also indisputably contribute to human evolution and behavior. Modeling a system with such diverse inputs and agents, most of which are distant indeed from measurable connections to genetic complexes, without accepting the possibility of selection at multiple levels (and inheritance at multiple levels) would appear to severely limit the potential applicability of models.

Along these same lines an expanded focus on epigenetic systems' agency in evolutionary change might benefit our investigations. DST and evolution in four-dimensional perspectives suggest that epigenetic systems, especially those involved in developmental patterns (including learning and language/ symbol acquisition) may play central roles in the evolution of human behavior. More than just tools to document developmental trajectories, a focus on epigenetic systems can play a core role in structuring/facilitating the available patterns of development, which in turn can have a long-term impact on the systems' pattern and potential for evolutionary change. The development of behavioral patterns, either in concert with epigenetic systems, or as extra-somatic systems running parallel to the somatic systems, can also act in the same manner.

Expanding beyond epigenetic systems of the soma (the body), behavioral and ecological inheritance are also worthy of greater focus. As explicitly described in niche construction, DST, and evolution in four dimensions (even in a sense by Dawkins as the "Extended Phenotype"), ecological inheritance can be a major agent in evolutionary change. Behavioral inheritance is likely of greater importance for humans than for many other organisms. Human cognitive power and ability to transmit large quantities of information on diverse topics enables humans to exploit information as a tool in forming adaptive responses to a greater degree than other organisms. This suggests that this ability alone can facilitate (or hinder, see DIT, EP, and maladaptation, Chapter 3) behavioral change across generations that can impact patterns of energy acquisition and distribution, and even reproductive success.

Because of the substantial potential for phenotypic (behavioral) plasticity in humans and the important implications of plasticity for many organisms (see phenotypic plasticity above), an increased focus on the range and patterns of this plasticity in humans might be important in models of human behavioral evolution. Humans are not infinitely malleable, but do have a variety of behavioral options not generally available to other organisms; we might have to develop more comprehensive tools to incorporate this type of plasticity into our models and hypotheses.

Given behavioral plasticity, the patterns of behavioral inheritance, cognitive complexity, humans' potential ability to rapidly change behavioral patterns, and the significant informational content of human communication, it seems that there is very much a role for behavior as an agent of evolutionary change in humans. Because of these same factors, there is the possibility that behavior can affect change across generations, even impacting reproductive success, without selection acting as a structuring or mediating agent, and still be inherited. So, our functional models (or "ultimate" explanation hypotheses) must be carefully constructed to incorporate or at least recognize this possibility.

There is a startlingly high degree of dynamism and feedback in the human–environment relationship and thus in our evolutionary history, present, and future. From the subjects reviewed in this book, it should be apparent that a number of factors must be introduced into any scenarios/ models for human behavioral evolution. No one perspective is going to be able to encompass a majority or possibly even a necessary minority of salient factors potentially impacting human evolutionary systems. Obviously, basic Neo-Darwinian theory acts as a baseline on which we can lay the framework for our investigations, and elucidating the patterns of selection must remain as a central facet in the construction of hypotheses regarding human behavioral evolution. However, the perspectives reviewed in this chapter strongly argue for the inclusion of a variety of additional facets in such hypotheses. Relying on relatively linear models of environmental selection on organisms and using proxy measures for fitness is probably not sufficient to answer most questions about human behavioral evolution. Therefore, our starting point in constructing hypotheses, heuristic models, and scenarios, requires the acceptance of a view wherein multiple perspectives can make valid contributions to the same question. It is unlikely that anyone will be able to fuse all of the perspectives reviewed her into a new mega-theory (such as Neo-Darwinism), but we can attempt to incorporate various elements from different perspectives into our approaches and analyses.

In 1951, Sherwood Washburn called for a "multidisciplinary and interdisciplinary approach" to the study of human evolution, morphology, and behavior. In Chapter 2, I referred to this call for a "New Physical Anthropology," the initial emergence of a modern evolutionary anthropology perspective. I would like to suggest at this juncture in time (2008) that we are indeed ready for such a new evolutionary anthropology that acts both as a space for integrative investigation and as a broker for linking and communicating across the various disciplines and perspectives involved in the quest to understand the evolution of human behavior. In the next chapter, I will elaborate on this notion and provide a set of examples that reflect an early, and notably incomplete but serious, attempt at this type of approach.

SUGGESTED READINGS

Odling-Smee, F.J., Laland, K.N., and Feldman, M.W. (2003) Niche construction: The neglected process in evolution; Monographs in Population Biology 37. Princeton: Princeton University Press.

Oyama, S., Griffiths, P.E., and Gray, R.D. (Eds.) (2001) *Cycles of contingency: developmental systems and evolution*. Cambridge, MA: The MIT Press.

West-Eberhard, M.J. (2003) Developmental Plasticity and Evolution. New York: Oxford University Press.

CHAPTER 8

A Synthesis and Prospectus for Examining Human Behavioral Evolution

> In anthropology, as elsewhere, progress will never result from destroying what has been previously achieved but rather from incorporating the past of our science into its present and future, enriching the one with the other and turning the whole process into a lasting reality. (Levi-Strauss 1968)

Over the course of the last seven chapters, we have reviewed the basal perspectives on the evolution of human behavior, examined the four main paradigms used in asking questions about the evolution of human behavior, reviewed the fossil and primate comparative record and introduced a set of emerging perspectives that enrich our understandings of evolutionary processes and human evolution. We reviewed a large set of proposals for the evolution of all, or aspects, of human behavior and compared and contrasted their main points and highlighted potentially underrepresented elements. In this chapter, I will attempt to tie much of this together in a twofold approach. Initially, I will lay out a broad perspective for an outline of human behavioral evolution, taking to heart the spirit of Levi-Strauss' quote above. Subsequently, I will take the main commonalities and potentially underrepresented elements from the 38 proposals highlighted in Chapter 6 and discuss each one in the context of what it might mean and/or how it might be best explained by comparative and fossil datasets, the paradigmatic perspectives, my own perspective, and how any of these ideas might actually be tested for validity.

As I present my views, you will notice that it is a hybrid of evolutionary biology and anthropology, or to take Washburn's terminology, what one might consider the new, new physical anthropology. This new physical anthropology is most correctly called biological and biocultural anthropology, although these terms encompass a diverse array of perspectives and paradig-matic orientations. I hope to demonstrate that there are benefits from much in the extant paradigmatic approaches [Neo-Darwinian (ND)-Sociobiology, Human Behavioral Ecology (HBE), Evolutionary Psychology (EP), Dual Inheritance Theory (DIT), Memetics], but that each individually cannot approach the kind of integrative information and theoretical toolkits that are required for advancing our understating of human behavioral evolution in the twenty-first century. I also hope to convince the reader that conflict among perspectives is less fruitful than collaboration, and that such collab-oration is indeed possible. At the start of this book, I reviewed a relatively simple example of behavioral evolution (the fox experiment and dog evolu-tion in Chapter 1) that acted as a test of hypotheses regarding the evolution of both morphology and behavior. The fox/dog example was simple, but drives home a specific point: *traits do not evolve free of the system of which they are a part.* Keep this in mind as we examine in more depth the commonalities and missing elements from the hypotheses and my views.

A SET OF MODEST PROPOSALS EMERGING FROM CHAPTERS 1 TO 7: SEEKING THE BROAD AND THE MINUTE FOCI

Here, I would like to propose a set of ideas as to how we might look at human behavioral evolution and construct integrated hypotheses that, potentially, can be tested using extant or accessible datasets. Rather than relying on one basal paradigm or perspective, I will draw liberally from those we have already reviewed, attempting to highlight both general and specific contri-butions and points of synthesis. First, I will lay out my general perspective and then we will examine the main commonalities and potentially under-represented elements from the 38 proposals highlighted in Chapters 5 and 6 from this perspective. To begin, I propose seven structural contexts that aid in establishing the basal parameters for asking questions about human evolution. These structural contexts emerge from serious consideration of the major perspectives we reviewed in Chapters 2 and 3 combined with ele-ments of the ideas in Chapter 7.

1. That human behavioral evolution must be primarily seen as a system evolving rather than as a set of independent or moderately connected traits evolving. While we might create hypotheses to explain specific behavioral patterns, they must be explicitly connected to broader themes and contexts. Human behavior itself is not a set of individual actions, but rather a consor-tium of action, experience, and innovation.

2. Niche construction is a core factor in human behavioral evolution. The ability of humans to modify their surroundings is central to any explanation of human behavior. These surroundings include the social, the biotic, and the abiotic. Understanding human evolution requires assessing the interac-tive and mutually mutable relationship humans have with their social and structural ecologies. We must accept the possibility that selection pressures can be modified as they are occurring and that human response to selective challenges need not always fit the standard ecological parameters of the selective force. That is, human toolkits (somatic and extra-somatic) might result in innovation that adds elements into a system that standard ecological and selection modeling cannot foresee or does not normally include. For example, behavioral innovation in the use of controlled fire as a response to pressures exerted by climate stress, predation risk, and the extraction of nutrition from complex food sources. We can already see this approach appearing in recent HBE and ND-Sociobiology models.

3. Ecological and social inheritance are core to human behavioral action and change. Emerging from DST and Jablonka and Lambs' proposal, this moves beyond general niche construction. Humans almost always exist in a place where there have been humans before them. Social and ecological parameters are impacted by the previous generations and individuals in subsequent human generations inherit a much larger amount of information than do any other organisms (at least since the advent of rudimentary language and tool use). Even when moving into new territories, humans carry some portion of the knowledge of past members of their group with them (social and material). This provides humans with a broader ability (more ways) to respond to challenges through a more diverse array of means than other organisms. It also might mean that humans can respond at quicker rates than most complex organisms when faced with strong selective challenges. It also means that humans may come upon multiple effective responses to the same challenges and potentially share them across individuals and possibly even groups.

4. Enhanced communication and information transfer is core to modeling and understanding human behavior. While already core to most perspectives on human behavioral evolution, it is worth reemphasizing that humans use their extensive ability to convey information to respond to the basic ecological challenges that they face; thus models should include a role for a type of communication not possible in other organisms.[1]

5. Feedback rather than linear models are central in human behavioral evolution. This is probably true for most evolutionary models in complex multicellular organisms; however it should be explicit in hypotheses and models for humans (as it already is in many). Feedback in a system implies that rather than moving from A to B, the system may modify itself during the processes of acting. If feedback is a component of a system, outcomes are not necessarily based on the initial behavioral pattern within the system. Human responses to predation pressures or foraging challenges might be

---

[1] It is highly possible that some or all cetaceans have a more complex communication ability than other organisms as well. Other highly social mammals, especially the primates, do use a wider array of social interactions to convey information; however, none approach the depth and density of information potentially transferable even with rudimentary language.

good examples, with constant modification of human behavior based on the experiences and patterns of the humans and of the predators/prey or forage targets.

6. We should consider the potential impacts of all forces that shuffle variation in evolutionary change; selection, gene flow, and genetic drift; and the possibility that selection can occur at multiple levels. Most hypotheses for the evolution of human behavior rely strictly on natural selection as the only significant evolutionary force in the structuring of human behavior. However, we should also include possible impacts from gene flow and drift in genetic, phenotypic, and behavioral responses. DIT and Memetics focus on the possibility that selection acts on human cultural behavior; here I extend that and suggest that patterns of flow and drift can impact behavior as well as genotypic factors. Selection need not always be invoked to explain the innovation and spread of behavior. When it is invoked, we should also be prepared to include models that accept selection as acting on levels beyond a selfish gene or selfish individual focus (as highlighted by Sober and Wilson 1998, Oyama 2000, Oyama et al. 2001, Odling-Smee et al. 2003 Wilson and Wilson 2007).

7. Our models must include a specific role for flexibility and plasticity in behavioral response as a baseline as opposed to assumptions of optimality striving or single trait maximization. It is most likely that the majority of human responses that result in behavioral change over time are not optimal, even if they do result in adaptation. It is likely that the majority of successful human responses reflect a pattern of plasticity and flexibility resulting from a cohort of selection pressures as opposed to specific selection for a particular adaptation in response to a single selective pressure. This suggests that explanations that focus primarily on the link of a particular behavior to a specific adaptive outcome may be poor models for many processes in human behavioral evolution.

Using these seven structural guidelines as a framework, we can attempt to examine major elements in human history (such as predation, material and social manipulation, foraging, the raising of young, mate choice, conflict, and cooperation) as facets of the human niche and attempt to model patterns of evolutionary change using modern human behavior, primate- and hominoid-wide trends, and the fossil record as testing grounds. Here, the focus is on biocultural engagement, not simply gene–culture coevolution, but true interpretation of humans as biocultural organisms.

Testability in behavioral models is difficult, especially when true controls are rare or impossible such as with humans or any other long-lived large-bodied organism. As in all of science, we can support and refute our hypotheses but never really confirm them 100%. This openness to imperfection of explanations and constant modification of perspectives is core to continued discovery in all of science but is especially relevant, and must be kept at the forefront, during investigations into human behavior (see Chapter 9). In addition to the seven structural guidelines, there are also a set of four questions we can ask about hypotheses or models of human behavioral evolution:

1. Are there data points from the fossil record that address elements of the hypothesis/model? Does any aspect of the fossil record affect the structure of the hypothesis/model?

2. Are there data points from the material/archeological record that address elements of the hypothesis/model? Does any aspect of the material record affect the structure of the hypothesis/model?

3. Are there any aspects/factors/patterns of the primate or mammalian comparative dataset that pertains to the hypothesis/model? There is danger of falling into the poor analogy/homology trap here. For comparisons to be appropriate you need to specify one or more of the following rationales for your comparison of the human and primate/mammalian elements; a phylogenetic fit (true homology), an ecological fit (true analogy), a social fit (social analogy), or a physiological fit (physiological homology).[2]

4. Does some facet/pattern of modern human behavior as evidenced via ethnographic observations, survey/interview research or experimental manipulation address elements of the hypothesis/model?

The types of datasets we use affect any hypothesis/model. Asking all four of these questions about each proposal or hypothesis about human behavioral evolution increases the chances of a higher quality, and thus more informative, result. It also makes the investigation more difficult, time consuming, and multi/interdisciplinary. Trying to be as inclusive as possible expands the potential validity of the hypothesis/model; however, one must avoid use of "common knowledge/cultural assumptions" or popular knowledge as baseline for these kinds of assessments as such biases can corrupt examinations of the four areas of questioning through unintentional filtering of data (see Chapter 9 for more on this).

LOOKING AT THE AREAS OF OVERLAP AND INTEREST FROM CHAPTER 6

In this section, we will apply the above perspective to elements of commonality and elements that should be further considered from the six themes from Chapters 5 and 6 (cooperation, conflict, diet/food, ecology/environment, sex/reproduction, and specific behaviors). For each, we will briefly examine relevant elements in the fossil data and comparative primate/mammalian comparative data, review what the traditional paradigmatic views

---

[2] Here, *analogy* implies a justified comparison due to functional similarities of the systems/traits of interest and *homology* indicates a justified comparison due to a phylogenetic (evolutionary lineage) connection of the systems/traits of interest.

(EP, HBE, ND-Sociobiology, Memetics, and DIT) might say about it, and what I think about it. Finally, we will address a few comments regarding possible testability of the ideas.

The citations used in this section are purposefully limited. I chose primarily recent review articles (when possible), seminal articles on the topic, or recent articles that address the issue particularly well. I did this so as not to rely on strings of citations making the reading and comprehension less fluid. This, however, does result in minimal citations throughout this chapter relative to the actual amount of work in each area discussed. If you are drawn to one or more of the areas, please follow up not only with the citations I provide but also delve a bit deeper into the literature. You will find that for many, but not all, of these topics, there is a rich and frequently quite diverse set of articles coming from many disciplines and theoretical perspectives.

Cooperation Commonalities

Intragroup Cooperation

Fossil Data: Cooperation within groups of humans and possible human ancestors can largely be inferred from a few factors in the fossil record. The primary indicator of cooperation is group living. The earliest (~3 million years ago) example of a fossil dataset reflecting group living are the *Australopithecus afarensis* (AL 333) remains from Hadar in East Africa described in Chapter 4. This sample represents a collection of approximately 13 individuals of varying ages who all appeared to have perished in the same event. This suggests that in early possible human ancestors, multiadult and mixed age–sex class groups occurred. Later finds of more recent human ancestors, such as those at Sima de los Huesos (Atapuerca, Spain) from approximately 4 to 500,000 years ago, support even larger multiadult groupings (Bermudez de Castro et al. 2004). At Sima de los Huesos, at least 32 individuals form a mixed age group using the same areas and working together on material and possible social elements, with the fossil accumulation in the cave possibly the result of active disposal of bodies in the cave by members of the group (Arsuaga et al. 1997, Bermudez de Castro et al. 2004). These fossils have numerous injuries and some evidence of disease, some of which did not result in the death of the individuals, suggesting the possibility of intragroup care. We see only a few individuals over the age of approximately 35 years. As we get closer in time to modern day there are more and more finds of groups of fossils together. Between 100,000 and 20,000 years ago, we find evidence of aged individuals and individuals with significant injuries that did not kill them, but would have left them challenged at obtaining food and protecting themselves, thus directly suggesting assistance from other group members. We also begin to see evidence of deliberate burials in the fossil record indicating collaboration by group members regarding a postmortem practice.

The archeological record from approximately 2.5 million years ago through the recent past is rich in human ancestor/human modified stones and the more recent record (1 million years on through the present) has evidence of humans modifying a wide array of inorganic and organic substances. These items all show both consistent and improving patterns across time indicating specific teaching/learning in the creation of the items. From quite early (~2 million years ago) there are indications of multiple tool makers at fossil sites with tools and, in many cases, the raw materials had been transported to the site from various distances. Both of these factors strongly, albeit indirectly, suggest cooperation with groups or at least within segments of groups. The fossil and archeological records provide both direct and indirect support to the assumption that intragroup cooperation predates *Homo sapiens* in the *Homo* and hominin lineage. This suggests that substantial intragroup cooperation is an important evolutionary baseline (preexisting condition) for human behavior.

Comparative Data: The vast majority of nonhuman primates live in multiadult mixed sex groups that exhibit moderate cooperation such as in antipredator defense and alarm calling, group defense in intergroup encounters, and food calling. Within groups, it is common for individuals to form coalitions and alliances over the course of social interactions. The style and pattern of such cooperative interactions depend largely on the social structure of the species in question and vary in duration and intensity. In many primates, philopatric[3] kin form cooperative alliances at higher frequencies than do non-kin and such alliances can be related to social manipulation, infant care, and foraging success (Bernstein 2007, Fuentes 2007, Gouzoules and Gouzoules 2007, Susman and Garber 2007). Slightly more complex cooperation is reported for chimpanzee males who form subgroups to patrol and defend their home range boundaries and also possibly use mild cooperation/coordination in hunting behavior (Stumpf 2007). There is also extensive cooperation between offspring and mothers and occasionally other adults during the process of tool use acquisition in chimpanzees. However, all nonhuman primate species display lower rates and intensities and types of cooperation than in modern human groups.

Paradigmatic Views (EP, HBE, ND-Sociobiology, Meme, DIT): As evident from the overviews of the specific paradigms and the hypotheses, selfish orientation, and individual cost/benefit analyses underlie the majority of explanations for cooperation. Cooperation is assumed to have a cost relative to going it alone, even when cooperation improves outcomes relative to individual action, the underlying explanatory motives remain oriented towards explaining increased individual fitness. ND-Sociobiology and EP are concerned with Tinbergen's ultimate level explanation for cooperation, which, under their rubric, must have some fitness benefit for actors in order to allow its maintenance in a population. EP might explain the maintenance of these behaviors via an evolved "module" of intergroup cooperation that

---

[3] Philopatric means staying in the group one is born into (natal group). In many primate species, either males or females are philopatric, but never both. In a few species, both males and females disperse from the natal group.

is now an adaptation. Memetics and DIT allow for cooperation as a possible cultural (or memic) adaptation or outcome, but still model it as being maintained primarily via a fitness benefit (be it reproductive, cultural or memic fitness). HBE looks for the immediate or proximate payoffs in the ecological, energetic, or mating/reproductive sense to explain why cooperation occurs. ND-Sociobiology and HBE also envision the possibility of a pattern of reciprocal exchange over individuals' lifetimes that offer some form of evolutionary benefit to the cooperating individuals. Most of the main paradigms also see intragroup cooperation as a core factor in intergroup competition. Darwin and E.O. Wilson, and thus most of their intellectual descendants, see competition between groups driving cooperation within groups, possibly giving better cooperating groups a selective advantage (see Sober and Wilson 1998 as this is a core factor in multilevel evolutionary schema; also see explicit positing of a model for this in Bowles 2006). All of the traditional paradigms see cooperation as something that "costs" the individual in some fitness measure; thus explanations for intragroup cooperation center around models of benefits derived by the individual participants. We have already reviewed these models and they include kin selection, tit-for-tat exchanges, and reciprocal altruism, for example (Chapters 2 and 5).

My Thoughts: Do we really need to explain the majority of intragroup cooperation via specific adaptive models? Is it possible that the most basic, or parsimonious, explanation is simply phylogenetic inertia? That is, general intragroup cooperation might be a broad pattern common to human ancestors and enhanced in early humans relative to other primates, but today a basic part of our phenotype. I do not mean a specific adaptive module, rather a general pattern that is maintained via selection, ecological and social inheritance, and has become a central facet of the human niche. Early in human, or hominin, evolutionary history, the selection benefits may have been as proposed by Darwin and E.O. Wilson (among many others) but the general patterns are a broad adaptation for cooperation with group members. We can then examine specific patterns of cooperation in groups, assess whether they are different from general cooperative trends and look for possible cultural, experiential, contextual, and/or selective (fitness-based) hypotheses to explain their occurrence. Here, daily cooperation in a variety of tasks and social exchanges would not require explaining, but situations such as the establishment of a new within-group hierarchy, negotiation after severe disputes, or the pattern of distribution of a highly valued and rare commodity might (such an approach is already common in many primatological and HBE scenarios).

An analogy for what I am proposing is the fact that humans have four limbs. This is a phylogenetic (evolutionarily historical) factor that no one currently tries to explain via specific hypotheses when discussing human behavior and morphology. We use our four limbs in mundane, but extremely important ways everyday, requiring no specific adaptive scenario. However, when we start to consider patterns of use that fall outside of generalized contexts, such as distance running or dancing, we can then focus on the specific use of the limbs and the context in which these uses occur and attempt to construct explanatory scenarios (hypotheses). However, these hypotheses should include the range of possibilities, not just evolutionary fitness-based solutions (i.e., natural selection as the only important factor).

Testability: How would we test for underlying causal factors of intragroup cooperation? HBE and biocultural anthropology have the strongest existing methodological approaches to testing specific behavioral patterns, collecting data ethnographically and physiologically. DIT and Memetics allow for the possibility that behavior is nonfitness based and this can be expanded to include cultural anthropological and sociological approaches to such questions. In cases of cooperation within groups, if we assume a broad basal phenotype of cooperation, focus on the details of the cooperative behaviors in question, and allow for the possibilities that there are not necessarily reproductive fitness enhancing factors underlying the behavior, we can construct a variety of hypotheses and attempt to test them. There are also a wide array of mathematical applications to testing such assumptions (see Heinrich et al. 2004 and Bowles 2006, for examples). Fossil and archeological datasets influence the concept of a broad basal pattern, not the modern specifics. Tests of the broad basal pattern then would involve reconstructions of fossil contexts and developing scenarios for the evolution/enhancement of such patterns of cooperation from a generalized primate or ape baseline. However, as with all reconstructive hypotheses, the reality of accurately testing them is far lower than hypotheses that apply to living humans.

Male–Female Cooperation

Fossil Data: Aside from finding mixed sex fossil assemblages, the fossil record has very little to offer regarding male and female cooperation not covered in the section on intragroup cooperation (above). In many of the earlier forms (some Australopithecines and early *Homo*) there is debate as to the sex of some fossils, so the record is cloudy even at the level of representation of males and females in the fossil record. Most hominin species prior to modern humans do appear to exhibit greater sexual dimorphism than current humans. Males in the early hominins are substantially larger than females, and recent *Homo erectus* finds suggest that even in that species dimorphism may have been significantly large than in modern forms (Spoor et al. 2007). In many mammals, and primates especially, sexual dimorphism is correlated with conflicts between males but is equivocal on male–female relationships (sometimes stronger bonds, other times more antagonistic ones). However, the extreme success of our species suggests that male–female cooperation has a long history, but the bones tell us very little.

Comparative Data: In the majority of primate species, there is little documentation of extensive heterosexual cooperation in multiadult groups. In two-adult and pair-bonded species, there is frequently a high degree of cooperation between the adult male and female; however, even in such groups, this is not a consistent pattern across species (Fuentes 2002). In some cercopithecine species (such as baboons and macaques), cooperative male–female relationships not necessarily tied to reproductive relationships can occur (sometimes referred to as "friendships") (Jolly 2007, Thierry 2007). In many species of monkeys, males and females form temporary alliances and coalitions involved in negotiating social hierarchies. This is less common in the apes, except perhaps in the gorillas where males and females do form strong bonds; however, these are usually related to reproductive as well as social interactions (Robbins 2007). High rates of cooperation between male and female adults do occur in some gibbon species; however, these apes are primarily found in two-adult groups, not necessarily comparable to humans or human ancestors.

Paradigmatic Views (EP, HBE, ND-Sociobiology, Meme, DIT): For the majority of the traditional paradigms, competition reigns as the main underpinning element in the relationship between males and females. All of these perspectives see a significant conflict of interest in mating strategies (most explicitly laid out in EP: males seek increased reproductive opportunities and females seek increased reproductive quality) tied to differential parental investment requirements and patterns by males and females. This results in males and females attempting to manipulate one another for selfish fitness-based reasons in their relationships. All also see sexual selection as playing a core role in the formation of strategies that lead to male–female competition and behavior. Simultaneously, most accept that males and females do need to collaborate, especially in regard to child rearing; however, these collaborations are construed as having emerged as competitive compromises. The human sexual division of labor is viewed by ND-Sociobiology and HBE largely as a form of cooperation, but arising primarily via the differential reproductive interests and physical capabilities of males and females. EP sees the different strategies as precluding a basal pattern of cooperation but actual behavior as a form of negotiated compromise between males and females. DIT sees an integration of cultural and physical aspects resulting in the division of labor, with the outcome also being a form of cooperative endeavor between the sexes. Memetics by definition would have competitive memes controlling these patterns. See sexual division of labor and heterosexual pair-bond for elaborations on these themes below.

My Thoughts: It is likely that humans exhibit a much higher degree of heterosexual cooperation than other primates or mammals. I am not as convinced that males and females practice such distinct mating strategies as is held by EP (and also in ND-Sociobiology) and this point is currently being debated in the sexuality literature (see Schmidt 2005 and the associated commentary for an overview of this debate). I am also not fully convinced that the conflict between the sexes deriving from differential parental investment precludes a heightened degree of cooperation. It might even be that increased intersexual cooperation is a means to ameliorate the conflicts over reproductive differences. I suggest that one of the unique factors in human behavioral evolution was the emergence of significant cooperation between sexes not only as a component of intragroup cooperation but also as it relates to child rearing. Humans have a very complex sexuality and patterns of social bonding, both of which I think are related to an ability to engage in cooperative interactions at a level not seen in other organisms. See heterosexual pair bond and sexual division of labor below for further elaboration of these ideas.

Testability: Testing both conflict and cooperation between the sexes relies heavily on behavioral observations, surveys, and interviews. However, a more rigorous physiological assessment of the actual differences and similarities in costs of reproduction and reproductive behavior between human males and females might also be important. We currently assume much higher costs for females than males, and this forms the basis for our assumptions of conflict, but actual measurements of both sexes' investment across long time frames are quite rare. We also are just beginning to see investigation into hormonal profiles and contexts of cooperative interactions between the sexes, and area that may open new avenues for testing predictions (Story et al. 2000, Carter and Cushing 2004). In addition, cross-cultural assessments of male and female cooperation and patterns of interaction are missing from the majority of the literature on human behavioral evolution. Ethnographic datasets from the Human Area Relations Files and a broad array of ethnographies might inform these approaches. Currently, practitioners of HBE have largely focused on gathering extensive datasets on a small set of pastoralist, horticulturalist, and foraging societies (Ache, Hadza, Yanomamao, and so on) and EP practitioners have focused on using broad surveys on large demographic samples and specific interview and game modeling with small samples to address these issues. DIT practitioners have to an extent begun to synthesize these two approaches in their datasets (Heinrich et al. 2004). However, most reconstructive approaches still use a generalized model of a fictitious hunter-gatherer population to assume patterns in human evolution; this limits our testing of hypotheses and should be replaced by the actual datasets that continue to emerge.

Same-Sex Cooperation

Fossil Data: As with the two cooperation categories above, the fossil record has little to say in regards to same-sex cooperation. As noted, the early hominins and even early members of the genus *Homo* tend to show greater degrees of sexual dimorphism than modern humans. This is generally thought to indicate higher levels of male–male competition for access to females and one-male–multifemale groups (Plavcan and van Schaik 1997a). In such a case, there is the assumption of higher female–female competition for social access to the main male in the group. However, there is no fossil evidence suggesting one-male groups in hominins or early humans, the only multiadult fossil finds include more then one adult male. Also, in the highly dimorphic fossils, dimorphism is generally related to overall body size and robusticity, but not canine tooth size (see Chapter 4 and primate comparative below). By the time we see archaic *H. sapiens* (~400–100,000 years ago, forms such as *Homo heidelbergensis* and the Neanderthals) fossil show levels of dimorphism similar to modern humans. Low levels of dimorphism are theoretically linked to less overt male–male competition.

Comparative Data: As noted above, early hominins and members of the genus *Homo* show high levels of dimorphism. In many primate species, such male-biased dimorphism is associated with heightened male–male competition for females (Plavcan and van Schaik 1997b). In particular, these species tend to show not only body size dimorphism but also very large canine tooth dimorphism that has been associated with male display and contest competition for females. In dominance contests, males do tend to form alliances and coalitions with select other males, but the longevity of such alliances varies widely. In these same species (such as baboons, macaques, and langur monkeys) related females tend to form strong coalitions and alliances called matrifocal units. These are essentially female kin networks. In these cases, unrelated females do not tend to form close bonds and alliances. Of all the apes, only in chimpanzees do we see strong male–male cooperative alliances and coalitions that are not necessarily kin based (Mitani et al. 2000). There appears to be a high degree of variability in same-sex cooperation across primates.

Paradigmatic Views (EP, HBE, ND-Sociobiology, Meme, DIT): The majority of these views do hold that high levels of same-sex cooperation can and do occur mainly for the exploitation of opposite sex, within-group dominance contests, or group defense during intergroup aggression (male) or protection from aggressive males and assistance with child rearing (female). As with the other facets of cooperation, most of these perspectives seek to examine the cooperative act, or pattern of such acts (EP), in terms of its potential fitness benefit to actors (or to culture units or memes for DIT and Memetics) and predominantly see cooperation emerging as a beneficial way to deal with the pressures brought on by competition (with other groups, costs of child rearing, with other members of same group, and so on).

My Thoughts: Although same-sex cooperation does occur in many primate species, usually only in one sex only, modern humans are different from other primates in that both sexes form strong same-sex cooperative alliances regularly. These cooperative relationships are frequently kin related, but that kinship can be biological or cultural, or both. There are also numerous examples of non-kin related same-sex cooperation in modern humans. It is possible that this is simply a by-product of the general pattern of cooperation that characterizes humans; however, there may be specific adaptive patterns in humans related to same-sex cooperative interactions and bonding (see pair-bonding below). Because cooperation and bonding are so ubiquitous in human groups, I think that a focus on the context of cooperation is extremely important to assess any specific function or adaptation aside from general cooperative behavioral patterns. In particular, a focus on the pattern of development of cooperation over individuals' lifetimes and the patterns of cooperative interactions within the society at large seems particularly relevant. Social inheritance of patterns and trends seems to be a strong factor in human behavior and it is possible that specific cooperative patterns, above and beyond the general trend towards cooperation, may arise in groups/societies via a variety of means. Careful assessment of context is important. We need to be especially careful of using nonhuman primate analogies based on assumptions about the behavioral affiliates of sexual dimorphism as it appears that humans and our ancestors may have shown different correlations between differential body size and behavior between the sexes.

Testability: As with the above two cooperative elements, the fossil record has a few hints but no clear answers. The material record also suggests cooperation in tool making early on and more recently in building projects, hunting, and foraging. The advent of agriculture requires intensive cooperation, but these are all indicators of general cooperative patterns and do not necessarily reflect specific same-sex scenarios. The approaches currently used by HBE and EP are of great value here as ethnographic data collection and cooperation game scenarios provide some of the only testable datasets for these patterns. However, we should also utilize cultural anthropological datasets more heavily to get contextualized ideas about patterns of cooperative behavior as they occur in the thick ethnographic context rather than isolated foci as in HBE and EP experiments. Because of the human ability to utilize linguistic and complex semantic elements in forming and disrupting cooperative alliances, we should be extremely wary of using nonhuman primate analogies in any testing role larger than confirming generalized basal patterns on which humans can expand.

Food Sharing

Fossil Data: The fossil physical evidence for increased metabolic costs (increased body and brain size, see Chapter 4) suggest that something occurred in human evolutionary history that allowed our ancestors to effectively meet increased energetic needs. It is widely assumed that this was a set of mixed foraging strategies that included hunting and gathering. The material record shows increased complexity of tool assemblages, especially those associated with archaic and modern *H. sapiens*. This increased complexity of the foraging record is robust material support for the sharing of food items. Both the tools and the foods require collaborative processing, suggesting that group effort, and thus group sharing, occurred.

Comparative Data: Food sharing is uncommon in most primates aside from mother–infant sharing (usually unidirectional mother to infant). Occasional food sharing between nonmother adults and immatures occurs in many primate species but is sporadic and not ubiquitous. Food sharing between adults is extremely rare. Chimpanzees are the one other primate species that appears to share food regularly. Both species of chimpanzee *Pan troglodytes* and *Pan paniscus* share prized food items among certain adults. This social food sharing is tied to negotiation of social alliances and hierarchies and cannot be explained via simple energetic or reproductive strategy models (Mitani and Watts 2001).

Paradigmatic Views (EP, HBE, ND-Sociobiology, Meme, DIT): Because of the role of food as a fitness proxy (energy), the sharing of food is seen as important, especially for HBE, EP, and ND-Sociobiology. Energy is expended in acquiring food, different individuals have differential ability at hunting/gathering and thus the distribution of collected energy (food) becomes a central factor in modeling human fitness acquisition and loss. HBE and DIT explicitly see much in food sharing as relationships between social prestige (cultural fitness or societal value) and nutritional requirements. It is often modeled that individuals, good hunters, for example, will take a loss in nutritional energy for the trade of benefit in social prestige [see the example by Hawkes and Bleige Bird (2002) in Chapter 3]. The sharing and theft of food are seen as a central area for examining the ways in which human behavioral strategies play out in specific social contexts. There is also the consideration, in all of these perspectives, that food sharing might serve as a model for using broader fitness currencies in modern societies. The use of monetary wealth or prestige goods as proxy for fitness in these perspectives derives largely from the basal pattern of food sharing and distribution and its assumedly central importance in human evolution.

My Thoughts: This is yet another human behavior that radically exceeds what we see in other primates and is likely a factor that gave a competitive edge to our ancestors. The basal pattern is obviously ancestral for our species and thus probably requires no specific functional hypotheses at this point. However, the contexts and patterns of food sharing behavior, as noted above, are of central concern as we try to understand how human behavior plays out across groups/societies/cultures. The role of nutrition and its relationship to social status are central questions for the study of human behavior. In the light of radically changing diets and health contexts for many human populations, the linkage or disequilibrium between such patterns is of great interest and biocultural anthropologists are currently making strong headway in examining such patterns and their physiological and potentially evolutionary impacts (see Ulijaszek and Lofink 2006, for a focus on obesity in a biocultural evolutionary perspective).

Testability: While there is no need to test general patterns of food sharing, as it is ubiquitous in humans, specific behavior and health correlates are relevant. Testing behavior related to food is relatively easy via observations and tying it directly into measures of nutrition is also easy, given the technologies we have for assessing caloric and other nutritional elements in foodstuffs. Given the recent and growing focus on human physiological plasticity and strategies that emerge during development in response to nutritional cues and stressors (such as the Barker hypothesis/metabolic syndrome hypotheses, see Godfrey and Hanson 2008 for review), a focus on the behavior surrounding food use and sharing may provide insight into modern human health, the possibility of Baldwin effects in modern humans, and the ways in which our physiologies may be changing/responding to the social and nutritional environments we have constructed.

Cooperation Factors that Deserve Further Examination

Intergroup

Fossil Data: Again, the fossil record show little evidence in support of intergroup cooperation. However, it is also important to note that it does not show evidence against intergroup cooperation. As early as 800,000 years ago, some *Homo* remains show evidence of postmortem modification by stone tools. This has been widely interpreted as cannibalism and is seen occasionally throughout the human fossil record (Walker 2001). Whether this indicates intergroup aggression (negating intergroup cooperation) is equivocal. Solid indications of intergroup violence and aggression, eventually warfare, become most evident in the more recent archeological record, especially in the last 10,000 years (Walker 2001). The same time period also shows increased intergroup trade and other forms of cultural and material exchanges.

   Comparative Data: There is no evidence for broad-scale intergroup cooperation in nonhuman primates. While most species are not territorial as strictly defined,[4] most do defend core areas of their ranges from groups of the same species and are rarely seen in calm spatial association with neighboring groups. In some species, such as gibbons, individuals may disperse into neighboring groups such that clusters of groups tolerate each other or even form affiliative "neighborhoods" based on kinship and familiarity (see Fuentes 2000). At best, nonhuman primates occasionally show tolerance and affiliation between groups, but there is no indication that any species regularly display any substantive level of intergroup cooperation.

   Paradigmatic Views (EP, HBE, ND-Sociobiology, Meme, DIT): All the major paradigms assume that intergroup competition is a core factor driving human behavioral evolution and that intergroup cooperation is rare. While both Darwin and E.O. Wilson held out the possibility for intergroup cooperation in human evolution, neither championed its possibilities.

   My Thoughts: I do hold out the possibility that intergroup cooperation has played a role in human behavioral evolution. Modern human groups do cooperate, sometimes. Given the fossil record, it is quite possible, as I suggested in Chapter 6, that the relatively high frequency of intergroup conflict is a recent phenomena in human evolutionary history. Not that it was not present in the distant past, but that sedentism, material hierarchies, unequal distribution of good, and agricultural patterns increased the value

---

[4] Strictly defined a territorial group maintains exclusive use of its entire home range defending all parts of it from incursion by conspecifics from other groups.

of intergroup conflicts and thus their frequency. The ethnographic record is rife with examples of groups cooperating in historical and modern times. Frequently, these cooperative interactions involve some form of complementary engagement, such as between forest gatherers and forest edge pastoralists or between groups that unify in the face of ecological challenges or even challenges from other groups. I propose that it is this flexibility, the ability to possibly partner with other groups rather than always competing with them, that gave our ancestors an advantage relative to other hominins or other mammals and facilitated our extremely successful expansion. Here, it is the extension of our generalized cooperative abilities beyond the local group that might have acted as a potential behavioral response to ecological or social pressures that allowed humans to excel. This again can be seen as setting up a particular kind of ecological and social inheritance that can alter the kinds of available options for humans in times of increased selective pressures. I am not suggesting that intergroup cooperation is ubiquitous or even particularly common, just that is does occur and might be an important factor in the human toolkit for dealing with selective pressures and is thus evolutionarily relevant.

Testability: To test my assertion of potential intergroup cooperation as having been adaptive for humans we can look to the archeological record and examine the rise of trading networks and regional affiliations via the transport of materials. Even as early as *H. erectus*, materials used in the construction of stone tools occasionally came from long distances away; this suggests possible alliances between groups related to the access and transport of such materials (but does not necessitate such cooperation). Using modern ethnographic datasets also allows us to test the relative density of intergroup cooperation in different areas of the planet, giving us an assessment tool of its frequency and patterns. Finally, game theory models that have long been held to show interindividual and intergroup competition have also recently been shown to also show increased cooperative patterns in many societies (Heinrich et al. 2004), opening the door for some intergroup cooperation.

Across Age Class

Fossil Data: The few examples of mixed age groups in the fossil record provide equivocal support to the notion that immatures contributed in a significant manner to the group through cooperative endeavors.

Comparative Data: The primate comparative datatset does not provide strong support for the role of immatures as true cooperative partners. While young individuals do participate in aggression and affiliation, they are generally not sought out by adults as cooperative partners. In some species, such as Barbary or Tibetan macaques (*Macaca sylvanus* and *Macaca thibetana*) males use infants as social tools in male–male interactions (Thierry 2007), but it is not accurate to portray the infants themselves as having substantial agency in the interactions. Older immatures begin to play larger roles in group social life but this is primarily as they begin to integrate into adult behavioral patterns. There is, however, a good deal of literature on the conflicts and affiliation patterns between immatures and adults, but little in it suggest frequent cooperative behavior related to specific outcomes.

Paradigmatic Views (EP, HBE, ND-Sociobiology, Meme, DIT): In general, immatures are relatively ignored in regard to cooperative contributions (except in the cooperative breeding hypotheses, see Chapter 5). EP and ND-Sociobiology focus frequently on the immature–adult conflict especially in regards to parental investment and issues such as weaning and decisions about reducing investment in older immatures relative to infants. Some HBE studies have looked at the contribution of older siblings to child rearing and general food gathering.

My Thoughts: Because of the widespread food sharing, the large costs of infant rearing and the complex social networks within human groups, it seems to me that immatures of different ages may have more important roles in human evolutionary history than other primates (see Hrdy 1999, Kramer 2004). For example, immatures' caretaking of siblings or younger group members and assistance in foraging are patterns that are very common in modern human groups. I suggest that cooperation between adults and immatures was more common and that immatures contributed more to the social and ecological functioning of the group in humans and our ancestors than in the other primates. This is another area where I see a human difference and a behavior pattern that gave us an edge in dealing with ecological pressures. If immatures are able to contribute in foraging success and survivorship of young, then there are benefits that might result in immature–adult cooperation being a salient factor in human behavioral evolution.

Testability: My assertion is relatively easy to demonstrate in modern human groups, but very difficult to test for past humans and human ancestors. Relative contribution to the material record by immatures is near impossible to assess without written, oral, or observational data. The best test of this perspective is probably to examine the patterns and contexts of immatures' contribution in modern human societies and the range of capabilities displayed by immatures and attempt to model scenarios of the past where this may have had an impact. I admit that this perspective is not going to ever be well documented or supported by these measures as having played an important role in our evolution.

Conflict Commonalities

Intergroup

Fossil Data: As mentioned in the intergroup cooperation section, the fossil record shows abundant evidence for intergroup conflict in the very recent past, but is largely equivocal for human remains that predate the advent of sedentism and agriculture. There is evidence of postmortem defleshing or modification of crania and other bones as early as 800,000 years ago, but no clear examples of damage clearly attributable to intergroup aggression/

conflict. It is equally likely that the defleshing is associated with ritual or nutritional cannibalism (intra- or intergroup) and/or some form of cultural postmortem modification. It is also not clear from the fossil record what kinds of population densities were typical of most human ancestors and early humans. It is generally assumed that densities were low, but whether they regularly reached levels that were sufficient to cause specific conflict over resources and/or space is not clear.

Comparative Data: While many species of primates defend core areas within their home ranges (see intergroup cooperation above), there is a wide range of patterns of between-group conflict. The majority of same-species between-group conflicts involve vocal and visual displays, occasionally escalating to the level of physical aggression. One species of chimpanzees (*P. troglodytes*) provide a much stronger case of serious intergroup conflict, with at least one subspecies (*Pan troglodyetes schweinfurthii*) exhibiting relatively frequent lethal intergroup conflicts (Wilson and Wrangham 2003, Stumpf 2007). These conflicts arise when border-patrolling groups of males encounter single individuals or small groups from neighboring communities (groups), usually resulting in the death or severe beating of one or more individuals. This behavior is not seen in *P. paniscus* or other ape species. Lethal intergroup aggression is occasionally seen in some cercopithecoid monkeys, such as baboons and macaques, but is extremely rare. Most severe conflict in such cases is intragroup.

Paradigmatic Views (EP, HBE, ND-Sociobiology, Meme, DIT): Given the emphasis on genetic relationships (biological kinship), cost/benefit fitness analyses of behavioral strategies, and a notion that competition is common in moving systems or traits towards fitness enhancement in all of these approaches, it is not surprising that intergroup conflict is central to their hypotheses. These views tend to assume that intergroup competition is a core factor driving human behavioral evolution and that intergroup cooperation is therefore rare. There is abundant evidence from modern human groups and in the more recent archeological datasets to support the contention that, at times, intergroup conflict is common in (or between) human populations. However, there is also equal support for the notion that at times intergroup cooperation is common. Because of the predominance of the underlying theme of a "struggle for existence" and competition between individuals for access to fitness enhancement (biological or cultural), competition is seen as a basal driver in evolutionary systems. In fact, there have been many recent proposals suggesting that intragroup cooperation arises directly from intergroup competition (Bowles 2006, Lehman and Keller 2006).

My Thoughts: I think it is likely that human ancestors and humans throughout time participate(d) in defense (against conspecifics) of core areas within their ranges, when needed. However, was there sufficient resource stress in the typical early human environment to lead to significant competition and therefore conflict between groups as a normative state? Is it also possible that one way in which humans, unlike most other organisms, dealt with ecological challenges was to cooperate between certain groups? We do not know much about dispersal patterns in early humans. What if genetic relationships and fictive/cultural kinship and alliances were widespread across relatively geographically close groups even early in our evolutionary history (as it often is today)? The use of language and symbol may have united local populations or subunits in such populations in a way not present in other primates or mammals. This could lead to patterns of local social and ecological inheritance (even niche construction) that favored the maintenance of intergroup cooperative alliances. At the same time, histories of conflict could also lead to social and ecological inheritances of continued conflict. It seems to me that both of these scenarios are equally valid and probably both had significant impact on human behavioral evolution. Specific ecological changes and climate shifts affecting resource availability would also play a major role in determining or facilitating intergroup conflict or cooperation. My position is that it is the human potential for both conflict and cooperation in complex and innovative ways (relative to other organisms) that has played a major role in human behavioral evolution, not just that conflict (competition) is the main driver of behavioral systems.

Testability: Obviously, any assessment of such human ancestral patterns relies on our ability to model resources stress in the past, to identify evidence of intergroup aggression and conflict in the fossil record and to reconstruct paleoclimates. Both traditional analytic population ecology models and their modified niche construction analogs are helpful in this endeavor (Fuentes et al. in review, Odling-Smee et al. 2003) as are the use of agent-based models to estimate habitat use and density-dependent decisions in human ancestors. Modern societies also provide a set of data with which to examine context of both conflict and cooperation between groups (Fry 2005, Bowles 2006).

Resources

Fossil Data: There is a broad assumption that resource stress, and therefore conflict over resources, played some role in human evolution. This rests on the assumption of limited resources relative to the number of individuals who seek to use them. However, reconstructions of many environments in which we find fossil hominins do not show extremely stressful environments (in the sense of extensive food/climate stressors). Also, recent analyses of human ancestors and other hominin fossils suggest that Pleistocene hominins had broad and flexible diets and thus flexible foraging patterns (Wood and Straight 2004). This implies that there were a variety of options for human ancestors and especially early humans in regards to nutritional resource stress. Obviously, as humans expanded their ranges into more arid and seasonal climates, resource stress would play a more important role. However, there is strong evidence that until recently most humans occupied relatively resource-rich areas and exploited both somatic and extrasomatic (material) means in acquiring nutrition and other resources. While it is undoubtedly the case that resource stress has played a role in human behavioral evolution at points in our history, its role as a continuous selective pressure eliciting conflict over resources or the intensity of its impact across different time frames is not clear from the current fossil record.

Comparative Data: Depending on the species and the location resource stress, and concomitant conflict over resources, plays quite different roles in primate societies. However, a basic tenet of behavioral ecology is that individuals and groups will enter into conflict over resources because individuals attempt to maximize their acquisition of resources (food, mates, space, and so on). Most comparative analyses of primate groups assume this state. However, there are only a limited collection of long-term studies of multiple groups within a population and their relationships over resources. These long-term studies show variable relationships between and within groups in regards to overt conflict over resources. Within-group conflict over resources is well documented in the majority of primates; socially mediated priority of access hierarchies are seen in nearly all primate species. In such dominance hierarchies the resources can be food items, mates, preferred social partners, sleeping sites, favored locations in a resting tree, and so on. The hierarchies emerge via contest competition for the resources and social negation between group members. Different individuals occupy different slots in the hierarchies across their lives. Because of the near ubiquitousness of such hierarchies in primates, it is generally assumed that conflict over resources (social and biotic) is a driving pressure for all primate species.

Paradigmatic Views (EP, HBE, ND-Sociobiology, Meme, DIT): In all of these perspectives adaptation is seen as a process that emerges to cope with extreme or particularly salient pressures, not necessarily minor events present in daily life. So even when the actual stress is not there groups and individuals are likely to respond as though there is stress and engage in conflict (hoarding/accumulation/control) of resources. EP sees this as an adaptive module driven (evolutionary past) response pattern and the rest see it as both ongoing and phylogenetic causes. Regardless of the origin of the particular behavioral pattern, there is an underlying assumption that individuals and groups will compete for access to resources in limited environments, and for social/physical control of access to them in resource-rich environments.

My Thoughts: The most basic underlying Darwinian evolutionary scenario holds that there is a limited good (potential fitness) and that life consists of organisms struggling to acquire sufficient amounts of that good to facilitate their passing of heritable material on to the next generation. This is a strong and useful metaphor, however it is not necessarily an actuality in all circumstances. The notion of the "struggle" for existence need not always translate literally to a struggle (conflict) over resources between individuals. A debate between Spencer and Kropotkin focused on this exact point (see Chapter 2). While conflict over resources has obviously played important roles at different times in human history, how does it affect human behavioral evolution? The fact that nearly all primate species have social hierarchies with differential access to resources by participants suggests that this is a basal pattern for humans as well. However, most researchers constantly note the exorbitantly high rates of apparent altruism in human groups. Traditionally, this is explained via kin selection, reciprocal altruism, and related selfish genetic scenarios such that this altruism is in reality a response to conflict and competition. Regardless of explanations, the fact that, behaviorally, humans seem to circumvent and control conflict over resources within groups so extensively seems to me an indication that conflict over resources is important, but that significant aspects of human behavior might have evolved to ameliorate and/or control it rather than to make individuals better at exploiting it/succeeding at it. Ultimately, my view coincides in many ways with the standard paradigms; however, rather than seeing this conflict as underlying or driving much behavior (making humans better at conflict), I see a suite of strategies to control and ameliorate the importance of conflict over resources within human groups (see also de Waal 2000, Sussman and Chapman 2004).

Testability: Of central importance is identification of what resources we are interested in (as being important within a system) and then developing mechanisms to quantify the availability and extractability of those resources within the system of focus. This is seldom done as we tend to assume that there are limited resources, even if socially constructed, and generate hypotheses from that assumption. Fossil reconstructions are quite difficult in this realm and primate/mammalian comparative approaches may be more metaphorical than homologous. This is an area where in-depth behavioral ecology combined with good ethnography (as in a strong HBE and Biocultural Anthropology) can provide the kind of rich cultural, social, and ecological context and datasets necessary to really assess the role of resource limitation and behavioral contests over those resources.

Same and Different Sex

Fossil Data: See male–female cooperation and same-sex cooperation above for an indication of what relevance we can (and cannot) find in the fossil record.

Comparative Data: See male–female cooperation and same-sex cooperation above for an indication of what relevance we can (and cannot) find in the comparative record.

Paradigmatic Views (EP, HBE, ND-Sociobiology, Meme, DIT): See male–female cooperation and same-sex cooperation above for the basal perspectives of the paradigmatic views on this topic.

My Thoughts: Obviously, there is conflict among and between the sexes. However, what type of conflict and what intensity of conflict and competition are involved has great bearing on the relevance for evolutionary patterns. Modern Neo-Darwinian perspectives include a strong focus on intersexual conflict and its causal relationship to the evolution of form and behavior (see sexual selection below). Specific to human behavioral evolution, some of the proposals reviewed in Chapter 5 and some main assumptions of the main paradigms (at least EP, HBE, and ND-Sociobiology) hold that it is the conflict between the sexes (primarily investment in reproduction and parenting) that has, in part, driven the evolution of pair bonds, sexual behavior, and mating patterns in humans. As a basal assertion, this has merit, and has been a core perspective from Darwin through modern Behavioral Ecology. However, how much of the specific behavioral patterns in modern humans are directly connected to these broad evolutionary conflicts is a difficult assessment. Also, intersexual conflict is generally assessed based on comparing assumed costs of reproduction for males and females; however, it is not always clear that these costs are as radically different as is assumed (Tang-Martinez 2000, Kokko and Jennions 2003, Borgerhoff-Mulder 2004); so their role in driving the evolution of mating patterns and behavior is not as clear-cut as one might assume.

Same-sex conflict is generally assumed to be related to conflict over resources (these resources being females for males and nutritional sources and/or protection for females). It is not clear how intense this has been in human evolution nor is it clear what behavioral outcomes result from this today. Because of the core role of the social group and the extremely high levels of intergroup cooperation, I am not convinced that same-sex conflict has driven a major portion of behavioral evolution in humans.

Testability: See the above comments in the same- and different-sex cooperation sections for this discussion.

Conflict Factors that Deserve Further Examination

Intragroup

Fossil Data: As difficult to asses as general conflict is, it is even more difficult to assess intragroup conflict from the fossil record. The dimorphism evident in the early hominin fossils, and possibly even in early *H. erectus* fossils, suggests some degree of male–male competition, but there are no direct data to test this. The cut marks on some fossils and the damaged state of others are too vague to provide any indication of intragroup conflict.

Comparative Data: Low levels of intragroup conflict are characteristic of nearly all multiadult group living primates. On average, this conflict does not result in serious injury and relative to affiliative ("friendly") interactions, makes up a very small percentage of any primate's daily activity (Sussman and Garber 2007). However, dominance contests and competition for mates is expected to be most intense within groups and thus these contexts can be considered as important for the evolution of behavioral patterns (Bernstein 2007, Manson 2007). Within-group interactions are the most common context in primates' lives and thus the possible pressures and responses to such patterns within and across populations can be reflective of, or influence, evolutionary change.

Paradigmatic Views (EP, HBE, ND-Sociobiology, Meme, DIT): As most behavior, including mating, occurs within the group, these intragroup inter-actions are assumed to be the template where most evolutionarily significant behavior plays out. All of the main perspectives see the conflict between indi-viduals (same sex or different sex) as core in understating the evolution of behavior (see above). However, the generalized notion of conflict within the group, beyond dyadic (two-individual) contests and their outcomes, is not a focus of these perspectives. DIT relies heavily on notions of group cohesion intermixed with individual "status striving" in their models. This perspec-tive has an inherent focus on the role of conflict within groups. Memetics relies on conflict between memes rather than individuals but does allow for competing memes to occur within groups. HBE, ND-Sociobiology, and EP all allow for multiple strategies within groups; however, the general assump-tion is that one or a few of these strategies is closer to optimal, and over time, should become the dominant or only one available for the populations.

My Thoughts: The possibility that complex conflict between multiple individuals within groups is important in an evolutionary sense is difficult to conceptualize. However, if we see this as an outcome of complex sociality and growing group size, it might become clearer. As human groups began to grow substantially in size, probably within the last 40–20,000 years, types and complexity of intragroup interactions also grew. The archeological rec-ord begins to show differentiation in burial goods, living structures and accu-mulations of substantial material goods over the last 20,000 years (at least) and indicating emergence of social hierarchies. The question here becomes, once social differentiation within groups becomes reified via unequal distri-bution of material goods (and "status"?) does this then act also as an evolu-tionary force resulting in differential reproduction? Or is it a form of social/ symbolic inheritance? Or both? This pattern is suggested by the traditional perspectives (above), but to date it is not fully clear that status acquisition ties in any way to heritable genetic (evolutionary) elements. It is possible that social complexity in material culture and social structure has a niche construction effect, altering selection pressures such that behavioral strate-gies for increased competition within human groups become more common relative to earlier periods in human evolutionary history. However, it is also equally as likely that inequality and within-group conflict are merely by-products of a system of increased social and material complexity and do not tie to reproductive changes and thus are genetically invisible but still socially inherited. Either way, this area deserves serious attention.

Testability: The material record and the fossil record are the most valu-able bodies of evidence for assessing the frequency and type of intragroup conflict in the past. Archeological evidence demonstrates the intertwined role of material inequality, resource stress, and intragroup conflict in numer-ous recent contexts (see Hawaii example, Kirch 2007). Correlating increased inequality and increased conflict shows us their relationship, but actual tests o̧f their possible impact on evolution are more difficult. Historical records and assessments of modern within-group conflicts can possibly allow for some connections between conflict and reproductive success. To demonstrate that the connection between inequality and conflict are more than just social outcomes, there must be some quantitative differential impact on reproductive success.

Interhominin

Fossil Data: The fossil record does indicate the potential for conflict between human ancestors and other hominins. Range overlap, dietary overlap, body size overlap, and possible behavioral overlap give credence to the idea that *H. erectus/ergaster* and *Paranthropus* spp. came into conflict over resources (Conroy 2004, Wood and Strait 2004, Ciochon and Fleagle 2006, see Chapter 4). There are apparent cut marks from stone tools found on a few hominin fossils during the period of overlap of *Homo* and *Paranthropus* in Africa (~2–1 million years ago).

  Comparative Data: In many areas where similar sized primate species coexist, they either exhibit strong niche separation, sympatric associations, or are in direct competition for resources with one another. Gibbons (apes) and leaf monkeys frequently compete for fruiting sources in Southeast Asia but gorillas and chimpanzees (both apes) tend to avoid one another in African forests where both forms occur. This suggests somewhat mixed support for the possibility of humans ancestor–other hominin conflict.

  Paradigmatic Views (EP, HBE, ND-Sociobiology, Meme, DIT): The possibility of such conflict is largely ignored by practitioners of these perspectives, with the occasional exception in proposals focusing on hunting. Some "man the hunter" scenarios suggest that humans may have hunted *Paranthropus*.

  My Thoughts: The transition by an early hominin group to the genus *Homo* is marked by subtle morphological shifts but resulted in substantial changes in evolutionary trajectory and history (Wood and Collard 1999, McHenry and Coffing 2000, Conroy 2004, see Chapter 4). Predation and other ecological pressures on Australopithecines and early members of the genus *Homo* may have been significant in this transition (Hart and Sussman 2005). These contexts might have stimulated a shift in behavior and modes of engagement with the environment that initiated a complex suite of changes facilitating the emergence of some key current features of humanity. It is possible that related to these predation pressures, specific patterns of conflict between *Homo* and other sympatric hominins became a core facet of human evolutionary history and that niche construction can facilitate understanding of this history (Fuentes et al. in review). If human ancestors were able to change their behavioral patterns resulting in reduced predation, this might have increased predation pressure on *Paranthropus*. In this scenario, the conflict is between two organisms occupying a similar and overlapping niche, with one able to modify the niche to the detriment of the other.

Testability: The fossil record provides the basic tests corroborating the overlap in diet and predator pressure for the two genera. It also shows that one genera survived and flourished while the other did not. Niche construction equations (Odling-Smee et al. 2003) integrated with ecological models for predation and carrying capacity can provide scenarios/outcomes to compare to the fossil record. Such comparison can refute or support scenarios proposed to explain human success relative to *Paranthropus* extinction (Fuentes et al. in review).

Intermammalian

Fossil Data: Members of the genus *Homo* coexisted with other hominins and many other large-bodied primates. This suggests, minimally, that during our evolutionary history we were sympatric with a number of other mammals who shared generally physiologies and diets.

 Comparative Data: See interhominin above.

 Paradigmatic Views (EP, HBE, ND-Sociobiology, Meme, DIT): Generally, the only appearance of conflict between humans and other mammals in the traditional paradigms is in hunting scenarios. However, all of these perspectives (except Memetics) explicitly recognize a primary role for competition over resources, thus opening the door for a role for interspecific conflict in human behavioral evolution.

 My Thoughts: Hart and Sussman (2005) argue that predation by large mammalian predators might have been a significant force in hominin evolution. I also suggest that resource competition might also be important, especially between hominins and possibly other large-bodied primates and pigs, with whom they share dietary/isotopic profiles (Lee-Thorp et al. 2003). Developing behavioral strategies to overcome such competition and predation might have played very significant roles in human behavioral evolution.

 Testability: As with interhominin conflict above, combining the evidence of overlap between human ancestors and other mammals with models from ecology might give some insight into conflict patterns. Also, specific dietary analyses through isotopic investigations (see Lee-Thorp et al. 2003, Wood and Straight 2004) might allow for more detailed comparisons of possible competition between fossil forms.

Diet/Food Commonalities

Food Sharing (See Cooperation/Food Sharing Above) — Hunting

Fossil Data: Evidence for meat consumption comes early in the history of our genus; however, material evidence for actual hunting comes later. By approximately 600,000 years, there is evidence for hunting materials (spears, for example) but stone tool assemblages as old as 1.6 million years ago contain tools that are capable of effectively processing large animals. As early as 2.5 million years ago there is evidence of butchery of mammals at East African sites (see Chapter 4). The fossil record does not show clear and consistent evidence for large-scale hunting until the last 2–300,000 years ago.

Comparative Data: Chimpanzees hunt and consume other mammals (frequently favoring other primates as prey). However, animal prey make up a very small percentage of the chimpanzee diet (Stumpf 2007). Orangutan females have been observed capturing and eating prosimian primates (Knott and Kahlenberg 2007), but gorillas and gibbons are not seen taking animal prey with any regularity. Baboons and macaques will capture and consume animal prey, but do so haphazardly and independently. Of all the nonhuman primates, only chimpanzees, humans' closest evolutionary relative, exhibit any group hunting.

Paradigmatic Views (EP, HBE, ND-Sociobiology, Meme, DIT): HBE, EP, and ND-Sociobiology place an emphasis on hunting as a major element (and selective advantage) in the evolution of human behavioral patterns. All see hunting and meat consumption/sharing as important cultural/evolutionary aspects of human prehistory and today. In these perspectives, hunting is frequently associated with male aggression, combat skills, and display of abilities/quality/status. Hunting has also been suggested to result in important sex differences between males and females (ND-Sociobiology and EP). HBE sees hunting by both males and females as important, but especially sees the advent of sharing and distribution of meat as an important behavioral factor in human evolutionary patterns.

My Thoughts: There is no doubt that organized hunting by members of human groups has played an important role in our history. The fact that chimpanzees also form groups to acquire prey might suggest that this is a relatively old pattern for hominins. However, there is no fossil evidence suggesting that humans relied heavily on group hunting early in our history. With the move from mainly forested to more mixed environments and habitual terrestriality, it is not clear that hunting would have been as effective as for the arboreal chimpanzees. Obviously, by the time we see material evidence for hunting weaponry in the fossil record, the act had become a mainstay in human patterns. However, unlike traditional approaches from Darwin to ND-Sociobiology, I do not see a necessary correlation between hunting and human aggression. I see hunting as more of an indicator of the increasingly important and complex levels of cooperation and coordination between individuals and within hominin/human groups.

Testability: To assess the relationship between hunting and aggression we can look to the fossil record and see if there are any correlations between the appearance of hunting technology and increased human (*Homo*) injury related to aggression. As indicated earlier in this chapter, the evidence for significant levels of skeletal damage easily associated with interpersonal aggression comes much, much later than evidence for increased importance of hunting. The other logical tests are to compare ethnographic evidence for the importance of hunting within a society and its relative levels of interpersonal violence. The recent fossil record suggests that increased violence comes with sedentism and agriculture rather than with foraging/hunting-gathering lifeways.

Diet/Food Factors that Deserve Further Examination

Plant Storage Organs

Fossil Data: There is little fossil evidence aside from isotopic and tooth wear data from both *Paranthropus* and *Homo* suggesting that this type of plant matter played a prominent role in the diets of hominins. There are no clear types of materials (tools) associated specifically with root/tuber extraction processing, but it is also possible that these were made of perishable (wood) materials and thus unlikely to be preserved.

Comparative Data: While many primate species will consume plant storage organs when given the chance, only a few actively seek them out (baboons and macaques primarily) and in these cases the roots are always relatively small and easily accessible, requiring no tool use.

Paradigmatic Views (EP, HBE, ND-Sociobiology, Meme, DIT): Both HBE and ND-Sociobiology have practitioners who suggest that underground storage organs have played important roles in humans' behavioral evolution (Hatley and Kappelman 1980, Winterhalder 1996, Wrangham et al. 1999, see cooking, tubers, and male guarding hypothesis).

My Thoughts: I like the idea that such food sources were exploited by early humans as such exploitation requires specific patterns of cooperation and food sharing. The energetic returns are high as are the processing costs. Unfortunately, with little to no fossil evidence until relatively recent human populations, it is difficult to give this food source too much credit for influencing our evolutionary trajectories.

Testability: The primary tests of support for this concept would be to find some evidence in the fossil record associated with *H. erectus* of extractions and use of root/tubers as a main/major food source. The concept is supported by the high number of modern human groups that exploit these types of food resources when they can.

Ecology/Environment Commonalities

Variable Environments

Fossil Data: A major segment of human evolution occurs between 2 and 1 millions years ago (the origin and radiation of *H. erectus*). Work by Richard Potts and others (Potts 1998, 1999, Kingston 2007) demonstrate a substantial amount of climatic and environmental fluctuations during this period, especially in East Africa. The fossil record also shows that during this period mammalian (including primate) species who were more generalist or flexible behaviorally, survived better than those who had more limited adaptive response ranges (Potts 1998, 1999).

Comparative Data: Those primate species who are most flexible in their physiological and behavioral patterns (baboons and macaques) are the most widespread of the nonhuman primates and are able to exploit the widest array of environments.

Paradigmatic Views (EP, HBE, ND-Sociobiology, Meme, DIT): While there is some implicit recognition of human flexibility in response to environmental stressors, little attention is given by these perspectives to the actual role that fluctuating and variable environments have had on human behavioral evolution (However see Wells and Stock 2007).

My Thoughts: I am an explicit supporter of Potts' (1998, 1999, 2004) variability selection hypothesis. The possibility that selection has favored broad flexibility in behavioral and physiological response to fluctuating environments rather than specific focused adaptations to specific environmental challenges seems to me to be a very fitting explanatory facet of human behavioral evolution (see however, Barret et al. 2002).

Testability: See Potts' publications (1998, 1999, 2004) for examples and discussion of the kinds of tests for these ideas. In short, they include mixing fossil, paleoclimate, and modeling datasets and matching them to actual outcomes of species survival and behavioral patterns/ecologies (see also Kingston 2007, Wells and Stock 2007).

Competition with Other Human Groups

Fossil Data: See intergroup cooperation and conflict above.

Comparative Data: See intergroup cooperation and conflict above.

Paradigmatic Views (EP, HBE, ND-Sociobiology, Meme, DIT): See intergroup cooperation and conflict above.

My Thoughts: See intergroup cooperation and conflict above.

Testability: See intergroup cooperation and conflict above.

Brain/Body Energetic Costs

Fossil Data: The transition from early *Homo* to *H. erectus/ergaster* (~2–1.6 million years ago) is marked by a substantial body size and brain size increase in the fossils. Estimated energy costs for *Homo* go up by as much as 40% during this time period. Such a radical change in the cost of running one's body suggests a change in behavioral patterns to increase energy intake/ conservation/efficiency (Aiello and Wells, 2002).

Comparative Data: No primates have the kind of brain development we see in humans. Some neotropical primates have large brain-to-body size ratios and other primates have relatively large bodies; however, none come close to the human brain's physiology costs. There are no living primates who share the kinds of neurological and physiological changes seen in humans. However, there is increasing evidence that all primates share a pattern of increased brain complexity associated with social complexity. Across primate species, there are patterns of correlations between increased brains size/complexity and social complexity as well (termed the "social brain hypothesis," Dunbar and Shultz 2007).

Paradigmatic Views (EP, HBE, ND-Sociobiology, Meme, DIT): It is explicitly assumed that the evolutionary/energetic cost of increased brain size correlates with increased energy consumption. This is usually proposed in the form of meat (hunting and scavenging) or possibly underground plant storage organs and the concomitant behavioral changes each of these foraging choices involves. There is also an association with increased infant care costs due to the longer postpartum (after birth) development of the brain in human children. The traditional perspectives increasingly see this increase in energetic costs as central to a suite of human challenges and also as part of the primate-wide pattern of selective relationships between social complexity and cerebral complexity (Dunbar and Shultz 2007).

My Thoughts: I agree. The shift in humans relative to other primates and hominins in cerebral physiology and infrastructure/development sets the stage for much of the complexity and flexibility seen in human behavioral systems. It is, in large part, what distinguishes us from other primates. It is an integral precursor to the expansion of cooperative complexity, symbol and language, large-scale alterations of the environment, and substantial social and structural niche construction. The increased costs of maintaining the brain and its development (child rearing) must have played central roles in establishing novel or enhanced patterns of behavior in *H. erectus* relative to other species.

Testability: The fossil record supports all of these assertions; the increase in brain size and cost are associated with increased complexity of tool use, range expansion, and behavioral complexity. Examination of the living primates' brains and social patterns can also be used to assess the increases, costs, and selective correlates in human brains via testing the social brain hypothesis. However, testing across the competing hypotheses for how this occurred (many covered in this book) can be difficult.

Food Stress

Fossil Data: This is related to general resource stress (above). There is strong evidence that early humans were relatively eurytopic (had flexible dietary patterns—Lee-Thorp et al. 2003, Wood and Strait 2004) as are modern humans. Members of the genus *Homo* do not appear to occupy fringe or extremely stressful habitats until later in human evolution (last 200,000 years or so) when highly effective toolkits (complex tools, clothing of sorts, and fire) are already available.

Comparative Data: There is considerable debate as to the role of food stress in many primate studies. Tropical-forest living primates undergo some annual stressors related to food availability, but not to the extent of more climatically variable seasonal environments. In fact, the distribution of most living primate species (circum-equatorial) suggests that primates, on average, range in areas that minimize food and climate stress. However, there are a number of primate species (such as members of the genera *Macaca*, *Papio*, or *Rhinopithecus*) that do inhabit extreme habitats.

Paradigmatic Views (EP, HBE, ND-Sociobiology, Meme, DIT): As with resource stress above, it is assumed by all the traditional perspectives that resource limitation, especially that of food, acts as a stressor for all organisms. The concept of limited food and the competition over it are core to all models in these paradigms.

My Thoughts: As with resource stress above, I am not sure that food stress in particular has always exerted the kind of selective force on humans and human ancestors as is commonly assumed. If human ancestors lived in relatively low densities and had flexible behavioral patterns including tool kits and a heightened level of cooperation within and possibly between local groups, foraging might not have been the main limiting factor acting as a selective force on the evolution of human behavioral patterns. This is not to say that foraging stresses have not exerted selective pressures on human populations at different points in our history, rather that it may not have always played as central a role as is frequently assumed.

Testability: Again, looking to the fossil record is difficult given the paucity of individuals represented there. However, looking at the development and relative nutritional status (as measured by skeletal elements and structures) in fossils and fossil populations (such as the large number at Sima de los Huesos, Bermudez de Castro et al. 2004) can give us an indication of past nutritional states reflecting possible impacts of food stress.

Ecology/Environment Factors that Deserve Further Examination

Human–Environment Mutability

Fossil Data: There is little evidence early in the human fossil record that we can clearly interpret as human–environment mutability as envisioned under niche construction scenarios suggested by Odling-Smee and colleagues (Odling-Smee et al. 2003). However, some patterns related to success of the genus *Homo* relative to other hominins might be interpreted as reflective of humans impacting their environments and in turn facing changing selective pressures (Fuentes et al. in review, Wells and Stock 2007).

Comparative Data: There is little to no investigation into this type of niche construction pattern in nonhuman primates to date, although it may be a beneficial avenue of inquiry (Fuentes 2007).

Paradigmatic Views (EP, HBE, ND-Sociobiology, Meme, DIT): While it is standard in all of these perspectives to see humans as impacting the environment or the environment impacting humans, true mutability as envisioned under the rubric of niche construction is less commonly addressed. A possible exception comes with DIT and Memetics wherein changing social concepts can modify the social/cultural context, which in turn can facilitate novel selection pressures at both physical and cultural levels.

My Thoughts: A predominant implication of human–environment mutability is that feedback effects (from such interactions) can have dramatic impacts on population dynamics. I suggest that cooperation and its relationship to niche construction can be an aspect of evolutionary processes as organisms modify the environment in significant ways and those modifications in turn alter evolutionary pressures. Such feedback effects are inherently nonlinear and probably play an important role in developing more accurate reconstructions of our evolutionary history. I agree with Odling-Smee et al. (2003) in that the perspective that humans and their environments are mutually malleable and changing together over time is an important contribution to explorations of our evolutionary past.

Testability: Again, as with many of the above elements, looking to the fossil record and attempting to seek support or refutation for niche construction models and their outcomes is one avenue for assessment. Also, enhancing our analytical and agent-based/simulation modeling toolkits to incorporate niche construction scenarios and testing them on other organisms can bolster the case for their relevance in humans.

Disease

Fossil Data: Aside from some data from the Atapuerca site (Sima de los Huesos, Bermudez de Castro et al. 2004) and more recent fossils (from the last 20,000 years), there is little evidence that disease (particularly infectious disease) played a major role throughout human evolution. However, since the advent of sedentism and larger communities, there is ample evidence that disease plays a significant role in human mortality.

Comparative Data: There is good evidence from a few primate populations (Chimpanzees at the Gombe and Tai sites for example) that disease outbreaks can have major impacts. However, the majority of these cases are related to overlap with humans and involve human-based diseases. There is a good deal of literature regarding bidirectional pathogen transmission between humans and other primates, but nothing related to fossil contexts (Engel et al. 2006). Recently, there has been an increase in interest in infectious diseases (especially sexually transmitted infections) and the evolution of primate behavior (Nunn and Altizer 2006). This may be relevant to studies of human evolution.

Paradigmatic Views (EP, HBE, ND-Sociobiology, Meme, DIT): Interestingly, despite the acknowledged importance of disease in modern human contexts, the traditional perspectives have been largely silent regarding disease in the evolution of human behavior.

My Thoughts: It is logical to assume that prior to sedentism, and increased densities in human populations, infectious disease was not a major force in human behavioral evolution. However, it is worth considering that avoidance of disease and coping with illness were, and are, relevant in the development of human behavior. Disease can act as a strong localized selective pressure. Behavioral traditions and perspectives regarding treatments or evidence of diseases or disease-prolific areas passed across generations could have formed important social and ecological inheritances. This then might have facilitated success for human groups and populations in areas of disease danger. These behavioral patterns would not be necessarily adaptive at the genetic level (no change to specific related allelic frequencies) but would nonetheless prove beneficial to the maintenance of some human groups and thus may have been influential in the patterns of human behavioral evolution.

Testability: Unfortunately, testing this proposal seems relegated to models and modern human systems as there will probably never be a large enough find of fossil samples pertaining to specific paleoenviroments to allow us to actually test for the presence and response to disease.

Predation Pressure

Fossil Data: Hart and Sussman (2005) review the fossil data for predation on hominins. They conclude that predation was indeed a source of strong selection and that human ancestors must have developed behavioral adaptations to deal with predation (as they did not develop morphological ones). Lee-Thorp et al. (2003) also illustrate, via isotope data, that large hyenids and cats were likely predators on *Homo*, *Australopithecus* and baboons during the Pliocene.

Comparative Data: Predation is an important selective pressure for many populations of nonhuman primates (Miller and Treves 2007).

Paradigmatic Views (EP, HBE, ND-Sociobiology, Meme, DIT): There has been very little attention given to the possibility that humans have evolved a variety of behavioral patterns in response to their role as prey. All the traditional perspectives tend to envision and model humans and human ancestors as predators (on other organisms and on ourselves).

My Thoughts: The transition by an early hominin group to the genus *Homo* and the changes from early members of the genus *Homo* to *H. erectus/ergaster* is marked by subtle morphological shifts but resulted in substantial changes in evolutionary trajectory and history. Predation and other ecological pressures on Australopithecines and early members of the genus *Homo* may have been significant in this transition. These contexts might have stimulated a shift in behavior and modes engagement with the environment that initiated a complex suite of changes facilitating the emergence of current features of human behavior. These shifts could have included a ratcheting effect (see Tomasello proposal Chapter 5) of biocultural complexity through niche construction and an increasing reliance on cooperative interactions in antipredator behavior, foraging, reproduction, and general health maintenance. Matthew A. Wyczalkowski, Katherine C. MacKinnon, and I recently outlined a potential model for these shifts using a nonlinear dynamics scenario involving niche construction and increased reliance on complex cooperation as an antipredator strategy in early humans. The model proposes that selective pressures of predation on early humans facilitated increasingly complex sociality, patterns of cooperation, and niche construction, which laid the foundation for the successful emergence and spread of the species *Homo* and potentially a concomitant decline for the genus *Paranthropus* (Fuentes et al. in review).

Testability: The data reviewed by Hart and Sussman (2005), additional evidence for predation on hominins, niche overlap, and competition between *Paranthropus* and *Homo*, and analytic models for niche construction through increased effectiveness of antipredator strategies by humans support this contention.

Sex/Reproduction Commonalities

Multiple Caretakers

Fossil Data: Little direct evidence for caretaking can be found in the fossil record. However, the increased energetic costs and developmental patterns associated with increased brain size (see above) suggest that it became more costly for humans to care for their young (see Kramer 2004). The lack of ability for human infants to self-attach to the mother (distinct from all other primates) also suggests extra caretaking costs. The fossils do not suggest how this caretaking occurred except that there is evidence that hominins lived in social groups rather than as dispersed individuals.

Comparative Data: In general, primate mothers are the main caretakers for the young. In many species of monkey, there is allomothering where nonmother females carry, care for, and offer affiliative social interactions to infants. There are also species where males provide allomaternal care [Savannah Baboons (*Papio papio*) and Barbary macaques (*M. sylvanus*), for example]. In the apes, allomothering is relatively rare, except in Gorilla groups where males may spend large amounts of time interacting affiliatively with infants and immatures. Even though ape offspring can be dependent on their mothers for extended periods, none equal the level of physical and social dependence seen in human infants.

Paradigmatic Views (EP, HBE, ND-Sociobiology, Meme, DIT): In general, these perspectives see child-rearing costs as primarily impacting mothers and as setting the stage for male–female conflict over reproductive investment. However, Sarah Hrdy (ND-Sociobiology practitioner) (Hrdy 1999, 2005, Chapter 5) proposed a cooperative breeding model for human behavioral evolution (see also Kramer 2004). In this model, allomaternal assistance formed a main aspect of human adaptive response during the Pleistocene evolution of the genus *Homo*. She argues that emerging complexity in kinship systems between and within groups enabled a broad set of caretakers and learning experiences for developing offspring. This helped offset potentially high infant mortality and depends upon complex cognitively active engagement between infants and caretakers.

My Thoughts: I agree with Hrdy's cooperative breeding hypothesis and see it as a central component of the broader adaptive suite of cooperation in human evolution.

Testability: Looking at modern ethnographic datasets, one sees that child-rearing strategies in the majority of human populations today involve multiple caretakers. As noted above, the fossil record suggests an increased cost of rearing a human infant from at least the advent of *H. erectus*, making it unlikely that single mothers were the only participants in our evolutionary past. These elements are reviewed in Hrdy (1999) and the models she proposes in her 2005 publication review the existing data and basic theoretical tests for this proposal. In general, the data presented support the hypothesis that humans lived in groups, that multiple caretakers were involved in raising infants and that this resulted in a significant pattern of human behavioral evolution.

Sexual Selection

Fossil Data: The fossil data relevant to sexual selection are similar to those for cooperation and conflict between the sexes. Male hominins appear to have been substantially larger than females through early *H. erectus*. The level of dimorphism decreases significantly over the last million years, but on average, male bone and muscle density remains above that of females in modern humans. The fossil record does not preserve soft tissue, however it is assumed by many that the relatively large genitalia on males and possibly breasts on females, in addition to patterns of hair retention, are related to sexual selection (due to the lack of supported alternative functional hypotheses for them).

Comparative Data: Sexual dimorphism in size and pelage patterns in primates are generally attributed to sexual selection. Most species demonstrate some form of dimorphism in morphology and behavior, possibly resulting from sexual selection.

Paradigmatic Views (EP, HBE, ND-Sociobiology, Meme, DIT): Sexual selection is seen as a core factor influencing human behavior from Darwin's original works through E.O. Wilson's contributions, and more recently explicitly argued for by Geoffery Miller (see Chapter 5). Different facets of sexual selection have been highlighted, but most involve male and female displays (behaviorally and physically), female body shape (such as waist-to-hip ratio) and male symmetry as indicators of fitness, and behavioral competition for status (both within and between sexes). All of these perspectives see sexual selection as acting on human behavior with a resultant differentiation in male and female sexual strategies.

My Thoughts: I remain less convinced than most that certain aspects of male and female morphology are the results of sexual selection. There is no convincing reason for penis size to have been selected for (especially given the variance in living human populations) as it is not related to fertility, insemination ability, general health, or sexual capabilities (King 2004).

Female breasts are a sexual focus in some societies, but by no means a majority of societies (King 2004). Their shape and size in adulthood are greatly influenced by cultural measures (modern bras for example) and neither size nor shape of breast is correlated to fertility, fecundity or lactation ability. There is also substantial disagreement about the use of waist-to-hip ratio and symmetry as indicators of human fitness. Behaviorally, there is some debate regarding the modes of analyses for assessing the differences and similarities in male and female behavioral sexual strategies and their relationship to fitness (Schmidt 2005 and commentaries therein). I remain skeptical of a high degree of behavioral specificity in adaptive mating strategies for humans. Rather, humans, more so than any other primate, exhibit a high degree of sexual behavior in a variety of situations (Fausto Sterling 2000, Middleton 2001). I am more inclined to look at local groups and populations and the patterns of social sexual activity and actual reproduction within them as variation within a broad theme of hypersexuality in humans. I remain unconvinced that there are clearly identifiable strategic differences between males and females; rather, I think that sexual activity is used for a variety of purposes (social and reproductive) in humans. Sexual selection undoubtedly has impacted human behavior and morphology, but I am not clear on which facets of our behavior and physical form are actually direct results of such evolutionary patterns. This perspective is directly contradictory to the major stances in EP, ND-Sociobiology, and HBE of specific correlations between human sexual practices and adaptive strategies.

Testability: many EP and ND-Sociobiology practitioners have published, widely using primarily, survey and interview techniques in modern humans groups (see EP example from Chapter 3) to assess sexual selective outcomes in human behavioral strategies. This and a comparative ethnographic approach are the only truly available tests. However, see Miller (2006) for a proposal regarding sexual selection that does utilize facets of the fossil record. Comparative analyses of sexual behavior across mammals and human societies also provide a template for assessing current physiological and behavioral variation in sexual behavior in humans (see overviews in Fausto Sterling 2000).

Female Advertisement/Concealed Ovulation/Receptivity

Fossil Data: There are no direct fossil data that reflect menstrual cyclicity, fertility, and their potential morphological or behavioral indicators.

Comparative Data: While chimpanzees and a few macaque species have been used as exemplars of female morphological and behavioral advertisement of sexual receptivity, overt physical signals of peak cycling are not that common in primates (Campbell 2007). Rather, primates tend to exhibit a wide range of female sexual behavior and advertisement. Many primates are seasonal breeders with mating and sexual activity only taking place during limited times of the year. Others exhibit sexual behavior year round.

Paradigmatic Views (EP, HBE, ND-Sociobiology, Meme, DIT): On average, EP and ND-Sociobiology have taken female "concealed ovulation" as an adaptive strategy by human females to confuse both receptivity and paternity and thus exert control over males seeking to reproduce (see male–female conflict above). In this case, females are sexually receptive continuously, but able to hide the evidence of actual ovulation so as to control which males father her young. Others (as in sexual selection above) suggest that the combination of female form (enhanced hips and breasts) and minimal overt signals of cycling act as both a signal of sexual fertility and a method for females to control male access to actual reproduction, setting up a variety of behavioral strategies by both males and females to gain an upper hand in regards to maximal reproductive output with a minimum amount of input.

My Thoughts: I was once told that a senior anthropologist, when asked about continuous receptivity in human females, responded "any male who believes that is true is either too old to remember or too young to know better." The available ethnographic, sociological, and psychological datasets for human sexuality and mating patterns show that females are not continuously receptive, that there can be associations with sexual activity and cycling but that interindividual variation in sexual activity in human females is stunningly enormous (Fausto Sterling 2000, Middleton 2001, King 2004). Also, and most importantly, all cultures have a wide array of restrictions and social controls on how, where, when, and with whom people mate. In addition, a recent broad overview suggests that not only are males not adept at telling when females are ovulating, females themselves are very poor at pinning down their own ovulatory peaks (Brewis and Meyer 2005). For me this suggests that we are mistaken in thinking that human females have hidden ovulation as an adaptation, that females are tricking males via continues receptivity, or that there are specific modern behavioral patterns in females that reflect human adaptations of sexual advertisement of fitness quality or suppression of cycling information. There is simply too much cultural overlay on sexual behavior, mating, and attractiveness, and lack of evidence for a "hidden" ovulation for these measures to reflect deep adaptations in their specific modern forms.

Testability: Ethnographic and psychological study of sexual behavior are probably the best approaches, but they are extremely difficult in practice. EP practitioners would probably disagree and hold that surveys and interviews can get at these elements, and they may be at least partially correct. Comparative approaches are probably not too beneficial, given the complex distribution in primate female's overt signals of cycling across primate species.

Nuclear Family

Fossil Data: None of the multifossil finds of hominins suggest a two-adult and offspring social structure. More recent archeological evidence including households and villages also reflect various living arrangements, usually involving multiple adults and children, frequently related, but not single mother–father and offspring clusters.

Comparative Data: Few primates (~3–5% of species) live in two-adult plus offspring groups and those that do vary in their featly to the two-adult and their (genetic) offspring model (Fuentes 1999, 2002). As in all mammals, this pattern of group living is quite rare.

Paradigmatic Views (EP, HBE, ND-Sociobiology, Meme, DIT): Underlying many assumptions of ND-Sociobiology and HBE are the notion that the basal unit of human grouping is the nuclear family (two adults and their offspring). This nuclear family as a core unit is also supported by basic kin selection calculations (Chapter 2). EP generally argues that this arrangement results from a compromise between male and female mating strategies and may or may not reflect actual mating patterns (and is seen as a larger "concession" for the male than the female). DIT and Memetics have not directly addressed this issue but one might assume that DIT could envision a gene–culture evolutionary sequence wherein the nuclear family became predominant and Memetics might see such patterns as a particularly strong meme. Some current practitioners of these perspectives do not focus on the nuclear family in many of their hypotheses and are clear to extricate monogamous mating from direct association with nuclear family living.

My Thoughts: There is no evidence from the fossil record, the comparative record, the archeological record or modern ethnographic datasets that the nuclear family is a basal unit of group living, social interactions, or even child rearing for much of human evolutionary history. Many societies do recognize a social unit consisting of one female, one male and their offspring but this is usually part of a larger social and kin network and frequently part of a larger group residence pattern. These patterns include neolocality (nuclear family alone), patrilocal (live with father's kin), matrilocal (live with mother's kin), avuncolocal (father's uncle's family), and many more. In humans, social arrangements of kinship and residence integrate various genetic, cultural, and historical factors (McKinnon 2005). Although nuclear family residence has become a more popular pattern over the last few centuries, there is little evidence that it was particularly common before that. This does not mean that pair bonds do not occur and are not related to mating success in humans, it does mean that the presence of pair bonds is not necessarily associated with a specific grouping or residence pattern where the adults of the bond and their offspring are socially and spatially separated from other such groups. Given this, I do not think that hypotheses for the evolution of human behavior should use a nuclear family structure as an independent, and core, unit in their formulation. However, two-adult bonds are quite important and their relation to offspring production is a fertile area for speculation for human behavioral evolution (see pair bonds below)

Testability: Testing the role of the nuclear family in human evolution is best done via the archeological record and comparison with modern human ethnographic datasets. Examination of the patterns of material remains for signs of nuclear family residence and recognition is critical to assessing the appearance of nuclear family living and its relative frequency in past populations. Examination of modern humans is also important. Much of the developed world, particularly North American society, prioritizes nuclear family residences at the current time; however, extended family (kin group) coresidence remains the most common residential pattern across the globe and care must be taken when reducing human evolutionary patterns to something that looks suspiciously like idealized histories of 1950s United States (McKinnon 2005).

Sex/Reproduction Factors that Deserve Further Examination

Male Advertisement

Fossil Data: Sexual dimorphism in the fossil record might be seen as a form of advertisement or even an honest signal of male fitness. It is also argued that male symmetry is an advertisement for fitness quality. Symmetry can be assessed from fossils, but without a baseline level of symmetry for the fossil's population, no real assessments can be honestly made, and given the paucity of the fossil record, population level assessments are not really feasible at this time.

   Comparative Data: There are a number of morphological and behavioral characteristics that are proposed as male signals ("advertisements") of fitness in most mammalian species—size, quality of pelage (fur), fighting ability, display ability, dominance rank, age, propensity to affiliate with a female's offspring. Very few assessments have resulted in quantifiable relationships between these traits and male fitness. On average, high dominance rank is correlated with some degree of reproductive success in most species; however, most males move through middle and high ranks over the course of their lifetime resulting in a relatively broad distribution of offspring across time and males. Because the attainment and maintenance of dominance varies so much across (and even within) species and the fact that dominance is a state and not a trait of any individual male (is not heritable), it is far from clear if this is a possible mechanism for male advertisement. It seems more likely that overt physical and behavioral characteristics of males act as advertisements.

   Paradigmatic Views (EP, HBE, ND-Sociobiology, Meme, DIT): Of these perspectives HBE and DIT focus specifically on male advertisement (or male signaling) in multiple hypotheses, particularly in "showing off" (see Chapter 3 HBE example) or status acquisition and sharing models. EP also focuses on male honest signaling via physical symmetry/attractiveness and also on male "cheating" in behavioral advertisements. ND-Sociobiology has relied, in the past, on male dominance and aggression as a form of advertisement; however, this is less common in more recent hypotheses. However, there is relatively little attention placed on males' attempts to attract females via advertising given how core this is to most animal species' systems. In these perspectives, especially ND-Sociobiology and EP, there is more attention on females' strategies to attract males, an uncommon pattern for most animals.

My Thoughts: This is a very interesting realm of inquiry that has not received sufficient attention (however see Miller 2006 and summary of his proposal in Chapter 5). In the vast majority of mammals, males advertise to females but in many modern human cultures females spend a good deal of effort advertising to males. This reversal might be a very recent phenomena (there is very little evidence of gender/sex differentiation in adornment potentially related to mate/sexual partner attractions until extremely recently in the archeological record; Adovasio et al. 2007), or it might not. Miller (2006) argues for a role of sexual selection in molding the human mind as a "mating machine" tied to increasingly innovative ways of advertising quality and fitness. I am not fully convinced of this, but it is a very interesting arena for inquiry. To be honest, I do not have a good explanation to propose as to why human males might not be as advertisement "prone" as other animals.

Testability: Probably the main tests to be conducted here are those in modern humans to discover whether and in what contexts males are "advertising" aspects of their fitness potential. Aside from competitive sharing and "showing off" in certain forager societies (mostly HBE work), the EP focus on male symmetry and female choice, and Miller's hypothetical assertions about the arts, language, innovation, and male quality there have been few actual attempts to discover this. Given the paucity of any gender differentiation in the fossil record prior to the last 20,000 years, it is unlikely that the fossil record will provide testable materials.

Specific Behavior Commonalities

Symbol/Language/Tool Use

Fossil Data: We know that *H. sapiens* has been using materials such as red ochre (a pigment) for at least close to 200,000 thousand years, from the very earliest evidence of our species (Marean et al. 2007). Did *H. erectus* use materials items for symbolic purpose, did the archaic humans at Atapuerca or Bodo do so? (see Chapter 4). The fossil record provides evidence of nonfunctional material use at least 180–200,000 years ago by *H. sapiens sapiens*, but earlier than that is less clear. Over the last 200,000 years there has been a steady increase in humans' use and manipulation of symbolic and linguistic factors in their behavior and the ways in which they respond to environmental and social pressures.

Comparative Data: Nonhuman primates, in free-ranging setting, do not appear to manipulate material for symbolic means. There has been a substantial documentation of regional- and group-level behavioral, nonfunctional, variants termed "cultural" by some primatologists (Whiten et al. 1999). However, there have been no instances of pigment use, creation of nontool items or language. In captive contexts, some apes have been taught to interact via human-based communication systems such as American Sign language and image-based keyboards, suggesting some capability under human training to exploit symbols. However, this type of symbolic communication has not been documented, ever, in free-ranging situations.

Paradigmatic Views (EP, HBE, ND-Sociobiology, Meme, DIT): All perspectives on human evolution acknowledge the use of symbol and language as major factors in human evolutionary success. DIT and Memetics focus explicitly on the use of language and symbolic cultural elements (broadly defined) as core factors driving human behavioral evolution. EP sees much of human symbol use as emergent from specific adaptive modules reflecting human abilities to manipulate social and symbolic elements to their (evolutionary) benefit. ND-Sociobiology specifically sees the complexity of human language and symbol use as reflective of a cognitive adaptation that facilitates such behavior (as in EP). HBE, largely, ignores language and symbol in favor of specific behavioral activities and quantifiable energetic and physical patterns that are quantitatively assessable.

My Thoughts: Symbol and language differentiate humans from other primates. The ability to participate in temporally disjunct and descriptively diverse, in-depth communication regarding a variety of events, sensations, and past/future plans gives humans an ability no other organism on this planet currently has. It provides a venue for social and ecological inheritance, a mechanism to increase plasticity in human behavioral response and to facilitate (or inhibit) niche construction and a range of responses to potential selective pressures. Importantly, it creates the potential for social and ecological feedback between members of a group that can occur at an extremely fast rate. Symbol and language facilitate the rapidity and flexibility that we see in human behavioral evolution. I suggest (as have many others) that this ability did not start with modern humans (*H. sapiens sapiens* ~200,000 years ago) but rather has deep roots in early *Homo* and specifically began to elaborate/expand in *H. erectus*. Early linguistic precursors and a complex communication system alongside rudimentary symbol use enabled a rapid and radical increase in groups' abilities to cooperate and exchange information with neighboring groups. This then led to rapid abilities to cope with ecological shifts and changes including those associated with rapid and enormous range expansion and fluctuating local climates (as seen in the fossil record ~2–0.5 million years ago). This also sets the stage for a behavioral evolutionary trajectory favoring flexible response patterns focused on communication/information exchange rather than specific adaptations to local ecological or social contexts. This could have also led to increasingly complex intragroup, and occasionally intergroup, cooperative behavior over time.

Testability: The material fossil record (as it indicates innovation in tool kits, range expansion, and success of the genus *Homo* relative to other hominins) provides general support for these assertions. More effective tests of early symbol/language use require the discovery of more specific details regarding the construction and dissemination of stone and nonstone tools, as this might reflect more complex communicative abilities. Possibly assessments of tool types' spread across regions compared with models that predict such spreads based in simple observation diffusion versus focused dissemination of specific knowledge might offer some insight. There is some contention that symbolic behavior is evident in the fossil record before 200,000 years ago' however, no clear-cut examples have yet been discovered. As more examples are uncovered, some trends and patterns in early and very simple symbol use may emerge.

Sexual Division of Labor

Fossil Data: Identifiable differences between male and female behavior are not evident in the fossil record prior to approximately 45,000 years ago (Adovasio et al. 2007). There is no association of gender/sex and stone tool making or the construction of any of the artifacts between approximately 2.5 million and 45,000 years ago or so. The fossil record does show sexual dimorphism in size and therefore possible strength dimorphism, which may be related to differential hunting and gathering behavior between males and females, but this is purely hypothetical based on some modern comparisons. Kuhn and Stiner (2006) suggest that the appearance of small forage items (seeds, for example) along with aspects of clothing and other possibly "female" based material items with *H. sapiens sapiens* fossils in Eurasia at this time and the lack of such items in Neanderthals (see Chapter 4) demonstrates that a sexual division of labor existed in modern humans and enabled them to out-compete Neanderthals.

Comparative Data: In the nonhuman primates, there is not a sexual division of labor aside from the fact that in most species (but not all) females are the primary caretakers of infants. In most species, both males and females engage in range defense. In chimpanzees, males are more likely than females to participate in hunts, border patrols, and intergroup lethal conflicts. In orangutans, females are the sex observed most frequently capturing and eating meat. There is generally, a near 100% overlap between males and females in forage targets as well, with Gorillas being the main exception (females and immatures forage in terminal branches while males do not).

Paradigmatic Views (EP, HBE, ND-Sociobiology, Meme, DIT): The sexual division of labor is a general assumption of all of these perspectives, with the underlying theme being that the division is adaptive. Memetics and DIT also include the possibility that cultural units/memes also facilitate/maintain the division. HBE and ND-Sociobiology see the sexual division of labor as a fitness enhancing strategy based on male–female differences in morphology wherein males focus on larger, higher payoff/larger loss work (such as hunting) while females focus on projects that are smaller (in energy/risk cost) with more consistent returns (such as gathering plant materials). EP sees these divisions as resulting from specific adaptive module tied to broad male–female behavioral differences ultimately associated with mating strategies. All of these perspectives see the sexual division of labor as "old" in the human lineage.

My Thoughts: Because the fossil record does not show any clear evidence of a sexual division of labor until relatively recently (much later than the appearance of modern *H. sapiens sapiens*, see Chapter 4) it is hazardous to assume its existence as a basal assumption in human behavioral evolution. All human populations today have some form of sexual division of labor (but the details of what males and females do varies substantially), so it is not far-fetched to think of it as characteristic of modern human societies. But when did it "evolve" or did it? I am not sure that the sexual division of labor is best seen as an adaptation (the result of selection for specific phenogenotype associations). Rather, these behaviors can be seen as human behavioral responses to different types of ecological and social contexts and pressures under the rubric of a highly cooperative social group. Members of such groups divide the "work" required to achieve energetic input, protection, child rearing, and so on across all members (including immatures, see cooperation across age class above). Some of these divisions fall along sex or gender[5] lines, some do not. Physical state, age, experience, social standing, and so on, all impact the types or roles individuals have within the group. Seeing the division of labor as a social solution to diverse types of challenges rather than specifically tied to sexual differences enables us to model it as part of the cooperative and flexible social pattern that is core to human success. This is not to say that some roles/behaviors are not tied to sex differences; males and females do differ in important morphological and physiological ways, but they also overlap in as many ways.

Testability: The suggestion by Kuhn and Stiner (2006) that humans outcompeted Neanderthals due to a sexual division of labor is contentious, but it does offer some methodological insight for testing such ideas. Focusing on a set of overt signals of different roles for individuals within groups in the archeological record can allow us to build a reasonable timeline for the appearance of such differences. As Adovasio et al. (2007) note, there is very little evidence for this differentiation along sexual lines prior to about 45,000 years ago, but that does not mean it does not exist. Perhaps detailed inspection of material remains from earlier times with an emphasis on reconstructing techniques of foraging and tool construction/transport/dissemination

---

[5] It is important to note that anthropologists treat "gender" as a socially constructed role and "sex" and the biological definition of male and female. Sex differences and gender differences tend to overlap but are not in a one-to-one relationship.

might reveal earlier differences. We cannot simply assume that sexual division of labor existed without any supporting evidence, but we can cast the net more broadly and focus on role differentiation within the group as an important precursor to more specific types of labor divisions over time in the evolution of human behavior.

Flexible Behavior

Fossil Data: The overviews by Potts (1998, 1999, 2004), Wood and Strait (2004), Wells and Stock (2007), myself (Fuentes 2004), and many others suggest that behavioral flexibility in response to ecological pressures was important throughout hominin evolution. The fossils themselves do not provide insight aside from their distribution across diverse ecozones (indicating human ancestral success in meeting diverse ecological challenges). The material record also indicates the use and increase in complexity over time of extra-somatic (not of the body) materials by the genus *Homo*, suggesting a level of flexibility and associated innovation not present in other organisms.

   Comparative Data: Primates, especially monkeys and apes, are behaviorally flexible and excellent problem solvers. While we do see some species-wide patterns of behavior, individual variation in behavior is the norm rather than the exception in primates. Individuals encounter diverse social situations across their lives and the ability to respond flexibly appears to be a common primate pattern. This then acts as a primate-wide baseline from which humans can expand (Dunbar and Shultz 2007, Hermann et al. 2007).

   Paradigmatic Views (EP, HBE, ND-Sociobiology, Meme, DIT): All of the main perspectives accept that humans exhibit flexible behavior. EP, HBE, and ND-Sociobiology see this behavioral flexibility as bounded by specific adaptive strategies (or modules for EP) such that certain types of behavior (that more explicitly tied to fitness enhancing for example) are less plastic than others. DIT and Memetics envision a larger role for cultural variation as a driver and thus a greater degree of flexibility, including maladaptive variants in human behavior.

   My Thoughts: The expansion of primate hypersociality and behavioral flexibility in humans is a core element in our success. The ability to respond to pressures (selective or otherwise) via diverse physical, behavioral, and cultural/material manners allows us a very broad range of reaction and thus higher likelihood of a successful (or at least sufficient) response. Humans are not capable of overcoming everything or infinitely flexible in response, but having such a large "toolkit" that draws on such a diverse set of sources enables us to develop multiple ways to deal with ecological pressures, other organisms, and each other. This also makes it difficult to identify specific adaptations in much that humans do. A common adaptation may be the ability for flexibility rather than a specific set of behavior (in most cases). This is not to suggest that certain behavioral patterns in humans are not the result of specific adaptive scenarios, rather my point is that most behavioral patterns probably arise from a generalized broader flexibility/range of potential behavior. Therefore the onus for those examining human behavioral evolution is on demonstrating that any given behavioral pattern is a specific adaptation and not part of the human ability to respond via diverse mechanisms.

Testability: Given human flexibility of behavioral patterns and responses, we should assume, as a null hypothesis, that any given behavior pattern we see is not the direct result of a specific adaptive scenario, even if we can identify potential fitness costs (this is contrary to most of the traditional perspectives). Measuring the range of behavioral response across contexts/situations rather than only seeking the ultimate fitness impact of a specific behavior might provide us with a better picture of the overall system and thus a deeper understanding of systemic patterns of behavior in humans rather than individual traits/behavior. If we can construct a reliable, testable scenario for adaptation, then we can set out a hypothesis for the behavior and seek to connect it to the larger human behavioral system.

Heterosexual Pair Bond

Fossil Data: As noted previously, the fossil record contains little that identifies specific patterns of male–female relationships. The reduction in sexual dimorphism moving from early *Homo* to *H. erectus* and then to the smallest level of dimorphism in modern humans might correlate with increasing importance of pair bonds as monomorphism is associated with pair bonding in many mammalian groups. See also male–female cooperation above.

Comparative Data: Many primate species do show varying degrees of pair bonding between adult females and males. In some species where two-adult groups are the norm, strong pair bonds emerge, however in others they do not (Fuentes 2002). Strong social and spatial associations between adult females and males also occur in species that are found in multiadult groups. However, it is important to note that pair bonds are not common in human's closest relatives, the chimpanzee, gorilla, and orangutan, but do occur in the smaller apes, the gibbons. In chimpanzees, males and females form temporary social pair-bond associations related to mating and in gorilla groups, males form strong bonds with multiple females. See also male–female cooperation above.

Paradigmatic Views (EP, HBE, ND-Sociobiology, Meme, DIT): ND-Sociobiology, HBE and EP tend to view female–male pair bonds as a main element in human social organization explicitly tied to reproductive strategies (see nuclear family above). There are a number of hypotheses proposed by these perspectives to explain pair bonds with most relating to a female's need for protection and paternal investment/quality and a male's need for paternity assurance and access to reproductive opportunity. Again, the pair bond is seen as a trade-off that is more in the female's favor than the males, such that the male should seek extra-pair reproductive opportunities if possible. DIT and Memetics theoretically allow for more flexibility of the social construction and maintenance of bonding patterns, but neither perspective has resulted in much published literature on the topic. Unfortunately, in all of these perspectives, marriage[6] is frequently used as homologous to pair bonds in the construction of hypotheses for human bonding and mating.

My Thoughts: The heterosexual pair bond has played a central role in hypotheses about human evolution for some time (Lovejoy 1981, see Chapter 5). While all human societies have marriage (see Footnote 6), it is less clear that heterosexual pair bonds are ubiquitous. At one extreme, some societies favor same-sex association and bonding over heterosexual associations, with males and females only coming together for reproductive purposes (Middleton 2001). Across modern human cultures, strong associations occur both homo- and heterosexually with and without sexual connotations (see below). There is evidence for physiological correlates of pair bonding in humans with males and females involved in pair bonds exhibiting complex hormonal (oxytocin and prolactin, for example) responses in association with social and physical interactions, including parenting behavior. However, I suggest that it is the pair bond that is of greatest interest here, not necessarily sex of the bonded individuals (see below).

Testability: Because of the overreliance on marriage as a proxy for pair bonding, many hypotheses proposed are actually looking at cultural constructions rather than evolutionary outcomes. Examination of pair bonds in humans should explicitly address the structural, behavioral, and reproductive factors of pair bonds (see Fuentes 2002) so that we can construct actual scenarios relative to the evolution of human behavior rather than cultural proxies. We need to look specifically at the physiologies of bonding, their behavioral correlates and the variation in patterns (or lack thereof) in pair bonds across modern humans. Clear and explicit measurements of what we mean by pair bond are core to constructing and assessing hypotheses.

Specific Behavior Factors that Deserve Further Examination

Pair-Bonding (General Same Sex and Different Sex)

Fossil Data: See intragroup cooperation and heterosexual pair bonds for a review of the relevant fossil information.

Comparative Data: The presence of both same-sex and heterosexual social bonds is prevalent in primate societies, called pair bonds in two-adult groups and friendships in multiadult groups; these associations have behavioral, and physiological correlates. In some species, heterosexual bonds are stronger; in others, same-sex bonds predominate. For example,

---

[6] Marriage is a complex cultural category that involves social, economic, and kinship variables and may or may not involve any specific bonding between the spouses. Marriage is not equal to pair bonds and may or may not reflect actual reproductive patterns and should not be used as shorthand for pair bonds in hypotheses about the evolution of human behavior (Fuentes 1999, McKinnon 2005).

in chimpanzees, strong associations between male dyads form, but in gorillas the stronger bonds are between males and females. However, long-term strong physiological and social ties between dyads are not found in all primate species. The strongest such pair bonds are found in neotropical primates that occur primarily in two-adult groups and mate more or less monogamously (such as the genera *Aotus* and *Callicebus*, Fernadez-Duque 2007, Norconk 2007).

Paradigmatic Views (EP, HBE, ND-Sociobiology, Meme, DIT): In ND-Sociobiology, EP and HBE alliances between males are proposed as important in human evolution, especially in the context of intergroup aggression, hunting and possibly control of females. However, none of these perspectives focus in the possibility that pair-bonding itself (homo- and heterosexually) is a major characteristic of human behavior.

My Thoughts: I suggest that strong physiological and behavioral bonds between individuals are of core importance in understanding human behavioral evolution. Co-opting the underlying physiology of the particularly strong mother–infant bond characteristic of primates (see Chapter 4) I suggest that in adulthood humans are able to use this physiological system to form one or more tight social relationships with other individuals. While individuals are able to form loose bonds with all or most members of their social group, certain relationships have much stronger ties behaviorally and physiologically. These special relationships can be same-sex or heterosexual and may or may not involve sexual activity (and if heterosexual, reproduction). Through these relationships we can envision enhanced pockets of cooperation within groups and the creation of social networks that provide social, behavioral and physiological benefits. As with language and symbol use, and the intensity and depth of intragroup cooperation, this pair-bonding ability also separates humans from other primates in the extent to which we carry it. I suggest that our success as a species is specifically the result of these three elements (language/symbol, heightened cooperation, and pair-bonding) combined with a highly flexible and manipulative behavioral capability.

Testability: As with heterosexual pair bonds above, specific behavioral and physiological measures of human participants in strong relationships must be undertaken to define the parameters of human bonding (much of this work is underway in biocultural anthropology, psychological and physiological studies). Once defined, we can look at the prevalence and impact of such relationships in areas such as health, stress, behavior, and even reproduction in attempts to construct testable scenarios about human behavioral evolution.

A MODEST PROPOSAL FOR A GENERAL FRAMEWORK OF OUR EVOLUTIONARY HISTORY

Having discussed these commonalties and perspectives and proposed my thoughts about each, I close this chapter with a brief summary of how

I envision a general framework/narrative for the evolution of human behavior.

First we have a baseline of elements that characterize the earliest direct human ancestor. These are drawn from comparative primate studies and the fossil record—we do not need to hypothesize about how these arose—they are the baseline for humanity. The earliest human ancestors existed in multiadult groups with a relatively high degree of social complexity, patterns of social bonding between individuals within the group and a level of interindividual cooperation and competition at least equal to that found in ape and monkey societies. Individuals exhibited substantial behavioral flexibility, at least as much as the modern apes, and a repertoire of vocal and gestural communication, but not language. Rudimentary tool use and manipulation of the environment was present as was sexual dimorphism in size, with males being larger than females resulting in some differences in behavioral roles between males and females. However, specific patterns of dominance relationships between individuals are not clear. These earliest human ancestors shared with their primate cousins specific type of "social intelligence" (Dunbar and Shultz 2007) such that "distinctive aspects of primate cognition evolved mainly in response to the especially challenging demands of a complex social life of constant competition and cooperation with others in the social group" (Herrmann et al. 2007) in addition to the external ecological pressures.

Between Approximately 2 Million Years and 500,000 Years Ago

In Africa, humans coexist with other hominins, namely members of the genus *Paranthropus*, frequently living sympatrically and possibly competing for space and food resources. Early in this time period, predators remain a significant selective pressure on all hominins. As humans move around and out of African they encounter diverse ecologies and novel environmental contexts stimulating an expansion of behavioral responses. Associated with this time period is a feedback process involving expanded behavioral flexibility and enhanced cooperative interactions along with increasing brain size and neurological complexity (augmenting cognitive power). Also, sexual dimorphism in size begins to decrease, possibly associated with some changing aspects of male–female roles (possibly more heterosexual cooperation) relative to ancestral forms.

The transition from early *Homo* through *H. erectus/ergaster* is marked by a shift in the locus of primary selection pressures, including increased energetic and child-rearing costs, to which *Homo* responds with further behavioral changes. These include enhanced intra- and occasionally intergroup cooperation associated with increased quality and content of information transfer (aiding foraging and antipredator success). Elements such as cooperative food collection (in scavenging, hunting, and exploitation of underground plant storage organs for example), substantial intragroup (and possibly intergroup) food sharing, and cooperative/multiple caretakers of young also appear during this period. This increased social complexity facilitates the cooption of caretaking physiology and alliance formation tendencies (general for primates) to facilitate the appearance of pair bonds between some individuals in groups. Predation, a major selective force earlier in human evolution, is lessened via these same cooperative behavioral shifts. This pattern is accompanied by the advent and augmentation of innovation in tool creation and utilization and an overall increased manipulation of extra-somatic materials and the environment, resulting in substantial niche construction by humans and its concomitant ecological and social inheritance patterns (true biocultural inheritance). Some role differentiation begins to emerge in human groups. During this period, the selective landscape for hominins in Africa shifts in a positive direction for members of the genus *Homo* and a negative one for members of the other living hominin genus, *Paranthropus*, who go extinct by 1 million years ago. At some point in this period humans begin using fire, but do not yet have full control over its creation and maintenance.

During this period, members of the genus *Homo* begin the transition from the generalized primate "social intelligence" cognitive abilities towards a modern human "cultural intelligence" cognitive pattern. This can be seen as a "release from proximity" in social organization where spatial and temporal proximity are no longer requirements for social relationships (Quiatt and Reynolds 1993, Gamble 1998). This uniquely human pattern involves a suite of powerful and multifaceted sociocultural cognitive skills that are tied to extremely intensive ontogenetic learning and long-term developmental processes (see Hermann et al. 2007).

500,000–45,000 Years Ago (Give or Take 10,000 Years)

The human brain ceases its increase in size but probably continues its trajectory of enhanced neurological complexity facilitating continued expansion of cognitive skills resulting in a nearly complete cultural intelligence. Human groups are exploiting a wide variety of resources at this point and begin to increase both their geographic range (into higher stress/more seasonal climates/ecotypes) and their pattern of energy acquisition (expanding the types and intensity of hunting and gathering). The full control and use of fire facilitates both of these aspects and increases the potential active period for humans (via light) leading to increased rates of mental and material cultural change (control of fire becomes a major niche constructing event). In this period, large game hunting becomes more common as does cooperative care of ill and elderly within groups. The human toolkit expands into more fine-tuned tools of diverse types and uses, resulting in the emergence of aesthetic traditions in some groups and populations.

The intense feedback between behavioral/cultural actions and ecological/social pressures/contexts and cognitive potential speeds up and continues driving behavioral and cognitive complexity in communicative ability and behavioral systems. Language of some form emerges, and humans continue to expand the density and complexity of their information sharing system. Role differentiation along age, sex, and some social lines becomes more commonplace in human groups and populations. Biocultural inheritance becomes more multifaceted, likely involving stories and mythos, and linguistic capabilities enable cultural histories and ideologies to be shared and disseminated across regions. Symbolic representation via material goods (wall painting, figurines, or iconographic materials) also arises during this period indicating the full integration of symbolic action and thought into human everyday life. Intragroup stratification (gender and social hierarchies) associated with material goods begins late in this period as do personal adornment and burial of the dead and/or postmortem modification. These patterns indicate increased complexity in social kinship structures, group and regional identities, and the emergence of intricate socioreligious systems. The frequency, complexity and importance of both intra- and intergroup conflict increase.

45,000 Years Ago Through Today

Human language and complex material culture are full blown, humans have a full cultural intelligence. The precursors of sedentism and agriculture influence the initiation of regional polities and large-scale socioreligious kinships with clan/tribal associations becoming commonplace. Conflict between groups and populations becomes more common as such units invest more and more in local material and mythical stakes. Across the globe, human interactions at the group and population levels become a complex mix of cooperative and conflictual histories and relationships having both material and sociohistorical components. A multifarious division of labor, gender stratification, material wealth stratification, social restrictions on mating, and the creation of socioeconomic unions of marriage all become standard (but not necessarily universal) components of human societies (Figure 8.1).

This is simply a generalized overview, a narrative emphasizing the systematic and interconnected nature of human behavioral evolution and the emergence of a human cultural cognition. It is based on what we know from the fossil record and what we can comfortably and relatively assuredly assume about the timing of broad behavioral patterns. It neither prioritizes natural selection nor cultural change but attempts to demonstrate how these, and other forces, are inextricably linked in a dynamic interplay with a type of behavioral complexity not seen in the evolutionary histories of other organisms on this planet. Within this framework, we can attempt to

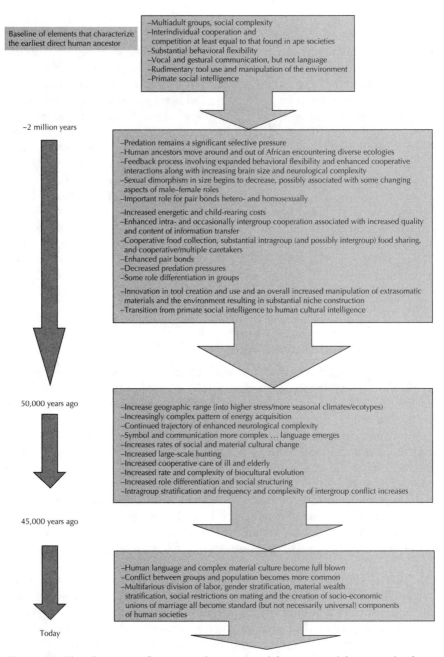

Baseline of elements that characterize the earliest direct human ancestor
–Multiadult groups, social complexity
–Interindividual cooperation and competition at least equal to that found in ape societies
–Substantial behavioral flexibility
–Vocal and gestural communication, but not language
–Rudimentary tool use and manipulation of the environment
–Primate social intelligence

~2 million years

–Predation remains a significant selective pressure
–Human ancestors move around and out of African encountering diverse ecologies
–Feedback process involving expanded behavioral flexibility and enhanced cooperative interactions along with increasing brain size and neurological complexity
–Sexual dimorphism in size begins to decrease, possibly associated with some changing aspects of male–female roles
–Important role for pair bonds hetero- and homosexually

–Increased energetic and child-rearing costs
–Enhanced intra- and occasionally intergroup cooperation associated with increased quality and content of information transfer
–Cooperative food collection, substantial intragroup (and possibly intergroup) food sharing, and cooperative/multiple caretakers
–Enhanced pair bonds
–Decreased predation pressures
–Some role differentiation in groups

–Innovation in tool creation and use and an overall increased manipulation of extrasomatic materials and the environment resulting in substantial niche construction
–Transition from primate social intelligence to human cultural intelligence

50,000 years ago

–Increase geographic range (into higher stress/more seasonal climates/ecotypes)
–Increasingly complex pattern of energy acquisition
–Continued trajectory of enhanced neurological complexity
–Symbol and communication more complex ... language emerges
–Increases rates of social and material cultural change
–Increased large-scale hunting
–Increased cooperative care of ill and elderly
–Increased rate and complexity of biocultural evolution
–Increased role differentiation and social structuring
–Intragroup stratification and frequency and complexity of intergroup conflict increases

45,000 years ago

–Human language and complex material culture become full blown
–Conflict between groups and population becomes more common
–Multifarious division of labor, gender stratification, material wealth stratification, social restrictions on mating and the creation of socio-economic unions of marriage all become standard (but not necessarily universal) components of human societies

Today

Figure 8.1 This diagram reflects a modest proposal for a general framework of our evolutionary history.

locate the origins and scenarios of maintenance for a multitude of human behaviors. From specific sexual behavior, to bullying, to the appearance of dietary taboos and the cross-cultural prevalence of music, specific behavioral patterns can be linked at various points to this generalized history. The challenge in trying to disarticulate the tapestry of human evolution is to assume a systems approach but attempt to find the nodes of interconnection between the fossil and archeological record, selective pressures, ecological contexts, cultural patterns, behavioral possibilities, and testable hypotheses. Using all of the tools in our toolkit, from theory to datasets (Chapters 2–8), we are better able (although not guaranteed) to develop answers that are closer to reflecting our actual histories than ever was possible within a single perspective or within purely evolutionary functionalist or culturally constructivist mind sets.

CHAPTER 9

Problem of Being a Modern Human and Looking at Our Evolution

BENEFITS AND FLAWS IN THIS PROSPECTUS

The first problem of being a modern human and looking into our behavioral evolution is really the theme of this book: that there are many different ways to do it. I suggest that we try to integrate these views, and expand them, as much as possible, in working toward a more synthetic approach. There are more benefits than detriments in doing this, despite its inherent complexity, the frequent danger of contradiction in assumptions, and the lack of simple straightforward answers to the questions in human behavioral evolution. I hope that students and practitioners reading this text can find at least some agreement with my contention, minimally to the point that you see enough potential (or salvageable) value in the differing perspectives to at least read articles and books that originate from them. It is apparent that the main benefits and detriments of this approach are inherent in the same two themes: the merging of disparate perspectives and the ability to produce testable hypotheses. These are simultaneously the strengths and weaknesses of the approach.

Merging Approaches and Perspectives

Chapter 1 began with the following quote:

> It was thus a prevailing, if not universal, belief of early writers on evolution, and one that crept well into the twentieth century, that not only did behavior evolve, but it also functioned as a principal instrument of species modification. (Robert Richards 1987, p. 70)

Human behavioral evolution occurs in large part because of the way in which humans behave. This sounds self-evident, but is in reality frequently overlooked. The agency that behavior has in its own patterns of change over time make constructing scenarios about its evolution more complex than trying to figure out the change in the morphology of a specific tooth or other physical traits (not that this is a particularly easy task either). The first seven chapters of the book focused on this theme via assessing theoretical perspectives, some datasets, overviews of various proposals, and my thoughts on what I see as the primary elements emerging from Chapters 1to 7.

Chapter 8 started with the quote:

> In anthropology, as elsewhere, progress will never result from destroying what has been previously achieved but rather from incorporating the past of our science into its present and future, enriching the one with the other and turning the whole process into a lasting reality. (Levi-Strauss 1968)

Most of the various dominant and emerging perspectives on human behavioral evolution can complement one another. The history of evolutionary approaches, much as with the history of anthropology, is filled with expansions and refinements of previous conceptualizations. We grow by cannibalizing existing perspectives, adding and changing as our datasets and methodologies mature and expand. Occasionally, outright rejections of past views occur, but usually some threads continue into the new forms and perspectives. Obviously, aspects of the current and emerging views reviewed here are incompatible in some cases, but rather than viewing the various perspectives as necessarily conflictual, we can attempt to see how each approach might complement others, looking both to areas of overlap and discord as we try to best assess our evolutionary patterns (i.e., Chapter 8).

I do not intend these statements to be naïve; many practitioners of these diverse perspectives do not agree and will not agree. However, that need not dissuade us from exploiting the findings and prospectuses of the various viewpoints in our quest for understanding. None of the perspectives reviewed in this book, by themselves, is the best way to describe, study, and propose scenarios for human behavioral evolution. What I intended in this book was to outline the various threads and to look at their areas of overlap and emerge with a renewed synthesis perspective. I contend that a commitment to evolutionary anthropology is one of the best ways to do that. Anthropology is situated in such a manner as to favor its ability to draw from the best of the social and biological sciences and fuse them as possible. However, viewing this project from an anthropological perspective also illustrates its pitfalls for modern humans more emphatically than from other disciplines (see next section below). Human behavior can result from aspects of adapted systems, from systems in flux, from systems contingent on cultural and individual experience, and from reactions to contextual stimuli. Such behavior may or may not have fitness impacts and/or heritable components. Behavioral patterns and potential are constructed by evolutionary histories, biocultural development, and social context and histories.

How do we keep this approach from being "overly holistic" and thus more or less unable to produce specific, usable, outcomes? We do so by formulating and testing questions at the junctures/intersections of facets of modern evolutionary and anthropological, psychological, and ethological theories combined with methodological toolkits provided by the social and biological sciences. We try to piece together the results from across disciplines and from across the perspectives reviewed in this book in order to attempt a broader, possibly multidimensional representation, of patterns and processes. Different junctures are best assessed using diverse disciplinary tools, and the predominant approaches will include hybridization between evolutionary, ecological, ethnographic, ethnological, psychological, and philosophical methodologies.

How Do We Test This and Why Are Testable Hypotheses Important?

As with all endeavors that strive to use the scientific method, the value lies in the tests. Without a real ability to refute and support assertions via methods that are transparent, or at least replicable, all such proposals are confined to the realm of philosophical musings.[1] In the case of the proposals and examples presented in this book, it is apparent that our strongest assertions will be amenable to testing via comparative primate and mammalian datasets or experiments and via data from the fossil record. However, comparative analogy is not always a real test.

Take, for example, sexual dimorphism in the living primates. In general, there is a pattern of correlation between such dimorphism and male–male conflict and male–female relationships. But, that relationship is not ubiquitous. That is, we do not know whether human ancestors' dimorphism correlated with the majority pattern in primates, the minority pattern, or neither. There is no way to fully test this. We can drive the range of phylogenetic error down by comparing across specific groups of primates, or just within the Hominoidea. However, even that is problematic as there has been such a winnowing of ape-type primate lineages over the last 15 million years. Those few remaining lineages, especially those that are closest to us, the so-called great apes, are all quite derived relative to ancestral hominoids (as are we). This means that we are missing a good description of ancestral hominoid behavior, our phylogenetic control group, beyond a very generalized concept (see end of Chapter 8: our baseline section).

This is where the fossil record becomes critical. In the last 20 years there has been an explosion in fossil discoveries and technologies, allowing us

---

[1] Not that this is necessarily a bad thing. Much of what Darwin and Wallace and their contemporaries proposed, much of what has emerged over the last 150 years in evolutionary theory, began as musings without a glimmer of testability. We need such philosophical underpinnings for all theory; however, the closer we can come to proposing testable hypotheses the closer we are to establishing more accurate views of our evolutionary histories.

to reconstruct paleoecologies. This is core to testing proposals for human behavioral evolution. However, even if this rate of discovery continues, we are still looking at an amazingly depauperate and biased sample. Remember, a majority of our fossil data for humans between 300,000 and 600,000 years ago comes from only one site in Spain (Atapuerca). Most important to our ability to test hypotheses are the material remains in the archeological record and the specific analyses of health and stress/use patterns in the bones themselves. These details enable us to test assumptions about lifestyle and behavior including actual dietary patterns, the tools used to access the foodstuffs, real health issues, and life histories as recorded in the bones. The archeological record also illustrates the manipulation of extra-somatic items and the contexts in which this occurred—also a fertile zone for testing hypotheses. However, there is the depositional bias. Those events and items closer to us in time are more common and more amenable to extractions of this kind of information. This biases us to a larger dataset for those ancestors closest to us in time, especially the last 50,000 years or so—the precise time when I suggest we might be seeing a dramatic change in patterns of behavior and conflict.

The solution? Strive to use the various perspectives (traditional and emerging) reviewed in this book to produce hypotheses that do not rely on a multitude of shaky assumptions about what specific traits in primates and human ancestors are adapted for. Look to systems in primate and modern human behavior, the patterns therein, and then attempt to identify such patterns in the fossil, paleoecological, and archeological records. Look at the quantifiable portions/facets of those patterns and hypothesize what their correlates would be in the fossil and material record. This has been demonstrated to be particularly effective in recent work in paleoanthropology, human behavioral ecology, and evolutionary anthropology on fossil diets and foraging behavior assessed via stable isotope analyses and material remains.

For example, dental and related fossil analyses indicate that *Paranthropus* was not particularly stenotopic (not a dietary specialist) and that *Homo* was not more eurytopic (dietary generalist) than *Paranthropus* (Wood and Strait 2004). Wood and Strait demonstrate that the Robinson's dietary hypothesis[2] is not supported across a majority of morphological and ecological variables—both genera appear relatively eurytopic. They argue that if this is the case, then dietary strategies and flexibility in foraging behavior may not fully account for the differential survivorship between the two genera. Wood and Strait (2004) propose examining at least seven variables for constructing hypotheses regarding the success of *Homo* and the extinction of *Paranthropus*. Those variables are locomotor mode, degree/mode of tool-use and/or production, predator avoidance/predation pressure,

---

[2] Robinson's dietary hypothesis is the proposal that *Paranthropus* was a specialist of herbivorous matter and it was this dietary specialty that facilitated its extinction as climates and ecologies changed.

competition from other primates or mammals, competition between *Homo* and *Paranthropus*, social group structure, and the capacity for learned behavior. All of these have some facets that can be assessed in the fossil record (some more than others) but all are seen as part of a system of relationships between the hominins rather than a specific trait or single adaptation that differentiated them.

Testing is difficult, but it is our strongest ally.

THE DIFFICULTIES WE ENCOUNTER WHEN RECONSTRUCTING OUR EVOLUTIONARY PATH AND ITS UNDERLYING CAUSES/PATTERNS

The second problem of being a modern human and looking into our behavioral evolution is the suite of biases and obfuscating factors that accompany being a human at this time and place. These factors are found in our educational and paradigmatic structures, elements introduced by niche construction and the fossil/archeological record, and the impact of current cultural patterns and beliefs.

Basic Educational and Paradigmatic Biases and the Problems These Bring

Throughout this book we refer to a set of traditional and emerging perspectives in evolutionary theory. Each of these has particular biases that direct the kinds of inquiries we undertake. A focus on a certain level of selection (genic or group, for example) structures the kinds of questions you can ask. The Tinbergen level of focus (see Chapter 3) also affects the way in which a question is asked. Assumptions about the role of function for behavior (fitness impacting), about explicit genetic linkages, and the heritability of behaviors leads us to emphasize particular aspects of our hypotheses. However, all of these biases are fairly well known and taking a comparative and integrative approach, as I suggested in the last chapter and above, allows one to moderate some of the negative impacts of such biases. A larger impact of these paradigmatic orientations lies in how they are translated into accessible information—journal articles, books, and most importantly textbooks/articles for teaching purposes.

The type of education we experience shapes the projects we choose to undertake. Given general university culture,[3] academics are constrained at

---

[3] Here, I am generally referring to the North American university systems, where students are not necessarily required to declare a major topic until their second or third years. This mode of "liberal arts" education creates a potentially broader general base, but has students specializing later in their undergraduate career. The rest of the world follows more of a European model laying a greater emphasis on specialization earlier on in the university career. However, many of the North American patterns are starting to appear in some United Kingdom and European universities.

the level of introductory courses to providing simplified explanations of human evolution and human behavior. This is due to the need for establishing a baseline about evolutionary processes, human/mammalian biology, and human cultural and individual variation. Simplification of basic themes and patterns enables instructors to cover a broad range of interrelated topics while providing a sufficient knowledge set for comprehension of the general patterns.

For example, when starting out teaching about genetics in introductory biology or anthropology courses, instructors tend to provide fairly simple linear descriptions of the processes by which segments of DNA (genes) produce proteins, which in turn affect traits. It is not until more advanced courses that more complex patterns of allele variation, translational and transcription variations, genomic regulatory systems, and more complicated elements such as transposons and intragenome variations in function are introduced.

The same is true for evolutionary theory. It is generally taught by introducing a relatively uncomplicated view of natural selection and applying that to a variety of situations. The famous black-and-white moths and tree bark color changes associated with industrialization in England is a well-used example of this. But unlike genetic/genomic theory, many treatments of evolutionary processes fail to become more complex in more advanced courses. When they do, the courses are often taught only in biology departments and all too infrequently attended by anthropology and psychology students interested in human behavior. If one does not receive enhanced and more accurate descriptions, you remain without a detailed grasp of how evolutionary patterns and processes truly function. This can result in the acceptance of simplistic, linear, "common sense," models (such as that proposed by Oliver Curry, see Chapter 1) without sufficient critical analyses resulting in a limitation in abilities, and interests, for critically assessing evolutionary patterns. Learning about complexity and being open to a diversity of views is an important factor in the ability to continuously enhance research quality and findings in the areas of human behavioral evolution.

Related to these instructional themes is the sheer diversity of disciplinary affiliation of researchers focused on facets of human behavioral evolution. Ranging from social scientists, such as anthropologists and psychologists, to behavioral biologists, genomicists and even philosophers, these researchers publish in a multitude of different academic journals. Collecting the diverse array of information is difficult for professional researchers and even more so for students. Having sufficient training and background to be relatively fluent across these disciplinary languages, bodies of theory, and modes of inquiry just adds to this burden.

So, our educational systems, the patterns of student training, and access to the relevant literature affects the shape and tenor of approaches to the study of human behavioral evolution. This is important to keep in mind as one peruses the literature on human behavioral evolution, and notices trends and patterns in perspective. These emerge both from intensive and repeated testing of particular hypotheses as well as from entrenchment of educational trajectories and reproduction of extant views. In this context, I suggest that assessing such proposals and data using the criteria outlined in Chapter 8 might facilitate disarticulating paradigmatic statements based on training from those that are more based on the actual outcomes of the research.

Human Niche Construction Matters

The fact of human niche construction, its potential to have altered/changed selective environments, and the suite of temporal and depositional patterns of the past also bias our questions about human behavioral evolution.

We have already, briefly, discussed the fossil record and the archeological record and their biases. We have very limited material evidence of behavior prior to the last few hundred thousands year ago and extremely limited, but growing, evidence of the range of morphological and material variation at any given time period in our past (prior to ~100,000 years ago). This forces a heavy reliance of reconstruction scenarios that use a variety of assumptions from the comparative primate record and modern human forager groups. It is quite common to use patterns of behavior exhibited by human forager groups living today as a baseline for our ancestral behavior. This is becoming less frequent as such groups are rarely practicing seminomadic foraging separate from industrial and agricultural practice anymore. One could even contend that none of these modern forager peoples were truly separate from these modern impacts and lifeways even during the 1950s–1970s when much of the anthropological and physiological research on such populations was initiated. Regardless, this reliance of datasets from a collection of Amazonian, Australian, Papuan (New Guinean), and South African forager and horticultural societies has structured the kinds of questions we ask. Commonalities and differences between them such as group sizes, marriage practices, and foraging patterns form many of the assumptions we have about past human behavior. This is a phylogenetic analogy approach that assumes that the similarities/patterns may be homologies for humans (same owing to similar ancestral state). However, there are a number of dangers inherent in this approach. We do not know the range of successful "ways" to be a human forager, and how many of these may not be represented in modern groups. Nor do we know how past action by humans has changed the structure of selection pressures (see niche construction below) and the resultant ecological and behavioral inheritance patterns. This is not to say that these comparisons are of no use; they are critical to our practice. Rather, it is simply another potential bias to keep in mind when assessing proposals and research findings.

More common in the past two decades is the assessment of such societies as they make the transitions to the more global cash economies and integration into their broader national identities. The focus then is on the patterns of behavior related to foraging, conflict resolution, marriage patterns (for example), and how they change relative to earlier patterns and what impacts that has on the physiology and behavior of such peoples. Understanding these patterns of change also can provide insight into the range of human response and possibly trajectories of response that occurred in the human past. It is difficult to use modern peoples and their ecologies as mirrors for the past. We must be very cognizant of social, political, and economic factors that manipulate behavior (and health) at rapid rates potentially producing results that are fully modern but cloaked with a few trappings of possibly historically relevant behavioral and/or ecological features. Unlike Darwin, Wallace, Spencer, and their colleagues, we know that all humans living today are fully modern in every way. The variation in economies, technologies, and ways of living are historical elements, not reflections of "primitiveness." There are no primitive humans today, only those in the fossil record.

But even that fossil record (in the broadest sense) is not so clear-cut. Humans have been described from our earliest ancestors as *Homo habilis*, the 'handy' person. I suggest that this is simultaneously correct and a misnomer. Yes, we are notably distinct from other organisms in part due to our alteration of extra-somatic (not of the body) material items and the creation of new toolkits. However, I suggest that this metaphor be taken further; we not only construct material items, we also engage in the construction and navigation of social structures and the conceptualizations of space and place to an extreme equaled by no other organisms. Because niche construction has occurred in areas where humans live (most of the planet for at least the last 15,000 years) we may have a limited potential to see that things were different before. That is, how much of the local ecologies of the reconstructions of the past are direct measures of human niche construction? How much are more reflective of current versus past patterns of ecological pressures? As humans change their environment, they do so in a number of ways. Behavioral niche construction might not leave an overt material record so that we model ecological parameters without realizing that they in fact were modified by the humans (or human ancestors) living there in ways we cannot see. This might be especially relevant when looking at modern foragers and extrapolating their contexts to those of our ancestors.

Because niche construction occurs, there remains a significant problem with the traditional notion of an environment of evolutionary adaptiveness (EEA): the idea that there was a particular past environment, or set of past environments, is the underlying context for the evolution of the main patterns of behavior seen in humans. This is explicitly addressed in more recent treatments of Evolutionary Psychology with the notion of the adaptively relevant environment (ARE) (see Chapter 3). However, there remains too much emphasis, both in public and in academia, on the notion that there was a specific environment or specific ecological factors that drove particular changes in specific traits resulting in the pattern of human behavioral evolution leading to the behavior we exhibit today. As we have already noted, it is very likely that the variation in ecologies and environments encountered and moved through by human ancestors played core roles in human behavioral evolution. To pinpoint specific factors of those environments as more relevant than others is very difficult, given our limitations in measuring potential niche construction by our ancestors. Modeling such scenarios including niche construction and its associated ecological and social inheritance as core factors in the models might be a way around this. Our largest difficulty is trying to guess at the relative strength of selection for any given ecological pressure. We can reconstruct paleoecologies/environments for *Homo erectus* in East Africa between 1.7 and 1.5 million years ago but we cannot assume that those pressures were not already modified via some behavioral niche construction. We have to include the possibility that such systems were in place. This is why using modern nonhuman primates as analogies (even for earlier human ancestors) can be a problem. Primates engage in niche construction, but nowhere near the level of modern humans; thus our ancestral ability to do so probably played an increasingly important role in our evolution since the split from other primate forms.

My point here is that past ecologies, or even human bodies, may already have borne the mark of human manipulation, well before the advent of agriculture and relatively complex material toolkits. This need not be the case in all situations, and might only be relevant in a very few; however, it should be a standard facet of our hypotheses and proposals for the examinations of human evolution in the context of ecological pressures.

Everyday Life, Gender, and Cultural Anthropology Matter

In addition to these historical contexts and potential problems, the impact of modern cultural context and experiential bias of everyday life (beyond academic views) affects how we see the past and thus how we ask questions about it. Issues such as gendered perspectives, relative levels of agency and diversity by practitioners, and basic cultural preconceptions structure our views. One relevant observation is that the review in Chapter 2 of the basis of evolutionary approaches and that in Chapter 7 of emerging theory have a salient difference; there are many more female researchers represented in the emerging theory than in the original approaches. Few women had agency or any impact on the structure of mainstream evolutionary theory between Darwin's publication in the late 1850s till the 1970s. Only in the last three decades has there emerged a substantial pool of female practitioners looking into evolutionary theory. There are numerous debates and discussions about how such gender disparities play out in theoretical formations and paradigmatic structures. But it is clear that there is at least a correlation between female participation and an expansion in perspectives in evolutionary theory.

It is worth noting that the increase in number of female primatologists had substantial impact in primatological methods and theory in the last three decades of the twentieth century (Strum and Fedigan 2000).

In addition, Adavosio et al. (2007) provide an interesting overview of biases in interpretations of the fossil and material records related to gender role division. They demonstrate, quite effectively, that cultural assumptions about gender roles permeate the literature on human evolution in regards to the fossil record. This is surprising as there is little to no direct evidence for any such patterns in the fossils or material record prior to the last approximately 50,000 years (see Chapter 4). The main "evidence" for earlier gender divisions comes from comparative data on modern human patterns (including foragers, but not limited to them) and extrapolations from nonhuman primates. This is not to say that those assumptions are incorrect, but rather to point out that they are loose assumptions that get a "pass" in rigorous analyses given that they "fit" so well with our current cultural behavioral realities. Without some actual data to support or refute such claims, we should be hesitant to accept them as actual patterns in early human ancestors.

There are numerous other assumptions about gender and general behavior that we impose on our assessments of the past—assumptions about male and female sexual behavior and interests, the male's tendency to be more physically aggressive, humans' drive for status via acquisition of material goods, and even the nature of human competitiveness as seen in team and individual sports. Importantly, humans today also exist almost completely within a cash economy, an amazingly recent phenomenon. Cash economies and their corollaries of symbolic presentation of goods and services, majority detachment from actual food production, and rapid patterns of display of status and power are associated with a broad suite of behavior that we take as basic human patterns. These might reflect some evolved patterns in human behavior, but the cash economy might just as easily have produced many of these patterns. We should be exceedingly careful in making one-to-one comparisons of behavior today, especially behavior that is fundamentally tied to specific socioeconomic, religious or historical systems, and the evolution of behavioral patterns in the human past.

While we humans do have agency in our behavior, there is also cultural historicity and contextuality that is tied to any behavior exhibited. It is important to note that modern cultural anthropology also creates an enriching context for examining human behavioral evolution. Anthropological inquiries are frequently concerned with who/what has agency in human behavior. Current answers to these questions in the anthropological literatures include elements from phylogenetic histories, cultural/social histories, current evolutionary pressures, current economic–political pressures, local context (ecological, cultural, environmental, familial, and so on), and experiential molding of individuals (physiological, behavioral, and perceptual molding), just to name a few. Therefore, there is most certainly an important place at our table for an integrated evolutionary approach that includes cultural anthropologies.

Following Tim Ingold (2001, 2007), I suggest that if anthropology, and all of those questing to understand human behavior, in general becomes more familiar with the offerings of the traditional and the "post Neo-Darwinian" emergent perspectives in evolutionary theory (see Chapters 3 and 7), we will see that there is indeed a significant space for mutual enrichment and overlap between evolutionary and cultural anthropological approaches. I also agree with Jon Marks' (2004) call for a true Darwinian anthropology; "A Darwinian anthropology should be as culturally sensitive as any other kind of anthropology" (Marks 2004, p. 191). Anthropology, in a general sense, should be concerned with evolutionary theory and incorporate relevant perspectives well beyond those that exclusively focus on the action of natural, and sexual, selection as the prime driver in evolutionary change (classic Neo-Darwinian orientation). I want to emphasize that we have expanded beyond Darwin's initial contributions, also noted by Marks (2004), and this book is an illustration, theoretically, of where and how this is happening as it most relates to the interests of those who prioritize a focus on human behavior.

Epilogue: Anthropology, Science, and People

SOME NOTES ON THE VALUE OF INTEGRATIVE ANTHROPOLOGICAL APPROACHES

There is no single answer to the question "what have we 'evolved' for?". The notion that we have evolved simple specific strategies to deal with the dynamic, complex challenges seems highly unlikely. Our adaptive zone is broad and cultural; therefore very specific, limited behavioral adaptations are unlikely to arise in human ancestry. Humans are biocultural organisms and that simple fact makes it most difficult to articulate and model our evolutionary histories. However, as I have repeated throughout this book, I maintain that an approach that melds evolutionary theory, emerging complexities in the understanding of evolutionary biology, and the methodologies inherent in anthropology will provide the most promising space to engage in such endeavors. This space is that occupied by what we can term a "biocultural perspective"; holistic, messy, but potentially highly profitable as a paradigm. Biocultural approaches provide the best way to understand human behavior, because rather than being obsessed with specific answers as an endpoint they can provide exciting new questions, which themselves are telling of rich possibilities. However, *Biocultural* is not simply the union of two things (e.g., Culture + Biology), it is a dynamic perspective on the multifarious structure of humans, their niches, and the interactions within and between them. It is, in short, what the promise of a real integrated anthropology could provide.

But why anthropology? Because culture (however defined) is ubiquitous, creatively used, symbolic, and exhibits emergent domains and patterns, it has agency in the molding of human behavior and physiologies. Because humans are mammals, primates, and hominins, our phylogenetic history involves trajectories that have agency in the development and transformation of our behavioral and physiological patterns. Because we humans participate in broad-scale behavioral cooperation and environmental manipulation our collective behavior has agency in the creation and modification of behavioral and physiological patterns. Because of all the disciplines interested in human behavior, anthropology is the most diverse in its foci (behavior, language, symbol, culture, material past and present, physiology, paleontology, and endocrinology, to name a few arenas of anthropological inquiry) and in its potential for acceptance of perspectives from other disciplines. Anthropologists[1] potentially have training, or at least a familiarity, across a broader range of the study of humanity than those trained in other disciplines. The focus of anthropology is humans and their culture in the broadest sense and anthropologists can bring a diverse set of methods to tackle such themes.

Anthropology is an approach that, in the ideal sense, could attempt to assess the variable inputs, stakeholders and agents within a given system.... biological, cultural, symbolic, historical, ecological. Unfortunately, such a perspective has not yet really been fully enacted as a paradigm itself. Few anthropologists are participants in both traditional evolutionary theory and emergent perspectives such as *Niche Construction* and *DST* paradigms while simultaneously participating in the more traditional approaches of the anthropological subdisicplines. This is very difficult; there is not much institutional support for it as it requires teaming up with individuals from other disciplines such as biology, psychology, public health, and so on. However, the conceptual models are available and the biocultural arena stands as the prime location for the implementation of such approaches

For example, Ulijaszek and Lofink (2006) recently published, in *Annual Reviews of Anthropology*, an article entitled "Obesity in Biocultural Perspective." In the article, they come close to the kind of integration I am proposing, but stop short of it. They provide an overview of morphological definitions of obesity (BMI based), population trends over the past 50 years, evolutionary hypotheses for "fat" and energy storage and utilization, genetic factors in obesity, physiological and neuro-endocrinological pathways of obesity, and sociocultural and socioeconomic aspects of obesity. They present the common conclusion that because humans have "biological tendencies" to maximize food intake and minimize energy expenditure and that high-energy food is easier to access and sedentization is rising, rates of obesity in humans will continue to increase. In each of the areas they cover, there are a number of researchers examining the various facets, but in their review the authors do not go quite far enough to integrate what they are almost explicitly stating: that niche construction is altering the proximate pressures and the physiological outcomes in humans, resulting in rapidly changing global

---

[1] It is worth pointing out that here I mean anthropologists who have what is usually termed four-field training. That is, they have had minimal course work across the subdisciplines of archeological, biological, linguistic, and sociocultural anthropology; they are familiar with the methodologies of the subdisciplines and have actually conducted research in more than one of the areas. There is also a subset of social anthropologists who have no training or course work in other disciplines, at any level. These individuals, I feel, are not generally predisposed to the integrative approaches I describe here.

context. When they speak of evolutionary pressures they imply the past, using "have undergone selection," and when they speak of cultural practice/behavior they envision the present and future. They are not truly synthesizing evolutionary and sociocultural facets of the system. They represent modern behavior as modifying ancient physiological sets to produce these new (assumedly maladaptive) results (akin to an evolutionary psychology perspective). Is it possible to perform a more integrated assessment wherein evolutionary pressures are not seen as things of the past, but as operating today? Can we extend on a modern Human Behavioral Ecology perspective wherein sociocultural patterns are changing the ecologies in which we live such that patterns of evolutionary pressure and our responses to them are themselves being modified? Can the factors they review be incorporated into a set of models that can both represent the system at hand and provide predictive outcomes?

I would like to argue "yes" to all of these questions, and I hope that after reading this book you would agree or at least see why I think like this. We could envision expanding Ulijaszek and Lofink's example using even greater and more explicit input of aspects from Human Behavioral Ecology, Niche Construction Theory, Dual Inheritance Theory and, obviously, Cultural Anthropology, to name a few. There are so many interesting ideas about human behavioral evolution but there should be a much greater attempt to integrate them in the production of dynamic models that allow for assessment, understanding, and prediction in human behavioral systems. It is worthwhile to look to anthropology as the academic space that has the best chance at housing this integration.

GETTING PAST CONFLICTS BETWEEN RESEARCHERS STUDYING HUMAN BEHAVIORAL EVOLUTION

Having just proposed that anthropologists are best suited to be the locus for this integrative approach, I am undoubtedly annoying (if not angering) readers who are not anthropologists or students of anthropology. Let me clarify; it is not that I think anthropologists are the only ones capable or qualified for this endeavor, it is just that the field of anthropology has the greatest potential to be a place where divergent perspectives get together and have the space and methodological diversity to tackle issues related to human behavioral evolution. It is fully possible that great advances in this approach will come from biologists, psychologists, or even philosophers. However, all the other disciplines interested in this theme either have foci beyond humans or are interested only in certain aspects of humanity, while anthropology, by definition, is interested in all things human and human related (past, present and future).

It should be evident from reading through this book, especially Chapters 2, 3, and 7 and the proposals in Chapter 5, that there are some substantial disagreements amongst researchers in the area of human behavioral evolution. My point here (and throughout) is that all of those interested in this area of research benefit from listening more intensively to one another and trying to see where overlaps occur and in exploiting them. I have probably learned much more and grown more effectively as a scholar by reading and assessing proposals that I do not agree with rather than those I do agree with. I have also had the experience and pleasure of being wrong. As scientists, we must realize that most of what we propose is wrong, and will eventually be refuted. Accepting that enables us to practice science as a methodology rather than as a contest or competition.

This is not to say we should all try to find one perspective to agree upon, which is neither realistic nor preferable. Rather, we need to be ready to be relatively open minded about proposals and paradigm shifts, especially as datasets change and no longer fit models as comfortably as they once did. Science advances by cannibalizing its history, mating with new information and perspectives and producing hybrid offspring, some of which flourish, most of which disappear without significant impact.

THE IMPORTANCE OF UNDERSTANDING THE RELATIONSHIPS BETWEEN RELIGION, SCIENCE, POLITICS, AND EXPLANATIONS FOR THE EVOLUTION OF HUMANITY

In the prologue to this book, I introduced the problems that creationism and essentialism have for humans, especially here in the United States, where such beliefs have a long history of affecting governmental policy and public opinion for the worse. However, I am not calling, as Richard Dawkins does, for an opting out of religion, nor do I think that holding the beliefs of a religion as core to ones ideology and lifestyle is a mistake. As I said in the prologue, I lump creationism and essentialism together because they occur in the religious and the secular alike. They are types of fundamentalist attitudes that occur across a wide range of belief systems. And both are equally damaging for humanity by causing erroneous and harmful views about who we are and why we behave in the ways we do to become common parts of public belief (with serious social and political impact). However, just as I argue for tolerance and mutual interaction between researchers, I also think that those interested in the evolution of human behavior should be interactive with those focused on religious, political, and social facets of being human. Humans everywhere are religious,[2] social, and political, and these realms are obviously important to us as a species. This suggests that those of us interested in human behavioral evolution should be paying particular

[2] Here I mean practice a particular belief system that creates their moral and ethical contexts. This includes atheistic and agnostic perspectives as well as those considered traditionally as "religions."

attention to the religious, social and political systems in which we live. We might have something to contribute to understanding these patterns and contexts. It is just as likely that interacting and engaging with our own religious, social and political contexts as participants and as scientists can give us insight into our own patterns and contexts. Remember, one of the main methodologies of anthropology is participant observation. You frequently need to be part of something to more effectively understand it.

In this same vein I encourage readers of this book to think about how what they know and what they research might impact public discourse on topics related to human behavior. Few days go by without significant news stories about gender, violence, differences amongst groups, social harmony and social disruption, and the human condition. Most of these stories if they have any reference to human evolution or to biocultural facets of humanity treat these elements in a simplistic and frequently misleading fashion. I am sure that students reading this book have been at parties or other gatherings where a peer made simplistic and incomplete or incorrect comments about the gender division of labor, the role of aggression in men or other items related to human behavioral evolution. In all such cases, consider your ability to share more accurate information about the subject. Popular ignorance is at least partially present because of the invisibility of most research findings in the public sphere. The information from the study of human behavioral evolution can be relevant and have an impact on our daily lives, but only if we help it to.

Appendix: Related Titles for Further Reference

It is worthwhile to note that there is more than a century and a half's worth of books examining the evolution of human behavior—many of which have influenced the way I think about the theme. Darwin's (1871) The Descent of Man and Selection in Relation to Sex is in large part just such a book and Carl Warden's (1932) The Evolution of Human Behavior is another. More recently, Lee Cronk's (1999) That Complex Whole: culture and the evolution of human behavior and Geoffrey Pope's (1999) The Biological Basis of Human behavior among others have also taken up the quest to explain the evolution of human behavior.

While there are a number of books that deal with views and proposals for human behavioral evolution in ways that overlap with this one, there is a select group that deserves special note. Below, I give a brief synopses of a handful of recent such books that have influenced me most and that I feel rise above the others. These are not all of the recent books that deal with this topic by any means, but they are the ones that I think are amongst the best or at least the most important recent contributions for students and practicing professionals interested in the evolution of human behavior. I am in their debt for influencing, in part, the way I chose to structure this book and the topics and materials I chose to present. Each of these has their own strengths and weaknesses and all are well worth reading in full. Here, I simply provide a brief overview of each for the inquisitive reader who wants to expand her/his knowledge base and perspectives (books listed in alphabetical order).

Louise Barret, Robin Dunbar, and John Lycett, J. (2002). Human Evolutionary Psychology. Princeton: Princeton University Press.

This book probably represents the most up-to-date version of a synthesis between evolutionary psychology and human behavioral ecology. The authors wrote this specifically to address the dearth of intermediaries between the primary literatures in these areas and undergraduate students/undergraduate coursework. There is substantial overlap in thematic approaches and contexts between this book and Cartwright's "Evolution and Human Behavior" (below). As with Cartwright's book, this is a traditionally structured text book. The 13 chapters begin with an introduction to what the authors call "the evolutionary approach to human behavior" presenting it as a logical integration of evolutionary psychology and human behavioral ecology. The second chapter introduces selfish genic theory and the basic premises of evolutionary psychology and some of behavioral ecology. The next eleven chapters tackle specific themes in human behavior and evolution with examples from the primary literature in evolutionary psychology, human behavioral ecology, primatology, and even occasionally, anthropology. Topics covered include mate choice and sexual selection, cooperation among kin, marriage and inheritance, language and cultural evolution. Each chapter contains a number of explanatory boxes for specific topics and ends with a succinct summary and suggestions for further reading. The back matter includes the bibliography, a glossary, and both author and subject indices.

John Cartwright (2000). Evolution and Human Behavior: Darwinian Perspectives on Human Nature. Suffolk: Palmgrave.

Cartwright's text and the text by Barret et al. are the most traditional college textbooks of those mentioned here. It is written primarily for upper division courses in human behavior, evolution or evolutionary psychology and biology. It is a very clear and extensive overview of human behavior and evolution from a specific type of evolutionary biological and evolutionary psychological perspective. Its twelve chapters provide an overview of the topic starting with historical chapters on evolutionary theory. Cartwright's overall perspective has a focus on a selfish gene orientation and a functionalist approach to understanding human evolution. Specific chapters then cover aspects of humanity such as mating behavior, sexual selection, sexual behavior, language, intelligence, intra- and intergroup conflict, and altruism and cooperation. The final chapter, "the use and abuse of evolutionary theory," is a defense against attacks on functionalist perspectives by the late Stephen Jay Gould and others and a strategy for the relevance and implications of Cartwright's integration of human sociobiology and evolutionary psychology. This text provides numerous examples from the primary research literature throughout, uses figures and tables very well, has a glossary, and lists suggested readings at the conclusion of each chapter.

Paul R. Erlich (2000). Human Natures: Genes, Culture, and the Human Prospect. Island Press (later released in soft cover by Penguin Books in 2002).

Rather than being a book geared toward classroom use, this is a popular book by an eminent biologist attempting to draw a broad overview of human evolution. It is a very engaging read, quite comprehensive, and extremely well footnoted. The preface and 13 chapters take a conversational tone and use snappy and well-crafted phrases for chapter titles (such as From Grooming to Gossip? and Gods, Dive-bombers and Bureaucracy). I first read this book during fieldwork and have to admit that its perspectives and arguments influenced me greatly. The contents are a broad overview and synthesis of published primatological, paleoanthropological, and archeological analyses intermixed with assessments of recent advances and discoveries in the fields of genetics and biological sciences (with ecology thrown in at various levels). All of which are applied to the basic questions of "where do we come form?" "where are we going?," and "why do we behave the way that we do?" Erlich unabashedly has a specific perspective and uses it to answer each of these questions, and he encourages the reader to share his views. An important facet of the book is that the extensive footnoting allows for serious assessment of his assertions and conclusions.

Walter Goldschmidt (2006). The Bridge to Humanity: How Affect Hunger Trumps the Selfish Gene. New York: Oxford University Press.

This is a brief, well-written argument for the primary role of "affect hunger" in human behavioral evolution. Affect hunger, or "the urge to get expressions of affection from others" acts as a cornerstone for the anthropologist Goldschmidt to weave a narrative about the relationship between biology and culture in the evolution of human behavior. Chapter 1 is an argument for an interrelationship between nature and nurture rather than a conflict. Chapters 2 though 7 take the reader, briefly, through issues in human evolution, definitions and functions of affect hunger, and facets of culture and cultural evolution. The final two chapters deal thematically with what Goldschmidt (following Segerstrale 2000) refers to as the conflict for the "soul" of science and of the study of humanity. He proposes that the concept of affect hunger acts as a bridge uniting the various perspectives, generally represented as sociobiological and evolutionary psychological approaches on one hand and cultural anthropological and sociological approaches on the other. Goldschmidt concludes with a comment that truly underlies the rationality for all the books mentioned here, including the one you are currently reading, "Understanding how we got to be human turns out to be one with understanding what humans fundamentally are like— which is what we really want to know."

Kevin N. Laland and Gillian R. Brown (2002). Sense and Nonsense: Evolutionary Perspectives on Human Behavior. Oxford, UK: Oxford University Press.

Of all the books I briefly review here, this one (along with Sussman's reader and the Barret et al. text) is probably the most widely used in courses on human evolution and behavior. It is generally well reviewed and eminently easy to read (quite well written). Part of the layout of the text you are currently reading owes a great deal to what I take to be a central component of the successful structure of Laland and Brown's book. The eight chapters consist of an introduction and explanatory guide, a history of evolutionary and behavioral thought from 1800 to 1900s, a chapter each on the current dominant paradigms of sociobiology, human behavioral ecology, evolutionary psychology, memetics, and gene–culture coevolution, and a final chapter entitled "comparing and integrating approaches." There is a good list of "further readings" chapter-wise and, of course, a bibliography and index.

Kenan Malik (2002). Man, Beast, and Zombie: What Science Can and Cannot Tell Us about Human Nature. New Brunswick, NJ: Rutgers University Press.

Malik, a philosopher and essayist who has a research background, produced a book that is somewhat different for the others mentioned here. Somewhere in-between philosophy, history, and a sociopolitical essay, the book's 14 chapters weave through narratives of the history of investigations into the evolution of human behavior, reviews and evaluations of the major current paradigms used in such endeavors and the books emerging from them, and a philosophical and theoretical treatise on negotiating the balance between naturalist and humanist views in categorizations of human nature. Malik, more so than others (except maybe Erlich), emphasizes the linkage between science and politics, the need to restore a "human quality" to both and the need to "reconcile subjectivity and rationality." He starts and ends the book with the premise that we are subjective and conscious beings with the unique capability for rational dialogue and inquiry, and that this is what enables us to ask what it means to be human. Although overlapping in some of the historical and overview content, this book acts more as a philosophical companion to the others noted here.

Robert W. Sussman (1999). The Biological Basis of Human Behavior: A Critical Review. Upper Saddle River, NJ: Prentice Hall.

Unlike the other books mentioned here, this is actually a "reader" or compendium of previously published articles tied together with brief linking essays by Sussman. The 59 reprinted, generally brief, articles come from many of the top researchers in the area of human behavioral evolution and a number of well-known science writers. Sussman expertly mixes the voices of differing perspectives letting the short essays and fragments represent perspectives from the "mouths" of major players. The book is divided into five parts: evolution, humans and primates; the evolution of human behavior; the biological basis of race and racism; the new biological determinism; and the brain, hormones, and human behavior. Each section has between 9 and 15 essays representing a range of different viewpoints on the topic at hand. Unlike the other books mentioned here, this reader provides an overview of the debates in brief, and is particularly geared toward stimulating discussion about these topics amongst undergraduate students (at which it seems to be very effective). Sussman emphasizes his belief that there is a biological basis to human behavior, but that there are no simple or simplistic answers to any questions about behavior and its complex evolutionary patterns.

Glossary

Acheulian tools: More complex and diverse than earlier forms and were added gradually to the toolkits of Homo. An important characteristic of the Acheulian toolkit is bifacial flaking, a process that produced strong, sharp edges with better control in the making than Olduwan tools.

Adaptability: The degree to which a species can survive and reproduce in a wide variety of environments.

Adaptations: Traits resulting from natural selection in response to environmental pressures.

Adaptive lag: "Left-over" adaptations to prior environments that may be maladaptive in the present context.

Adaptively relevant environment: Those features of an environment that an organism must interact with to achieve reproductive success.

Altruism: Acts that have a net loss of fitness to the actor but a net gain in fitness to the receiver.

Autocatalysis model: The model put forward by E.O. Wilson to describe patterns of human evolution.

Baldwin effect: "Ontogenetic adaptations are really new, not preformed; and they are really reproduced in succeeding generations, although not physically inherited." Behavioral traits (learned or innovated) acquired in the course of an organism's lifetime can be passed on to offspring eventually becoming adaptations, even without initially having a genetic underpinning.

Codetermination: The dual inheritance and interaction of biological and cultural units.

Cultural units: Core to Dual Inheritance Theory these units are seen as discrete packages or particles that can be beliefs, behaviors or other cultural elements and are seen as acting roughly analogous to genes and alleles (variant forms of genes) in the context of population genetics and their relationship to evolutionary patterns.

Dominance: The set of relationships that results in different relative abilities to acquire desired goods/resources.

Ecological selectionist logic: A perspective deriving from Neo-Darwinian (sociobiological) understandings of selection combined with a focus on specific types of ecological pressures that affect energetic expenditure/gain as it relates to potential fitness of individuals.

Encephalization Quotient: Brain to body size ratio for mammals.

Environment of Evolutionary Adaptiveness: The proposal that the prime context for the selection of human behavioral patterns was in the lifeways of Pleistocene hunter gatherers, not necessarily to modern circumstances (as we spent 99% of our evolutionary history as Pleistocene foragers and less than 1% in modern contexts). The EEA is during this Pleistocene period.

Epigenetic: Organic systems outside of, or in addition to, the DNA that can affect genetic expression, development and biological function.

Ethology: Study of the expression and development of behavior as measured though observation.

Eurytopic: A dietary generalist.

Evolutionary Stable Strategies: Behavioral strategies that have the highest fitness value relative to other strategies in a given environment.

Expensive tissue hypothesis: Brains are very energetically expensive tissue. Hominin guts size decreases as relative brain size increases in the mid-Pleistocene fossil record. Researchers have suggested that an increase in meat consumption making large guts less necessary (due to the processing and absorption qualities of meat versus plant matter) allows increased energetic investment in brain tissue, which results in large neocortexes.

Facilitation: Interactions between species or potentially between groups within a species that results in a positive selective environment for all interactants.

Foramen magnum: The hole where the spinal column enters the skull.

Gene flow: The process by which genetic material and complexes move, or are limited in their movement, through and between populations (largely through migration and nonrandom mating).

Genetic drift: The process by which random events affect the frequencies of alleles from generation to generation.

Genotype: The genetic makeup of an individual.

Group selection: Natural selection acting at the level of intergroup interactions.

Hominins: Humans and all their ancestors and relatives after the split with any other ape lineage.

Hominoid-wide trends: Those behavior patterns that we see in all, or most, hominoids (apes and humans) but not in other primates.

Kin selection: The behavioral favoring of your close genetic relatives.

Levallois technique: Stone tool making technique that provides higher quality (than Acheulian) end products that can be refined for a wide variety of uses.

Megadontia quotient (MQ): A measure of premolar/molar tooth area relative to body size.

Megadontia: Larger postcanine teeth (molars and premolars) than would be expected for the size of the body.

Memeplexes: Clusters of memes that can be best described as cultural trends, patterns and beliefs.

Memes: Cultural units that are replicators, existing in a parallel, cultural, system roughly analogous to genes.

Mutation: Novel changes in the DNA sequences. The only way new genetic sequences (alleles) are introduced.

Natural selection: The filtering of phenotypes (and their genotypes) by factors in the environment, resulting in an overrepresentation of better fit phenotypes (and their associated genotypes) within a population in a given environment over time. The traits they carry that help them do well in the environment are called adaptations.

Niche construction: The building and destroying of niches by organisms and the mutual dynamic interactions between organisms and environments.

Obligate mutualists: Organisms that coincide in their patterns and mutually, beneficially, influence one another.

Olduwan tool industry: Earliest hominin tool industry; very simple modifications made to certain types of rocks to produce sharp flakes and edged choppers.

Optimality theory: In a given system with multiple variants selection will push the system towards optimal solutions (patterns of behavior that maximize fitness).

Phalange: Finger or toe bones.

Phenogenotypes: The human biocultural complex made up of integrated behavioral, morphological and genetic complexes.

Phenotype: The morphology and behavior of an individual.

Phenotypic plasticity: The potential production of multiple phenotypes from a single genotype, depending on environmental conditions.

Philopatric: Staying in the natal (birth) group.

Primate-wide trends: Those behaviors or behavior patterns that occur in all, or most, primates.

Prisoner's dilemma: A choice game wherein two players are given the options to cooperate or compete with each choice's payoffs depending on the choice of the other player.

Reaction norm: The trajectory of phenotypes (final forms) that can potentially be produced by a single genotype exposed to a variety of different environmental conditions.

Reciprocal altruism model: Unrelated organisms can enter into relationships that can be characterized as fitness value exchanges. One organism undergoes a fitness cost for another with the assumption that the other will return the fitness benefit at some time in the future.

Satisficing: Behavior might not reach optimal levels but still be sufficiently beneficial in an evolutionary fitness context.

Shearing complex: A characteristic dental condition in which the lower first premolar is somewhat sharpened or flattened from rubbing against the upper canine as the mouth closes.

Standard Social Science Model: Proponents of the Evolutionary Psychology perspective sees the SSSM as the antithesis of their endeavor. They describe it as practiced by cultural anthropologists, "humanist" biologists, and other social constructivists who believe that mental organization of the adult is absent in the infant and must be acquired from their social world and that biological construction goes on in the womb, but is complete except for growth at birth with social forces being the main agents responsible for the remaining construction of the individual.

Stenotopic: A dietary specialist.

Strategies: Patterns of behavioral response that emerge via selection and result in fitness benefits in a given ecological context.

Tri-inheritance vision model: Human behavior results from information acquiring processes at three levels: population genetic processes, ontogenetic processes and cultural processes.

Typological approaches: A focus on the use of "types," fixed structures, and morphological measurement to assess and examine human morphology and behavior.

Bibliography

Adovasio, J.M., Olga, S., and Jake, P. (2007) *The Invisible Sex: Uncovering the True Roles of Women in Prehistory*. New York: Smithsonian Books.

Aiello, L.C. and Wells, J.C.K. (2002) Energetics and the evolution of the genus *Homo*. *Annual Review of Anthropology* 31:323–338.

Aiello, L.C. and Wheeler, P. (1995) The expensive tissue hypothesis: the brain and the digestive system in human and primate evolution. *Current Anthropology* 36:199–221.

Alexander, R.D. (1987) *The Biology of Moral Systems*. New York: Aldine de Gruyter.

Ardey, R. (1966) *The Territorial Imperative*. New York: Atheneum.

Arnold, K. and Aureli, F. (2007) Postconflict reconciliation. In C.J. Campbell, A. Fuentes, K.C. MacKinnon, M. Panger, and S.K. Bearder, Eds. *Primates in Perspective*. New York: Oxford University Press, pp. 592–608.

Arribas, A., and Palmqvist, P. (1999) On the ecological connection between saber-tooths and hominids: faunal dispersal events in the lower Pleistocene and a review of the evidence for the first human arrival in Europe. *Journal of Archaeological Science* 26:571–585.

Arsuaga, J.L., Bermudez de Castro, J.M., and Carbonell, E. (1997) The Sima de los Huesos hominid site. *Journal of Human Evolution* 33:105–421.

Asfaw, B., White, T., Lovejoy, O., Latimer, B., Simpson, S., and Suwa, G. (1999) *Australopithecus garhi*: a new species of early hominid from Ethiopia. *Science* 284:629–635.

Aureli, F. and de Waal, F.B.M. (2000) *Natural Conflict Resolution*. Berkeley: University of California Press.

Axlerod, R. (1984) *The Evolution of Cooperation*. New York: Basic Books.

Axlerod, R. (1997) *The Complexity of Cooperation: Agent Based Models of Competition and Collaboration*. Princeton: Princeton University Press.

Axlerod, R. and Hamilton, W.D. (1981) The evolution of cooperation. *Science* 211:1390–1396.

Baldwin, J.M. (1896) A new factor in evolution. *American Naturalist* 30:441–451.

Barkow, J.H., Cosmides, L., and Tooby, J. Eds. (1992) *The Adapted Mind: Evolutionary Psychology and the Generation of Culture*. New York: Oxford University Press.

Barrett, L., Robin, D., and John, L. (2002) *Human Evolutionary Psychology*. Princeton: Princeton University Press.

Begun, D.R. (1999) Hominid family values: morphological and molecular data on the relations among the great apes and humans. In S.T. Parker, R.W. Mitchell, and H.L. Miles. *The Mentalities of Gorillas and Orangutans.* Cambridge, MA: Cambridge University Press, pp. 3–42.

Bermudez de Castro, J.M., Martinon-Torres, M., Carbonnel, E., Sarmiento, S., Rosas, A., Van Der Made, J., et al. (2004) The Atapuerca sites and their contribution to the knowledge of human evolution in Europe. *Evolutionary Anthropology* 13:24–41.

Bernstein, I.S. (2007) Social mechanisms in the control of primate aggression. In C.J. Campbell, A. Fuentes, K.C. MacKinnon, M. Panger, and S.K. Bearder, Eds. *Primates in Perspective.* New York: Oxford University Press, pp. 562–570.

Blackmore, S.J. (1999) *The Meme Machine.* Oxford, Oxford University Press.

Blackmore, S. (2003) Consciousness in meme machines. *Journal of Consciousness Studies* 10(4–5):1–12.

Blurton-Jones, D. (1984) A selfish origin for human food sharing: Tolerated theft. *Ethology and Sociobiology* 5:1–3.

Boehm, C. (1999) *Hierarchy in the Forest: The Evolution of Egalitarian Behavior.* Cambridge, MA: Harvard University Press.

Boehm, C. (2004) Large game hunting and the evolution of human sociality. In R.W. Sussman and A.R. Chapman, Eds. *The Origins and Nature of Sociality.* pp. 270–287. New York: Aldine de Gruyter.

Borgerhoff-Mulder, M. (2004) Are men and women really so different? *Trends in Ecology and Evolution* 18(3):119–125.

Bowlby, J. (1969) *Attachment.* New York: Basic Books.

Bowles, S. (2006) Group competition, reproductive leveling, and the evolution of human altruism. *Science* 314:1569–1572.

Boyd, R. and Peter, R.J. (2005) *The Origin and Evolution of Cultures.* New York: Oxford University Press.

Brewis, A. and Meyer, M. (2005) Demographic evidence that human ovulation is undetectable (at least in pair bonds). *Current Anthropology* 46(3):465–480.

Brown, P., Sutikna, T., Morwood, M.J., Sowjono, R.P., Jatmiko, Wayhu Saptumo, E., et al. (2004) A new small-bodied hominin from the Late Pleistocene of Flores, Indonesia. *Nature* 431:1055–1061.

Brunet, M., Guy, F., Pilbeam, D., Mackaye, H.T., Ahounta, D., Beauvilain, A., et al. (2002) A new hominid from the upper Miocene of Chad, Central Africa. *Nature* 418:145–151.

Brunet, M., Guy, F., Pilbeam, D., Lieberman, D.E., Likius, A., Mackaye, H.T., et al. (2005) New material of the earliest hominid from the upper Miocene of Chad. *Nature* 434:752–755.

Bruno, J.F., Stachowicz, J.J., and Bertness, M.D. (2003) Inclusion of facilitation into ecological theory. *Trends in Ecology and Evolution* 18(3):119–125.

Campbell, C.J. (2007) Primate sexuality and reproduction. In C.J. Campbell, A. Fuentes, K.C. MacKinnon, M. Panger, and S.K. Bearder, Eds. *Primates in Perspective.* New York: Oxford University Press, pp. 423–436.

Carter, C.S. and Cushing, B.S. (2004) Proximate mechanisms regulating sociality and social monogamy in the context of evolution. In R.W. Sussman and A.R. Chapman, Eds. *The Origins and Nature of Sociality.* New York: Aldine de Gruyter, pp. 99–121.

Cartwright, J. (2000) *Evolution and Human Behavior: Darwinian Perspectives on Human Nature.* Suffolk, UK: Palmgrave.

Cavalli-Sforza, L. and Feldman, M. (1981) *Cultural Transmission and Evolution.* Princeton: Princeton University Press.

Ciochon, R.L. and Fleagle, J.G. (Eds.) (2006) The human evolution source book (2nd edn.). *Advances in Human Evolution Series.* Upper Saddle River, NJ: Pearson Prentice Hall.

Conroy, G.C. (1997) *Reconstructing Human Origins: A Modern Synthesis.* New York: Norton.

Conroy, G.C. (2004) *Reconstructing Human Origins: A Modern Synthesis* (2nd edn.). New York: Norton.

Cronk, L. (1999) *That Complex Whole: Culture and the Evolution of Human Behavior.* Boulder, CO: Westview Press.

Daly, M. and Wilson, M. (1988) *Homicide.* New York: Aldine de Gruyter.

Darwin, C. (1871) *The Descent of Man and Selection in Relation to Sex.* London: John Murray.

Dawkins, R. (1976) *The Selfish Gene.* Oxford: Oxford University Press.

Dawkins, R. (1982) *The Extended Phenotype.* Oxford: Oxford University Press.

Deacon, T.W. (1997) *The Symbolic Species: The Co-evolution of Language and the Brain.* New York: W.W. Norton.

de Heinzelin, J., Desmond Clark, J., White, T., Hart, W., Renne, P., WoldeGabriel, G., et al. (1999) Environment and behavior of 2.5 million year old Bouri hominids. *Science* 284:625–629.

Dennell, R. (1997) The world's oldest spears. *Nature* 385:767–769.

Dennet, D. (1991) *Consciousness Explained.* London: Penguin books.

Dennett, D. (1995) *Darwin's Dangerous Idea.* New York: Simon and Schuster.

de Waal, F.B.M. (1996) *Good Natured.* Cambridge, MA: Harvard University Press.

de Waal, F.B.M. (2000) Primates—a natural heritage of conflict resolution. *Science* 289:586–590.

Dobzhansky, T. (1972) On the evolutionary uniqueness of man. In T. Dobzhansky, M.K. Hecht, and W.C. Steere, Eds. *Evolutionary Biology*, vol. 6. New York: Appleton-Century-Crofts, pp. 415–430.

Donohue, K. (2005) Niche construction through phenological plasticity: life history dynamics and ecological consequences. *New Phytologist* 166:83–92.

Dressler, W.W. (2005) What's cultural about biocultural research? *Ethos* 33:20–45.

Dressler, (2008) Explaining health inequalities. In C. Panter-Brick and A. Fuentes, Eds. *Health, Risk and Adversity.* New York: Berghahn Books, pp. 175–184.

Dufour, D.L. (2006) The 23rd annual Raymond Pearl Memorial Lecture. Biocultural approaches in human biology. *American Journal of Human Biology* 18(1):1–9.

Dunbar R.I.M and Shultz, S. (2007) Evolution in the social brain. *Science* 317:1344–1347.

Engel, G., Hungerford, L.L., Jones-Engel, L., Travis, D., Eberle, R., Fuentes, A., et al. (2006) Risk assessment: a model for predicting cross-species transmission of Simian Foamy virus from Macaques (*M. fascicularis*) to humans at a monkey temple in Bali, Indonesia. *American Journal of Primatology* 68:934–948.

Erlich, P. (1999) *Human Natures: Genes, Cultures and the Human Prospect.* Washington, DC: Island Press.

Erlich, P. and Feldman, M. (2003) Genes and cultures: what creates our behavioral phenome? *Current Anthropology* 44(1):87–107.

Falk, D. (2004) Prelinguistic evolution in early hominins: whence motherese? *Behavioral and Brain Sciences* 27:491–541.

Falk, D., Hildebolt, C., Smith, K., Morwood, M.J., Sutikna, T., Jatmiko (2005) Response to "Comment on the brain of LB1 Homo floresiensis." *Science* 310:236c.

Fausto-Sterling, A. (2000) *Sexing the Body: Gender Politics and the Construction of Sexuality*. New York: Basic Books.

Fehr, E. and Gachter, S. (2002) Altruistic punishment in humans. *Nature* 415:137–140.

Fernadez-Duque, E. (2007) Aotinae: Social monogamy in the only nocturnal haplorhines. In C.J. Campbell, A. Fuentes, K.C. MacKinnon, M. Panger, and S.K. Bearder, Eds. *Primates in Perspective*. New York: Oxford University Press, pp. 139–154.

Flack, J.C., Girvan, M., de Waal, F.B.M., and Krakauer, D.C. (2006) Policing stabilizes construction of social niches in primates. *Nature* 439:426–429.

Foley, R. (2001) The evolutionary consequences of increased carnivory in hominids. In C.B. Stanford and H.T. Bunn, Eds. *Meat-Eating and Human Evolution*. Oxford: Oxford University Press, pp. 305–331.

Fry, D. (2006) *The Human Potential for Peace*. New York: Oxford University Press.

Fuentes, A. (1999) Re-evaluating primate monogamy. *American Anthropologist* 100(4):890–907.

Fuentes, A. (2000) Hylobatid communities: changing views on pair bonding and social organization in hominoids. *Yearbook of Physical Anthropology* 43:33–60.

Fuentes, A. (2002) Patterns and trends in primate pair bonds. *International Journal of Primatology* 23(4):953–978.

Fuentes, A. (2004) It's not all sex and violence: integrated anthropology and the role of cooperation and social complexity in human evolution. *American Anthropologist* 106(4):710–718.

Fuentes, A. (2006) The humanity of animals and the animality of humans: a view from biological anthropology inspired by J.M. Coetzee's Elizabeth Costello. *American Anthropologist* 108:124–132.

Fuentes, A. (2007) Social organization: social systems and the complexities in understanding the evolution of primate behavior. In C. Campbell, A. Fuentes, K. MacKinnon, M. Panger, and S. Bearder, Eds. *Primates in Perspective*. Oxford University Press, Oxford/New York pp. 609–621.

Fuentes, A., Wyczalkowski, M.A., and MacKinnon, K.C. (in review) Niche construction through cooperation: a nonlinear dynamics contribution to modeling resilience and evolutionary history in the genus. *Homo Current Anthropology*.

Galick, K., Senut, B., Pickford, M., Gommery, D., Treil, J., Kuperaunge, A.J., et al. (2004) External and internal morphology of the BAR 1002_00 *Orrorin tugenensis* femur. *Science* 305:1450–1453.

Gamble, C. (1998) Paleolithic society and the release form proximity: a network approach to intimate relations. *World Archeology* 29(3):426–449.

Gaulin, S.J.C. and McBurney, D.H. (2004) *Evolutionary Psychology* (2nd edn.). Upper Saddle River, NJ: Pearson/Prentice Hall.

Gibson, K.R. (2005) Epigenesis, brain plasticity, and behavioral versatility: alternatives to standard evolutionary psychology models. In S. McKinnon and S. Silverman, Eds. *Complexities: Beyond Nature and Nurture*. Chicago, IL: University of Chicago Press, pp. 23–42.

Gibson, M.A. and Mace, R. (2005) Helpful grandmothers in rural Ethiopia: a study of the effect of kin on child survival and growth. *Evolution and Human Behavior* 26:469–482.

Godfrey, K. and Hansen, M. (2008) The developmental origins of health and disease. In C. Panter-Brick and A. Fuentes, Eds. *Health, Risk and Adversity*. New York: Berghahn Press.

Goldschmidt, W. (2006) *The Bridge to Humanity: How Affect Hunger Trumps the Selfish Gene*. Oxford: Oxford University Press.

Goodenough, U. and Deacon, T.W. (2003) From biology to consciousness to morality *Zygon* 38(4):801–819.

Goodman, A.H. and Leatherman, T.L. Eds. (1998) *Building a New Biocultural Synthesis*. Ann Arbor, MI: University of Michigan.

Gould, L. and Sauther, M. (2007) Lemuriformes. In C.J. Campbell, A. Fuentes, K.C. MacKinnon, M. Panger, and S.K. Bearder, Eds. *Primates in Perspective*. New York: Oxford University Press, pp. 46–72.

Gouzoules, H. and Gouzoules, S. (2007) The conundrum of communication. In C.J. Campbell, A. Fuentes, K.C. MacKinnon, M. Panger, and S.K. Bearder, Eds. *Primates in Perspective*. New York: Oxford University Press, pp. 621–635.

Haile-Selassie, Y. (2001) Late Miocene hominids from the middle Awash, Ethiopia. *Nature*, 412:178–181.

Hahn, R. (1999) *Anthropology in Public Health: Bridging Differences in Culture and Society*. Oxford: Oxford University Press.

Hamilton (1964) The genetical evolution of social behavior. Parts I and II. *Journal of Theoretical Biology* 7:1–52.

Hart, D.L. and Sussman, R.W. (2005) *Man the Hunted: Primates, Predators, and Human Evolution*. New York: Basic Books.

Hatley, T. and Kappelman, J. (1980) Bears, pigs, and Plio-Pleistocene hominids: a case for the exploitation of below ground food resources. *Human Ecology* 8:371–387.

Hauser, M. (2006) *Moral Minds: How Nature Designed Our Universal Sense of Right and Wrong*. New York: Harper Collin Publishers.

Hawkes, K. (1991) Showing off: tests of an hypothesis about men's foraging goals. *Ethology and Sociobiology* 12:29–54.

Hawkes, K. and Bliege Bird, R. (2002) Showing off, handicap signaling, and the evolution of men's work. *Evolutionary Anthropology* 11:58–67.

Hawkes, K., O'Connell, J.F., Blurton-Jones, N.G., Alvarez, H., and Charnov, E.L. (1998) Grandmothering, menopause, and the evolution of human life histories *Proceedings of the National Academic Science USA* 95:1336–1339.

Hawkes, K., O'Connell, J.F., and Blurton-Jones, N.G. (2003) Human life histories: primate trade-offs, grandmothering socioecology, and the fossil record. In P.M. Kappeler and M.E. Pereira, Eds. *Primate Life Histories and Socioecology*. Chicago, IL: The University of Chicago Press, pp. 204–227.

Hawkes, K. and Paine, R.R., Eds. (2006) *The Evolution of Human Life History*. Santa Fe, NM: School of American Research Press.

Heinrich, J., Boyd, R., Bowles, S., Cammerer, C., Fehr, E., and Gintis, H. (2004) The foundations of human sociality: economic experiments and ethnographic evidence from fifteen small-scale societies. Oxford: Oxford University Press.

Helman, C. (2001) *Culture, Health and Illness*. London: Arnold

Herrmann, E., Call, J., Hernandez-Lloreda, M.V., Hare, B., and Tomasello, M. (2007) Humans have evolved specialized skills of social cognition: the cultural intelligence hypothesis. *Science* 317:1360–1366.

Hrdy, S.B. (1999) *Mother Nature: A History of Mothers, Infants and Natural Selection.* New York: Pantheon.

Hrdy, S.B. (2005) Evolutionary context of human development: the cooperative breeding model. In C.S. Carter, L. Ahnert, K.E. grossmann, S.B. Hrdy, M.E. Lamb, S.W. Porges, and N. Sachser, Eds. *Attachment and Bonding: A New Synthesis.* Cambridge, MA, The MIT Press, pp. 9–32.

Ingold, T. (2001) From complementarity of obviation: on dissolving the boundaries between social and biological anthropology, archeology and psychology. In S. Oyama, P.E. Griffiths, and R.D. Gray, Eds. *Cycles of Contingency: Developmental Systems and Evolution.* Cambridge, MA: The MIT Press, pp. 255–280.

Ingold, T. (2007) The trouble with evolutionary biology. *Anthropology Today* 23(2):13–17.

Irons, W. (1998) Adaptively relevant environments versus the environment of evolutionary adaptiveness. *Evolutionary Anthropology* 6:194–204.

Jablonka, E. and Lamb, M. (2005) *Evolution in Four Dimensions: Genetic, Epigenetic, Behavioral, and Symbolic Variation in the History of Life.* Cambridge, MA: The MIT Press.

Jolly, C.J. (2007) Baboons, mandrills, and mangabeys: Afro-Papionin socioecology in a phylogenetic perspective. In C.J. Campbell, A. Fuentes, K.C. MacKinnon, M. Panger, and S.K. Bearder, Eds. *Primates in Perspective.* New York: Oxford University Press, pp. 240–251.

Kaplan, G. (2004) What's wrong with social epidemiology, and how can we make it better? *Epidemiologic Reviews* 26: 124–135.

Kaplan, H., Jane L., and Robson, A. (2003) Embodied capital and the evolutionary economics of the human life span. In J.R. Carey and S. Tuljapurkar, Eds. *Life Span: Evolutionary, Ecological, and Demographic Perspectives, Supplement to Population and Development Review,* vol. 29. New York: Population Council, pp. 152–182.

Kelley, E.A. and Sussman, R.W. (2007) An academic genealogy on the history of American field primatologists. *American Journal of Physics and Anthropology* 132:406–425.

King, B.M. (2004) *Human Sexuality Today* (5th edn.). Upper Saddle River, NJ: Pearson-Prentice Hall.

Kingston, J.D. (2007) Shifting adaptive landscapes: progress and challenges in reconstructing early hominid environments. *Yearbook of Physical Anthropology* 50:20–58.

Kirch, P.V. (2007) Hawaii as a model system for human ecodynamics. *American Anthropologist* 109(1):8–26.

Knauft, B.M. (1991) Violence and sociality in human evolution. *Current Anthropology* 32(4):391–428.

Knauft, B.M. (1994) Culture and cooperation in human evolution. In L.E. Sponsel and T. Gregor, Eds. *The Anthropology of Peace and Nonviolence.* Boulder, MO: Lynne Riener, pp. 37–67.

Knott, C.D. and Kahlenberg, S.M. (2007) Orangutans in perspective: forced copulations and female mating resistance. In C.J. Campbell, A. Fuentes, K.C. MacKinnon, M. Panger, and S.K. Bearder, Eds. *Primates in Perspective.* New York: Oxford University Press, pp. 290–304.

Kokko, H. and Jennions, M. (2003) It takes two to tango. *Trends in Ecology and Evolution* 18(3):103–104.

Kramer, P.A. (2004) The behavioral ecology of locomotion. In D.J. Meldrum, C.E. Hilton, Eds. *From Biped to Strider: the Emergence of Modern Human Walking, Running and Resource Transport.* New York: Kluwer/Plenum Publishers, pp. 101–115.

Krebs, J.R. and Davies, N.B. (1997) *Behavioral Ecology: An Evolutionary Approach* (4th edn.). Oxford: Blackwell.

Krieger, N. (2001) Theories for social epidemiology in the 21st century: An ecosocial perspective. *International Journal of Epidemiology* 30: 668–677.

Kuhn, S.L. and Stiner, M.C. (2006) "What's a mother to do" the division of labor among Neanderthals and modern humans in Eurasia. *Current Anthropology* 47(6):953–980.

Laland, K., Odling-Smee, J., and Feldman, M.W. (2000) Niche construction, biological evolution, and cultural change. *Behavioral and Brain Sciences* 23:131–175.

Laland, K.N. and Brown, G.R. (2002) *Sense and Nonsense: Evolutionary Perspectives on Human Behavior.* Oxford, UK: Oxford University Press.

Leakey, M.G., Feibal, C.S., McDougall, I., and Walker, A. (1995) New four-million-year-old hominid species from Kanapoi and Allia Bay, Kenya. *Nature* 376:565–571.

Leakey, M.G., Feibal, C.S., McDougall, I., Ward, C., and Walker, A. (1998) New specimens and confirmation of an early age for *Australopithecus anamensis. Nature* 393:62–67.

Leakey, M.G., Spoor, F., Brown, F.H., Gathogo, P.N., Kiarie, C., Leakey, L.N., et al. (2001) New hominin genus from eastern Africa shows diverse middle Pliocene lineages. *Nature* 410:433–440.

Leatherman T. (2005) A space of vulnerability in poverty and health: political-ecology and biocultural analysis. *Ethos* 33:46–70.

Lee, R.B. and DeVore, I., Eds. (1968) *Man the Hunter.* Chicago, IL: Aldine Publishing Company.

Lee-Thorp, J.A., Thackeray, J.F., and Van Der Merwe, N.J. (2000) The hunters and the hunted revisited. *Journal of Human Evolution* 39:565–576.

Lee-Thorp, J.A., Sponheimer, M., and Van Der Merwe, N.J. (2003) What do stable isotopes tell us about hominid dietary and ecological niches in the Pliocene? *International Journal of Osteoarcheology* 13:104–113.

Lehman, L., and Keller, L. (2006) The evolution of cooperation and altruism—a general framework and a classification of models. *Evolution* 19:1365–1376.

Leonetti, D.L., Nath, D.C., Heman, N.S., and Neill, D.B. (2005) Kinship organization and the impact of grandmothers on reproductive success onmatrilineal Khasi and Bengali of Northeast India. In E. Voland, A. Chasiotis, and W. Schiefenhoevel, Eds. *Grandmotherhood: The Evolutionary Significance of the Second Half of Female Life.* New Brunswick, NJ: Rutgers University Press, pp. 194–214.

Levi-Strauss, C. (1968) Concept of primitiveness. In R.B. Lee and I. DeVore, Eds. *Man the Hunter.* Chicago, IL: Aldine Publishing Company.

Lewontin, R. (1983) Gene, organism and environment. In D.S. Bendall, Ed. *Evolution Form Molecules to Men.* Cambridge, UK: Cambridge University Press.

Livingstone, F.B. (1958) Anthropological implication of sickle cell gene distribution in West Africa. *American Anthropologist* 60:533–562.

Lovejoy, O. (1981) The origin of man. *Science* 211:341–350.

Lovejoy, O. (1993) Modeling human origins: are we sexy because we're smart or smart because we're sexy? In T. Rasmussen, Ed. *The Origin and Evolution of Humans and Humanness*. Boston, MO: Jones and Bartlett Publishers, pp. 1–28.

Lumsden, C.J. and Wilson, E.O. (1981) *Genes, Minds, and Culture: The Coevoltuionary Process*. Cambridge, MA: Harvard University Press.

Malik, K. (2002) *Man, Beast, and Zombie: What Science Can and Cannot Tell Us About Human Nature*. New Brunswick, NJ: Rutgers University Press.

Manson, J.H. (2007) Mate choice. In C.J. Campbell, A. Fuentes, K.C. MacKinnon, M. Panger, and S.K. Bearder, Eds. *Primates in Perspective*. New York: Oxford University Press, pp. 447–464.

Marean, C.W., Bar-Matthews, M., Bernatchez, J., Fisher, E., Goldberg, P., Herries, A.I.R., et al. (2007) Early human use of marine resources and pigment in South Africa during the Middle Pleistocene. *Nature* 449:905–908.

Marks, J. (2004) What, if anything, is a Darwinian anthropology? *Social Anthropology* 12(2):181–193.

Matsuzawa, T., Tomonaga, M., and Tanaka, M. (2006) *Cognitive Development in Chimpanzees*. Tokyo: Springer.

Mayr, E. (1963) *Animal Speciation and Evolution*. Cambridge, MA: Harvard University Press.

McDade, T.W. (2001) Lifestyle incongruity, social integration, and immune function in Samoan adolescents. *Social Science and Medicine* 53:103–114.

McDade, T.W. (2002) Status incongruity in Samoan youth: a biocultural analysis of culture change, stress, and immune function. *Medical Anthropology Quarterly* 16:123–150.

McDade, T.W. (2003) Life event stress and immune function in Samoan adolescents: toward a cross-cultural psychoneuroimmunology. In J. Wilce, Ed. *Social and Cultural Lives of Immune Systems*. New York: Routledge, pp. 170–188.

McDade, T.W. (2008) Beyond the gradient: an integrative anthropological perspective on social stratification, stress, and health. In C. Panter-Briack and A. Fuentes, Eds. *Health, Risk, and Adversity*. New York: Berghahn Books.

McHenry, H.M. and Coffing, K. (2000) *Australopithecus* to *Homo*: Transformations in body and mind. *Annual Review of Anthropology* 29:125–146.

McKenna, J.J. (1978) Biosocial functions of grooming behavior among the common Indian langur monkey (*Presbytis entellus*). *American Journal of Physical Anthropology* 48(4):503–509.

McKenna, J.J. (2007) *Sleeping with Your Baby: A Parent's Guide to Cosleeping*. Washington, DC: Platypus Media.

McKenna, J.J., Ball, H.M, and Gettler, L.T. (2007) Mother-infant cosleeping, breast-feeding and sudden infant death syndrome: what biological anthropology has discovered about normal infant sleep and pediatric sleep medicine. *Yearbook of Physical Anthropology* 45:133–161.

McKinnon, S. (2005) On kinship and marriage: a critique of the genetic and gender calculaus of evolutionary psychology. In S. macKinnon and S. Silverman, Eds. *Complexities: Beyond Nature and Nurture*. Chicago, IL: University of Chicago Press, pp. 106–131.

Mesnick, S.L. (1997) Sexual alliances: evidence and evolutionary implications. In P.A. Gowaty, Ed. *Feminism and Evolutionary Biology: Boundaries, Intersections, and Frontiers*. New York: Chapman and Hall, pp. 207–260.

Middleton, D. (2001) *Exotics and Erotics: Human Cultural and Sexual Diversity*. Prospect Heights, IL: Waveland Press.

Miller, G. (2006) *The Mating Mind: How Sexual Choice Shaped the Evolution of Human Nature*. London: Doubleday.

Miller, W.B. and Rodgers, J.L. (2001) *The Ontogeny of Human Bonding Systems: Evolutionary Origins, Neural Bases, and Psychological Mechanisms*. Boston, MA: Kluwer Academic Publishers.

Miller, L.E. and Treves, A. (2007) Predation on primates: past studies, current challenges, and directions for the future. In C.J. Campbell, A. Fuentes, K.C. MacKinnon, M. Panger, and S.K. Bearder, Eds. *Primates in Perspective*. New York: Oxford University Press, pp. 525–542.

Milton, K. (1999) A hypothesis to explain the role of meat-eating in human evolution. *Evolutionary Anthropology* 8(1):11–21.

Miner, B.G., Sultan, S.E, Morgan, S.G., Padilla, D.K., and Relyea, R.A. (2005) Ecological consequences of phenotypic plasticity. *TRENDS in Ecology and Evolution* 20(12):685–692.

Mitani, J.C., Merriweather, A., and Zhang, C. (2000) Male affiliation, cooperation and kinship in wild chimpanzees. *Animal Behavior* 59:885–893.

Mitani, J.C., and Watts, D. (2001) Why do chimpanzees hunt and share meat? *Animal Behavior* 61:915–924.

Morgan, C.L. (1891) *Animal Life and Intelligence*. London/New York: Edward Arnold.

Morgan, C.L. (1896) *Habit and Instinct*. London/New York: Edward Arnold.

Morgan, C.L. (1896) Of modification and variation. *Science* 4:733–740.

Nekaris, A. and Bearder, S.K. (2007) The Lorisiform primates of Asia and Mainland Africa: diversity shrouded in darkness. In C.J. Campbell, A. Fuentes, K.C. MacKinnon, M. Panger, and S.K. Bearder, Eds. *Primates in Perspective*. New York: Oxford University Press, pp. 24–45.

Nell, V. (2006) Cruelty's rewards: The gratifications of perpetrators and spectators. *Behavioral and Brain Sciences* 29:211–257.

Norconk, M.A. (2007) Sakis, Uakaris, and Titi monkeys: behavioral diversity in a radiation of primate seed predators. In C.J. Campbell, A. Fuentes, K.C. MacKinnon, M. Panger, and S.K. Bearder, Eds. *Primates in Perspective*. New York: Oxford University Press, pp. 123–138.

Nunn, C.L. and Altizer, S. (2006) *Infectious Diseases in Primates*. Oxford, UK: Oxford University Press.

O'Connell, J.F., Hawkes, K., Lupo, K.D., and Blurton-Jones, N.G. (2002) Male strategies and Plio-Pleistocene archeology. *Journal of Human Evolution* 43:831–872.

Odling-Smee, F.J., Laland, K.N., and Feldman, M.W. (2003) *Niche Construction: The Neglected Process in Evolution*. Monographs in Population Biology 37. Princeton: Princeton University Press.

Oyama, S. (2000) *Evolution's Eye: A Systems View of the Biology-Culture Divide*. Durham, NC: Duke University Press.

Oyama, S., Griffiths, P.E., and Gray, R. D. (2001) Introduction: what is developmental systems theory? In S. Oyama, P.E. Griffiths, and R.D. Gray, Eds. *Cycles of Contingency: Developmental Systems and Evolution*. Cambridge, MA: MIT Press, pp. 1–12.

Panger, M. (2007) Tool use and cognition in primates. In C.J. Campbell, A. Fuentes, K.C. MacKinnon, M. Panger, and S.K. Bearder, Eds. *Primates in Perspective*. New York: Oxford University Press, pp. 665–676.

Panter-Brick, C. and Fuentes, A. (Eds.) (2008) *Health, Risk and Adversity*. New York: Berghahn Books.

Pederson, C.A. et al. (2003) Group report: beyond infant attachment: the origins of bonding later in life. In C.S. Carter, L. Ahnert, K.E. grossmann, S.B. Hrdy, M.E. Lamb, S.W. Porges, and N. Sachser, Eds. *Attachment and Bonding: A New Synthesis*. Cambridge, MA: The MIT Press, pp. 385–428.

Pederson, C.A. (2004) Biological aspects of social bonding and the roots of human violence. *Annals of New York Academic Science* 1036:106–127.

Pigliucci, M. (2001) *Phenotypic Plasticity: Beyond Nature and Nurture*. Baltimore, MD: Johns Hopkins University Press.

Plavcan, J.M. and van Schaik, C.P. (1997a) Interpreting hominid behavior on the basis of sexual dimorphism. *Journal of Human Evolution* 32: 345–374.

Plavcan, J.M. and van Schaik, C.P. (1997b) Intrasexual competition and body size dimorphism in anthropoid primates. *American Journal Physical Anthropology.* 103:37–68.

Pope, G. (1999) *The Biological Basis of Human Behavior*. Boston, MA: Allyn and Bacon.

Potts, R. (1998) Environmental hypotheses of hominin evolution. *Yearbook of Physical Anthropology* 41:93–136.

Potts, R. (1999) Variability selection in hominid evolution. *Evolutionary Anthropology* 7(3):81–96.

Potts, R. (2004) Sociality and the concept of culture in human origins. In R.W. Sussman and A.R. Chapman, Eds. *The Origins and Nature of Sociality*. New York: Aldine de Gruyter, pp. 249–269.

Power, C. and Aiello, L. (1997) Female proto-symbolic strategies. In L.D. Hagar, Ed. *Women in Human Evolution*. London: Routledge, pp. 153–171.

Quiatt, D. and Reynolds, V. (1993) *Primate Behaviour: Information, Social Knowledge, and the Evolution of Culture*. Cambridge: Cambridge University Press.

Rawls, J. (1971) *A Theory of Justice*. Cambridge, MA: Harvard University Press.

Richerson, P.J. and Robert, B. (2005) *Not by Genes Alone: How Culture Transformed Human Evolution*. Chicago, IL: The University of Chicago Press.

Richards, R. (1987) *Darwin and the Emergence of Evolutionary Theories of Mind and Behavior*. Chicago, IL: University of Chicago press.

Rivas, E. (2005) recent use of signs by Chimpanzees (Pan troglodytes) in interaction with humans. *Journal of Comparative Psychology* 19(4):404–417.

Robbins, M.M. (2007) Gorillas: diversity in ecology and behavior. In C.J. Campbell, A. Fuentes, K.C. MacKinnon, M. Panger, and S.K. Bearder, Eds. *Primates in Perspective*. New York: Oxford University Press, pp. 305–320.

Sapolsky, R.M. (2004) Social status and health in humans and other animals. *Annual Review of Anthropology* 33:393–418.

Savage-Rumbaugh, S. and Lewin, R. (1994) *Kanzi: the ape at the brink of the human mind*. New York: Doubleday.

Schlichting, C.D. and Pagliucci, M. (1998) *Phenotypic evolution: a reaction norm perspective*. Sunderland, MA: Sinauer.

Schmitt, D.P. (2005) Sociosexuality from Argentina to Zimbabwe: a 48-nation study of sex, culture, and strategies of human mating. *Behavioral and Brain Sciences* 28:247–311.

Scott, E. (2005) *Evolution vs. Creationism: An Introduction*. Berkeley, CA: University of California Press.

Sear, R. and Mace, R. (2008) Who keeps children alive? A review of the effects of kin on child survival. *Evolution and Human Behavior* 29:1–18.

Segerstrale, U. (2000) *Defenders of the Truth: The Battle for Science in the Sociology Debate and Beyond*. Oxford: Oxford University Press.

Selye H. (1976) *The Stress of Life* (Revised edn.). New York: McGraw-Hill.

Senut, B., Pickford, M., Gommery, D., Mein, P., Cheboi, C., and Coppens, Y. (2001) First hominid from the Miocene (Lukeio Formation, Kenya). *C.R. Academy of Science Paris* 332:137–144.

Sigmund, K., Christoph, H., and Martin N.A. (2001) Reward and punishment. *Proceedings of the National Academy of Sciences USA* 98:10757–10761.

Silk, J.B. (2007) Social component of fitness in primate groups. *Science* 317:1347–1351.

Simpson, S.W. (2002) *Australopithecus afarensis* and human evolution. In P.N. Peregrine, C.R. Ember, and M. Ember, Eds. *Physical Anthropology: Original Readings in Method and Practice*. Upper Saddle River, NJ: Prentice-Hall, pp. 103–123.

Skinner, M.M. and Wood, B.A. (2006) The evolution of modern human life history—a paleontological perspective. In K. Hawkes and R. Paine, Eds. *The Evolution of Modern Human Life History*. Santa Fe, NM: School of American Research Press, pp. 331–400.

Smith, E.A. (2000) Three styles in the evolutionary analysis of human behavior. In L. Cronk, N. Chagnon, and W. Irons, Eds. *Adaptation and Human Behavior: An Anthropological Perspective*. New York: Aldine de Gruyter, pp. 27–46.

Sober, E. and Wilson, D.S. (1998) *Do Unto Others: The Evolution and Psychology of Unselfish Behavior*. Cambridge, MA: Harvard University Press.

Soltis, J., Boyd, R., and Richerson, P.J. (1995) Can group functional behavior evolve via cultural group selection? An empirical test. *Current Anthropology* 36:473–494.

Spencer, H. (1851) *Social Statics: Or, the Conditions Essential to Human Happiness Specified and the First of Them Developed*. London: Chapman.

Spencer, H. (1855) *Principles of Psychology*. London: Longman, Brown, Green and Longmans.

Spencer, H. (1872) *Principles of Psychology* (2nd edn.). London: Williams and Norgate.

Spencer, H. (1892) *Social Statics, Abridged and Revised: Together with the Man versus the State*. New York: D. Applegate.

Spencer, H. (1893) The inadequacy of natural selection. *Contemporary Review* 63:152–166, 439–456.

Spencer, H. (1893) *The Principles of Ethics*. New York: D. Appleton and company

Spoor, F., Leakey, M.G., Gathogo, P.N., Brown, F.H., Anton, S.C., McDougall, I., et al. (2007) Implications of new early *Homo* fossils from Ileret, east of Lake Turkana, Kenya. *Nature* 448:688–691.

Stamps, J. (2003) Behavioural processes affecting development: Tinbergen's fourth question comes of age. *Animal Behavior* 66(1):1–13.

Stanford, C.B. and Bunn, H.T. (2001) *Meat-Eating and Human Evolution*. Oxford: Oxford University Press.

Stearn, J.T. (2000) Climbing to the top: a personal memoir of *Australopithecus afarensis*. *Evolutionary Anthropology* 9:113–133.

Stinson, S., Bogin, B., Huss-Ashmore, R. and O'Rourke, D. (2000) *Human Biology: An Evolutionary and Biocultural Perspective*. New York: Wiley-Liss.

Storey, A.E., Walsh, C.J., Quinton, R.L., and Wynne-Edwards, K.E. (2000) Hormonal correlates of paternal responsiveness in new and expectant fathers. *Evolution and Human Behavior*, 21(2):79–95.

Strum, S.C. and Fedigan, L.M. Eds. (2000) *Primate Encounters: Models of Science, Gender, and Society*. Chicago, IL: University of Chicago Press.

Stumpf, R. (2007) Chimpanzees and bonobos: diversity within and between species. In C.J. Campbell, A. Fuentes, K.C. MacKinnon, M. Panger, and S.K. Bearder, Eds. *Primates in Perspective*. New York: Oxford University Press, pp. 321–344.

Sussman, R.W. (1999) *The Biological Basis of Human Behavior: A Critical Review* Upper Saddle River, NJ: Prentice Hall.

Sussman, R.W. and Chapman, A.R. (2004) The nature and evolution of sociality: introduction. In R.W. Sussman and A.R. Chapman, Eds. *The Origins and Nature of Sociality*. New York: Aldine de Gruyter, pp. 3–22.

Sussman, R.W. and Garber, P.A. (2004) Rethinking sociality: cooperation and aggression among primates. In R.W. Sussman and A. R. Chapman, Eds. *The Origins and Nature of Sociality*. New York: Aldine de Gruyter, pp. 161–190.

Sussman, R.W. and Garber, P.A. (2007) Cooperation and competition in primate social interactions. In C.J. Campbell, A. Fuentes, K.C. MacKinnon, M. Panger, and S.K. Bearder, Eds. *Primates in Perspective*. New York: Oxford University Press, pp. 636–651.

Symons, D. (1979) *The Evolution of Human Sexuality*. New York: Oxford University Press.

Symons, D. (1990) Adaptiveness and adaptation. *Ethology and Sociobiology* 11:427–444.

Tang-Martinez, Z. (2000) Paradigms and primates: Bateman's principle, passive females, and perspectives from other taxa. In S.C. Strum and L.M. Fedigan, Eds. *Primate Encounters: Models of Science, Gender, and Society*. Chicago, IL: University of Chicago Press, pp. 261–274.

Tattersal, I. (1998) *Becoming Human: Evolution and Human Uniqueness*. New York: Oxford University Press.

Tattersal, I. (2004) Emergent behaviors and human sociality. In R.W. Sussman and A.R. Chapman, Eds. *The Origins and Nature of Sociality*. New York: Aldine de Gruyter, pp. 237–248.

Thierry, B. (2007) The macaques: a double-layered social organization. In C.J. Campbell, A. Fuentes, K.C. MacKinnon, M. Panger, and S.K. Bearder, Eds. *Primates in Perspective*. New York: Oxford University Press, pp. 224–239.

Tomasello, M. (1999) The human adaptation for culture. *Annual Review of Anthropology* 28:509–529.

Trivers, R. (1971) The evolution of reciprocal altruism. *Quarterly Review of Biology* 46(10):35–57.

Trut, L.D. (1999) Early canid domestication: the farm-fox experiment. *American Scientist* 87:160–168.

Ulijaszek, S.J. and Lofink, H. (2006) Obesity in biocultural perspective. *Annual Review Anthropology* 35:337–360.

Ungar, P.S., Grine, F.E., and Teaford, M.F. (2006) Diet in early homo: a review of the evidence and a new model of adaptive versatility. *Annual Review of Anthropology* 35:209–228.

van Schiak, C.P. and Janson, C.H. (2000) *Infanticide by Males and Its Implications* Cambridge: Cambridge University Press.

Waddington, C.H. (1959) Canalization of development and genetic assimilation of acquired characters. *Nature* 183:1654–1655.

Walker, A., Leakey, R.E., Harris, J.M., and Brown, F.H. (1986) 2.5 myr *Australopithecus bosei* from west of Lake Turkana, Kenya. *Nature* 322:517–522.

Walker, P. (2001) A bioarchaeological perspective on the history of violence. *Annual Reviews in Anthropology* 30:573–596.

Wall-Scheffler, C.M., Geiger, K., and Steudel-Numbers, K.L. (2007) Infant carrying: the role of increased locomotory costs in early tool development *American Journal of Physical Anthropology* 133(2):841–846.

Wallace, A.R. (1864) The origin of human races and the antiquity of man deduced from the theory of "natural selection." *Journal of the Anthropological Society of London* 2:158–187.

Ward, C.V., Leakey, M.G., and Walker, A. (2001) Morphology of *Australopithecus anamensis* from Kanapoi and Allia Bay. *Journal of Human Evolution* 41(4):255–368.

Warden, C. (1932) *The Evolution of Human Behavior*. New York: The Macmillan Company.

Washburn, S. (1951) The new physical anthropology. *Transactions of the New York Academy of Science* 13(2nd ser.):298–304.

Washburn, S. (1973) The promise of primatology. *American Journal of Physical Anthropology* 38:177–182.

Washburn, S.L. and Dolhinow, P. (1972) *Perspectives on Human Evolution* 2. New York: Holt-Reinhart.

Washburn, S.L. and Jay, P. (1968) *Perspectives on Human Evolution* 1. New York: Holt-Reinhart.

Washburn, S.L. and Lancaster, C.S. (1968) The evolution of hunting. In R.B. Lee and I. DeVore, Eds. *Man the Hunter*. Chicago, IL: Aldine Publishing Company, pp. 293–303.

Watanabe, J.M. and Smuts, B.B. (2004) Cooperation, commitment, and communication in the evolution of human sociality. In R.W. Sussman and A.R. Chapman, Eds. *The Origins and Nature of Sociality*. New York: Aldine de Gruyter, pp. 288–312.

Wells, J.C.K. and Stock, J.T. (2007) The biology of the colonizing ape. *Yearbook of Physical Anthropology* 50:191–222.

Werner, E.E. and Peacor, S.D. (2003) A review of trait-mediated indirect interactions. *Ecology* 84:1083–1100.

West-Eberhard, M.J. (2003) *Developmental Plasticity and Evolution*. Oxford University Press, New York.

White, T.D., Suwa, G., and Asfaw, B. (1994) *Australopithecus ramidus*, a new species of early hominid from Aramis, Ethiopia. *Nature* 371:306–312.

Whiten, A., Goodall, J., McGrew, W.C, Nishida. T., Reynolds. V., Sugiyama, Y., et al. (1999) Cultures in chimpanzees. *Nature* 399:682–685.

Williams, G.C. (1966) *Adaptation and Natural Selection: A Critique of Some Current Evolutionary Thought*. Princeton: Princeton University Press.

Wilson, D.S. and Wilson, E.O. (2007) Rethinking the theoretical foundation of Sociobiology. *The Quarterly Review of Biology* 82(4):327–348.

Wilson, D.S. and Sober, E. (1994) Reintroducing group selection to the human behavioral sciences. *Behavioral and Brain Sciences* 17(4):585–608.

Wilson, E.O. (1975) *Sociobiology: the New Synthesis*. Harvard: Belknap press.

Wilson, M. and Wrangham, R (2003) Intergroup relationships in chimpanzees. *Annual Review of Anthropology* 32:363–392.

Winterhalder, B. (1996) Social foraging and the behavioral ecology of intragroup resource transfer. *Evolutionary Anthropology* 5(2):46–57.

Wood, B.A. (1992) Origin and evolution of the genus *Homo*. *Nature* 355:783–790.

Wood, B. and Collard, M. (1999) The changing face of the genus *Homo*. *Evolutionary Anthropology* 8:195–207.

Wood, B. and D. Strait (2004) Patterns of resource use in early *Homo* and *Paranthropus Journal of Human Evolution* 46:119–162.

Wrangham, R.W. (1999) Evolution of coalitionary killing. *Yearbook of Physical Anthropology* 42:1–30.

Wrangham, R.W. and Peterson, D. (1996) *Demonic Males: Apes and the Origins of Human Violence*. New York: Houghton Mifflin Company.

Wrangham, R.W., Jones, J.H., Laden, G., Pilbeam, D., and Conklin-Brittain, N.L. (1999) The raw and the stolen: cooking and the ecology of human origins. *Current Anthropology* 40(5):567–594.

Zahavi, A. (1975) Mate selection—a selection for handicap? *Journal of Theoretical Biology* 53:205–214.

Zahavi A. (1977) The cost of honesty (further remarks on the handicap principle). *Journal of Theoretical Biology* 67:603–605.

Zihlman, A.L. and Bolter, D.R. (2004) Mammalian and primate roots of human sociality. In R.W. Sussman and A.R. Chapman, Eds. *The Origins and Nature of Sociality*. New York: Aldine de Gruyter, pp. 23–52.

Index

Page numbers in *italics* indicate boxes/figures/tables

Acheulian tools, 88, 91, 93
adaptability, 40, 109, 141, 165, 178
adaptationist perspective, 45, 48, 49n.1
adaptations, 7, 41, 42, 44, 45, 46, 47, 49,
    51, 122, 157, 165–168, 178, 194,
    222, 228, 242
  and behavior/behavioral change,
    62, 190, 193, 218, 226, 249
  and cooperation and bonding,
    198–199
  and coping with pressures, 206
  and inheritance, 117, 161–162
  and niche construction, 173, 175, 177
  and selection pressures, 118
  specific, 214, 226, 229, 230
  and traditional Neo-Darwinian
    theory, 174
The Adapted Mind: Evolutionary
    Psychology and the Generation of
    Culture (1992), 45–47
adaptive lag, 42, 46, 55, 62
adaptive patterns, 20, 38, 107, 198
adaptive problems, 45, 47, 48
adaptive psychological mechanisms, 62
adaptive specificity, 47
adaptive trade-offs, 40
adaptively relevant environment (ARE),
    46, 48, 245
Adovasio, J.M., 228
advertisement behavior, 155, 225
affect hunger, 116–117, 256
affiliative ("friendly") relationships,
    66, 201, 208, 219

Africa/African continent, 3, 43, 74, 76,
    81, 82, 83, 84, 87, 88, 91, 92, 93,
    100, 177, 210, 233, 234
African apes, 33n.2, 68, 69, 71, 87, 153
African hominine lineages, 71
African hominoids, 68
age–sex class groups *See* age–sex
    classes/age–sex class groups
age–sex classes/age–sex class groups,
    104, 192
aggression, 27, 32, 33, 99, 101, 102, 103,
    105, 112, 118, 122, 123
  and dominance relationships, 67
  form of advertisement, 224
  and relationship with hunting, 212
  See also aggressive conflict; intergroup
    aggression; male aggression
aggressive conflict, 33, 105, 112
  See also aggression; intergroup
    aggression; male aggression
agonistic ("unfriendly") relationships, 66
agriculture, 94, 199, 203, 213, 235, 246
Aiello, L.C., 90, 125
Alexander, Richard D., 110
  The Biology of Moral Systems, 110
alleles, 24, 25, 53, 171, 243
alliances, 44, 66, 67, 193, 196, 198, 205,
    232, 234 *See also* coalitions
allomaternal assistance, 113, 219
altruism, 49, 20, 21–22, 98
  cooperation link with, 141, 255
  core factor in human societies, 23–24
  fitness factor in, 30–31

altruism (*contd.*)
  response to conflict and
    competition, 207
  and "tribal" psychology, 103
  and Wilsonian Sociobiology, 29
  See also altruistic behavior; altruistic
    punishment; reciprocal altruism/
    reciprocal altruism model
altruistic behavior, 21, 31, 109–110,
    145 *See also* altruism; altruistic
    punishment; reciprocal altruism/
    reciprocal altruism model
altruistic punishment, 98, 110–111,
    116 *See also* altruism; altruistic
    behavior; reciprocal altruism/
    reciprocal altruism model
Alvarez, H., 119
anatomically modern humans, 83, 84,
    92, 103
ancestors, 3–4, 10, 64, 69, 75, 80, 148,
    199, 218, 241
  and aggressive or violent behavior, 123
  competition with other human groups
    and, 153, 200, 202, 203
  complex meme clusters in, 106
  niche construction by, 246
  and true imitation, 59
animals, 3, 12, 13, 17, 18, 22, 86, 91, 93,
    141, 148, 151, 155, 170, 225
  altruistic behavior in, 31
  and DIT, 53
  group living in, 31, 38
  intragroup (beyond kin-biased)
    cooperation among, 55
  and moral sense and system of
    values, 97
anthropoids/anthropoid primates, 4, 65,
    98, 108
anthropology/anthropological, 62–63,
    95–96, 112, 160, 239, 240, 243,
    247–248, 249–253
  biocultural approaches in, 165–168,
    177–179, 200
  ethnographic accounts, 32
  and evolutionary psychology, 45
  research trajectories of the 1960s and
    1970s in, 27–28
  and SSSM specific approach, 48–49
  treatment of gender and sex in, 228n.5

See also biocultural anthropology/
    biocultural anthropological
antipredator abilities *See* antipredator
    strategy/antipredator defense
antipredator behavior *See* antipredator
    strategy/antipredator defense
antipredator defense *See* antipredator
    strategy/antipredator defense
antipredator strategy/antipredator
    defense, 44, 76, 193, 218, 219, 233
    See also predation avoidance
apes, 3, 7, 65, 67–72, 97, 114, 124, 195,
    204, 219, 233, 240
Aramis site (northern Ethiopia), 71
arboreal environment, 71–76, 86
arboreality, 68, 72, 86, 212
archeological record, 3–5, 11, 63, 64, *158*,
    176, 191, 192, 225
  and emergence of social
    hierarchies, 209
  of encephalization and behavioral
    complexity, 128
  interconnection with fossil record,
    237, 244
  of intergroup cooperation, 202
  of intragroup cooperation, 193
  of lifestyle and behavior, 241–242
  of material culture of modern
    humanity, 92
  of nuclear family as basal unit,
    223–224
  of use of fire, 89
  of violence and aggression, and
    warfare, 201
Ardey, R., 102
  The Territorial Imperative (1966), 102
Ardipithecus ramidus, 71, 72
Ardipithecus ramidus kadabba, 71
Ardipithecus ramidus ramidus, 71
Ardipithecus subspecies, 74
Asian great ape (orangutan), 68
Atapuerca site (Spain), 217
atlatl (spear thrower), 92, 93
attention (innovation of human mind), 17
Aureli, F., 112
  Natural Conflict Resolution (2000), 112
Australia/Australian, 93, 277
Australopithecus afarensis, 70, 72, 74,
    75–76, 79, 80, 192

Australopithecus anamensis, 71, 72, 74
Australopithecus bahrelghazali, 74
Australopithecus garhi, 77, 78–80, 87
autocatalysis model, 32–34, 98–99
avoidance strategies *See* predation
    avoidance
Axlerod, R., 111

baboons, 27, 196, 198, 204, 212, 213, 218
Baldwin and Morgans' organic
    evolution *See* Baldwin's organic
    evolution/Baldwin effect
Baldwin, Mark James, 21, 22–24
    Baldwin effect "the Baldwin effect",
        22, 23
    "evolutionary biopsychology", 23
    "organic evolution", 23
    organic selection, 22
    physical heredity, 23
    social heredity, 23
Baldwin's organic evolution/Baldwin
    effect, 22, 23, 44, 52, 55, 173, 174,
    179, 181
Barbary macaques (*Macaca sylvanus*),
    202, 219
Barkow, J.H., 46, 49n.1, 118
Barrett, L., 46
    Human Evolutionary Psychology
        (2002), 254
basal assumptions/basal perspectives
    (of evolution of human
    behavior), 16–36, 52, 187, 207
    of Baldwin's theory of "organic
        selection", 23–24
    of Darwin's focus on natural and
        sexual selection, 17–18
    of Dawkins' theory of genic level
        selection, 34–36
    of Hamilton's theory of kin selection, 30
    of "Modern Synthesis" paradigm, 24–25
    of Morgan's theory, 22–23
    of Spencer's multidisciplinary
        approach, 21
    of Tinbergen's ethological approach, 28
    of Trivers' reciprocal altruism model, 31
    of Wallace's focus on human mind,
        19–20
    of Washburn's "New Physical
        Anthropology", 26–27

of Wilsonian sociobiology and
    autocatalysis model, 29, 32–33
basal patterns, 67, 75, 122, 195, 196, 199,
    200, 207
basal perspectives *See* basal
    assumptions/basal perspectives
    (of evolution of human behavior)
basal traits, 17
basic gene function, 25–26
behavior patterns, 39, 64–66, 96,
    203, 230
behavioral adaptations, 22, 30, 36, 39,
    218, 249
behavioral capabilities, 65, 126, 232
behavioral ecology, 38, 96, 101,
    165–166, 206, 255 *See also* human
    behavioral ecology (HBE)
behavioral evolution *See* human
    behavioral evolution/behavioral
    evolution
behavioral factors, 39, 155–157, 164,
    168–169, 184–185
behavioral flexibility/flexible behavior,
    98, 116–117, 126, 128, 225–227,
    229, 233, 236
behavioral inferences, 86–94
behavioral inheritance, 161, 162, 173–174,
    179, 185, 244
behavioral innovation, 189
behavioral interactions, 65–68
behavioral patterns, 5, 7, 8, 10, 19, 40–42,
    97, 112, 168, 202, 210, 214–215,
    216, 218, 235, 239, 247
    of competition for access to resources,
        206–207
    of competition for dominance and
        mates, 208
    of cooperation, 198–199
    human-impacted change in, 11
    influence of feedback on, 189–190
    response to ecological pressures, 165
    role of epigenetic systems in, 185
    and selective pressures, 14, 38–39
    and sex differences, 141
    "tameness", 12–13
    and transmission of information,
        162–163
    See also human behavioral patterns;
        specific behavioral patterns

behavioral phenotypes, 163–169 *See also* phenotypic plasticity

behavioral plasticity, 108, 109, 124–125, 163–164, 181, 182, 183–184, 185, 206 *See also* phenotypic plasticity

behavioral potentials, 11, 17–18

behavioral proclivities, 21–22

behavioral responses, 24, 28, 42, 157, 164, 169, 180–181, 190, 230, 233
    DIT as a solution, 52
    pressures, 39, 202, 226, 228

behavioral strategies, 38, 40–42, 62, 148, 204, 211, 221
    niche construction, 209
    show-off behavior, 44
    in specific social contexts, 200

behavioral traits/human behavioral traits, 13, 170, 175, 181

behavioral trajectories, 10, 163

behavioral variants, 57, 164, 175–176

behavioral variation, 40, 126, 164, 165, 221

belief systems, 94, 252–253

beliefs, 41, 53, 56, 58, 94, 106, 114, 242, 252

Belyaev, Dimity K., 11–12

biased cultural transmission/biased transmission, 56

bidirectional pathogen transmission, 217

big game hunting, 33, 43 *See also* hunting

biocultural anthropology/biocultural anthropological, 180, 183, 187–188, 195, 200, 207, 232 *See also* anthropology/anthropological

biocultural human, 177–178

biocultural inheritance, 234, 235

biocultural innovations, 88–90

biocultural organisms, 190, 249

biological adaptation, 49, 105

biological determinism, 257

biological fitness, 53, 54, 106

biosocial patterns, 52

biotic pressures, 168

bipedal anatomy, 3, 70, 71, 80, 125, 152 *See also* bipedal locomotion

bipedal locomotion, 69, 72, 96, 98, 125, 152 *See also* bipedal anatomy

"blackbox" linkages, 161, 181, 182

Blackmore, S.J., 105, 58, 59
    The Meme Machine, 105

blade tools/blade tool kits, 92–93

Bliege Bird, R., 42, 43, 44, 121

Blurton-Jones, N.G., 119, 120

body shape, 10, 220

body size, 3, 10, 44, 72, 76–77, 83, 84, 86, 90, 100, 168, 198, 199, 210 *See also* larger body size

Boehm, C., 119
    Hierarchy in the Forest: The Evolution of Egalitarian Behavior, 119

Bolter, D.R., 108

bonding patterns, 124, 156, 231

Bouri geological formation (Ethiopia), 78

bow and arrow, 93

Bowlby, J., 45, 118

Boyd, R., 52, 53, 55, 103, 104, 161n.2
    Not by Genes Alone: How Culture Transformed Human Evolution (2005), 103
    "obligate mutualists", 53
    The Origin and Evolution of Cultures (2005), 104

brain, physiology costs of, 214–215

brain size, 3, 59, 77, 80, 87, 90, 107, 199 *See also* encephalization/ increased encephalization; increased brain size

Brown, G.R., 48, 175, 256
    Sense and Nonsense: Evolutionary Perspectives on Human Behavior (2002), 256

Bunn, H.T., 99
    Meat-Eating and Human Evolution (2001), 99

burials/burial sites, 92, 94, 192, 209, 235 *See also* human remains

Call, J., 104

caloric requirements/caloric intake, 86, 90, 128, 200

caloric return/caloric payoffs, 43, 44

canids, 11, 144

canine dimorphism *See* canine tooth dimorphism

canine tooth dimorphism, 72, 83–84, 198

cannibalism, 92, 201 *See also* nutritional
    cannibalism
caretakers, 8, 99, 113, 227
caretaking behaviors, 65, 104, 119, 120,
    203, 219, 234
Cartwright, J., 127, 128, 157, 158,
    254, 255
    Evolution and Human Behavior:
        Darwinian Perspectives on Human
        Nature (2000), 128, 254
Cavalli-Sforza, L., 52
cercopithecine species, 196
cercopithecoid monkeys, 204
Chad, 70, 74
changing environments, 23, 88
Charnov, E. L., 119
child care *See* child rearing
child rearing, 141, 148, 159, 196, 197,
    198, 203, 223, 228
child survival, 40
childhood, 8, 104, 108, 121
child-rearing assistance, 44
child-rearing costs, 141, 148, 198, 203,
    219, 220, 233
child-rearing strategies, 220
children, 33, 40, 119, 215, 223
chimpanzees, 3, 70, 71, 74, 87, 123,
    141, 161n.3, 200, 204, 212, 217,
    230, 232
    female participation in hunts, 227
    food sharing among, 199
    male–male cooperative alliances
        among, 198
    memory recall in, 68
    tool use acquisition in, 193
Chomsky, N., 45, 115
    universal grammar, 45
climates, 41, 103, 168, 173, 189, 205, 215,
    226, 234, 236, 241
coalitions, 66, 67, 102, 125, 128, 193, 196,
    198 *See also* alliances
coevolution *See* gene–culture
    coevolution/DIT
cognitive abilities/cognitive skills,
    20, 29, 59, 98, 102, 104, 106, 114,
    124, 234
cognitive adaptation, 46, 226
cognitive capabilities, 19, 20, 115, 116,
    129–130, 184

cognitive complexity, 3, 116, 124,
    185, 235
cognitive function, 18, 58, 59, 102
cognitive mechanisms, 42, 48
cognitive modularity, 47
cognitive patterns, 234
cognitive powers, 59, 97, 110, 185, 233
community/family altruism, 22
comparative data, 153, 191, 247 *See also*
    traditional paradigmatic views
    (EP, HBE, ND-Sociobiology,
    Memetics, and DIT)
comparative primatology, 64–68, 128,
    153, 158
competition, 18, 20, 34, 39, 53, 58, 66,
    121, 141, 150, 159, 170, 179, 204,
    205, 208, 220, 233, 242
    altruism response to, 22, 207
    between sexes, 157, 196, 197–198
    for resources, 66, 151–153, 198, 210,
        211, 216
complex behavior, 18, 112
complex information transfer, 109, 114,
    116, 171
complex learning, 110
conditional strategies, 36
conflict, 10, 149–151 *See also* intergroup
    conflict; intragroup conflict
    commonalities in, 133–135, 149–150,
        158, 203–207
    factors needing further inquiry,
        208–212
conflict negotiation, 112, 122, 140, 157
conformity, 33
Conklin-Brittain, N.L., 100
contest competition, 38, 144, 198, 206
context sensitivity, 166, 170, 180
controlled use of fire/making and
    controlling fire, 59, 89, 91, 93, 100,
    189, 215, 234
cooking, 93, 100–101, 176, 213
cooperation, 22, 55, 67, 96, 98, 105,
    106, 112–119, 124, 128, 147–148,
    207–208, 228, 232, 255
    among kin and non-kin, 110
    among males, 99, 100, 141, 145
    in child rearing, 145–146
    commonalities in, *158*, 133–135,
        149–150, 192–200, 211–213

cooperation (*contd.*)
  at community level, 108
  factors needing further inquiry,
      201–203
  female–female, 126, 141, 145
  interindividual, 233
  major element in human evolution,
      149, 157, 217, 220
  male–female, 121, 126, 141, 145, 230
  patterns of, 130–140
  in predation avoidance, 123
  and tit-for-tat strategy, 111
  See also intergroup cooperation;
      intragroup cooperation/
      intragroup care
cooperative alliances, 193, 198, 199, 205
cooperative breeding, 113–114, 203,
      219, 220
cooperative caretaking, 120
cooperative child rearing, 145–146, 197
cooperative endeavors, 20, 196, 202
cooperative hunting, 91, 128, 141, 193
cooperative patterns, 57, 114, 125,
      199, 202
coordination, 91, 156, 193, 212
core factors, 18, 23, 62, 99–100, 111, 129,
      183, 201, 220, 226, 246
  in intergroup competition, 201, 204
  in intragroup cooperation in
      intergroup competition, 194
  in niche construction, 188–189
  in plasticity, 165–169
  in xenophobia, 157
co-sleeping, 8
Cosmides, L., 46, 49n.1, 118
costly signaling hypothesis, 43–44, 126
  See also show-off hypothesis
costs, 30, 40, 111, 181, 193–194, 197–198,
      199, 204, 213–218, 228
cranium/cranial, 20, 70–74, 76, 82–84
creationist perspectives/creationism,
      8–11
Cronk, L., 254
  *That Complex Whole: culture and
      the evolution of human behavior*
      (1999), 254
cruelty, 7, 102–103
cultural anthropology/cultural
      anthropological, 48, 195, 199,
      246–248, 250, 256

cultural behavior/cultural behavioral,
      8, 45, 52, 106, 177, 190, 247
cultural change, 54, 56, 175, 234, 235
cultural component (of evolution), 5–7
cultural environments, 46, 105, 106,
      177, 247
cultural fitness, 53, 54–55, 106, 200
cultural group selection, 9, 55–56
cultural information, 36, 45, 53–54, 115
cultural inheritance, 54–55, 167
cultural innovation, 34–36, 89
cultural intelligence, 234, 235
cultural mind, 7
cultural niche construction, 176
cultural patterns, 6, 36, 52, 107, 116, 177,
      237, 242
cultural processes, 79, 175
cultural traits (memeplexes), 58
cultural trends, 58, 183
cultural units, 53–54
cultural variations, 40, 49, 54, 55, 56, 91,
      118, 171, 229
culture variants, 53, 54, 57, 62, 169,
      171, 175
culture, 5, 40, 45, 222, 249–250, 254, 256
  See also information
"culturgens", 53
current behaviors, 3, 47, 62, 165, 184
Curry, Oliver, 9–10, 243

Daly, M., 102
  Homicide (1998), 102
Darwin, Charles, 10n.6, 17–19, 20, 21–24,
      30, 32, 54, 55, 95, 97, 150, 155, 157,
      173, 182, 183, 194, 201, 208, 212,
      240n.1, 245
  *The Descent of Man and Selection in
      Relation to Sex* (1871), 17–19, 97, 254
  The Origin of Species (1859), 10n.6
Darwinian anthropology, 38, 248 *See also*
      human behavioral ecology (HBE)
Darwinian evolution (natural
      selection), 54
Darwinian evolutionary process, 52, 103
Darwinian "fitness", 59
Darwinian perspectives, 21
Darwinian process, 47
Darwinian selection, 22
Dawkins, Richard, 34–36, 57, 105, 172, 252
  The Selfish Gene (2006), 34–36

Dawkinsian "extended phenotype"
        ideas, 173. 185
Dawkinsian "genes", 57
Dawkinsian genic selfishness, 37
Dawkinsian memes, 53, 171
Dawkinsian selfish gene perspective,
        58, 170
de Waal, Frans B.M., 112
    Good Natured, 112
Deacon, T.W., 115, 116
    *The Symbolic Species: The Co-Evolution of
        Language and the Brain* (1997), 116
"decision rules", 36
Dennet, D., 58, 105
    Darwin's Dangerous Idea (1995), 105
dependency period, 65, 119, 120
design features, 45, 47, 48, 51
determinism, 9n.4, 257
development, 6, 14–15, 19–21, 85, 100,
        102, 108, 114, 124, 162, 165, 170,
        180, 200, 216
    of animal behavior, 28
    of behavioral patterns and
        strategies, 112
    of behavioral phenotypes, 163, 171
    brain, 214, 215
    of cooperation, 199
    gene-based conceptualizations of, 171
    human behavior and patterns in,
        18, 23, 185, 218, 249
    influence of DNA in, 161
    misunderstanding of SSSM and, 49
    of organisms, 25, 26, 163, 164, 169
    of traits, 183
developmental linkages
    see developmental trajectories
developmental plasticity, 110, 165–166
developmental systems theory (DST),
        26, 163–165, 165, 169–172, 178,
        179, 183–184, 189, 250
    concept of extended inheritance in, 173
    and ecological inheritance, 174–175
    and four-dimensional evolution,
        180–181, 185
developmental systems *See* developmental
        systems theory (DST)
developmental trajectories, 182, 185
diet, 75, 86–88, 90–91, 96, 120, 151–153,
        191–192, 200, 201, 211–213
    and differential survivorship, 241

of Pleistocene hominins, 205
    taboos in, 237
dietary patterns/diet patterns, 87, 90,
        93, 139–140, 215, 241
dietary practice/food, 96, 129
dietary strategies, 88, 241
differential access to resources, 66, 207
differential survivorship, 88, 241
disease, 111, 153–154, 159, 192, 217–218
dispersal patterns, 31, 66–67, 205
dispersed social groups, 65
DNA, 25–26, 34, 161, 171, 243
DNA sequences, 5, 180, 260
Dobzhansky, Theodosius, 28
dog evolution (fox/dog example),
        11–13, 188
domesticated animals, 10, *12*
domestication, 12–13, 273
dominance hierarchies, 31, 66, 206
dominance/dominance relationships/
        dominance systems, 66, 67
Dual Inheritance Theory (DIT), 17, 37,
        48, 188, 251 *See also* gene–culture
        coevolution/DIT; traditional
        paradigmatic views (EP, HBE,
        ND-Sociobiology, Memetics,
        and DIT)
Dunbar, R., 254
    Human Evolutionary Psychology
        (2002), 254
dwarfism, 12, 83, 105
dyadic (two-individual) contests, 209
dyads, 232

Early Australopithecines, 71–76
East Africa/East African, 72, 76, 80, 88,
        89, 91, 192, 212, 213, 246
East Asia/East Asian, 82, 88, 91
ecological anthropology, 38
ecological challenges, 40, 41, 42, 117,
        189, 202, 205, 229
ecological contexts, 39, 40, 41, 51, 207, 237
ecological engineering, 173–174 *See also*
        ecosystem engineering
ecological impacts, 7, 165–169
ecological inheritance, 117, 172, 173–175,
        185, 205, 218, 226
ecological pressures, 152–154
"ecological selectionist logic", 39
ecological variables, 41, 88, 173, 241

ecology/ecological, 38, 136–138,
     152–153, 168n.5, 213–218, 256
ecosystem, 168, 173
ecosystem engineering, 117, 172–173, 174
     See also ecological engineering
egalitarianism, 119, 122, 144
embodied capital theory, 120–121
emotional bonding/emotional bonds,
     8, 110, 124
empathic altruism, 105
encephalization quotient, 77–78
encephalization/increased
     encephalization, 77, 125 *See also*
     brain size; increased brain size
endocrinological pathways, 178–179
enhanced neurological complexity, 234
energetic costs, 59, 158, 214–215, 219
enhanced protein/caloric intake
     See caloric requirements/caloric
     intake
environment, 5, 18, 19, 23, 25, 33, 43, 99,
     106–107, 136–138, 152–153, 172,
     174, 183–184, 186, 191–192, 201,
     205, 206, 212, 213–218, 233, 247,
     249–250
   arboreal, 71–76
   and environment of evolutionary
     adaptiveness (EEA), 45–46, 48,
     62, 118, 183, 245
   and females dominance, 66
   genic level selection and, 34–36
   humans adaptability to, 40, 41–42,
     117, 225, 234, 244, 245–246
   influence on humans/organisms, 26,
     51–54, 93–94, 97, 105, 109
   and selection pressures, 20–21, 22, 173
environmental challenges, 177, 214
environmental factors *See*
     environmental factors/
     environment factors
environmental factors/environment
     factors, 17, 105, 153, 159, 168,
     216–219
environmental fluctuations, 107, 164, 213
environmental pressures, 33, 46, 96, 116,
     118, 129, 152–154, 164, 172–173,
     206, 210
epigenetic cognitive plasticity, 109
epigenetic development, 109

epigenetic inheritance/epigenetic
     inheritance affect, 161, 162
epigenetic processes, 37, 109
epigenetic systems, 162, 181, 185
Erlich, P., 104, 105, 255, 256, 257
     *Human Natures: Genes, Culture, and the
     Human Prospect* (2000), 254
Eskimos (Esquimaux), 18
essentialist perspectives, 8–11
ethics, 99, 106, 115
ethnographic datasets, 9, 42, 55, 197,
     220, 223–224
   Human Area Relations Files, 197
ethology, 28, 30, 38, 240
eugenics movements/eugenicists, 9, 10n.6
Eurasia/Eurasian, 81, 82, 83, 88, 89, 91,
     92, 227
eurytopic (generalist foragers), 88, 215,
     214, 241
evolution of the mind, 19–21
evolutionary (genetic) advantage, 9
evolutionary anthropology of behavior,
     26–28
evolutionary biology, 32, 44–45, 180–186
   biological/biocultural
     anthropology-based approach,
     187–191, 233–237
   emerging approaches to, 165–179
   traditional Neo-Darwinian and
     affiliated approaches to, 160–164
evolutionary change, 5–11, 62–63,
     156–157, 164, 185–186, 190–191,
     208, 248
evolutionary history, 3, 8, 10, 29, 46,
     51, 101, 102–103, 108, 186, 194,
     205, 223
   alternative explanatory approaches
     to, 165–179
   causal roles in, 161–163
   cooperation in, 151, 152–154
   feedback effects on, 217
   genic level selection and, 34–36
   and natural selection process, 17–19,
     24–26, 182–184
   proposed general framework for,
     232–237
   and sympatric hominins, 210, 211
evolutionary hypotheses, 170, 250
evolutionary impacts, 150, 169, 182, 200

evolutionary medicine, 7–8
evolutionary models, 24, 27, 42, 189
evolutionary past, 6, 153, 206, 217, 220
evolutionary patterns, 53, 122, 127,
         141, 163, 168, 169, 181, 221, 239,
         243, 257
    influence of plasticity on, 169
    intensity of conflict and competition
         on, 207–208
evolutionary perspectives, 9, 21, 38, 111,
         160, 200, 256
evolutionary problem, 43, 50
evolutionary processes, 6, 26, 45, 53,
         170, 174, 187, 217, 243
evolutionary psychology (EP), 17, 37,
         40, 44–52, 95, 107, 109, 129, 160,
         188, 245, 251
    The Adapted Mind, 45–47
    goals and methods, 47–48
    SSSM specific approach, 48–52
    See also traditional paradigmatic
         views (EP, HBE, ND-Sociobiology,
         Memetics, and DIT)
evolutionary scenarios, 9, 11, 15, 141,
         174, 206
evolutionary sociobiology, 32–34
Evolutionary Stable Strategies (ESS), 38
evolutionary theory, 27–28, 37, 42, 44,
         48, 240, 246, 248
    alternative approaches to, 165–176
    "biocultural' approach to, 177–179
    four dimensions of, 160–163
    paradigmatic biases in, 242–244
evolutionary time, 29, 46, 47, 109, 156,
         177–178
evolutionary trajectories, 46, 115, 210,
         213, 218, 226
evolutionary understanding, 29
evolved psychological mechanisms,
         45, 46, 118
expensive tissue hypothesis, 176–177
experience, 19, 23, 27, 28–29, 65, 109,
         113, 115, 177, 188, 228, 239,
         242–243
    constant modification of human
         behavior, 190
    inherited resources, 170
experiential biases, 54, 246
extended inheritance, 170, 173, 174–175

extinction, 20, 55, 56–57, 71, 76, 88, 98,
         211, 234, 241–242
extra-somatic factors/elements, 106, 116,
         156, 170, 184–185, 189, 229, 245

facilitation, 19, 168
Falk, Dean, 122
familial pair-bonding, 119
family altruism, 21
feedback loops, 169, 177
feedback systems, 58, 107, 174
Fehr, Ernst, 110
Feldman, M.W., 52, 104, 117, 178
female advertisement, 221–222
female receptivity, 101, 154, 221–222
females counterstrategies, 100, 101, 102
fitness, 18, 29, 39–41, 42–44, 52, 54,
         55–56, 106, 108, 109, 126, 163–164,
         196, 206, 224, 227, 229–230,
         239, 242
    and aggressive behavior, 101–102, 123
    altruism/altruistic punishment and,
         22, 30–31, 110–111
    benefit, 30, 39–40, 43, 44, 58,
         193–194, 198
    body shape and, 220–221, 222
    competition and, 204
    conflicts and, 148–149
    costs, 30, 39–40, 43, 100, 150, 230
    health across populations, 177–178
    impact of natural selection on, 32
    impact of variation in memes on,
         57–58, 59, 195
    measures of/proxy measures of, 26,
         47, 62, 181–182, 186, 194–195, 200
    and pair-bonding, 124
    values, 31, 39, 54, 57, 101, 106, 109
Flack, Jessica C., 112
flexible behavior *see* behavioral
         flexibility/flexible behavior
Foley, Robert, 100
food investments, 101 *see also*
         meat/meat acquisition
food resources, 90, 101, 213, 233
food sharing, 39, 43, 101, 119–120, 152,
         155, 199–201, 203, 211–213, 234
    cooperative, 144–145
    increase in group size, 128
    intragroup, 121, 151

food stress, 152, 215–216
food/foodstuffs, 13–14, 65, 39–40,
        56, 59–60, 65, 75, 86, 139–140,
        151–152, 200–201, 203, 206,
        211–213, 215, 241, 247, 250
    basal assumptions, 32–34, 42–43
    behavioral innovation in, 189
    competition for, 67, 216
    cooperative collection of, 233
    and nutritional ecology, 38
    See also food sharing; food stress
forager groups/human forager groups,
        43, 44, 46
foragers *See* hunter-gatherers/foragers
foraging behavior, 88, 92, 100, 241
foraging patterns, 205, 244
foraging rates, 168
forager societies, 102, 225
foraging strategies, 100, 152, 199
foraging success, 193, 203
foraging, 94, 123, 141, 190, 218, 244–245
foramen magnum, 69, 70, 71
forested environment *See* arboreal
        environment
fossil analyses, 88, 241
fossil data, 33, 69, 187, 191 *See also*
        traditional paradigmatic views
        (EP, HBE, ND-Sociobiology,
        Memetics, and DIT)
fossil datasets, 33
fossil record, 27, 64, 88, 92, 106, 151, 156,
        169, 184, 190, 191, 233, 235, 240,
        242, 244, 245, 247
    human, 68–85
    of increased encephalization, 128
    mid-Pleistocene, 176
    of utilization of tools, 90
fossils, 69, 70, 71–73, 76–85, 87–88, 184,
        192, 195, 198, 216, 219, 229, 247
    of *A. afarensis*, 75
    of anatomically modern humans,
        92–93
    assessment of symmetry from, 224
    of *H. erectus*, 208, 214
    of *H. sapiens sapiens*, 227
friendships, 32, 110, 196, 231
Fry, D., 122
    The Human Potential for Peace (2006), 122
Fuentes, A., 108, 112

Gachter, S., 110
Galton, Francis, 18
    Hereditary Genius (1869), 18
Garber, P.A., 123
Gaulin, S.J.C., 49
gene flow, 13–14, 24, 37, 81, 170, 190
gene pool, 13, 14, 29, 53, 174
gene–culture coevolution/DIT, 23, 37,
        52–57, 62, 151, 160, 161nn.1, 2,
        176n.6, 178, 190, 256
    five elements of, 103
    role for selection on behavior in, 182
    tri-inheritance vision model
        (TIV) and, 175
    See also Dual Inheritance Theory
        (DIT); traditional paradigmatic
        views (EP, HBE, ND-Sociobiology,
        Memetics, and DIT)
genera *Aotus*, 232
genera *Australopithecus*, 153
genera *Callicebus*, 232
genera *Homo*, 151
genera *Macaca*, 216
genera *Papio*, 216
genera *Paranthropus*, 153
genera *Rhinopithecus*, 216
"General Adaptation Syndrome", 178
generalist foragers (eurytopic), 88
generations, across, 5, 11–12, 22–23, 25,
        26, 34, 36, 55, 164, 169, 181, 182,
        185, 189
    culture change, 53, 56
    niche construction behavior, 173–174
    passing information, 162–163
    specific outcomes, 168
    treatments of diseases, 218
genetic complexes, 27, 185
genetic drift, 14, 24, 37, 170, 190
genetic inheritance, 54, 174, 177, 183
genetic material, 6, 24, 26, 106, 126, 180
genetic predisposition, 33, 54
genetic sequences, 11, 162, 181–182
genetic units, 32, 53
genetic variants, 24, 53
genetic variation, 11, 14, 25, 55, 181
genic level selection, 34, 168
genic selection, 34, 62, 117, 181
genic selfishness, 37
genic-based sociobiology paradigm, 24

genotypes/genotypic levels, 12, 26, 180
genotypic levels *See* genotypes/
 genotypic levels
genus *Homo*, 5, 46, 76–77, 79–85, 87–92,
 94, 99–100, 106–107, 109–110,
 113–125, 151–153, 156–157, 195,
 198, 211, 212, 214–219, 226–227,
 229–234, 241–242, 245
 diets of hominins, 213
 increase in brain size of, 86
 intragroup cooperation predates, 193
 and "ratchet effect", 104
 sexual dimorphism in, 197
 social complexity in, 103
 use of stone tools by, 201, 210
genus *Paranthropus*, 76, 77, 78–81, 86–88,
 151, 153, 210–211, 213, 219,
 233–234, 241–242
geography/geographical, 5, 24, 80–81,
 82–83, 91, 152, 205. 234
gibbons, 75, 201, 210, 212, 230
Gibson, Kathleen R., 107, 109
Girvan, Michelle, 112
Goldschmidt, Walter, 116, 256
 *The Bridge to Humanity: How Affect
 Hunger Trumps the Selfish Gene*
 (2006), 116, 256
Gombe stream reserve (Tanzania), 217
Goodenough, Ursula, 115
gorilla groups *See* gorillas/gorilla
 groups
gorillas/gorilla groups, 68–72, 153, 196,
 210, 212, 219, 227, 230, 232
grandmothering, 96, 119–120
Gray, R. D., 169, 171
Griffiths, P.E., 169, 171
grooming/mutual grooming/social
 grooming, 65–66, 67, 76
group extinction, 55, 56, 98
group hunting, 212
group living, 31, 65, 66–67, 176, 192,
 208, 223
group selection, 24, 30, 33, 55, 56, 61,
 103, 114, 119
guilt, 32, 103, 110

Hadar (East Africa), 75, 192
Hamilton, William D., 30–31, 36, 37, 111
 kin selection, 30–31

handedness, evolution of, 99
handicap principle, 43, 122
Hare, B., 104
Hart, D.L., 123
 *Man the Hunted: Primates, Predators,
 and Human Evolution* (2005), 123
Hatley, T., 101
Hauert, C., 111
Hauser, M., 114, 115
 *Moral Minds: How Nature Designed
 Our Universal Sense of Right and
 Wrong* (2006), 114
Hawkes, K., 42, 119, 120
health issues, 7–8, 250
herbivorous bovids, 75
heredity, 23, 161, 163
heritable components, 6, 14, 239
heritable variation, 161, 163, 181
Hernandez-Lloreda, M.V., 104
Herrmann, E., 104
heterosexual pair-bonding
 See heterosexual pair bonds/
 heterosexual pair-bonding
heterosexual pair bonds/heterosexual
 pair-bonding, 125, 156, 197,
 230–231, 232
heterosexual cooperation, 141, 145,
 195–196, 233
high-risk behavior, 121
higher traits, 17
 "quadrumana", 17
historical perspectives (of human
 behavior), 16–36
historicity, 47, 247
Hobbes, Thomas, 150
hominin/human characteristics, 64
Homininae (subfamily), 3, 69
hominins, 59, 68–72, 74–75, 76–80, 82–85,
 86–87, 90–91, 122–123, 125, 141,
 149, 153–154, 159, 202, 205–206,
 210–213, 215–216, 218–220, 222,
 227, 233–234, 242, 249
 and arboreal environment, 86
 conspecific competition in, 124
 cruelty in forager society of, 102
 evolution, 107, 115, 127, 150, 194,
 211, 229
 food sharing among, 144–145
 fossil species, 76

hominins (*contd.*)
  and group living, 128
  large neocortexes of, 176
  physiology/hominin physiological, 106
  sexual dimorphism in, 197–198
  species, 123, 151, 195
Hominoidea (superfamily), 3, 240
hominoid-wide trends, 64, 190
Homo antecessor, 82, 91
Homo erectus, 81–85, 88–89, 100–101, 103,
      118–119, 153, 195, 202, 208, 210,
      213–215, 220, 225, 226, 233, 246
  dimorphism, 195
  male–male competition, 208
  reliance on hunting, 90
Homo ergaster, 82, 83, 90, 100, 153, 210,
      214, 218, 233
Homo floresiensis, 83, 89
Homo habilis, 79–80, *81*, 82, 86, 87–88, 245
Homo heidelbergensis, 82–83, 198
Homo material culture, 91
Homo neanderthalensis, 83 *See also*
      Neanderthals
Homo rudolfensis, 73, 79–82, 86–87
Homo sapiens, 5, 32, 81, 106, 193
hormone patterns, 14
Hrdy, Sarah B, 113, 114, 219, 220
  Mother Nature: A History of Mothers,
      Infants and Natural Selection
      (1999), 114
human adaptations, 29, 46, 48, 62, 102,
      113, 116, 120–121, 161, 222
human aggression, 212
human ancestors, 69, 192, 194, 196,
      203–204, 205, 210–211, 216, 218,
      233, 240–241, 245–247
human behavior *See* human behavioral
      evolution/behavioral evolution
human behavioral ecology (HBE),
      17, 37, 38–44
  commonalities in:
    conflict, 203–207
    cooperation, 192–200, 211–212
    ecology/environment, 213–215
    sex/reproduction, 219–223
    specific behavior, 225–230
  factors needing further enquiry:
    conflict, 208–212
    cooperation, 201–202

ecology/environment, 216–218
    sex/reproduction, 224
    specific behavior, 231–232
  See also Darwinian anthropology
human behavioral evolution/behavioral
      evolution, 3–4, 30, 34, 68, 95–97,
      127–129, 152–157, 180, 183–197,
      201, 203–207, 211, 214, 228, 230,
      232, 235, 238–239, 241, 243–247,
      254, 256
  avoidance of disease and, 217–218
  conflicts between researchers on,
      251–253
  evolutionary psychological
      perspectives on, 22–24, 44–52
  high levels of cooperation in, 141–149,
      219–220
  intergroup competition and, 150–151
  and offspring production, 223–224
  relevance of early theories of, 5–15
  and use of language and symbols, 226
human behavioral patterns, 10, 19, 67,
      97, 112, 141, 212, 216, 218, 226–230
human behavioral phenome, 96, 104–105
human behavioral traits *See* behavioral
      traits/human behavioral traits
human biocultural behavior, 181
human bodies, 3, 20, 120, 246
human childcare, 120
human children *See* children
human cognitive abilities, 20, 124
human cooperation, 110, 113
human cultural behavior, 106, 118, 190
human culture, 47, 58, 105–106, 115,
      225, 231
human development, 21, 97, 113, 170
human differences, 9, 203
human–environment mutability,
      216–217
human evolution, 8–15, 21, 24, 27, 33,
      52, 58, 68–85, 96
  comparative primatology, 64–85
  cultural account of, 86–94
  current studies in, 254–257
    academic approaches to, 243–248
    dealing with religious, social, and
      political dimensions in, 252–253
    proposal for evolutionary history,
      233–237

See also hypotheses/theories (human evolution)

human evolutionary history, 10, 157, 199, 201–202, 203, 209, 210, 233

human evolutionary patterns, 148, 162, 170, 171, 212, 224

human flexibility, 109, 214, 230

human forager groups *See* forager groups/human forager groups

human forms, 3

human fossil record, 68–85

human genome, 9

human groups, 13, 18–20, 40, 57, 92, 111, 113, 114–115, 153, 158–159, 193, 203, 212, 213, 214, 218, 234–235

  altruism in, 207

  cooperation and bonding in, 198

  increased competition within, 209

human histories, 10, 150, 157, 190, 206–207

human infants, 119, 141. 219, 220 *See also* infants

human lineage, 75, 116–117, 125, 153, 168n.4, 228 *See also* lineage

human mating strategies, 50, 221

human mind, 17–20, 21–36, 126, 225

  information processing mechanisms of, 45–47

  memes, 57–59

human morality, 97, 110

human niche construction *See* niche construction

human patterns *See* human traits/ human patterns

human phenotypic expression, 48

human populations, 10, 41, 106, 110–111, 177, 200, 204, 213, 216–217, 220, 228

human potential, 10, 205

human psyche, 47–48

human psychological mechanisms, 47

human remains, 94, 203 *See also* burials/burial sites

human sociality, 113, 119, 123

human societies, 6, 11, 23–24, 56–57, 110, 221, 231, 235 *See also* modern human societies

Human Sociobiology *See* ND-Sociobiology

human toolkit, 189, 202, 234

human traits/human patterns, 171, 212, 234, 247

human variation, 28, 178 *see also* plasticity

humanity, 9–10, 15, 17–20, 22, 92, 97, 99, 114, 116, 210, 233, 250, 251, 252–253, 255–256 *See also* modern humanity

humankind, 6, 18–19, 98, 113

hunter-gatherers/foragers, 43–44, 46, 99, 118, 121, 141–142, 155, 175, 197, 200, 210 *See also* Pleistocene hunter-gatherers

hunting, 43–44, 59, 86–87, 90–94, 98–100, 123, 199–200, 210–213, 215, 227–228, 232, 233–234

  egalitarianism among groups, 119

  and embodied capital, 120–121

  and expression of cruelty, 102

  males risk-taking behavior, 33, 47, 121–122, 125, 155

  measure of individual fitness in, 39

  and nutritional intake, 128, 141, 151, 176

  weapons for, 20

  See also cooperative hunting; fitness costs

hypotheses/proposals/theories (human evolution), 157–159, 182–183, 191, 249–250, 252–253

  biases and related problems in, 242–244

  biocultural approach, 177–19

  concepts of limited use, 180–181

  conflicts among researchers, 251–252

  criteria of selection of, 95–97

  evolutionary biological approach, 165–176

  factors needing further enquiry:

    conflict, 208–212

    cooperation, 201–202

    diet/food, 213

    ecology/environment, 216–218

    sex/reproduction, 224

    specific behavior, 231–232

  integrative proposals, 188–189, 232–237

  overlapping themes in comparisons:

    conflict commonalities, 203–207

hypotheses/proposals/theories (human evolution) (*contd.*)
  cooperation commonalities, 192–200, 203
  diet/food, 211–212
  ecology/environment commonalities, 213–215
  sex/reproduction commonalities, 219–223
  specific behavior commonalities, 225–230
perspectives with scope for expansion, 184–186
shared themes in comparisons, 129, 158
  conflict patterns, 133–135, 149–150
  cooperation patterns, 129–132, 141, 144–145, 147
  environment/ecologic patterns, 136–138, 152–153
  food/diet patterns, 139–140, 151–152
  sex/reproduction patterns, 142–143, 154
  specific behavioral patterns, 146–147, 155–156
See also human evolution

imagination, 17, 94
imitations, 17, 23, 52, 57–59, 103, 104–105
immatures, 141, 145–146, 148, 199, 202–230, 219, 227, 228
increased brain size, 125, 126, 128, 176, 214, 215, 219, 233 *See also* brain size; encephalization/increased encephalization
increased encephalization *See also* brain size; encephalization/increased encephalization; increased brain size
indoctrinability, 33
infanticide, 99, 101, 155
infants, 8, 65, 75, 90, 113, 123, 128, 202–203, 219, 220, 227 *See also* human infants
information, 53, 65, 68, 103, 106, 113, 162–163, 185, 188, 189, 226
information processing mechanisms, 45, 48

information sharing, 9, 105, 113, 114, 123, 235 *See also* culture
information transfer/transmission, 100, 106, 107, 108, 115, 118, 156, 162, 170, 171, 189, 233
Ingold, T., 247
inherent morality, 114–115
inheritance, 6n.1, 18, 22, 23, 42, 52–54, 160–161, 185, 255 *See also* extended inheritance
inheritance patterns, 54, 173, 234, 244
inherited environments, 117
innovations, 17, 104, 106–107, 188, 189, 190, 225, 227, 229, 234
instinct/instinctive, 19, 21, 22. 99, 103 *See also* tribal-social instincts hypotheses
intelligence, 9, 22, 97, 98, 126, 255
interactive developmental system, 171
intergenerational contexts, 165, 167
intergroup aggression, 98, 101, 201
intergroup alliances, 149, 202
intergroup competition, 20, 30, 103, 119, 150, 152, 153, 157, 194, 201, 202, 204
intergroup conflict, 98, 100, 103, 141, 156, 208–210, 235, 255 *See also* conflict; intragroup conflict
  commonalities in, 203–205
  focus of hypotheses, 150–151
  frequency of, 201–202
intergroup cooperation, 99, 104, 107, 113, 117, 122, 148–149, 151, 201–203 *See also* cooperation; intragroup cooperation/ intragroup care
intergroup violence, 201
interhominin conflict, 210–211
interindividual affiliation/ interindividual bonding, 123, 124
interindividual aggression, 112
interindividual competition, 202, 204, 233
interindividual cooperation, 233
interindividual social negotiation, 122
interindividual variation, 222
intermammalian conflict, 211
International Sexuality Description Project (ISDP), 50–51
interpersonal violence, 213
intersexual aggression/coercion, 101

intersexual differences, 50, 51
intragroup care *See* intragroup
    cooperation/intragroup care
intragroup conflict, 112, 149–150,
    208–210 *See also* conflict;
    intergroup conflict
intragroup cooperation/intragroup care,
    55, 92, 99, 104–115, 121, 129–130,
    141, 149–150, 155, 192–195, 197,
    201–202
  in evolution of genus *Homo*, 114
  food sharing, 151–152
  selection pressures and, 119
  "tribal" psychology, 103
intrasexual competition, 101
intraspecific competition, 38

Jablonka, E., 160, 161, 162, 163,
    165, 171, 173, 174, 175, 178,
    182, 189
Jake, P., 228
Janson, C.H., 102
  *Infanticide by Males and Its
    Implications*, 102
John, L., 46
Jones, J.H., 100

Kaplan, H. 120
Kappelman, J., 101
Kenya, 69, 71, 74
Kenyanthropus platyops, 74
kin selection, 29–36, 37, 40, 67, 103, 105,
    110, 117, 119, 122, 128, 141, 145,
    163, 194, 207, 223
kin support, 40
Knauft, B.M., 113
Koro Toro (Chad), 74
Krakauer, D.C., 112
Kropotkin, Petr, 22, 206
Kuhn, S.L., 227, 228

lactation ability, 90, 221
Laden, G., 100
Laetoli (Tanzania), 72, 74
Lake Turkana (Kenya), 71, 74
Laland, K.N., 48, 117, 172, 173, 174, 175,
    176, 178, 216, 217, 256
  *Sense and Nonsense: Evolutionary
    Perspectives on Human Behavior*
    (2002), 256

Lamb, M., 160, 161, 162, 163, 165, 170,
    171, 173, 174, 175, 178, 182, 189
Lancaster, C.S., 99
Lancaster, Jane, 120
language (communication), 17, 19, 33,
    44, 50, 68, 98–99, 103, 113, 114–115,
    117, 155–156, 157–158, 162,
    184–185, 189, 205, 215, 225–227,
    232–233, 235, 243, 250, 255
  benefits of feedback system, 107
  of genus *Homo*, 104–106
  of late-Pleistocene *Homo*, 91–92
  motherese in evolution of, 122–123
  primary role in cooperation, 116
  result of mental prowess, 97
large bodies, 68, 91, 153, 211, 214
large brains, 69, 79, 91, 126, 214
larger body size, 80, 90, 214 *See also*
    body size
Late Pliocene/Early Pleistocene forms,
    86–88
learning, 6, 23, 47, 104, 110, 113, 120, 170,
    175, 193, 219, 243
  Darwinian process, 47
  epigenetic systems, 185
lethal aggression *See* lethal conflict/
    lethal aggression
lethal conflict/lethal aggression,
    101, 118, 122, 227
lethal violence *See* lethal conflict/lethal
    aggression
Levallois technique, 81
Levi-Strauss, C., 187
Lewontin, R., 165, 172, 174
lifeways, 46, 213, 244
lineage, 3–5, 7, 29, 33n.2, 59, 64, 68–69,
    71, 74–75, 193, 240 *See also* human
    lineage
Livingstone, F.B. 177
local ecologies, 7, 41, 51, 105, 182–183,
    226, 245
local environments, 18, 51, 97,
    173, 174, 175
Lofink, H., 250, 251
long learning, 120, 124, 125
longevity, 31, 56, 57, 62, 128, 198
Lorenz, Konrad, 28
Lovejoy, O., 124
lower animals, 17
Lower Paleolithic period, 93

Lumsden, C.J., 52, 53
    "culturgens", 53
Lycett, J., 254
    Human Evolutionary Psychology
        (2002), 254

Macaca sylvanus (Barbary macaques),
        202, 219
Macaca thibetana (Tibetan macaques), 202
macaques, 196, 198, 204, 212, 213
Mace, R., 40
Mad Cow Disease, 162
maladaptation, 42, 46, 55, 62, 96, 183,
        185, 229, 251
maladaptive behavior *See* maladaptation
male aggression, 157, 212, 253 *See also*
        aggression; aggressive conflict;
        intergroup aggression
male dominance, 33, 98, 128, 156, 224
male guarding, 100, 213
male honest signaling, 224
male risky behavior, 46–47, 155
male signaling, 224
male–female cooperation, 195–197
male–female pair-bonding/male–female
        pair-bonds, 125, 126, 128
Malik, K., 257
    *Man, Beast, and Zombie: What Science
        Can and Cannot Tell Us about
        Human Nature* (2002), 257
Malthus, T.R., 150
Marks, J., 248
material culture, 64, 80, 87, 90–92, 98,
        107, 175, 209, 235
mathematical models, 29–31, 52, 54,
        61, 62
mating mind, 125, 155
mating patterns, 10, 154, 156, 208, 222, 233
mating strategies, 50, 126, 196, 223, 228
    See also sociosexuality
mating success, 39, 223
mating systems, 51
Matsuzawa, Tetsuro, 68
Mayr, Ernst, 172
McBurney, D.H., 48, 49
McDade, T.W., 178, 179
McKenna, J.J. 8
    co-sleeping, 8
meat consumption, 121, 176

meat distribution/meat sharing, 43, 44
meat/meat acquisition, 99–100, 152
    see also food investments
Mediterranean region, 92
megadontia quotient (MQ), 76–78, 80, 83
memeplexes, 36, 57–58, 105, 106
memes, 36, 53, 57–59, 61–62, 105–106,
        169, 171, 182, 196, 198, 209, 227
Memetics, 17, 37, 52, 57–59, 62–63,
        95, 160, 161n.1, 171, 181, 188,
        231, 256 *See also* traditional
        paradigmatic views (EP, HBE,
        ND-Sociobiology, Memetics,
        and DIT)
    conflict between memes, 209
    and cooperative interactions,
        194, 196, 198
    core factor in behavioral evolution, 183
    and natural selection, 180, 182, 190
Mendelian genetic system, 31, 32
menopause, 119
mental evolution, 33
mental facilities, 17, 22
mental prowess *see* intelligence
Mesnick, S.L., 102
Middle Paleolithic period, 93
Miller, Geoffery, 125, 220, 221, 225, 229
    *The Mating Mind: How Sexual Choice
        Shaped the Evolution of Human
        Nature* (2006), 126
Miller, W.B., 124
    *The Ontogeny of Human Bonding
        Systems: Evolutionary Origins,
        Neural Bases, and Psychological
        Mechanisms* (2001), 124
Milton, Katherine, 100
Miner, B.G., 165, 168
Miocene, 64–68, 71
modern behavioral patterns, 34, 222
modern foragers, 90, 244, 245
modern human groups, 20, 92, 94, 97,
        193, 201, 203, 204, 213
modern human societies, 97, 110, 148,
        151, 176, 203, 228 *See also* human
        societies
modern humanity, 33, 92, 98, 150
    See also humanity
    biocultural approaches to study of,
        177–179

modern humans, 8–9, 20–21, 34, 94,
106, 153, 177–180, 183–184,
195, 197–198, 208, 215, 220–221,
224–225, 230, 246
anatomically modern humans, 92, 103
Baldwin effects in, 201
bipedal anatomy in, 70
brain size increases in, 86, 109
cranial remains of genus *Homo*, 80–85
fossils of, 72–76, 78–79
megadontia quotient of, 77
role of cooperation in, 113, 141, 144
sexual division of labor in, 227
stone tool remains of, 86–88
symbols and language of, 226
"Modern Synthesis" paradigm, 24–26
molecular anthropology, 28
monkey societies, 65, 233
monogamy, 50–51, 124–125, 126, 152,
154, 159
monomorphism, 75, 230
moral experience, 115–116
moral instinct, 115
moral sense, 19, 21, 97
moral values, 19, 98
moralistic aggression, 32, 110
morality, 21, 115
Morgan, C. Lloyd, 21, 22–23, 44, 52, 173,
174, 179, 181
Animal Life and Intelligence (1891), 22
"the Baldwin effect", 22
Habit and Instinct (1896), 22
"Of Modification and Variation,"
(1896), 22
Morgan, S.G., 168
morphological changes, 3, 83
morphological studies, 27
morphological traits, 12, 156, 164
motherese, 122–123
mother–infant bond, 65, 123, 124, 232
Mousterian industry, 91–93
multiadult groups/grouping pattern,
68, 75, 192, 193, 195, 197, 208, 230,
231, 233
multilevel selection, 113, 114
multimale/multifemale groups, 68, 128
multiple caretakers, 104, 114, 123, 145,
155, 219–220, 234
mutation, 13, 24, 26

mutual grooming *See* grooming/mutual
grooming/social grooming

natal groups, 67, 193n.3
The National Center for Science
Education, 8n.3
natural selection, 17, 19–22, 24, 26, 29,
34, 37, 45–48, 53–55, 57, 62, 126,
170, 182–183, 190, 195, 235, 243
and altruism, 30–31
and functional behavior, 32
and gene focused model, 161n.1
and niche construction, 117, 172,
174–175
outcomes of, 58
present behavioral patterns and, 41
ND-Sociobiology, 37, 59–63, 95,
163–165, 180 *See also* traditional
paradigmatic views (EP, HBE,
ND-Sociobiology, Memetics,
and DIT)
Neanderthals, 84, 91–92, 198, 227, 228
See also Homo neanderthalensis
negotiation, 67, 194, 200
Nell, Victor, 102
Neo-Darwinian approaches, 160–161,
163, 165, 182
Neo-Darwinian (ND)-Sociobiology
See ND-Sociobiology
Neo-Darwinian behavioral theory,
163, 174, 177
Neo-Darwinian definition of
evolution, 171
Neo-Darwinian history, 37
Neo-Darwinian natural selection, 57
Neo-Darwinian selection theory, 55
neural plasticity, 109
neuro-cognitive complexity, 7
neurological complexity, 59, 233
neurological pathways, 179–180
new physical anthropology, 26–28, 62,
186, 187–188
New Synthesis/new synthesis
(of approaches), 27, 29–36, 37,
54, 160
niche construction, 7, 117, 114, 163,
165, 172–177, 183–185, 205, 211,
215, 218–219, 234, 244–246,
250–251

niche construction (*contd.*)
  and human behavioral evolution,
    188–189
  and human behavioral response, 226
  and human–environment mutability,
    216–217
  phenotypic plasticity in, 169
  and social complexity, 209
  theory on the phenogenotype, 178
  and TIV model, 179
nomadic forager model, 122
nonadaptationist perspectives, 49n.1
nonfunctional developmental processes,
    62, 160–164
nonfunctional symbolism, 93–94
nongenetic developmental processes, 62
nonhuman animals, 141, 169
nonhuman primates, 8, 27, 108, 112, 193,
    201, 212, 214, 216, 218, 225–226,
    227, 246, 247
non-kin, 67, 110–111, 141, 193, 198
nonmemetic developmental processes, 62
nonseasonal reproduction, 12
Nowak, M.A., 111
nuclear family, 33, 98, 101, 154–156,
    222–224, 230
nutrition/nutritional, 38, 44, 65, 101,
    120, 128, 141, 145, 154, 200
nutritional cannibalism, 94, 204 *See also*
    cannibalism
nutritional ecology, 38
nutritional requirements, 43, 128, 200
nutritional stressors/nutritional stress,
    154, 200, 205, 208

O'Connell, J.F., 119, 120
obligate mutualists, 53
Odling-Smee, F.J., 172, 173, 174, 175, 176,
    178, 216, 217
offspring, 5, 8, 14, 25, 30, 43, 65, 67, 75,
    99, 101, 113, 119–121, 125, 219,
    222–224, 252
  cooperation with mother, 193
  transmission of traits, 170
Olduwan tool industry, 73, 87–88, *89*, 93
Olga, S., 228
ontogenetic explanations (of behavior),
    28–29
  of Tinbergen, 163–165

ontogenetic learning, 66, 234
ontogenetic processes, 117, 175, 176
ontogenetics/ontogenetical, 23, 168–169
ontogeny (life experience), 65, 67, 163,
    164, 172
optimality models, 38–40, 42, 164
  reduction of reliance on, 180–181
optimality theory, 38, 39–40, 42, 163,
    164, 180, 190
orangutan (Asian great ape), 68–69, 212,
    227, 230
organic evolution *See* Baldwin's organic
    evolution/Baldwin effect
organism–environment dynamic,
    169, 172
organism–environment interaction,
    168, 174, 184
organism–environment systems,
    166, 171, 183
organisms, 5–7, 11, 19, 25–26, 38–39,
    52–53, 87, 93, 103, 115, 117–118,
    124, 129, 141, 145, 151
  altruism in, 30–31
  differential survival in, 34–36
  functional organization of, 46
  preservation in, 23
  tit-for-tat strategy in, 111
Orrorin tugenensis, 69–70, 72, 74
Oyama, S., 169, 171
  "developmental dualism"
    approach, 169

Padilla, D.K., 168
pair bonding *See* pair bonds/pair bonding
pair bonds/pair bonding, 100–102, 119,
    125, 126, 156, 158, 159, 195–197,
    199–200, 208, 223, 230–232, 234
paleoanthropology/paleoanthropological,
    62, 74, 151, 241, 256
paleoclimates, 205, 214
Pan paniscus, 200, 204
Pan troglodytes, 199–200, 204
Pan troglodytes schweinfurthii, 204
Papio papio See savannah baboons
paradigmatic approaches (to human
    behavioral evolution), 188 *See also*
    traditional paradigmatic views
    (EP, HBE, ND-Sociobiology,
    meme, DIT)

comparison tables of, 129
    conflict patterns, 133–135
    cooperation patterns, 130–132
    environment/ecological patterns,
        136–138
    food/diet patterns, 139–140
    sex/reproductive patterns, 142–145
    specific behavior patterns, 146–149
paradigmatic views (EP, HBE,
        ND-Sociobiology, meme, DIT) *See*
        traditional paradigmatic views
        (EP, HBE, ND-Sociobiology,
        meme, DIT)
Paranthropus boisei, 73, 76, 77, 78, 86, 87
Paranthropus robustus, 77–78, 86–87
parental investment/differential
        parental investment, 50, 196, 203
Peacor, S.D., 168
Peterson, D., 101, 103, 124
    *Demonic Males: Apes and the
        Origins of Human Violence* (1996),
        101, 103
phenogenotypes, 117, 176–177,
        178, 228
phenotypes, 26, 54, 163–165, 172, 174,
        180, 182, 184
phenotypic plasticity, 48, 165–169, 172,
        174–175, 178, 185–186 *See also*
        behavioral phenotypes; behavioral
        plasticity
philopatric species, 67, 193
phylogenetic histories, 5, 42, 247, 249
phylogenetic relationships, 17
physical traits, *12*, 69, 239
physiological patterns, 106, 249–250
physiological traits, 62, 177
physiology, 13, 29, 42, 100, 116, 124, 164,
        169, 179, 197, 200, 217, 215, 232,
        247, 249, 250
Pilbeam, D., 100
plant foods, 86–87, 100, 120
plant storage organs, 213
plant underground storage organs
        (USOs), 120
plastic responses, 23, 28, 168, 182
plasticity, 23–24, 28, 52, 98, 105, 106–107,
        108, 109, 190, 200–201 *See also*
        behavioral plasticity; phenotypic
        plasticity; plastic responses

effects on organism–environment
        interaction, 168–169
Platonic Idealism, 8n.4
Pleistocene foragers, 46
Pleistocene hominins, 76–79
Pleistocene Hominins—Early, 88–90
Pleistocene Hominins—Late, 90–94
Pleistocene *Homo*, 89
Pleistocene hunter-gatherers, 46, 118
        See also hunter-gatherers/
        foragers
Pleistocene period, 46–47
Ponginae, 69
ponginines See orangutans
Pope.G., 254
    The Biological Basis of Human Behavior
        (1999), 254
population genetic processes *See*
        population genetics
population genetics, 28. 53, 176
population densities, 34, 153, 204, 154
populations, 10, 13–15, 18, 24–26, 28, 31,
        39–40, 41–42, 52, 67, 81–83, 88,
        117, 154, 170, 171, 177, 179, 205,
        208, 221, 224, 234, 235, 244
    cooperation based on reciprocity in,
        111, 114
    fitness values in, 106
    health disparities within and
        between, 178
    imitation in, 59
    interactive feedback and, 174, 176
    lethal conflict between, 122
    "post Neo-Darwinian"emergent
        perspectives in evolutionary
        theory, 248
Potts, R., 107, 108, 213, 214
    variability selection hypothesis, 214
predation, 38–39, 44, 153, 189, 190, 210,
        211, 218–219
    cruelty in, 102–103
    major selective force in, 234
    man the hunted, 123
    susceptibility to, 67
predation avoidance, 29, 90, 76, 90,
        123, 241 *See also* antipredator
        strategy/antipredator defense
predation pressure, 87, 123, 189, 210,
        218, 241

primate lineages, 64, 240
primate plasticity, 108 *See also* plasticity
primate societies, 21, 67, 112, 206, 231
primate species, 65–67, 92, 153, 193,
    195–196, 198–200, 206–207, 210,
    214, 215–216, 222
  consumption of plant storage
    organs, 213
  pair bonding, 230
  social ties between dyads, 232
primate taxonomy, *4*
primates *See* primate species
primate-wide trends, 64, 67, 156
primate-wide trends, 64, 67–68, 156
primitive traits, 64, 72, 79
prisoner's dilemma, 31, 111
prosimians, 65, 212
prosociality/prosocial, 97, 115, 116
protection, 65, 100, 198, 208, 228, 230
protohuman evolutionary history, 102
proto-religious behavior, 59
proximate explanations (of human
    behavior), 28
pseudo-Lamarckian perspective, 21, 22
psychological adaptations, 47, 48, 118
psychological mechanisms, 42, 44–46,
    47–48, 62, 118
psychosocial stress/psychosocial
    stressors, 178, 179
public health, 7–8, 250

"ratchet effect", 90, 104, 117, 218
Rawls, J., 115
  A Theory of Justice (1971), 114
reaction norm concept, 164, 165–168
reasoning, 17, 62
reciprocal altruism/reciprocal altruism
    model, 31–32, 36, 37, 109–110,
    116, 117, 119, 141, 194, 207
    See also altruism; altruistic
    behavior; altruistic punishment;
    tit-for-tat strategies/tit-for-tat
    reciprocities
  cooperative punishment and, 145
  hunting by human males, 43–44,
    118, 128
  intragroup competition and, 150
  and tit-for-tat strategies, 111
religion, 9, 58, 99, 116, 252–253

religious beliefs, 9n.4, 33, 58, 106
Relyea, R.A., 168
reproduction, 6, 51, 57, 96, 142–143,
    154–155, 219–224
  costs of, 90–91, 128
  and evolutionary change, 34–36
  and practice of cruelty, 102
reproductive benefits, 44, 47
reproductive cycling, 98, 119, 128, 222
reproductive outcomes, 48
reproductive success, 13, 38, 53, 181,
    210, 224
  adaptively relevant environment
    (ARE) and, 46–47
  energy acquisition and distribution
    and, 185
  impact of behavior on, 185
  measures of, 41, 42, 62
  selective forces in, 38–39, 163
resource conflict/resource stress,
    205–207
resource distribution, 68, 121
resources, 38
  differential access to, 66–67
Richerson, P.J., 52, 53, 55, 103, 104, 161n.2
  *Not by Genes Alone: How Culture
    Transformed Human Evolution*
    (2005), 103
  "obligate mutualists", 53
  The Origin and Evolution of Cultures
    (2005), 104
rituals/ritual practices, 59, 94, 99, 103,
    125, 204
RNA interference, 162
Robin, D., 46
Robinson's dietary hypothesis, 88, 241
Robson, Arthur, 120
role differentiation, 229, 234, 235

Sahelanthropus tchadensis, 70–71
same and different sex conflict, 207–208
same-sex cooperation/same-sex alliances,
    101, 141, 145, 197–199, 207
Samoa, 178, 179
satisficing, 42
savannah baboons (*Papio papio*), 27, 219
Schmitt, D.P., 49, 50, 51
  Sociosexual Strategies Index (SOI), 50
scramble competition, 38–39

Sear, R., 40, 41
sedentism, 201, 203, 213, 217, 235
selection pressures, 20, 23, 46, 48,
    63, 108, 110, 117–119, 170,
    172–174, 177, 189, 190, 217,
    233–234, 244
  of caretaking, 65
  cultural variants and, 54
  ecological, 40–41
  and EEA, 46–47, 62
  and inherent morality, 115
  and niche construction, 176, 209
  of predation, 38, 123
selection scenarios, 48, 53
selective advantages, 97, 105, 162,
    194, 212
self-awareness, 3, 58, 115
selfish genes/selfish gene system,
    29, 34–36, 57
selfish herd concept, 38
"selfish meme" system *See* selfish
    genes/selfish gene system;
    selfish memes
selfish memes, 57, 58, 59
selfish signaling theory, 110
Selye, H., 178
sense of beauty, 17
serial monogamy, 126
sex differences, 51, 141, 155. 212, 228
sex ratios, 51
sexes, 18–19, 67, 128, 142–143, 154,
    196–197, 198, 207–208, 219–224
  canine teeth similarity in, 75
  competition between, 141, 150–151,
    128, 157
  cooperation between, 126, 141, 128,
    150, 157
  differences between men and women,
    18–19, 72, 125
  division of labor between, 98, 156
sexual activity, 33, 125, 221, 222, 232
sexual behavior, 33, 50, 154, 208,
    221–222, 234, 247, 255
sexual dimorphism, 66, 72, 74, 78, 81,
    197, 220, 224, 227, 230, 233, 240
  correlated with conflicts between
    males, 195
  correlations between differential body
    size, 199

sexual division of labor, 33–34, 119–122,
    125, 156–157, 196–197, 227–229
sexual selection, 10, 17–19, 98, 100, 159,
    207–208, 220–222, 225, 255
  behavioral flexibility and, 126
  male advertisement, 155
  male–female competition, 196
  modern behavioral patterns, 34
  selective advantages in, 97
sexual strategies/sexual strategies
    theory, 50–51, 101, 220–221
sexuality, 50, 154, 196–197, 222
sham menstruation, 125
shearing complex, 69, 71, 72
show-off hypothesis, 43–44, 47 *See also*
    costly signaling hypotheses
Sigmund, K., 111
Silk, J.B., 108
silver foxes (*Vulpes vulpes*), 11, *12*
Sima de los Huesos (Spain), 192, 216, 217
Skinner, M.M., 83, 84
small foraging groups, 103, 118
Smith, Adam, 150
Smuts, B.B., 113
Sober, E., 113, 114
  *The Evolution and Psychology of
    Unselfish Behavior*, 113
social alliances, 44, 200
social animals, 19, 115
social behavior, 10, 19, 30n.1, 32, 67,
    75–76, 97, 108, 109, 117, 126–127,
    151, 232
social complexity, 18, 92, 98, 103,
    105, 108, 115–117, 209, 214–215,
    233, 234
  cooperative patterns in humanity, 114
  emergence of motherese, 123
  pattern of conflict negotiation, 112, 122
  propagation of memes and
    memeplexes, 106
social constructivism, 9, 48
social Darwinism, 21
social environments, 22, 23–24, 170, 179
social grooming *see* grooming/mutual
    grooming/social grooming
social groups, 9, 67, 87, 90, 123, 219
social inheritance, 22, 189, 194, 199, 202,
    234, 246
social insects, 32

"social intelligence", 126, 233, 234
social learning, 52, 103, 162
social mammals, 11, 129, 141, 189n.1
social mind, 7
social negotiation, 67, 122
social relationships, 19, 65, 67, 98, 112,
    156, 231, 234
social roles, 66, 98, 106
social status, 39, 178–179, 200
social structure, 18, 28, 32, 51, 94, 112,
    122, 177, 193, 209, 222, 245
    male–female pair-bonding underlies,
        125
    reducing fitness differences, 114
    threat of predation, 123
sociality, 17–18, 67–68, 103, 107, 113,
    209, 219
societies, 5, 18, 21, 23, 43, 102, 108, 113,
    150, 199, 205, 212–213, 221, 244
    and affect hunger, 116
    nuclear family in, 224
    plastic and creative processes in, 109
    reciprocal altruistic patterns in, 110, 202
    recognition of social unit in, 223
    same-sex association and
        bonding in, 231
sociobiology *See* ND-Sociobiology
sociocultural anthropology, 250n.1
socioecological environments, 40, 41
socioecological pressures, 38
socioeconomic hierarchies/socioeconomic
    class distinctions, 10, 94
Sociosexual Strategies Index (SOI),
    50–51
sociosexuality, 50–51 *see also* mating
    strategies
Soltis, J., 55, 56
somatic defense capabilities, 153
South Africa, 78, 79, 83, 86, 87, 89, 244
Southeast Asia, 88, 898, 210
space/space use, 65–66, 204, 206, 233,
    245 *See also* spatial associations
spatial associations, 8, 65, 201, 230
specialist foragers (stenotopic), 88
specific behavioral patterns/specific
    behavior, 146–147, 155–156, 188,
    195, 208, 222, 225–230, 231–232, 237
Spencer, Herbert, 21–24, 30, 31, 32, 44,
    52. 206, 245
    "law of intelligence", 22

The Principles of Ethics, (1893), 22
Principles of Psychology (1855, 1872),
    21–22
*Social Statics: Or, the Conditions
    Essential to Human Happiness
    Specified, and the First of Them
    Developed* (1851), 21
"Synthetic Philosophy" program, 21
standard social science model (SSSM),
    45, 48–49
Stanford, C.B., 99, 100
    Meat-Eating and Human Evolution,
        99, 100
status, 39, 44, 103, 179, 209, 212, 220, 247
status acquisition, 209, 224
stenotopic (specialist foragers), 88
Stiner, M.C., 227, 228
stone tool technology, 82, 87–88, 91
Strait, D., 88, 229, 241
strategic pluralism/strategic pluralism
    theory, 50, 51
stressors, 154, 159, 178, 200, 205, 214,
    215, 216
subfamily *Homininae*, 3, 69
sudden infant death syndrome, 8
Sultan, S.E, 168
superfamily Hominoidea, 3, 240
"survival machines", 34, 126
survivorship, 39, 88, 203, 241
Sussman, R. W., 123, 218, 219, 257
    *The Biological Basis of Human Behavior:
        A Critical Review* (1999), 257
    *Man the Hunted: Primates, Predators,
        and Human Evolution* (2005), 123
symbolic communication, 68, 183, 226
symbolic inheritance *See* symbolic
    inheritance systems
symbolic inheritance systems, 160–161,
    162, 175, 209
symbolic/linguistic communication, 68,
    225–227
symbolically marked groups, 103
sympathy/sympathetic behavior, 10, 20,
    21, 32, 110
sympatric hominins, 210, 211

Tattersal, I., 106, 107
    *Becoming Human: Evolution and
        Human Uniqueness* (1998), 106
terrestrial locomotion, 68, 86

territoriality, 33, 100, 111, 122
testable hypotheses, 240–242
testability (in behavioral models),
        190–192, 195–232, 240n.1 *See also*
        traditional paradigmatic views
        (EP, HBE, ND-Sociobiology,
        Memetics, and DIT)
theft and sharing of food, 100–101
theoretical perspectives, 16, 34, 180,
        192, 239
thermoregulation, 65, 90
Tibetan macaques (*Macaca thibetana*), 202
Tinbergen, Niko, 28–29
    "On aims and methods of ethology",
        28–29
tit-for-tat cooperation, 111 *See* tit-for-tat
        exchanges; tit-for-tat strategies/
        tit-for-tat reciprocities
tit-for-tat exchanges *See* tit-for-tat
        cooperation; tit-for-tat strategies/
        tit-for-tat reciprocities
tit-for-tat strategies/tit-for-tat
        reciprocities, 111, 122, 150, 194
        See also reciprocal altruism
tolerated theft, 43
tool use, 225–227
Tomasello, M., 104–105
Tooby, J., 46, 49n.1, 118
trade-offs, 40, 68, 90, 120, 230
traditional Neo-Darwinian
        perspectives/traditional
        Neo-Darwinian thought,
        160, 174, 182
traditional paradigmatic views
        (EP, HBE, ND-Sociobiology,
        Memetics, and DIT):
    commonalities in:
        conflict, 203–207
        cooperation, 192–200, 211–212
        ecology/environment, 213–215
        sex/reproduction, 219–223
        specific behavior, 225–230
    factors needing further enquiry:
        conflict, 208–212
        cooperation, 201–202
        ecology/environment, 216–218
        sex/reproduction, 224
        specific behavior, 231–232
traits, 5, 181–183, 188, 191n.2, 204, 224,
        230, 243

tribal-social instincts hypotheses, 103, 176
tribes, 20, 103
tri-inheritance vision model (TIV), 175,
        176n.6, 178, 179
Trivers, Robert, 30, 31–32, 111
    reciprocal altruism, 31–32
Trut, L., 11–12
tubers, 75, 86, 100, 213
twenty-first century evolutionary the-
        ory, 160–186
two-adult groups, 195–196, 223, 232
two-adult plus offspring groups, 222,
        223

Ulijaszek, S.J., 250, 251

van Schiak, C.P., 102
    Infanticide by Males and Its Implications
        (2000), 102
variable environments, 107, 109, 121,
        152, 159, 213–214, 215
violence, 10, 213, 253
vocalizations, 65, 122
Vulpes vulpes (silver foxes), *12*

Waddington, C., 172
Wallace, Alfred Russel, 19–21, 22, 23, 30,
        54, 182, 240n.1, 245
    evolution of the mind, 19–21
Warden, C., 254
    The Evolution of Human Behavior
        (1932), 254
warfare, 33, 34, 56, 98, 157, 201
Washburn School, 27
Washburn, Sherwood, 26–28, 30, 62, 99,
        186, 187
    "New Physical Anthropology",
        26–28
    savannah baboons, 27
Washburnian Biological Anthropology, 17
    new physical anthropology, 26–28
Watanabe, J.M., 113
weapons/weaponry, 20, 44, 76, 212
Wells, H.G., 10
    The Time Machine (1895), 10
Wells, J.C.K., 90
Werner, E.E., 168
West Africa/West African, 176
West-Eberhard, Mary Jane, 165, 169
Williams, G.C., 34

Wilson, D.S., 113, 114
  *Do Unto Others: The Evolution and
    Psychology of Unselfish Behavior*
    (1998), 113
Wilson, E.O., 29–30, 32–34, 53, 95, 98
  autocatalysis model of human
    evolution, 33–34, 98–99
  "culturgens", 53
  social insects, 32
  Sociobiology: the New Synthesis (1975),
    30, 98
  ultimate explanations (of human
    behavior), 30
Wilson, M., 102
  Homicide (1998), 102
Wilsonian Sociobiology, 29

Winterhalder, B., 101, 103
  *Demonic Males: Apes and the
    Origins of Human Violence* (1996),
    101, 103
Wood, B.A., 83, 84, 88
woodland environments *See* arboreal
  environments
Wrangham, Richard W. 100, 101, 102
  *Demonic Males: Apes and the Origins of
    Human Violence* (1996), 101

xenophobia, 33, 58, 106, 118, 157

Zahavi, A., 43, 122
  handicap principle, 43
Zihlman, A.L., 108